THE DYNASTY YEARS

'We hear a lot about "critical thinking" nowadays, but Jostein Gripsrud actually does it, lucidly and logically, in one of the most sensible books I have read about the meanings and demeanings of television. One need not agree with Gripsrud's every assessment of *Dynasty* to learn from his clear-headed analysis and critique of the *Dynasty* phenomenon. His reflections on the static and wishful academic celebrations of American television that he rightly calls "anaemic" are sorely needed.' *Todd Gitlin, University of California, Berkeley*

'Jostein Gripsrud's study of *Dynasty* brings together in a fresh and striking synthesis the main elements of contemporary cultural critique and opens an original perspective on the processes and consequences of one of the main themes of our era – the internationalization of popular culture.' *Nick Browne, University of California, Los Angeles*

'In this polemical study, Jostein Gripsrud takes *Dynasty* as the first soap opera ever encountered on Norwegian television and the accompanying campaigns both for and resisting this "event" as an opportunity to challenge the "post-modern" focus on consumption at the expense of production and the "text". Both rigorous and wittily provocative, this study lays bare the cultural, epistem-ological and political implications of a range of analytical and interpretive strategies, and, steering between the Scylla of capitalist determination and the Charybdis of populism, seeks out a new position from which to speak of cultural politics for the 90s. A clarifying and stimulating book.' *Christine Gledhill, University of Staffordshire*

Jostein Gripsrud is Professor in the Department of Media Studies, University of Bergen, Norway. His articles have appeared in numerous journals including *Screen, Cultural Studies* and *Critical Studies in Mass Communication*.

COMEDIA
Series editor:
David Morley

THE DYNASTY YEARS

Hollywood Television and Critical Media Studies

Jostein Gripsrud

A Comedia book
published by Routledge
London and New York

First published 1995
by Routledge
11 New Fetter Lane, London EC4P 4EE

Simultaneously published in the USA and Canada
by Routledge
29 West 35th Street, New York, NY 10001

© 1995 Jostein Gripsrud

Typeset in Baskerville by J&L Composition Ltd, Filey, North Yorkshire
Printed and bound in Great Britain by
Biddles Ltd, Guildford and King's Lynn

British Library Cataloguing in Publication Data
A catalogue record for this book is available from the British Library

Library of Congress Cataloging in Publication Data
Gripsrud, Jostein
The Dynasty years: Hollywood television and critical media
studies / Jostein Gripsrud.
p.   cm. – (Comedia)
Includes bibliographical references and index.
1. Dynasty (Television program)   2. Soap operas – United States
– History and criticism.   3. Soap operas – Norway – History and
criticism.   I. Title.   II. Series.
PN 1992   .77.D9G751995
791.45'72 – dc20
95–12935

ISBN 0–415–08598–5
0–415–08599–3 (pbk)

For Silje and Synne

CONTENTS

CONTENTS

PLATES

PREFACE

It is now about ten years since I started the research which has resulted in this book. A major reason why it has taken so long to complete is that I have been busy organizing, administrating and teaching media studies at the University of Bergen. But a project as ambitiously comprehensive as this necessarily takes a lot of time, particularly since for me, with a background in the social history of literature and popular culture, it has served as an introduction to the wider, complex field of modern media studies.

I have learnt a lot over the years, not only from reading scholarly work, but also from talking to more experienced people in the field, including, not least, many of those whose work I criticize on some accounts in this book. I wish to express my gratitude to all the colleagues, too many to name here, in several countries, in film, television, (mass) communication and cultural studies, whose interest in my work, advice and friendliness I have enjoyed. I hope a somewhat polemical tone here and there will not seriously damage my chances for future discussions with those I criticize – our disagreements will hardly come as a surprise to most of those concerned. In most cases, I also share (and draw on) some of their perspectives and conclusions.

I would, moreover, like to thank the many women and men who kindly devoted time and effort to helping me in my work at a more practical level. They include, first of all, Esther Shapiro, Robert and Eileen Pollock, Curtis Harrington and others involved in the production of *Dynasty*, whom I interviewed. Thanks also to Wendy Wilkinson for helping to arrange some of these interviews. I am very grateful to the late Beverle Houston and Nick Browne for helping to arrange my stays as Visiting Scholar at USC and UCLA (in 1987 and 1993). James Monaco kindly allowed free use of Baseline Inc.'s database on the US entertainment industry – thank you. Geir Waagsbø and his market research company in Bergen, Norway (Salgs-og Markedsinstituttet), helpfully provided vital services at discount prices. Thanks also to Stein Roger Bull and Per Selstrøm at the Norwegian Broadcasting Corporation, and to the staff at Kristelig Kringkastingslag's office in Oslo, whose archives were very useful.

The Film and Series Department at the Norwegian Broadcasting Corporation made an extremely important contribution to my work when they, free of charge, gave me copies of hundreds of letters from viewers about *Dynasty*, and Professor Eva Lundgren, now at the University of Uppsala, Sweden, generously allowed me to use transcripts of interviews she conducted in one of her projects.

Financial support was essential to the completion of a project such as this one. I wish to express my sincere gratitude for the funding my project received from the University of Bergen, and for the generous grants from the Norwegian Research Council, without which my research in Los Angeles would not have been possible.

I have benefited greatly from information from, and discussions with, friends and colleagues all over Scandinavia, and particularly in my own department at the University of Bergen. Thanks to you all. Special thanks go to Tone Kolbjørnsen for the very rewarding discussions we have had, and for general existential support. In the final rounds of writing, I also enjoyed expert criticism and advice on different parts of my manuscript from Michael Bruun Andersen and Irene Iversen; Toril Moi and Klaus Bruhn Jensen, in particular, read and commented on draft versions of different (parts of) chapters, while Peter Larsen did a splendid job in helping me to organize the textual analysis and to avoid too many misunderstandings.

Most of all, though, I would like to thank Dave Morley for his extremely important support and always thorough, thoughtful commentaries to the drafts of chapters as they finally began to appear. Without his friendship, patience and critical encouragement, this book would still only be a good idea.

The patience shown by my two daughters, Silje and Synne, in the decade it took to get this work done is even more impressive and of a very different nature. It is one of many very good reasons why I dedicate the book to them.

Bergen, February 1994
Jostein Gripsrud

Note on translations: All translations from non-English sources are by the author, unless otherwise indicated in the bibliography.

INTRODUCTION
Signalling a position

Whatever else sociology may be, it is a result of consistently asking: (1) What is the meaning of this – whatever we are examining – for our society as a whole, and what is this social world like? (2) What is the meaning of this for the types of men and women that prevail in this society? And (3) how does this fit into the historical trend of our times, and in what direction does this main drift seem to be carrying us? No matter how small-scale what he is examining, the sociologist must ask such questions about it, or he has abdicated the classic sociological endeavor.

(Mills 1967: 572)

'THE ULTIMATE DOLLHOUSE FANTASY FOR MIDDLE-AGED WOMEN' IN CONTEXT

This book is a critical discussion of central theoretical and methodological positions in recent media and cultural studies, conceived as a wide, cross-disciplinary field, stretching from social scientific mass communication research and cultural sociology to film, television and literary studies. Throughout, theoretical and methodological issues are related to an analysis of a specific instance of transnational communication: the US television serial *Dynasty* and its reception in a small country in northern Europe, Norway.

The public sphere and everyday life were going through rapid and deep changes all over western Europe in the early 1980s. These changes were in part technologically induced and related in particular to the medium of television: the advent of satellite television, the concurrent rapid spread of cable systems and the market breakthrough for domestic VCRs. All of this happened more or less at once. In many countries, these developments led to heated debates about the implications of a transnationalized and commercialized television. Some predicted the downfall of all cultural values worth mentioning, while others cheered the arrival at last of multichannel opportunities of choice for pleasure-thirsty peoples who had been subjected too long to dreary public service broadcasting monopolies.

Not accidentally, American TV serials in the genre that came to be known as

1

'prime-time soap operas' were in many countries seen as emblems of the new situation by both sides in these debates. *Dallas* was the first of these shows, and its central role in the transnational media-political debates of the decade is seen in the catchphrase for the nightmare vision of European television of the future: 'wall-to-wall *Dallas*'. First formulated by either the then Director of the BBC Michael Checkland or the then French Minister of Culture Jack Lang, it was repeated by representatives of official culture and public service broadcasting institutions in many countries.

In Norway, the role of *Dallas* was played by *Dynasty*, which, according to one of its producers, Esther Shapiro, is 'the ultimate dollhouse fantasy for middle-aged women' (Klein 1985: 37). The first episode, shown in Norway on 7 May 1983, marked the beginning of what I call the *Dynasty* event: an intense public debate about the serial and its cultural implications which would last for more than a year. I found the basic positions clearly recognizable as present-day versions of historical instances I had studied before: a cultural elite attacking what seemed to be the genre preferences and tastes of 'ordinary people'. But the context was obviously very different from those I knew from my previous historical research on popular cultural forms and formations. The text discussed was televisual, not literary or theatrical; it was also produced in Hollywood, USA, not in some Norwegian valley or city; the debate took place in the media of a quite different public sphere. The public discussion was, however, clearly also a struggle over general cultural issues as well as those more specifically related to broadcasting policies. *Dynasty* and the debate it created thus suggested themselves as empirical material for a project which would investigate the historically well-known tensions between cultural elites and ordinary people in a contemporary setting. In this setting, issues of cultural democracy and broadcasting policies necessarily had to be seen in the light of very complicated transnational processes and relations with economic, technological, political and cultural dimensions.

My project was from the beginning intended to be a many-sided investigation of *Dynasty*, regarded as a complex media phenomenon, comprising both its origins in the US, its text, and its public and domestic reception in Norway, and aimed at reaching a historical understanding. The simple fact that *Dynasty* was first shown in the US in the very week in which Ronald Reagan was inaugurated as president, became a major hit during his presidency, and was cancelled more or less as he left the White House, could in itself be said to support an interest in the serial as a 'sign of the times'. A historical understanding of an 'event' like *Dynasty* and its reception means grasping what a unique slice of cultural history may be said to 'contain' or (re)present of more general socio-cultural forces at play in the ongoing shaping of our lives and life worlds. The main methodological principle in this basically hermeneutic project would be one of contextualizing the event, placing it in ever wider circles of relevant factors, much in the manner of the so-called 'Contextualist' approach in historical research:

The Contextualist proceeds, [Stephen] Pepper tells us, by isolating some (indeed *any*) element of the historical field as the subject of study, whether the element be as large as 'the French Revolution' or as small as one day in the life of a specific person. He then proceeds to pick out the 'threads' that link the event to be explained to different areas of the context. The threads are identified and traced outward, into the circumambient natural and social space within which the event occurred, and both backward in time, in order to determine the 'origins' of the event, and forward in time, in order to determine its 'impact' and 'influence' on subsequent events.

(White 1990: 18)

At the same time, it has been important to maintain the centre of attention at the centre of the event: the *Dynasty* serial itself.

The three-year grant I received was specifically intended for a project devoted to the exploration of theoretical foundations for media studies in the humanities. My *Dynasty* project was in my view well suited for such a purpose, because it necessitated thinking through just about every relevant theoretical and methodological problem in mainstream mass communication research as well as in film, television and general media and cultural studies. It tied reflections on these matters to both a wide variety of empirical data and highly controversial media–political issues. Max Weber once argued that 'nothing should be more sharply emphasized than the proposition that the knowledge of the *cultural significance* of *concrete historical events and patterns* is exclusively and solely the final end which, among other means, concept-construction and the criticism of constructs also seek to serve' (Weber 1969: 111). While I would insist that theoretical discourse has a degree of autonomy and that its role cannot be reduced to the task of constructing 'useful' propositions and 'concepts' for empirical research, I do think that theoretical work would benefit from the insight that it ultimately will have to confront concrete historical material, including specific texts.

The theoretical points I try to make in this book are, then, the outcome of 'impure' theoretical thinking: reflections on theoretical issues with a view to both a certain empirical material and issues of a 'practical' political nature.

'FERMENT IN THE FIELD'

In the empirical and/or empiricist corner of mainstream (mass) communication research, the scholarly climate of the 1980s was signalled by the much-quoted title of the *Journal of Communication*, no. 33, 1983: 'Ferment in the Field'. The issue contained articles which raised a fundamental debate over epistemological presuppositions within the mainstream of (mainly American) communication research, and returned to the categorization of research which Paul F. Lazarsfeld once (1941) used in the title of a highly interesting piece he published in the journal of the so-called 'Frankfurt School', *Zeitschrift für Sozialforschung/Studies*

3

in Philosophy and Social Science: 'Remarks on Critical and Administrative Communications Research'.

Lazarsfeld argued that the kind of research he devoted his own time to, administrative research, was done in the service of any agency which wanted increased empirical knowledge in order to make its use of mass communication media more efficient. Critical media research, on the other hand, studied, in a more hermeneutic or 'speculative' way, media communication in the light of general social and cultural trends, and also asked whether these trends were positive or negative with respect to certain fundamental values. Lazarsfeld's soon forgotten main point was that the administrative research needed the critical research as a source of ideas and perspectives; without it, his own kind of research would suffer severe intellectual impoverishment. Later developments confirmed this prediction to a considerable degree.

Of course, by the time intellectual 'ferment' reaches a journal like the *Journal of Communication*, it has been going on for quite some time outside the most prestigious or dominant quarters of an academic field. But the 'Ferment in the Field' issue was not only somewhat delayed in relation to developments within the field of (mass) communication research, it was more significantly also in many ways delayed in relation to epistemological and research-political discussions that had taken place in neighbouring fields and disciplines, especially in Europe, from the late 1950s on. The *Positivismus-Streit* (i.e. the struggle over positivism) in German sociology played an important role in preparing the 1960s 'student revolution' all over western Europe, and heavily influenced developments in the humanities as well as in the social sciences. American-dominated mass communication research must have been just about the last academic corner to be reached and influenced by the reverberations of this struggle, and that fact is telling, in more ways than one, of the intellectual status and social role of this tradition. It must to a remarkable degree have been insulated from what went on elsewhere in the academic communities of the 1960s and 1970s.

By the time the critique of 'positivism' reached mainstream mass communication research, in other social science disciplines it had become less dogmatic in its critique of empiricist methodology. It no longer stood for an almost total rejection of statistical methodology. Instead, it employed such methodology for socially critical and theoretically informed empirical work. The by now well-known research conducted by Pierre Bourdieu and his colleagues in France is but one example. The notion of methodological triangulation, i.e. the simultaneous use of many approaches to the same problematic or phenomenon, was towards the end of the 1970s more in line with the prevailing thinking about methodology in central social science disciplines than any clear-cut dichotomy between 'number crunchers' on one side and those in favour of 'qualitative' or 'interpretive' methodologies on the other (cf. Denzin 1970; Jick 1979). Still, such a dichotomy structured many of the struggles within the field of mass communication throughout the 1980s. The result was an unfortunate blurring of important distinctions between methodological, theoretical and political issues. Such distinctions need to be made if the equally important relations between them are to be properly understood. It is not accidental that research which is not rooted in a fundamentally critical understanding of society has a marked preference for certain statistical methodologies, but this does not imply that such methodologies are of no use to research which is conducted from a socially critical hermeneutic position.

I hope to demonstrate this point in practice in this book. It is methodologically pluralistic, in the sense that a plurality of sources and data, gathered in a variety of ways, are employed to shed light on various dimensions of the phenomenon under scrutiny. I have interviewed people involved in the production and distribution of the serial, and analysed its text from various angles; I combine quantitative audience surveys with several forms of qualitative data in the analysis of the show's reception in Norway. I try to bring all of this material together as an object for historical and political interpretation which is theoretically informed by what might be called an updated version of the non-dogmatic marxist tradition to which I owe my basic intellectual orientation.

THE FRANKFURT SCHOOL REVISITED

I owe part of the inspiration to work in the fashion sketched above to Theodor Wiesengrund Adorno, a – or the – leading figure in the research tradition known as the Frankfurt School. It may seem a bit strange to British and American readers that I refer to pieces by Adorno of over thirty years ago – and open this introduction with a quote from someone as unfashionable as C. Wright Mills – when sketching the overall approach attempted in this book. I will try to explain why I have decided to be so markedly untrendy. The fact that Wright Mills recommended the writings of the Frankfurt School as the best source for learning about 'the classic sociological endeavor' is not the only reason.

There are two reasons besides the obvious (that I think Adorno was basically right in making the points I refer to). First, there is a strong tendency in recent Anglo-American 'critical' media and cultural studies to write as if the history of studies in our field started in the mid-1970s or last year, and that just about every important idea and insight was produced in France, Britain or the US. I want to demonstrate the value of looking further back and also beyond the franco- and anglophone traditions. Second, and even more important, this book is written in part to counter the widespread dismissal of the Frankfurt School not only in Anglo-American media and cultural studies but also in mainstream mass communication research. Innumerable papers, articles and books have in an almost ritual fashion written off the Frankfurt School as an impossible source of inspiration on the grounds that it is elitist and pessimistic. It is never stated why much of the relevant work of the Frankfurt School is regarded as 'elitist'. The point that its 'elitist' contempt was not least directed against the contemporary bourgeoisie, ruling elites and their academic associates is normally forgotten. And no one has ever taken the trouble to explain why optimism is now to be seen as a hallmark of critical media and cultural studies.

This book draws on the Frankfurt School in two ways: particular concepts and theories (such as Jürgen Habermas's *public sphere*) have provided ways of thinking about various issues and types of questions to be asked; the book's argument(s) will in many cases develop in critical dialogue with texts and positions belonging to that tradition. I have found reading and rereading Adorno particularly rewarding for a number of reasons.

Adorno's rejection of epistemological empiricism and empiricist forms of social science research is well known, not least since it was an important factor in a certain chapter in the history of modern mass communication research. Paul F. Lazarsfeld hired him to do audience studies at his Office of Radio Research in 1939. More specifically, Adorno was supposed to study the ways in which people listened to radio music, using survey methodology. He was chosen for this task on the basis of his writing on the sociology of music earlier that decade. But Adorno decided that the transformation of his theoretical ideas about music and forms of listening to simple categories in a survey was 'like squaring the circle' (Towers 1977: 13; Adorno 1969 :347).

This was, however, not a total rejection of empirical studies of social and cultural practices. The Institute for Social Research in Frankfurt had early on done empirical studies of German society – here the mathematician-cum-psychologist Lazarsfeld had also contributed with statistical work – and Adorno was involved in the five-year project behind *The Authoritarian Personality* (1950). Still, he started the *Positivismus-Streit* (the struggle over positivism) in West Germany with his article on 'Sociology and Empirical Research' (first published 1957), in which the epistemology underlying the total reliance on empiricist methodology in most post-war sociology was harshly attacked. He pointed out, for instance, that the 'objectivity' of survey methodology was in the methodology itself, not in the knowledge it produced, since that was merely a quantified summary of subjective opinions. He stressed that there was a significant difference between a social science worthy of such a name and research he regarded as very difficult to distinguish from 'pre-scientific informa-tion-gathering for administrative purposes' (Adorno 1972: 156). It is worth noting in the context of this book that Adorno's view here has since been echoed by M. Wober in a discussion of research on television audiences: '[T]he data produced by "audimetry" [techniques for audience measure-ment] provides much raw material for research; but in itself it does not constitute research or even half of research' (Wober 1981: 410, quoted in Morley 1992: 174).

Adorno signalled a more open attitude to the use of statistical methods in empirical studies in his *Musiksoziologie* (first published 1962). Half jokingly he says this book contains so many fruitful questions it will keep the empirical sociology of music meaningfully busy for a long time. The 'translation' of theoretical concepts to operational ones is not regarded as absurd or impossible, only very difficult. He does not reject all attempts at verifying or falsifying the book's 'theorems', but insists that such attempts should stick to the basic principle of the theorems. Research should

> understand and analyse subjective ways of relating to the music in relation to the phenomenon itself and its decidable content, instead of disregarding the quality of the object, treating it merely as stimulus for projections and limiting itself to registration, measurement and ordering of subjective reactions or sedimentary ways of relating. A sociology of music, where music means more than soap or cigarettes in market research, does not only demand an awareness of society and its structure, or informational knowledge about musical phenomena, but a full understanding of the music itself in all its implications.
>
> (Adorno 1976: 10)

In addition, Adorno demands a historical understanding of the object of research. He argues that a mere registration of 'facts' without regarding their dynamic historicity will tend to make research apologetic, make it represent an uncritical acceptance of existing conditions as they are. Consequently, significant research in the sociology of music, or media sociology, which is to meet Adorno's demands, cannot be conducted by just any average mainstream sociologist – or mass communication researcher. Still, the guidelines that serious work in this field has to consider the (whole) *social context*, the *qualitative dimensions of the media texts themselves*, and the *historicity of both* when studying the interplay between music/media and audiences seem to me highly valuable.

Towards the end of his life (he died in 1969), Adorno also indicated a more nuanced understanding of the mass media and their relations to their audiences than that which informs the (in)famous essay on 'the culture industry' in his and Horkheimer's *The Dialectic of Enlightenment* (written in 1944, first published 1947). Umberto Eco has provided anecdotal evidence of this. He met Adorno in the 1960s when he was himself trying to carve out a position 'between' the Frankfurt School and American communication sociologists 'who accepted the world as it was'. Adorno told Eco that 'if the *Dialectic of Enlightenment* had not been written in the U.S.A. in the forties [. . .] but in Germany after the war, and in relation to [anlässig] an analysis of television, then his judgements would have turned out less pessimistic, less radical' (Eco 1984: 11). More significant than this afterthought is Adorno's own writing about the results of a particular empirical project at the Institute of Social Research in Frankfurt in the 1960s, on the reception of the media coverage of a particular royal wedding. Interviews with audiences revealed a striking 'double consciousness' in their relation to the event and the media's treatment of it – at once joyfully involved and sceptically distanced. Adorno regarded the results of this project as a clear indication of the need to revise some of the perspectives in the culture industry essay. The culture industry would probably never be totally successful in its efforts to colonize and manipulate the minds of its audiences (Adorno 1991: 169). I doubt whether many Anglo-American students and scholars have ever heard of Adorno as one who intelligently theorized the potential for 'resistance' in popular audiences and was a champion of qualitative audience studies.

RECENT 'QUALITATIVE' AUDIENCE STUDIES

It is true that Adorno and Horkheimer in their essay about the culture industry did not show much faith in or have high hopes for the consumers of this industry's products. Recent theory and research in the field known as qualitative audience studies or studies of reception are more in line with Adorno's modifying realizations in the 1960s. On the other hand, much writing in Anglo-American media and cultural studies over the last fifteen years or so has tended to go to the other extreme, celebrating a powerful, sovereign consumer/audience member/people as if the utopia of complete self-determination was already realized in the western world.

I am, in other words, not writing only in a dialogue with certain positions of the Frankfurt School. The book is also conceived as a critique of certain tendencies within the tradition(s) of cultural studies and qualitative audience or reception studies that have developed so rapidly in mass communication and cultural studies. Productive researchers in cultural and audience studies such as Dave Morley, Ien Ang, James Lull and John Fiske, and – in important ways belonging to a different category – Elihu Katz and Tamar Liebes have made significant contributions to an improved understanding of how television 'works' in relation to its audiences. But in some of this work there are serious shortcomings and misunderstandings, particularly with regard to overarching theoretical perspectives. These weaknesses have become even more pronounced as the 'cultural studies' approach to audience studies has become fashionable and mixed with elements of trendy 'postmodernist' theories. Banalized bits and pieces of poststructuralist thought ('deconstruction') have led to a misunderstood over-rating of the instability of meaning and a disregard for how all communication is constrained by material, social and semiotic conditions (cf. for instance Corner 1991). Also, it has more generally led to a relativism which often extends to any notion of truth and to questions of values. This is part of the reason why too much of this kind of work takes part in the above-mentioned populist celebration of the sovereign audience and its members. Such a position is often also tied to an oversimplified social analysis, in which complex modern societies and their culture(s) are understood to a much too large degree through more or less interchangeable dichotomies like dominant/dominated, powerful/powerless, high culture/low culture, male/female, the power bloc/the people. An adequate understanding, one which may for instance guide practical media-political and cultural interventions, requires somewhat finer conceptual tools. In spite of these and other criticisms, which will be further developed elsewhere in this book, the new wave of qualitative audience studies has certainly, as stated above, produced valuable insights and raised important questions. Even if writing within this new 'school' will be among my main targets for criticism, I will also be drawing on its results.

This book will try to demonstrate that we need more nuanced ideas about how socio-cultural structures and forces on the one hand and individuals and their minds and choices on the other work in relation to each other in the reception of media texts. But, at least equally important, I also hope to show that studies of audiences, their verbal and non-verbal responses and relations to particular texts, can never provide all the answers to the question of what these texts *mean*. Texts also carry meanings that are of no immediate interest to us as ordinary, everyday members of audiences. They work in ways we cannot talk about in interviews and in ways we do not betray in our observable behaviour. And the study of various features of a text, the study of relations between different texts, possibly in different media at different times, may be highly interesting in itself, no matter what the immediate 'effect' or 'reception' among various audiences is or has been.

IS THERE A TEXT?

The text is the central element in the simple, linear model of communication, which retains its obvious logical adequacy even if semiotics and reception theory severely complicate its straightforwardness. The text is the primary link between producers and audiences. It must draw on shared semiotic resources in order to communicate at all, even if a significant gap between encoding and decoding remains. It must to a greater or lesser extent, in some way or other, speak of and address various kinds of social experiences.

The centrality I claim for the text in the process of communication is of course dependent upon the existence of the text as a definable object separate from both producers and recipients. Some people have argued quite seriously and influentially that there is no text in this sense. The emergence of the reader as a central figure in all kinds of textual studies has led to a number of theories which may, for most outsiders, seem quite silly. John Fiske's (1989b) attempt to 'dissolve' the categories of 'texts' and 'audiences' and Jane Feuer's (1989) attempt to dissolve the distinction between the text, contexts and 'reading formations' (cf. Chapters 3 and 4 in this book) are merely repercussions or repetitions of arguments previously put forward in literary studies. The struggles in that field to overcome the limitations and impossible presuppositions of, first, romanticist and empiricist fixation on the author and his/her biography and intentions, and, later, New Criticism's insistence on the autonomy of the work, have over the last few decades resulted in hyperbolic and ultimately untenable positions parallel to those of Feuer and Fiske. The most extreme position taken does away with the notion of the text as a carrier of meaning altogether, and thereby ends in a principally argued relativism only restrained by the pseudo-sociological notion of 'interpretive communities'. The issue is so central to the whole conception of this book that I will deal with it in some detail here.

In the very title of his book *Is There a Text in This Class?* (1980), Stanley Fish raises the possibility of a 'non-existence' of the text. Chapter 14, an essay entitled 'How To Recognize a Poem When You See One', is a particularly entertaining and clearly argued version of his basic points: that 'meanings are the property neither of fixed and stable texts nor of free and independent readers but of interpretive communities that are responsible both for the shape of readers' activities and for the texts those activities produce' (Fish 1980: 322). Fish recounts an experiment with a group of students which, according to him, demonstrated that readers are able to produce coherent meanings out of a text constructed by mere coincidence. He concludes that these meanings were all in the heads of readers, produced in accordance with shared, academic-institutional interpretive principles existing prior to the actual reading of the text. One may counter Fish's position at a philosophical level. But one may also have a more practical, closer look at his experiment. It then becomes evident that his conclusion is wrong.

In 1971 Fish was teaching two morning classes, one after another, in two different subdisciplines, stylistics and seventeenth-century English religious poetry, in that order. An 'assignment' (a reading list, consisting of authors' names) from the first class remained on the blackboard when the students in the second, on religious poetry, entered the room. It looked like this:

Jacobs-Rosenbaum
Levin
Thorne
Hayes
Ohman(?)

Importantly, Fish had also, after the first group of students left, drawn a frame around this list of names, and written 'p. 43' above it. He told the second class of students that what they saw on the blackboard was a religious poem of the kind they had been studying, and asked them to interpret it. And so they did. 'Jacobs' was seen as referring to Jacob's ladder, though the ladder was here replaced by a rose tree (Rosenbaum), which referred to the Virgin Mary, since she was often characterized as a rose without thorns – etc. Relations between the various meanings of the individual words were discovered, and larger 'structural patterns' (Fish 1980: 325) discerned. To Fish, it seems that his students 'did not proceed from the noting of distinguishing features to the recognition that they were confronted by a poem; rather, it was the act of recognition that came first' (ibid.: 326). The experiment thus, according to Fish, shows that '[it] is not that the presence of poetic qualities compels a certain kind of attention but that the paying of a certain kind of attention results in the emergence of poetic qualities' (ibid.: 326). This point is then extended and generalized to mean that 'Skilled reading [. . .] is a matter of knowing how to *produce* what can thereafter be said to be there. [. . .] Interpreters do not decode poems; they make them' (ibid.: 327). Eventually, this is extended even further, to a general epistemological principle: '[A]ll objects are made and not found, and [. . .] they are made by the interpretive strategies we set in motion' (ibid.: 331). Not surprisingly, then, Fish ends up by wanting to 'eliminate' the subject-object dichotomy (ibid.: 336).

To me, the importance of institutionalized or group-specific 'interpretive principles' in the formation of readers' experience of texts is indisputable. It is a foundational insight in the sociologically and hence pragmatically inflected semiotics I myself and quite a few others are interested in. What Fish fails to account for is the equally indisputable importance of that which these principles of interpretation are applied to: the object of interpretation, the text. In fact, it is admitted by Fish himself elsewhere in the same book (1980: 165) that he cannot say what his 'interpretive acts' are interpretations of. A closer look at his own class-room example might have been helpful to him, even if his position would have needed some significant revision as a result.

First, his students might have been harder to fool into believing that what was on the blackboard was a poem had it not been written in the graphic shape shown above. Would they have believed him if he had said it was a novel? The definition of 'poetry' as texts with lines of uneven length is an old joke among teachers of literature, at least in Norway. The point here is that the teacher's lie about the text's genre was supported by an observable and quite significant graphic feature of the text itself. Second, it may be very indicative of authoritarian relations in Fish's American class-room of 1971 that not a single student questioned the professor's claim. It is striking that Fish does not reflect on this, since an institutional analysis of reading practices seems to be of central interest to him. Among my (Norwegian) students of the 1980s and 1990s there would certainly have been several undisciplined rascals who would have laughed or protested. What happened in Fish's class-room was a result of authoritarian relations. Once a figure of authority had told them which *genre* the text belonged to, and they could see with their own eyes that the text had a familiar shape and some recognizable, relevant words, they were eager to demonstrate that they were good students. Isn't 'class-room activity' sometimes part of the basis for grading in the US? Third, and most important, the students were not the first to 'see' that the list of names 'was' (or rather could be) a poem, as Fish presents it (ibid.: 337). The first to see this was actually Fish himself, probably for the reasons I have just mentioned, and this recognition ('this list actually has the shape of a poem, and some of these names are biblical') must have triggered his hoax. How he came to think of the experiment, his 'creative impulse', is significantly missing from his account of it. I suspect this is so because it would have quite effectively undermined his argument.

The interpretation(s) offered by Fish's students were not accidental in relation to the words on the blackboard. The professor's claim that this was a religious poem of the kind they had been analysing for weeks was actually supported by names with a biblical ring to them (Jacobs and Levine). Rosenbaum was also mistakenly categorized as a 'Hebrew' name, probably because US students would associate it with Jewish people, and their teacher, Fish, did not complicate things by pointing out that it is in fact German. Thorne could, in the religious context provided by the course and the teacher, only refer to the crown of thorns – etc. Fish claims that his students could have done the same with any list of names, and cites names 'drawn from the faculty of Kenyon College' (ibid.: 328): Temple, Jordan, Seymor, Daniels, Star, Church. He does not state which faculty he excluded from this list of obvious candidates for religious interpretation. But I would really like to see Fish turn the following list of names into a seventeenth-century religious poem: Gentikow, Gripsrud, Hausken, Johansen, Kolbjørnsen, Larsen, Larsen (surnames of those currently employed in the humanities section of my department).

Moreover, the 'interpretation' suggested by Fish of the 'poem' made out of names taken from Kenyon College (ibid.: 328) is by no means identical to the one his students made of their list of names. The same interpretive principles are employed, but the meanings are different; they were, in other words, different 'poems'. The only possible reason is that the signifiers have shifted – the object of interpretation is not the same. This means that Fish will have to revise the position he formulates elsewhere in his book, that the shared 'interpretive strategies' of 'interpretive communities' will 'determine the shape of what is read rather than, as is usually assumed, the other way around' (ibid.: 171). Principles of interpretation may determine the shape of interpretations, but not the shape of that which is interpreted. Within a certain linguistic (not necessarily institutional) community, which may well span the globe, letters, words and other kinds of (combined) signs are given a basic meaning by deeply entrenched conventions which form the basis for all attempts at communication. The fact that the meanings of words (and particularly sentences and longer texts) may change with a change of context, of pragmatic circumstances, does not change this.

Likewise, it is possible to reach interpersonal agreement on a number of elementary features of any kind of text. There are characters named 'God' and 'Jesus' in the Bible, and the storylines in that book can in most cases easily be agreed upon. One may check points of elementary disagreement simply by opening the book: 'Was there a storm blowing when Jesus walked on water or wasn't there?' 'Did this happen before or after he made a deaf man blind?' 'He never made a deaf man blind!' Atheists, Buddhists, Lutherans or Muslims can easily take part in such clarifications as long as their elementary linguistic competence allows them to read. There is, in other words, a considerable space for interpersonally acceptable *descriptions* of (certain important dimensions of) texts, even if, as in the case of the Bible, very different *interpretations* may even give rise to military actions.

According to Jonathan Culler (1983: 73ff.), what has emerged from the debates over what the text and its readers respectively contribute to the outcome

12

of their encounter is that a precise, general theoretical determination of it is quite impossible. He argues that theories of reading will always end up with a 'monism', positing either that 'everything' is supplied by the text or that 'everything' is supplied by the reader. Culler regards this as resulting from 'the impossibility of establishing well-grounded distinctions between fact and interpretation' (1983: 75) in general. Referring to the philosopher Richard Rorty's argument about physics in *Philosophy and the Mirror of Nature* (1980), Culler suggests that a main reason why one should keep 'the notion of a given text with unchanging, discoverable properties' is that it 'provides an excellent backdrop for arguments about interpretation and accounts of changing inter-pretations' (1983: 78). It simply makes for better stories, 'stories of reading', just as, according to Rorty, the notion of physics 'finding' rather than 'making' facts of an unchangeable nature provides an excellent backdrop for our 'stories' of social and cultural change. The idea that the text exists independently of the reader and also 'manipulates' him or her is retained mainly for aesthetic reasons:

> The story of manipulation will always reassert itself, first because it is a much better story, full of dramatic encounters, moments of deception, and reversals of fortune, second, because it deals more easily and precisely with details of meaning, and third, because this sort of narrative confers value on the temporal experience of reading. A reader who creates everything learns nothing, but one who is continually encountering the unexpected can make momentous, unsettling findings. The more a theory stresses the reader's freedom, control, and constitutive activity, the less* likely it is to lead to stories of dramatic encounters and surprises which portrays reading as a process of discovery.
>
> (Culler 1983: 72)

*The sentence reads 'more likely', but this must logically be a printing error.

There is of course something to this argument. But we do not need to establish a general, fixed theoretical distinction between 'subject' and 'object' to acknowledge the existence of these two poles of any act of perception and interpretation. The relations between them most probably vary considerably from the reading of traffic lights to the reading of James Joyce, from the observation that flames are hot to the theory of the Big Bang. Doing away with the notion of an object altogether also leads to the epistemological position formulated by Stanley Fish: his 'fiction' about what reading is 'relieves me of the obligation to be right [. . .] and demands only that I be interesting' (1971: 180). In my view, being interesting is important but not sufficient. While pretending to be absolutely and definitely right would be foolish conceit, not being wrong is an important goal, not only for interpreters of texts, but also for, say, seismic experts and engineers who design bridges in southern California.

Moreover, Rorty's and Culler's argument does not take into consideration the simple fact that people actually do learn something from reading. It is not just a convenient, aesthetically gratifying fiction. That is why schools and universities make people read books, that is why Culler and others keep writing and publishing. If all we get out of reading scholarly texts is already in our heads, reading would not be worth the trouble, students could go home or out to work immediately. And why should the reading of other kinds of texts be any different in this respect? It is true, of course, that we already know a lot about any individual text in any medium before we start reading it, today's newspapers as well as the next episode of *Dynasty*. We are culturally and socially conditioned; knowledge of codes and conventions is part of any kind of literacy. But we do not really know texts until they are read (not even then completely), and we may in principle always be surprised. The more precise (and highly complex) relations between subjects and objects, between readers and texts, must be decided by semiotically informed empirical studies. The existence of the texts as entities separate from readers is evident.

IN DEFENCE OF TEXTUAL INTERPRETATION

Once it is made plausible that the text really exists, new challenges are found in current theories of criticism. To regard the text as the central element in the communication process and to see textual analysis and interpretation as absolutely central to media research meets stubborn resistance not only from empiricist media sociology. It now also has to be legitimized within criticism itself, both as a necessary part of reception studies and, more generally, as a central area of textual studies as such.

For instance, Janet Staiger (1992: 9, 212) repeatedly argues that 'reception studies is not textual interpretation'. According to Staiger, such studies '[i]nstead [. . .] seek to understand textual interpretations as they are produced historically' (ibid.: 9), they seek 'a historical explanation of the activities of interpretation' (ibid.: 212). What Staiger attempts, then, is to separate the study of receptions from a study of the texts they are receptions of. In my view, it is logically impossible to arrive at an understanding of historically produced interpretations without performing an interpretation of the text(s) in question. The texts will also, in many cases, be the best set of data remaining from the historical encounter between two parties – the text and an audience. The fact that the researcher's own interpretation of the text will often differ from those which can be historically (re)constructed highlights the fact that *all* receptions are historically determined, and the difference (if there is one) may lead to fruitful questions. Why did this or that feature of the text seemingly go unnoticed? Was it 'read' unconsciously? Did it touch on what was 'unspeakable' then? To me, only a practical interest in limiting the scope of university courses can make a clear-cut division between interpretation of texts and interpretation of reception (which is, by the way, always also an interpretation of texts) understandable.

14

The other attacks on textual interpretation are of a different nature. While the goal of New Criticism was that of producing ever better, more adequate interpretations of autonomous works through close reading, the goal of structuralists and semioticians has been to 'move through texts towards an understanding of the systems and semiotic processes which make them possible' (Culler 1983: 12), in line with the (linguistic) Saussurean study of *parole* (instances of speech) in order to establish *langue* (the basic elements and the rules for their combinations). In fact, the activity of interpretation has been regarded by some as not really a task for literary studies – 'one thing we do not need is more interpretations of literary works', 'the interpretations of individual works is only tangentially related to the understanding of literature' (1983: 5).

I for my part sympathize with the grand semiotic project, even if in many ways it must be said to have collapsed. But it is hard for me to see how it can exclude interpretation of individual texts as a legitimate and indeed necessary part of research. One cannot move 'through' a text to reach its foundational codes and processes without reading it and thus implicitly performing some kind of interpretation. The very selection of which texts to 'go through' also presupposes that some kind of interpretation has taken place. Questions which for instance interested Fredric Jameson in his *Marxism and Form* (1971), such as why interpretation of a particular text seems 'necessary' and what such a 'necessity' signifies, cannot logically be answered unless the text in question is interpreted in some way, to some extent. In the present book about the *Dynasty* event, it seems to me that a need for some interpretation of the text has been pretty well established by the facts about its reception. Its massive success and the differentiated response to it beg the question of what it was all about. And contrary to Culler and others he has been chosen to represent here, I would hold that interpretation of works is what textual studies are ultimately about, both since that is what reading as a social phenomenon outside academia is to a considerable extent about, and since the interest in *langue* is ultimately motivated by an interest in *parole*.

Jonathan Culler's arguments against interpretation are so easy to counter because he himself does not quite believe in them. They were originally formulated primarily for reasons of institutional politics within academic literary studies in the US in the mid-1970s: 'Fulfillment of the interpretive task has come to be the touchstone by which other kinds of critical writing are judged, and reviewers inevitably ask of any work of literary theory, linguistic analysis, or historical scholarship, whether it actually assists us in our understanding of particular works' (Culler 1981: 5). It is in other words in the defence of theoretical work against a narrow-minded, instrumentalist demand for 'useful theory' that Culler takes his polemical position.

Culler's arguments were first published as early as 1976 (in the article 'Beyond Interpretation'). But they were in part echoed much more recently in film studies, in David Bordwell's *Making Meaning: Inference and Rhetoric in the Interpretation of Cinema* (1989). The energetic argument in this book is: (a) that the business of interpretation ('Interpretation, Inc.') has for too long been the absolute central concern of film studies; (b) that what were once promising theories, concepts and analytical moves have been largely routinized, blunted, reduced to received truths serving as a basis for scholastic exercises with little or no import outside the hierarchical power-games of the interpretive institution of academic film studies. Bordwell's book is not least 'a report on how a particular tribe thinks and talks' (1989: xiv), i.e. an 'anthropological' or 'ethnographic' study of the practices of criticism and the tacit principles and values that regulate them.

As with Culler, Bordwell's position must be understood in light of institutional politics; his attack on 'interpretation' is conditional and actually limited to (a) the total *dominance* of interpretation and (b) the lack of conceptual rigour and other traditional scholarly virtues he finds in much current criticism. In fact, he sees '[t]he virtues of innovative interpretive criticism' as so obvious that no 'lengthy defense' is needed:

> Conceiving of the text as symptomatically revealing cultural tensions introduced a powerful frame of reference. To claim unity across an auteur's output, to posit that cinema contains 'three looks', and to suggest that a genre may constitute an intersection of nature and culture organized a great deal of information within a new perspective. Many exemplars deserve praise because they have introduced conceptual schemes that reorient our understanding. They have activated neglected cues, offered new categories, suggested fresh semantic fields, and widened our rhetorical resources. Innovative frames of reference have heightened our awareness of what can be noticed and appreciated in artworks.
>
> (Bordwell 1989: 256)

This praise of 'innovative' interpretations is furthermore complemented by two (at least institutionally) valuable main functions of 'ordinary criticism': that of '*domestication*, the taming of the new' and that of '*differentiation*, the reshaping of the known' (1989: 256f.).

What I will be doing in this book is not likely to qualify as 'innovative interpretive criticism' in Bordwell's terms. It will contain a little of both forms of 'ordinary criticism'. More importantly, it will also basically adhere to some of Bordwell's own suggestions for alternatives to the kinds of interpretation he criticizes. Not only will I build my inquiry 'around questions and hypotheses more than "applications"' (ibid.: 263), I will also be asking questions similar to those Bordwell recommends:

> First, how are particular films put together? Call this the problem of the film's *composition*. Second, what *effects* and *functions* do particular films have? If criticism can be said to produce knowledge in anything like the sense applicable to the natural and the social sciences, these two questions might be the most reasonable points of departure.
>
> (ibid.: 263)

One can sense here, as often with Bordwell, how close he is to what may be called a 'scientistic' ideal of scholarship, implicitly idealizing the empiricist self-image prevalent in the social sciences. His two simple questions may still be regarded as fundamental and actually extremely difficult to answer. This book may be seen as an attempt to answer them in the case of *Dynasty*.

I should note here that the way I conceive of 'composition' is also inspired by a now classic critique of interpretive practices in the arts: that of Susan Sontag in her essay 'Against Interpretation' (1964). Sontag's point was that various 'hermeneutics' of art tend to completely disregard the 'manifest' or 'superficial' dimensions and qualities of art in order to deep-dive directly for some thematic meaning hidden underneath. In her view, such reductionist and aesthetically insensitive practices should be replaced by an 'erotics' of art, focusing on 'meaningless' sensual, experiential dimensions. Sontag's argument is still important for meaning-fixated interpreters to keep in mind. In my view, though, even 'erotic' dimensions of texts may appear loaded with meaning from certain points of view, which relate these dimensions to historically produced social and cultural conditions.

'Neither causal nor functional explanation is the aim of film interpretation', says Bordwell (1989: 257). In Chapter 5 of this book, a partial explanation of the reception portrayed in the previous chapters is a significant part of what I am seeking. The other main aim of the analysis is to provide a basis for some hopefully qualified thoughts on the historical significance of the whole *Dynasty* event, the text included. That is definitely an interpretive effort, and one I deem absolutely legitimate and necessary, even if it may be less acceptable to those who wish to limit the kinds of questions asked in research to those which may be answered with near absolute certainty and rigour. The classic opposition between understanding (*Verstehen*) and explanation (*Erklärung*) was in part dismantled already by Max Weber, who claimed that sociology 'is a science concerning itself with the interpretive understanding of social action and thereby with a causal explanation of its course and consequences' (Weber 1968: 4). Any communication is social action. It is hard to see why an absolute opposition between understanding/interpretation and explanation should be reintroduced in our field.

MAIN ARGUMENTS: A BRIEF OVERVIEW

This book is, then, in part a study of the *Dynasty* phenomenon in Norway, and this particular media event is regarded as a 'symptom' or 'discursive intersection' of fundamental changes in both international and national structures of media and culture. These changes are related to at least four major, interrelated tendencies: (1) radical internationalization of culture and the media, spearheaded by television; (2) increasing commercialization of the media, both printed and electronic, i.e. changes in content that stem from increased competition for audiences; (3) changing relations between high and low/popular culture, in terms both of the social composition of audiences, and of aesthetic 'transgressions'; (4) relative weakening of the traditions and institutions of popular enlightenment, both in broadcasting and in the public sphere in general. Finally, I also intend to regard the event and the *Dynasty* text itself in relation to general socio-cultural trends in modern societies, and to the particular cultural, political or ideological climate of its decade, on both sides of the Atlantic Ocean.

The book represents in many ways an attempt to come to terms with the various political, cultural and theoretical impulses and challenges of the last fifteen years or so, what one might call 'the postmodern scene'. Though I am critical of many features of my theoretical and Scandinavian socio-cultural background, this book basically makes a conditional, negotiated defence of 'traditional' critical positions. While presenting what is a form of reception research, and also theoretically acknowledging the importance of reception studies, the book argues in favour of emphasizing the powerful role of production in the process of media communication. It argues against more or less unrestrained relativism in evaluation of the aesthetic and socio-political value of texts, in both populist and more general postmodernist versions. It also advocates a re-evaluation of the work of critical intellectuals, opposing certain fashionable 'anti-elitist' positions. Politically, the book argues for the importance of certain basic principles and traditions of public service broadcasting, though acknowledging that there was a need for some rather drastic changes in broadcasting and general cultural policies around 1980. The *Dynasty* event was basically a symptom of this need.

The empirical side of my research focused on 'reception' as a multidimensional process (public and domestic, collective and individual). Several forms of reception data were gathered and analysed: collections of clippings from newspapers and weeklies, letters to the Norwegian Broadcasting Corporation (NRK), audience survey data, etc. But I also attempted to assess the relative importance of production (industry organization and practices, the role of creative personnel) to the processes of meaning production, and my research included interviews with producers and others involved. The process of distribution (including marketing, programming) was also researched. I interviewed and corresponded with a PR company, certain print media and their personnel. Particularly important here was an analysis of print media coverage as part of the marketing of the serial. A major element in my research was the problematic analysis of the serial's text, where problems included deciding the 'object' of analysis, what generic categories were relevant (such as the serial's relation to filmic melodrama), and how more specifically to define and understand its textual characteristics, including the often overlooked use of music. I tried to pay particular attention to an analysis of how the *Dynasty* text invited audience involvement (various forms of identification, 'spectator positions'). On the other hand, I also emphasized a study of important dimensions of the text which one can hardly expect ordinary viewers to think or care much about in their immediate encounters with the show – such as its relation to Umberto Eco's distinction between 'open' and 'closed' texts, and the socio-cultural implications of the never-ending serial format.

The book's main argument in relation to current theoretical and methodological debates is that a *critical* knowledge-interest calls for a comprehensive historical understanding of the communication process(es), and that this necessarily entails a fundamentally *hermeneutic* approach to research issues. It necessitates a thinking together of a wide variety of empirical data in a theoretical framework constructed from discourses at quite different levels of abstraction. The book seeks to demonstrate that such an approach allows for a transgression of certain established borders between research traditions defined in terms of favoured methods or research fields (quantitative vs qualitative methods, political economy vs cultural studies, production vs reception studies). It argues that a fundamentally hermeneutic approach may allow for more relevant and substantial *political* distinctions between critical and affirmative research. The interesting oppositions in research should not be drawn on the basis of which methods and data researchers make use of, but rather on the basis of which questions are asked and which perspectives guide the interpretation of data. The difference between critical research and other kinds of research is not a difference between what is 'mainstream' and what is 'marginal' within the research community and hence dependent on academic conjunctures, as once suggested by Ien Ang (1989: 97). It is rather, as once suggested by Lazarsfeld (cf. p. 4), a matter of how research is related to certain political and ethical values and social conditions at large.

The book's argument in relation to the political, cultural and aesthetic issues involved in the *Dynasty* event and the surrounding debates, could briefly be summarized as follows. The 1980s brought a new awareness and validation of cultural difference which is essential to democratic cultural policies. In part contrary to the established marxist view of 'the market' as a leveller of cultural differences, transnational market forces may in this case be said to have helped produce this awareness. They did so 'positively' by way of highlighting the significance of popular texts and tastes which had been excluded from public broadcasting and official culture, and, at the same time, 'negatively' by posing an imaginable threat to a variety of other cultural forms, ranging from national, regional and ethnic specificities to the institutions and norms of a democratically functioning public sphere.

The 1980s – and the *Dynasty* event representing the decade in this book – may thus on the one hand be said to have demonstrated how the cultural market and mass-mediated culture under the prevailing social conditions of capitalism are valuable indicators of broadly popular interests, concerns, pleasures and hopes. However, the book also argues, in accordance with traditional critiques of the cultural industries, that these industries also exploit and shape these interests, concerns, pleasures and hopes in socially and ideologically affirmative ways. Consequently, the market does not represent 'freedom', as opposed to political,

19

authoritarian 'repression'. The clashes of interests and opinions in informed or enlightened political discourse, not least on where limits to the rule of the market should be drawn, remain the only means of ensuring and developing cultural democracy.

More or less in line with this pragmatic but still critical view of the relation between the market, culture and politics, the book suggests a pragmatic perspective on the questions of 'cultural value' so central to the debates on prime-time soaps and other popular genres. The argument is that genres are used for specific purposes, address specific problems, provide specific pleasures, produce specific types of insights and experiences. Thus, the cultural value of *Dynasty* cannot be directly compared to that of Dennis Potter's/BBC's *The Singing Detective* or Milton's *Paradise Lost*. But I would still argue, as I have done elsewhere (Gripsrud 1991b), that comparative judgements can and should be made about the cultural significance of specific genres, and about individual texts belonging to them, in light of, for instance, their ability to treat certain important issues interestingly, in new, more or less original ways, in a challenging or just pleasant manner. Such judgements always rely on more general standards of moral or political value. These standards may vary with historical, social, cultural and political contexts and positions, but still have a considerable degree of stability and cross-cultural acceptance. A critique of media output will always have to be based in such general standards, for which some degree of universal recognition is demanded – though not necessarily granted. There is a continuous cultural struggle over definitions of values, as there must be in democracies, in which the kind of people known as 'intellectuals' participate.

The book, then, implicitly and explicitly, argues for a conditional reappraisal of the value of critical intellectual work. Though socially marginal, the 'cultural capital' of intellectuals always separates them both from 'the people' and from those in positions achieved by economic capital primarily. They are, in their very marginality, privileged in their access to various forms of knowledge and reflective thought that are indispensable to any political project of emancipation, of social, political and cultural democracy.

1

HOLLYWOOD SPEAKS

To write a history of the culture of the popular classes exclusively from inside those classes, without understanding the ways in which they are constantly held in relation with the institutions of dominant cultural production, is not to live in the twentieth century.

(Hall 1981: 231)

STUDIES OF MEDIA PRODUCTION

The research literature on media production is quite sparse if compared to the overwhelming number of publications concentrating on various forms of audience research (in mass communication and some cultural studies) and textual analysis/criticism (in literature, film and other arts). This is particularly the case in the area of television fiction, in spite of what was once called 'the pervasiveness and importance of television drama in relaying social meanings and cultural forms' (Murdock 1976: 184). Some of the most useful work has been done by mass communication researchers who belong to what may be termed hermeneutically oriented social science (e.g. in the UK, Burns 1977; in the US, Cantor 1971, 1981; Gitlin 1985). But these contributions rarely if ever include thorough analysis of that which is produced, texts, and never encompass also the moment(s) of reception.

In various kinds of media research in the humanities, studies of production processes have been few. Since the late 1960s there has been a growing interest in reception in some circles. This has challenged the previous near-total concentration on the texts and their histories, but production studies have still suffered from low interest – not least for theoretical reasons. To include, as I do in this book, a study of the production of texts in what is basically a study of reception, has been out of the question in critical film, media and cultural studies since their discovery of Althusser, his therapist Lacan and later a couple of essays by Roland Barthes and Michel Foucault (Barthes's 'The Death of the Author' (1982) and 'From Work to Text' (1982) and Foucault's 'What Is an Author?' (1979)). Structuralist and poststructuralist critique of the romanticist ideology of authorship developed another

21

untenable position: 'Whereas the ideology of authorship presents writers as ventriloquists who speak through their works, structuralist criticism, led by Barthes, casts them in the role of dummy, manipulated by the hidden hands of language' (Murdock 1993: 131). Consequently, notions of authorial intention (and 'auteurism') have been considered reactionary and hence declared stone dead. Since the mid-1970s the whole idea that the production of media texts in some ways might determine some of what audiences get out of them has been slightly suspect in significant parts of the academic community in these fields.

The most notable exception to this general picture in film studies is Bordwell, Staiger and Thompson's *The Classical Hollywood Cinema* (1985), which meticulously describes classical studio production, but, conversely, hardly discusses issues of reception in relation to their analyses at all. The useful and in many ways very solid study of the US independent production company MTM Enterprises (Feuer, Kerr and Vahimagi 1984) is as far as I know the only book of its kind in television studies. It includes analyses of specific shows (*The Mary Tyler Moore Show, Lou Grant* and *Hill Street Blues*), but not of reception. An interesting case study of the production and textual characteristics of the BBC serial *Doctor Who* (Tulloch and Alvarado 1983) similarly lacks actual analysis of its reception. The only study of television I know of which covers both production, text and reception is David Buckingham's book about *EastEnders* (1987). Buckingham's is also the only study of television reception I know of besides my own which really seeks to integrate an empirical analysis of public debate and printed media coverage. But on the other hand it limits the analysis of 'ordinary' viewers and their 'readings' of the text to interviews of sixty young people between 7 and 18 years old, and does not really consider the social differentiation of the total audience (cf. Chapter 3 below).

This situation is both puzzling and deplorable if one considers the social functions of various forms of media studies. They are academic disciplines which deliver candidates for careers in the media industries on the one hand and as prospective teachers and critics on the other. The lack of attention to the determinations of media communication on the production side has been coupled with a wave of writing which has pointed out and celebrated the ability of audiences to make their own 'aberrant' or 'oppositional' meanings out of whatever material they are offered. If the conditions, intentions and practices of producers are more or less irrelevant to an understanding of texts and receptions, there is little reason why universities should bother to educate people for these positions. It might as well be left completely to the businesses in question. If, on the other hand, media audiences are by themselves perfectly able to act as fully competent, critical 'readers' of media texts, who needs critical studies, why spend time learning textual analysis?

THE ROLE OF PRODUCTION – IN THEORY

The theoretical climate in which an interest in authorship and production processes is marginalized may be related to the 'postmodern' mood of much cultural and literary criticism since the late 1970s. Elements of poststructuralist philosophy and textual theory have been used to critique fundamental assumptions of previous 'modernist' notions of historical developments (the 'grand narratives') as well as the spatial and temporal metaphors employed in the study of communication and cultural phenomena ('transportation of messages', 'high' and 'low' culture, etc.). Included in this highly generalized and often dubious critique of 'modernism' prevalent in critical theoretical work these days has also been a more or less political condemnation of the traditional marxist subordination of consumption to production in the analysis of historical forces and social power. The logic of such condemnation is well exemplified by Andreas Huyssen in the following passage:

> There seem to be fairly obvious homologies between this modernist insistence on purity and autonomy in art, Freud's privileging of the ego over the id and his insistence on stable, if flexible, ego boundaries, and Marx' privileging of production over consumption. The lure of mass culture, after all, has traditionally been described as the threat of losing oneself in dreams and delusions and of merely consuming rather than producing.
>
> (Huyssen 1986: 199)

This kind of 'homological' thinking in effect places Marx's privileging of production over consumption as just another instance of male bourgeois ideology. Theories which claim to be logically consistent constructions of basic principles underlying social developments or to explain the structures and processes of the human psyche are immediately equated with specific normative ideas about art and culture. What happens is that very different scholarly and more loosely critical discourses on very different subjects are only regarded from a 'formal' rhetorical point of view; they are not regarded in the light of their relative validity in terms of adequacy or degree of *truth*, to use a word postmodernists always avoid or put in quotation marks (even if they still claim that their general ideas about history, society and culture are basically correct).

While it is certainly true that there are interesting 'similarities' between the ideas Huyssen mentions, they can neither be countered nor criticized in the same way. It is perfectly possible to agree with basic points in both Marx's and Freud's theories without subscribing to ideas about 'purity' in art and the dangers of 'losing oneself' in popular culture. The latter idea is, for instance, obviously related to the classical 'Protestant' work ethic, in which production is also given priority over consumption – but a moral priority, not one of social theory and analysis. 'Homological' thinking, such as that represented by Huyssen here, may imply the erasure of distinctions between social fields that are central to an adequate understanding of society and culture. It may also lead to a disregard of important distinctions in the traditional bourgeois ideology it is intended to characterize. Bourgeois ideology has always distinguished between different kinds of production and consumption, and not all forms of 'losing oneself' have been feared or tabooed. One of the reasons for this is that mainstream bourgeois ideology has always kept remnants of romanticism sacred, so that, for instance, 'being carried away' when listening to serious music has been perfectly legitimate. Artists who may have held ideas about the 'purity and autonomy of art' may likewise have stressed the importance of irrational or spiritual elements in (the proper appreciation of) art.

Marx's own dialectical discussion of the relationship between production and consumption in the introduction to *Grundrisse* (1973) is in fact well worth rereading in our context. It is a logical (not 'homological') analysis of a basic economic relationship, pointing out that production is always consumption and that consumption is always production, in a number of ways. He also metaphorically foreshadows a fundamental idea in literary reception theory when pointing out that 'a railway on which no trains run, hence which is not used up, not consumed' is a railway only potentially (Marx 1973: 91). Still, what he concludes is that even if consumption and production are 'moments of one process', production is 'the point of departure for realization and hence also its predominant moment; it is the act through which the whole process again runs its course' (ibid.: 94).

This is a totally abstract, logical point, which in a sense has nothing to do with the *Dynasty* phenomenon as a concrete historical 'event'. But even so, it directs one's attention to an investigation of production's relation to consumption in terms of relative dominance in the historically specific field of television production and consumption. If we now leave the level of grand abstractions and turn to the case of the television industry, it is in fact empirically evident that the 'consumption' (reception) of a TV serial like *Dynasty*, in Norway and elsewhere, was to a certain extent determined by its American production.

Not only was the production of *Dynasty* in Hollywood, rooted in circumstances specific to the competition in the American TV industry for American markets, a logical precondition of any consumption of the product in Norway (and some ninety other countries). Production, according to Marx's abstract logic, 'also gives consumption its specificity, its character, its finish'. Production produces the 'manner of consumption', Marx argues, and he goes on to exemplify: 'Hunger is hunger, but the hunger gratified by cooked meat eaten by knife and fork is a different hunger from that which bolts down raw meat with the aid of hand, nail and tooth' (1973: 92). This classic formulation is in fact worth remembering when one studies the reaction of Norwegian viewers to the fictional format which *Dynasty* presented to them for the very first time: the open-ended soap opera, created for commercial broadcasting. According to Marx's analysis, this specific kind of product would demand a specific 'manner of consumption', which implies a certain subjective experience of the product in question, and thus also produces a certain consumer subject.

24

Transferred to the area of TV 'consumption', this line of thinking suggests that a specific form of televisual fiction demands a certain attitude or way of watching from its audiences which differs from that of other (actual or conceivable) televisual forms. In my view this is quite plausible, and as a hypothesis it lends itself to empirical validation. As I will try to show in the next chapters, *Dynasty* was extremely popular with large audience groups because it could answer an accumulated desire for entertainment in the form of popular drama. In other words, a quite unspecified 'need' for narrative entertainment was experienced as 'satisfied' by Norwegian audiences by the form of the prime-time soap opera, a genre they did not know beforehand and consequently could not 'demand' except as an international 'event' they wanted to be acquainted with. If this line of reasoning seems acceptable, one might say that the introduction of *Dynasty* delivered a specific kind of object for an accumulated need or desire which in principle might also have been met by other conceivable objects, for instance an aesthetically and ideologically different form of family melodrama. The extremely powerful position of US television production in the transnational television market in effect decided how the 'need' was to be met, and thus also what kind of television consumers or audiences would be produced from the 'consumption of the object' (attitudes to television, viewers' competence, ideological inputs, etc.).

THE POWER(S) OF US TELEVISION PRODUCTION

Dynasty was able to play its role on account of the world dominance of the American television industry. This dominance is in part based on the sheer size of the industry, related to the size of its domestic market. The production volume is currently more than 250,000 programming hours per year (Syvertsen 1992: 175). A year has 8,760 hours. Since shows successful in the American domestic market have normally already earned more than enough to pay for production costs, prices in foreign markets can be kept surprisingly low, adjusted to the financial possibilities of different customers. The NRK paid approximately US $1,500 per episode of *Dynasty* in 1983. In comparison, the NRK would at that time have had to pay about $20,000 for a Norwegian feature film, and the production of a particular half-hour satirical comedy (designed for the Montreux television festival) had cost about $6,000 per minute (*Nationen*, 4 June 1983). Examples of maximum prices paid per half hour for US series in 1985 are Italy $48,000, Canada $20,000, West Germany $18,000, UK $14,000, France $10,000, Japan $7,000, Sweden $2,500, Chile $375, Bermuda $45 (Hoskins and Mirus 1988: 511, quoting *Variety*, 17 April 1985). In Canada, production of drama costs about ten times as much as the import of American merchandise (ibid.).

American television's world dominance is of course also supported by generations of US world hegemony in general, and in cultural production particularly. Not only is an effective distributional apparatus at hand, the US has through the work of its cultural industries also long been established as a common 'mythic universe' to people all over the world. The cultural heterogeneity of the US domestic market has probably also helped to make the marketing of almost any American cultural product quite easy. They are from the outset constructed for audiences with a wide range of cultural backgrounds. All of these things contribute to an explanation of American television's international dominance.

Neglecting these elementary factors of economic, political and cultural power on the side of production when investigating 'the apparent ease with which American television programmes cross cultural and linguistic frontiers' (Katz and Liebes 1986: 187) necessarily leads to what must be termed apologetic research. One must then search for the answer only in a kind of magic either inherent in the programmes themselves or/and in the relationship between the programmes and their viewers. This is in fact the basic premise of, for instance, Katz and Liebes's project on *Dallas*. Their project's ultimate aim is, it seems, to 'explain the diffusion of a programme like *Dallas*' (ibid.: 187) in a perspective which is clearly opposed to those of research traditions in which US cultural 'imperialism' or cultural dominance is regarded as undesirable or at least problematic. In Katz and Liebes's project the explanation for the 'diffusion' of US television is only sought for in the interactive relationship between viewers and the text. They do not ask why the text is there to be interacted with in the first place.

Dallas is credited by Liebes and Katz with the capacity to stimulate the imagination and social interaction of different audiences. But without the power of production as part of the interpretive framework, it is impossible to ask, for instance, if other kinds of production might not only stimulate audience activities in a similar way, but also provide a form of entertainment which would address the viewers' lives more specifically, with a different influence on their way of looking at their conditions of existence.

I wish to stress again what I said in the introduction to this book, that this does not mean that research such as that of Katz and Liebes is without interest. As a contribution to a better understanding of how viewers interact with television texts, their work is important, and I will be drawing on their efforts in Chapter 3. Still, the interpretation of their observations should take place in a framework that differs from their own – a perspective which acknowledges the many-sided power of the American television industry over viewers' reception(s).

HOLLYWOOD IN US TELEVISION

The fact that Hollywood is the centre of both the film and television industries is an indication of how intimately the two are intertwined. This has been so since the mid-1950s. The film industry initially regarded television as an unwanted competitor. As cinema attendance showed signs of decline, this attitude was replaced by the considerably more profitable policy of cooperation in the role of supplier. The New York-based production of live anthology dramas died out, and Hollywood's filmed episodic series became the staple fare of US TV fiction (Barnouw 1975: 166, 193ff.).

There were a number of reasons for this development. For television, the shift from live transmissions to the more controllable production on film – both in terms of content and in terms of expenses – held many advantages. The series format meant that production could be rationalized and costs more precisely calculated. Live programmes transmitted from New York in the late afternoon would become prime-time viewing in California because of the four hours of time difference between the coasts. Filmed series could be distributed to the various local stations in advance, and thus make it possible for programming to be adjusted to the different time-zones in the US. They could also be redistributed or 'syndicated' after the first showing. They facilitated the shift from the financing system where a single company sponsored a whole programme to spot advertising. This increased the creative control of the networks, since no single company could claim the right to decide whether a programme served its interests any more. It also reduced the risk taken by advertisers, who could now spread their advertising across different programmes. Last but not least, the audience attendance of an established series could be more accurately predicted than that of a one-off anthology drama, with the help of A.C. Nielsen's ratings.

The geographical move from New York to Hollywood was also one of cultural significance – from a traditional centre for 'high' culture in the US, to the traditional centre for 'low' culture. The television historian Eric Barnouw mentions the worries sponsors had over the ideological implications of the kind of drama the New York artists had produced in the early and mid-1950s. These dramas, one suspected, tended to work against the interests of sponsors. Commercials and dramas dealt with the same problems, 'people who feared failure in love and in business'. But while the commercials suggested that the problems could be easily solved by a new deodorant or a new floor wax, the dramas 'made them complicated. They were forever suggesting that a problem might stem from childhood and involved feelings toward a mother or a father. All this was often convincing – that was the trouble. It made the commercial seem fraudulent' (Barnouw 1975: 163). This points to the very significant differences between film and commercial television, as businesses and as discursive regimes.

> Historically, the corporate interests that produced theatricals [movies for cinemas] were served by a narrative that was created as an end in itself. The TV narrative serves a different design; it must at once be a suitable 'environment' for commercials and a mechanism for delivery of an audience of a certain demographic composition.
>
> (Vianello 1984: 217)

Television's business in the US is in other words basically to deliver audiences for advertisers, or 'textualizing the interaction of audience and advertizers' (Browne 1984: 178). This has of course profoundly influenced the aesthetics of American television drama, from the structure of its stories (such as their adjustment to the rhythms of commercial breaks) to the looks of its actors (most shows dominated by actors looking as if they normally worked in commercials for cosmetics). The strict, commercially motivated formulas and schedules regulating drama production for network TV leave, it seems, extremely little room for personal, creative or ideologically deviant manoeuvres by the industry's personnel. US television drama is the epitome of commercial cultural production.

THE PRODUCER'S MEDIUM

While television was long researched mainly for its more or less detrimental influences on the population, there was from the mid- and late 1970s on an increased academic interest in television's texts. The quantitative forms of content analysis, such as counting the number of murders or sexual innuendoes per hour, were supplemented by various forms of structuralist and other forms of qualitative textual analysis. The purpose was often that of exposing, in a rather straightforward fashion, the bourgeois, misogynist or racist ideology of most TV texts. This analytical interest meant that television was now taken more seriously as a cultural phenomenon, as the dominant image-making institution in the US and other western societies. In effect, this also meant granting a new kind of respectability to the television medium, acknowledging the kinds of craftsmanship and creativity involved in the production of programmes.

Film had in the early 1960s secured its status as an art form through the so-called auteur theory, which was less a scholarly theory than a conception of film criticism (formed by film directors) that identified the director as the individual creative genius behind a filmic text and its (sometimes) unique style. In the early 1980s, two academic friends of television, Horace Newcomb and Robert S. Alley, launched a parallel idea of television as 'the producer's medium' (Newcomb and Alley 1983). The research of Muriel Cantor (1971) had a decade earlier demonstrated how central the producer's role was in US television, but Newcomb and Alley also argued something else. The central point of their book, mainly consisting of rather polite interviews with various American TV producers, was to demonstrate that certain producers are able to leave the imprint of a personal style on their products, thereby in effect qualifying their shows as 'art'.

The reason for picking the producer as the person responsible for a distinctive style or approach in TV productions lies in the way production has been organized in the American system. (Changes may be on the way as this is written, in 1993.) The networks are normally directly responsible only for the production of news programming; all entertainment and fiction is produced by formally independent production companies. These may either suggest ideas for new shows to the networks, or they may be asked by the programme development sections of the networks to develop certain ideas into scripts and pilot episodes. The networks then pay 80 per cent of production costs for the exclusive rights to the first two screenings of the shows. This means that the profits of the production company – the producer – depend on syndication sales to 'independent' (non-network, local) stations and abroad, the revenues from which belong exclusively to them. Thus, the producer's profits also depend on the show's first-run network success: without it, syndication and export sales will be minimized. With this arrangement, it is secured that the goals of the producers are completely in line with those of the network: creating a commercial success is the first priority.

Newcomb and Alley (1983: xiv) say, in the introduction to their book, that the producer's chance to achieve an artistic expression lies in his or her ability to transform constraints into 'a creative profile'. This is of course perfectly in line with the originally French auteur theory's argument about certain Hollywood directors. TV's dominant series format prevents the director having the same role as in film. The directors (and writers) may change, while the series – and its producer(s) – remain. The producer is thus the most stable member of a series' behind-the-camera staff. He or she does have a central creative role, but this role, unlike that of most film directors, includes a financial responsibility and interest. The US television producer is a very special kind of artist, if that is an appropriate term at all – he or she is at least as much a business executive.

AARON SPELLING, THE PRODUCER TYCOON

US television's own presentation of a successful producer is not without interest here. ABC's entertainment news programme, *Hollywood Close-up* of 9 November 1985, contained a report about and an interview with *Dynasty*'s producer, Aaron Spelling – and his wife, Candy. The main point of the reportage was that Spelling, like Blake Carrington, was a self-made man from a poor background in Texas. Only three days earlier he had dreamt that he was in the grocery store with his mother, and she couldn't pay the bill. His office is now so large it could house an airplane, according to the reporter, and he is able to supply Candy with all the jewellery she loves so much. Spelling was allowed more than a full prime-time minute to praise his wife, and the reporter said to her that she is 'married to one of the most romantic men I have met in my life'. Candy: 'I think I'm going to cry . . . '

The interesting thing here is not so much that the programme stressed the similarities between the Spellings and the Carringtons (the whole thing was actually part of the promotion for *Dynasty*'s spin-off *The Colbys*), but rather that there was no mention at all of any specific style or artistic idea informing Spelling's long-time work in the business. It was very much a business portrait

29

(and a quite hilarious one, too), not at all reminiscent of the 'portrait of an artist' genre. The whole presentation of Spelling, in short, confirmed Adorno and Horkheimer's remark in the *Dialectic of Enlightenment* that the various culture industries in no way try to hide their fundamental nature as business enterprises. On the contrary, they 'publish the incomes of their executives so as to remove all doubts about the social necessity of their finished products' (Adorno and Horkheimer 1981: 144).

But Aaron Spelling is actually 'in a class by himself', according to Todd Gitlin (1985: 136). Previously a TV actor and writer, he became tremendously successful as a producer from the late 1960s on, so successful he was able to 'transform the face of television' through his 'distinct style' (ibid.: 137).

> For upscale viewers and finicky critics, there was Spelling-Goldberg's more tasteful and realistic *Family*, but mostly Aaron Spelling produced what he called 'fast-food entertainment': high gloss, glamorous settings, shot in bright, primary colors, with plots, lines, and gestures stamped out so predictably they look as if they have been programmed by a home computer that not only carries out the programs locked in its memory but has been programmed to write variations.
>
> (ibid.)

Spelling has also been known to prefer 'tennis-match dialogue', simple lines and counterlines from characters A and B shot over the other's shoulder; and he is supposed to insist on a 'show and tell' technique in which something is first shown and then in the next scene talked about by the characters. This not only makes each point of the story very clear to the slowest and most inattentive in the audience, it also makes most viewers know more than the principal characters at any given moment. Someone explained to a frustrated director who had quarrelled with Spelling over this that it was a principle taken from children's theatre:

> The villain walks out onstage and says, 'Heh-heh-heh, I have the secret matchbook, and I am going to hide it. I am going to put it behind this basket, and the heroine will never find it. Heh-heh-heh!' And he walks off. Now the heroine comes out and says, 'Where oh where is the secret matchbook?' And all the kids in the audience say, 'It's behind the basket, it's behind the basket!' That's what Aaron does. He believes that that's what the American audience is, you see.
>
> (ibid.: 138)

Gitlin adds: 'And, by any network standard, it all works.'

The success of principles of children's theatre in dramatic fiction intended for adults is not often reflected on in recent television criticism. Adorno has, however, tied an (expressed!) interest in producing for a child's cultural level to a wider perspective on the culture industry's social effects:

This potential, however, lies in the promotion and an exploitation of the ego-weakness to which the powerless members of contemporary society, with its concentration of power, are condemned. Their consciousness is further developed retrogressively. It is no coincidence that cynical American film producers are heard to say that their pictures must take into consideration the level of eleven-year-olds. In doing so they would very much like to make adults into eleven-year-olds.

(1991: 91)

This is of course a 'tendentious' interpretation of overheard remarks (Adorno lived in Los Angeles in the 1940s) and of an observable feature of many Hollywood productions. It is also tied to what may well be an exaggeration of the extent to which modern western societies leave their rank-and-file members powerless by various ideological and socio-structural means. The central point of the argument remains and should still be considered disturbing: if the culture industry constantly addresses its audiences as child-like, as relatively simple-minded and thus ultimately dependent on some authority other than themselves, this might in the long run affect the self-image of these audiences. They might, over, say, a couple of generations, become more child-like, less self-determined and easier to control by various powerful social agencies than they would have become if they were addressed differently, more demandingly, as adults. This is, as Adorno argues in the (in)famous 'Culture Industry' essay, especially possible since people are largely deprived of self-determination in other areas of social life – at work and in relation to political decisions at many levels of government.

SPELLING MEETS THE SHAPIROS: DIFFERENT TYPES OF PRODUCERS

It is not hard to see that some of the characteristics Gitlin attributes to Spelling productions could be found in *Dynasty*. But *Dynasty* was not an exclusive Aaron Spelling production. He coproduced it with Esther and Richard Shapiro, who had the idea for the show, but not a production company of their own. These were people who had a somewhat different background, which needs to be looked into if the role of the producers is to be understood in *Dynasty*'s case. I concentrate on Esther Shapiro in the following, because for many reasons it is fair to say that she played the leading role in the *Dynasty* project.

Esther Shapiro studied comparative literature at the University of Southern California and was influenced by the political upheavals of the 1960s, mainly the women's movement. She met Richard several years later at a screen-writing course at UCLA. They started to cooperate on scripts for TV shows in several genres (*Ironside* was one of them), with no particular success (or failure, for that matter). They also worked on daytime soaps for a few months (personal communication; interview with Esther Shapiro, March 1988). But from the

31

early 1970s on, when the production of made-for-TV movies was really grow-ing, the Shapiros had the opportunity to 'strut their social concern' (Klein 1985: 37) in writing several 'socially relevant' pieces. The best remembered of these is probably Esther's *Sarah T. Portrait of a Teenage Alcoholic* (1975), but she also wrote (with her husband) *Minstrel Man* (which won the Prix Italia, according to Shapiro in an interview with Norwegian television, 25 January 1984) and *Intimate Strangers* (both 1977). Richard, among other things, also did the screen-play of a feature film, a comedy set in 1908 Colorado called *The Great Scout & Cathouse Thursday* (1975/6) (information drawn from the database of *Baseline Inc.*, January 1987). The couple were known in the business as highly competent craftspeople and called on as 'script doctors' on several occasions.

Esther Shapiro became vice-president in charge of mini-series at the ABC network for almost three years in the late 1970s, and soon established a reputation as a strong-willed executive with a particular interest in ideas that (the male) executives above her would find daring or outright dangerous. She has been credited with developing such mini-series as *Roots – The Next Generation*, *Masada* and *Winds of War* (Crotta 1985). Most remarkable is the story of how she struggled to get an adaptation of Marilyn French's novel *The Women's Room* produced. A whole campaign was necessary to have the idea pass the upper levels, involving among other things changing the signs on the executive men's rooms' doors to 'Women's Room' (Klein 1985). The original idea was to do the adaptation as a mini-series, but Shapiro had to accept a 'downgrading' of the project to a single movie-of-the-week, and the network ran a 'disclaimer', a statement on screen 'assuring viewers the show was set in the past and not meant to be relevant to current times' (Faludi 1992: 183). Even if network executives had predicted a rating of 11 per cent or less, the movie in fact ended up with an extremely strong share of 45 per cent, making it one of the most successful TV movies ever (Gitlin 1985: 195). It is not unlikely that the struggle over *The Women's Room*, which she has called 'the most gruelling experience' of her career (Faludi 1992: 183), was part of the reason why Shapiro left ABC shortly after.

Shapiro was a pioneer in breaking down the compact uniformity in US television's executive circles. A study of US television's 'elite' published in 1983 found a striking social homogeneity: they were 99 per cent white, 98 per cent male, 83 per cent from metropolitan areas, 59 per cent raised as Jewish (Cantor 1992: 73). This study did, however, use a sampling criterion, associa-tion with more than one show, which blinded it to the fact that 'a minirevolution has occurred for women in television production' (ibid.: 73) since the early 1970s, when there were virtually no female producers. In the 1986–7 season, thirty-seven women were listed as executive producers, supervising producers or producers (ibid.). Esther Shapiro was then, along with Terry Louise Fisher of *L.A. Law,* a sign of this beginning of a broader change in the position of women in the industry.

The main point of all this is to give an idea of what the teaming of the

Shapiros and Aaron Spelling in the production of *Dynasty* meant in terms of competences and aesthetic and political orientations. Spelling was probably the most successful producer of mainstream television at the time. His preferred style was that of 'high gloss' and 'glamour' in terms of mise-en-scène and quite heavy-handed storytelling even by television industry standards. In political terms, he was hardly the most progressive person around. As a producer 'type', he resembles most what Muriel Cantor (1971) has called 'old-line producers', people with little formal education but broad, long-term experience, who have no problem with commercialism and tend to see their audience as 'unsophisticated' (ibid.: 199). The Shapiros were highly skilled script-writers with a background mostly in 'realistic' and often 'socially relevant' productions. Politically they were liberals (in the American sense), with Esther's interest in feminist issues possibly putting her at odds with the then almost totally male top rank of executives both in the network(s) and elsewhere in the business. As producer types, they seem to fall in Cantor's two other categories: 'film makers' and 'writers-producers'. Film makers are people who have formal education in film/ television and who tend to regard work in feature film production as their 'real' goal. They therefore tend to see their work in television as a practical necessity, a means of acquiring further knowledge of the 'business' and a financial basis for film work; hence they rarely have a problem with adjusting to the demands of commercialism, and are not inclined to be interested in social 'messages'. They also 'consider themselves to have artistic tastes that are superior to those of the television audience' (Cantor 1971: 191), but know television is just not the place for elevated taste. I speculate that this is more or less where Richard Shapiro might belong, also because of his feature film record. Esther Shapiro, on the other hand, seems to be an obvious representative of the 'writer-producer' category. A majority of these have college education in a relevant field, and started out as script-writers. They become producers mainly to maintain control of what they have written, and often get in (a degree of) conflict with both networks and their own production companies. This is related to their emphasis on creative control, and their quite strong interest in 'new ideas and the political aspects of story writing' (ibid.: 194). The writers-producers are thus 'closer to the ideal of the lone creator, more similar to the artist, composer, novelist, and playwright than the other two types' (ibid.: 201). They are in a sense the group of producers who take the television medium most seriously, and correspondingly, in Cantor's study, tend to believe 'that the viewing audience is more intelligent than the networks believe it is' (ibid.: 196).

While the economic functions, organization and textual formats of US television production present producers with certain fundamental premises for their work, all of these factors are also reproduced and to some extent shaped by the people who act within their confines. The 'author' may from a certain point of view be theoretically 'dead', but in practice she or he or they live on and act as productive mediating instances in the ever ongoing (re)production of texts, in the institutional contexts of various media. The experiences, skills, aesthetic and political inclinations of the 'author' are not inconsequential. *Dynasty* is a case in point.

MOTIVATIONS, RATIONALIZATIONS – AND REAGANISM

When Esther Shapiro left ABC, she had 'a commitment from a back-end deal' (Gitlin 1985: 140) to write a script. 'They wanted us to do . . . anything we wanted. They needed a kind of serial, because *Dallas* was on another channel', Shapiro said in her interview with me in March 1988. It was, in other words, clear that they were supposed to come up with an idea that could become ABC's answer to the CBS success. This institutional, competitive element was rarely mentioned when Shapiro was asked in interviews about the background for *Dynasty*. More often, the idea for the show would be presented as the product of 'free' artistic creativity, in line with traditional romanticist ideas of the author/artist, and the show would also be tied to high culture 'forerunners'. When asked by an NRK (Norwegian Broadcasting Corporation) reporter how she got the idea for *Dynasty*, her answer was that

> we were much inspired by *I, Claudius*, on British television, and I have always been a Roman history buff. And I was fascinated by the idea of . . . of . . . of . . . the machinations of those families and what they did to each other. They would poison each other, they would do whatever, all kinds of mayhem. And it was endlessly fascinating. And if you look at Shakespeare, all the really good things, or at Dickens, always came from those kinds of family situations.
>
> (NRK-TV, 25 January 1984)

The story Esther Shapiro told me in my interview with her was a little bit different. Esther and her husband Richard took a vacation in Hawaii, and she says they 'began to think of all the things you were not supposed to do for television'. Shapiro then describes the background for the idea of the serial as follows:

> A lot of it was . . . business, like an oil crisis, older women who are not really acceptable as the main characters, the very rich are no-no, [. . .] They don't *seem* rich on *Dallas*. I mean, you don't see servants, you didn't see big cars, there were good old boys. And I love old mansions. [. . .] But the basic reason, I think, underneath it all, was that the portrayal of women on American television has always been that of a sex object, not the central character, and when we did have a central character it would only be in comedy, like Lucille Ball or somebody else. And, getting older myself, I kept thinking there's not going to be a lot of future here. What about . . . if we really did an older woman's fantasy? There's nothing to watch on television for most women [. . .], while there's been a lot of escapist fiction for men. Detectives with gold chains around their neck, jumping over fences. There's

nothing for women. And somehow or other, the pubescent male executives at the networks found it totally acceptable that we could deal with men's fantasies, but women had to be portrayed, it seems to me, either as victims, or as a woman who has lost a child. I mean, you have to have some really horrendous thing happen to you in order to be taken seriously. [. . .] And because I had my own secret ambitions – I've always wanted to run a Fortune 500 company – there were no really female role models for that, so in many ways Blake Carrington is my role model. I want to be Blake Carrington. [JG.: I *am* Blake Carrington.] Yes [*laughter*], I say that all the time. But my husband thinks I'm very much like Linda [Evans, i.e. 'Krystle Carrington'] because, he says, 'you're so moral, I mean, you work in this business and you never, you know, cheat anybody'. But I think that, when it comes down to litigation and all that, I'm pretty much like Alexis.

There are several points to be made here. First, the Shapiros were given an unusual amount of freedom by the network, even if their expectation of a competitor to *Dallas* was clear. This had its explanation in the couple's reputation in the business, their previously demonstrated skills in complying with the demands of a format while at the same time being inventive and even creative within them. A striking instance of how smart Esther Shapiro could be in relation to network executives was something she mentioned elsewhere in my interview with her. Since she knew these powerful men mostly had wives older than most women appearing on prime-time TV, she had calculated that they would feel personally flattered by having mature women presented as glamorous and sexually attractive. This was her best chance of having them accept the idea of breaking the monopoly of young women in prime time.

Second, Shapiro's fascination with 'the very rich', those too rich to have been considered appropriate for television's working- and middle-class audiences, was very much a personal one. It was not only taken from hunches of 'what was in the wind' or survey results indicating a particular ideological trend. The Shapiros started writing the script at least 15–16 months before the show premiered – in the week of Ronald Reagan's inauguration as president. One may wonder why they did not do something which was more in line with the 'socially relevant' material they had gained most of their experience with. But, as Shapiro explained in another interview, 'all of that seemed written out' (Klein 1985: 37). In other words, there was with the Shapiros, as with the majority of the voters in the presidential election in 1980, a feeling that it was time for something other than the climate of the 1970s. That *Dynasty* became a fantasy show about the lives of super-rich people was not just inspired by *Dallas*: it was just as much inspired by the political and cultural 'climate' in general.

Successful writers and producers in the industry are, then, not only very receptive of cultural trends, or 'cultural barometers'. They are, to a considerable degree, part of the audience they strive to attract. This is not to deny the active research into 'signs of the times' which is a significant part of a normal working day for people such as Esther Shapiro. She told me she gets up at 5.30 in the morning and then spends hours reading a wide selection of newspapers and magazines. As for surveys and other 'scientific' information on audiences and their responses to a serial's plot developments or characters, Shapiro, like other creative personnel, denies their influence. According to them, such material only 'confirmed what we already knew', it always comes *post factum*, after the production is already done.

Third, the emphasis in Shapiro's account on the wish to do a women's show, and particularly something for 'older' women, is believable particularly because of her previous efforts in that direction. She stressed this point also in her interview with NRK-TV (cf. p. 34). But *Dynasty* would not have been '*Dynasty* as we know it' (cf. Chapter 5 of this book) without Alexis, and she was in fact not part of the original conception of the show. This has also been pointed out by Gabrielle Kreutzner and Ellen Seiter (1991: 167): 'Few critics and viewers may remember that *Dynasty* started out as a *Dallas* clone, distinguished from its model by the creator-producer's explicit attempt to make the Ewings look rather pedestrian and petit-bourgeois.' Alexis was introduced in the first episode of the second season, and she was the creation of two new writers who were brought in at that time: Robert and Eileen Pollock. They had written daytime serials for years, and they immediately saw that the show was in need of a real 'bitch'.

In other words, the Shapiros were not the people who gave the show its decisive twist of feminine power challenge and its melodramatic enactment of the ultimate feminine stereotypes. Much of what Shapiro recounts as the motivation for the show must accordingly be seen as a kind of backward projection of what *Dynasty* came to be after the first season. *Dallas* also went through considerable changes after its first conception and first season, when it actually was a series, not a continuing serial. But that show's producers and writers seem to have had less of a problem remembering these changes, which they claim were made in part by accident, in part as a result of audience response (Silj *et al.* 1988: 12–21). For Shapiro, on the other hand, there were political values at stake here, which may have made accurate memory more difficult. Some of what she said in the interview with me indicated that Alexis had turned the show around in Shapiro's mind too. She stressed that she wanted to portray women who were 'in charge of their lives', not 'victims'. But the first season of *Dynasty* had Krystle, the subservient secretary, married to her brutal boss Blake Carrington, and the psychiatrically troubled Mrs Claudia Blaisdel as central female characters. The only woman with some noticeable transcendence of a traditional role was Fallon, Carrington's daughter, who as a father-fixated adolescent living at home, could hardly be seen as being 'in charge of her life'. This is why Esther Shapiro said that she identified with Blake Carrington; there were no females worth identifying with, if one wanted powerful self-images. In the above quote from my interview with Shapiro, it is worth noting how she slides from talking about identification with Blake

36

Carrington to talking about her similarities with Alexis. The latter is in a sense a female version of him, and she came in later.

The central ambition seems to have been to produce a fantasy show about struggle for 'control'. The domain of 'big corporations' would then be a suitable setting, not only because it is known to be a place where power is exercised and fought over, but also because it is a sphere so remote from most people that it is an adequate space for the play of fantasy. It is known to exist, but it is unknown territory. The feminist interest gets fused with the fascination with extreme wealth through the issue of power. Later in the interview, Shapiro also said that it is always good to see the rich 'get it'. In other words, the show could play to the (anticipated) widespread ambivalence towards the milieu in question; it was attractive because of the wealth and power associated with it, while at the same time also repulsive because of the moral corruption attributed to these very assets. The show would thus portray power and control as not entirely desirable. This ambivalence takes on a different and politically clearly problematic meaning when it is placed in the feminist perspective. It may actually lead to the question whether (women's) power or control is really worth the struggle.

In her interview with NRK-TV, Esther Shapiro suggested an additional interesting perspective on the social functions of *Dynasty*'s big business fantasy. She insisted that the show was humorous and entertaining, and 'certainly not political'. When the reporter asked 'what's so funny about suicide, rape, that people are getting divorced', Shapiro interrupted him with the following answer:

> Each of those things is not humorous. But when you put all those things together, it's like tying somebody to a railroad track, and a train is coming, and you say 'oh, by the way, that person has cancer too, and a few other things'. All those things could not happen to a single family. But I think it does go back to something I've said before. We have a, certainly in America, a society where life is fairly grim, in terms of the reality of having to work and what your expectations can be. And personally. . . . So many people are, you know, married to people they don't like, they have children they don't like, they work at jobs that they hate. They are quite repressed, there is no catharsis. So to come home, and watch people play out those . . . all those . . . rape, and those fantasies of telling each other off and . . . and cheating in business, and doing all of that stuff, I think it's a great release. If you took the same story and put it in a very, very grim, very lower middle class, it would be almost impossible to watch. But there is some sort of pleasure in knowing that the rich have worse problems than you do, and let them have it, you know.

Shapiro's analysis here is probably on to an important element in the social function of *Dynasty*, especially for 'very lower middle-class' viewers (note the smooth euphemism taken from American strata sociology!). While her own preferred perspective is obviously that of (ironic) humour, the fun of 'too

37

much', the cathartic effect she suggests for the many people who hate their lives (and have reason to do so) is not one of irony. It depends on taking the show at face value to a considerable extent. Shapiro in other words points to the likelihood of socially stratified receptions of the show.

The ambivalence towards big business is probably as old as American corporate capitalism. But the ambivalence in *Dynasty* may also be seen in the light of more specific ideological conditions in the late 1970s. The coincidence that *Dynasty* was shown for the first time as Ronald Reagan moved into the White House suggests how we need to think of media production as always embedded in wider social, cultural and political contexts. That both *Dallas* and *Dynasty* were the first TV shows ever to be set in the headquarters and homes of big business families, might also be tied to the powerful ideological offensive in the second half of the 1970s of corporate America, which used the media in a number of ways in order to change what the business community regarded as a widespread 'hostility' to (big) business since the 1960s. Peter Dreier (1985) has described a five-part 'selling job' undertaken from 1974 on, which in various ways, directly and indirectly, by uses of financial power, produced both signifi- cantly increased and more favourable coverage of big business in the media, particularly the print media. The five elements Dreier lists are: (1) so-called 'advocacy advertising' in major newspapers and magazines; (2) exclusive joint seminars for corporate and media executives; (3) endowments for programmes in business reporting at journalism schools; (4) several new awards for 'excel- lence' in business reporting; and (5) increased support for conservative think- tanks and other business-friendly expertise which journalists use as sources. Dreier summarizes the results of these measures in a way which indicates their success in helping to prepare the ideological climate for both Reaganism and the arrival of yuppies as dominant media culture heroes of the 1980s:

> Since 1978, almost every major newspaper in the country has expanded its business pages and added staff to cover business. A few, such as *The New York Times*, *The Boston Globe*, *The Washington Post*, the *Chicago Tribune*, and others, have added special business sections. (In contrast, there are only about twenty-five full-time labor-reporters on American newspapers.) [. . .] Much of it is simply boosterism – glowing stories of new investment plans, fawning profiles of corporate executives, summaries of quarterly and annual corporate reports. Stories about personal finance – how to start a new business, where to invest your savings, problems of finding a second home – take up much of the remaining space. There is almost no investigative reporting on these pages and little good to say about unions or consumer groups. Their focus is on 'upscale' readers, not inflation-pinched working folks.
>
> (1985: 302f.)

This is of course not to argue that a big business conspiracy was behind both *Dallas* and *Dynasty*. It only goes to show that particularly powerful actors did

38

their best to change the public's perception of corporate America, and society at large along with it, at the time when these shows were developed. And even if, as Esther Shapiro in her own way pointed out, *Dynasty* had to negotiate the fascination and idealization of big business with (remnants of) a widespread negative attitude towards it, my analysis of the serial's text will demonstrate that the show never questioned the role of Blake Carrington as guarantor of national prosperity and security.

SOAP EXPERTISE: THE POLLOCKS

Robert and Eileen Pollock had about twenty-five years of writing experience when they started working on *Dynasty*. ('We started working in television in the fifties', they told me in my taped interview with them, June 1987.) They had done a couple of books (like an 'autobiography' of Maurice Chevalier), but most of their experience came from writing daytime soaps in New York, such as *General Hospital*. They were also the first writers of daytime serial drama to receive an Emmy (for a show called *The Doctors*).

As *Dallas* became a success, they decided to create a soap opera by themselves, i.e. they wrote a 'bible' for a new show. A 'bible' is a manuscript of about 150 pages, written much in the style of a novel, presenting characters and describing main story developments in a serial for one or possibly two years. Their 'bible' did not sell, but it somehow landed in Aaron Spelling's office, at a time when *Dynasty* was in need of people who could do stories. Such people were, according to the Pollocks, harder to find than people who could do scripts. So, from episode 14 to episode 85, they did both the story and the outlines, i.e. the organizing of storylines into episodes. Ed de Blasio worked on the scripts along with freelance writers. The staff was then expanded and the division of labour altered so that the Shapiros and the Pollocks created the 'bibles', and someone else who, according to the Pollocks, 'is better at structure', did the outlines in cooperation with the Pollocks. This person then worked with three groups of writers who did the scripts and, as my interviewees said, 'also put some of their input into the story'. By the time the scripts reached the directors, they were thus definitely a collective product.

In my interview with her, Esther Shapiro talked quite a lot about what her intentions with *Dynasty* were, what the social significance of it was or was supposed to be. She spoke in the manner of a creator. The Pollocks spoke of their work in a different way, even if they were very clear about who had invented Alexis. They presented themselves first and foremost as industry professionals, as people who made their contributions out of knowledge of form rather than out of a need to express themselves or make any kind of 'socially relevant' statement.

Episode 13 of *Dynasty* ended when a heavily veiled character with sunglasses and a wide-brimmed hat entered the courtroom where Blake Carrington was on trial for murder. Fallon said to her brother Steven, 'Oh, my God, that's mother!' The plan for the following season then was to have 'mother', Blake's former wife, played by, for instance, Sophia Loren for about four episodes. Her name was supposed to be Madeleine. Eileen Pollock recounts their intervention at this point as follows:

Bob and I heard all this, and we were quite dismayed. First of all, you learn from many, many years of writing with continuing serial form, that you *never* create a major, core family character for four episodes. You would then create a character who is good for four *years*, for for ever, but *never* just for a quick little in-and-out. So first of all we said 'this name will have to go'. There was no concept about the character, so Bob and I sat down and created Alexis, and the first thing we did was name her Alexis. The second thing we did was start to structure a woman filled with vengeance. But, and again this comes back to so many years of understanding form, if you write a villain – and I think this is true, really, the closest form to this is the novel – if you write a villain who is all black, first of all she's a bore, or he's a bore, secondly they wear out their welcome, they cease being fun to the audience after a few chapters or a few weeks, because you always know what they're going to do. The really good and successful villains and villainesses have many textures, many colours, and in their own point of view, they have justification, or what we call 'they're on the side of the angels'. [. . .] And so we said 'what is it that drives Alexis?', and we said, what drives her, is a rage, an absolute rage, against this man whom she is not really finished with yet, she has really unfinished emotional business with him. Her rage against him, is that he not only broke the marriage – which he probably had a right to do, he caught her, you know, in bed with the gardener man – but the fact that he exiled her from her children. He sent her out of not only his marriage and his life and the country, but sent her away from her children, so that she was robbed of the experience as a mother of being able to experience her children growing up. The one really good core of Alexis, which we've never violated, is her love for her children, and that hunger to somehow make up for those years that were lost. [. . .] And her kids, as you may recall, were in one large amount of need of that love, because they had an awful lot of problems of their own with just dear old dad. And so Alexis – who did so very many naughty things, most of the naughty things I invented, the nice things Bob invented – became a villainess you love to hate.

I have quoted so extensively in order to demonstrate how a professional like Eileen Pollock speaks of her (and her husband's) 'invention'. The need for a character like Alexis was very clear to them simply as a demand given by the form itself – the open-ended, family-centred drama. They first of all gave her a name which is sexually a lot more ambiguous than 'Madeleine', with its connotations of something very traditional, innocent and motherly feminine. 'Alexis' was obviously thought to signal not least the character's high level of self-determination and goal-oriented activity. But the Pollocks did not think of her as anything in the way of a 'feminist role-model'. Her enormous rage and thirst for vengeance was due to her having been deprived of the full experience of motherhood, her 'naughty' behaviour was to be seen as a somewhat twisted expression of motherly love for her children. Alexis is thus, to the Pollocks, both a formal 'must' and a kind of mythic mother, one who has been deprived of her children, and therefore behaves (like some animal) in accordance with her 'instincts'. This immediate ability to tap into the mythic resources of our culture while fulfilling the demands of the formula is precisely the hallmark of true culture industry professionalism.

THE ROLE OF THE NETWORK AND INFORMATION ABOUT THE AUDIENCE

The network, ABC, initiated the production of *Dynasty* by inviting the Shapiros to write a serial which could compete with *Dallas* on CBS. They also had to approve both the original idea and later developments, such as the introduction of Alexis and the more explicitly ironic 'camp' elements. The situation for network television in the US around 1980 made a show able to grab and hold the attention of both 'upscale' and 'very lower middle-class' viewers particularly interesting and valuable. Long-term demographic changes had in effect produced an audience significantly different from that of previous decades. In 1957, 45 per cent of the civilian labour force were high school graduates, in 1978 the proportion was 73 per cent. The traditional difference between men and women in terms of educational level had almost disappeared, and 60 per cent of women between 18 and 64 had entered the work force. Around 1980, only 7 per cent of all US households were of the kind with a father at work and a mother at home with two school-age children (Bogart 1985: 10ff.). In other words, television's (potential) audience now contained larger groups of well-educated people, and a majority of women, who could no longer be unproblematically counted as primarily important as a daytime audience, in a stronger, more self-determined position in relation to men. According to Brian Winston, writing in 1981, ABC's own research revealed

> that 16 percent of the population, core culture-aficionados, do not watch television very much at all. These elusive folk – 'light watchers' – are also better educated and richer than the population generally. A further 24 percent are described as 'culturally receptive' – active PTA members and the like, who watch *60 Minutes* and network news but give television a low priority. Together these make a sizable, largely untapped universe.
>
> (Winston 1985: 474)

This research inspired ABC's initiatives in the already booming market for cable television, but it may also have opened the eyes of network executives to the potential of a 'feminine' show like *Dynasty*, with its combination of melodramatic fantasy (for anyone) and 'camp' irony (particularly for the more educated).

The Pollocks also talked quite openly about the role of the network in the production of the show. All scripts were sent to the network for comments before the shooting. These comments were mostly recommendations, which the Pollocks would sometimes follow, sometimes not. Every finished episode (music not yet added) would be screened for network representatives who primarily would check if anything conflicted with 'broadcasting standards'. In fact, the network's censorship here was primarily a check on sexual elements, such as nudity and explicit language in this area. The network's censor would sometimes (if rarely) demand that something should be left out or redone. The Pollocks described for instance how network rules applied to scenes where a man had flung a woman on a bed and then proceeded to lie on top of her. He was then only allowed to have two-thirds of his body on top; the last third should be 'visibly beside her'. In one case, in a 'perfectly married couple', the husband was shown playing a sensual version of 'little piggie went to market' with his wife's toes. Eileen Pollock remembered that he came as far up as the kneecap before the scene was cut; when the censor protested, they had thought it was because this was too far up. But it was the way the scene had portrayed the foot sensually as a fetish that he had reacted against. The Pollocks finally concluded that the man was probably a foot fetishist, but they still had to change the scene to comply with his demands.

It seems quite probable that the network pretested *Dynasty* in one of the many ways available – from 'concept'-testing to prescreenings at Preview House on Sunset Boulevard (cf. Gitlin 1985 on these techniques). But none of the people I interviewed ever mentioned such procedures. The network would sometimes have surveys done to check the popularity of certain characters, but these were said rarely, if ever, to have influenced developments. According to the Pollocks, both surveys and letters to the producers from members of the audience would come too late to have any real effect: the next three months were already canned (cf. Shapiro on p. 36). But they did mention that the number of letters to particular actors or actresses would be noticed. A considerable increase in the number of letters received by Heather Locklear (Sammy Jo), for instance, was taken as confirmation of the success of a recent change in her character.

To the Pollocks, the advice they would get at their local drugstore was more useful to their writing than anything they could get by way of 'research'. Not least because of the time factor (that shows are produced way ahead of the time when reactions from audiences could be registered), it seems that both the creation of 'bibles' and the writing of specific episodes develop largely without any specific input from surveys or fan mail. (I will return to important mod-ifications below.) The producers and writers have to trust their knowledge of the formula and their 'hunches' most of the time. Ultimately, though, the ratings and/or demographics decide. Even if network executives may at times refuse to take 'statistics' seriously if they 'believe in' (or don't believe in) a show (cf. Gitlin

1985), sooner or later the needs of the advertisers will have to be given decisive weight.

The relative dependence upon 'statistics' could be demonstrated by the simple example of how *Dynasty* got its name. The original name suggested was 'Oil'. This name was tested along with seven other possibilities in a national telephone survey. 'Oil' came out last in the ranking, while 'Mile High' was number one. *Dynasty* was number six, but was still preferred (Gitlin 1985: 39). According to Shapiro (in my interview), 'Oil' was out of the question because of its being last in this test. The fact that 'Mile High' was not chosen even if it was the 'winner' in the survey shows that there is ample space for 'hunches' and 'feelings' when executives make their decisions in the business. The same goes of course for decisions on whether or not to put a show on the air, maintain or drop it if it sags in the ratings, etc. The tastes and preferences of the few people who make the decisions, aesthetic or political, are of the greatest importance with respect to what television actually presents to its audiences.

Executive producers and writer-producers do not think of themselves as artists in the traditional sense. I asked the Pollocks if they would regard *Dynasty* as 'art', and the answer was that the word smacked too much of pretensions, of snobbism. Robert Pollock: 'I'll say this for *Dynasty*, though: it's one hell of a *story*!' They still have an interest in presenting themselves as 'creative' people, as people who make decisions on a self-determined, 'internal' basis of knowledge and 'feeling'. While this is also the fact in the ordinary run of a serial, it is probably less true when it comes to major changes in the show's development. For instance, when *Dynasty* changed from a story very much about battles in the Colorado oil fields to become what Shapiro once called 'the ultimate dollhouse fantasy for middle-aged women' (Klein 1985: 37) it had for a long time (in its first season) done quite poorly in the ratings. The producers then found out that the audience was not particularly interested in stories about oil workers – but they were fascinated by what went on in the Carrington castle (ibid.: 35). And the serial changed accordingly in the second season, where in many ways the mansion itself played a leading role. It is obviously quite safe to say that all the information about what the audience wanted did not stem from the producers' local drugstore. A variety of possible sources probably also included network testing of various dimensions of the show, different future developments, etc. This is not to say that the new direction of the show in any way broke with the tastes and ideas of its creators; it just points to the decisive role played by audience research of various kinds at certain key points in the serial's development.

THE PROLETARIAN WRITERS

I have so far talked about the top-rank levels of the production hierarchy: executive producers and writers, and the networks. Although the lower ranks have considerably less influence on the development of a show, they all contribute in their respective fields.

The contracted writers who finished each episode's script would get an outline of about seventeen pages. This draft 'outlined every scene, every emotion' in the episode, as one writer (who did not wish to be named) put it in an interview with me. In the course of one week, the outline was to be transformed to a full script of about sixty pages. This meant to 'dialogue it, physicalize it, behaviourize it for the camera'. The point was to try to 'feel each scene' and try to make the characters human by drawing on one's general life experience. The script would then be accepted or adjusted by those working as story editors. They would have to check such things as story and character consistency, since the contracted episode writers had not necessarily seen any previous episodes at all, and also to look ahead, and ask themselves: 'Will this line be useful for future developments, say, four episodes from now?'

These lower-level writers have very limited influence on a serial. Cantor (1992: 77) cites research which claims that writers in television have 'little or no control over any aspect of his or her writing, except the invention of dialogue and incident', and their work 'is rewritten as a matter of routine', changed without permission by story editor, producer, director or actors. At the same time, according to Cantor's own research, writers form the group which most clearly regard themselves as artists in the traditional sense. 'Most writers say that they would like to write drama or other fiction that is more "highbrow" or socially significant than the material they must write for television' (ibid.: 77). Accordingly, one might expect that many writers would experience a conflict between what they were actually doing and their individual hopes to 'express themselves', to have more or less full creative control. Since the outline of each episode was so detailed, their job was less 'writing' than 'rewriting'. The thousands of aspiring writers in Hollywood would still be very interested in getting the opportunity to work on a successful show like *Dynasty*. A job on *Dynasty* would pay well, make them thoroughly familiar with the demands of serial form and hopefully give them some kind of foothold in the business. Their situation would provide a combination of two ambitions: they would hope to demonstrate their ability to conform to the demands of the formula and the show in question, and still in some way stand out with a good idea or two, and show some kind of distinctive touch, which could land them other and possibly more interesting jobs.

In March 1988, the Writers' Guild of America began a strike which lasted twenty-two weeks, and managed to demonstrate the importance of writers' work since the autumn season started more than a month later than usual. But according to Cantor (ibid.: 79f.) little was actually achieved. I got a peculiar little insight into the class struggle in Beverly Hills after my interview with Esther Shapiro was over. The interview took place a day or two after the strike started. She very kindly offered to drive me to where I was staying, in her white Jaguar, with her secretary in the back seat, since she was anyway going out to 'show support' at the picket line. There was in other words little doubt about the successful writer-producer's personal bond to the less fortunate, basically quite powerless group she herself came out of.

A DIRECTOR'S STORY, AS TOLD BY CURTIS HARRINGTON

After the Pollocks had given the scripts their final touch, they would be sent to the director contracted for that particular episode. A director would normally be contracted for three weeks. Seven working days were normally spent on preparations, seven (or six-and-a-half) on shooting. The fifteenth day was there as a 'cushion', in case anything went wrong. (I am writing in the past tense because *Dynasty* is no longer produced, but these are standard procedures in the production of serials of similar kinds.)

The director of a TV serial episode has far less leeway than the director of a feature film – or a TV film for that matter. He or she is not involved in casting, except for very minor, incidental roles, where s/he may be consulted. The script is 'written in stone' when it goes to shooting, and the producers keep a liaison person on the set who monitors that everything proceeds according to the way the episode is written. If a line is to be changed, however slightly, a phone call has to be made to the producers' office for approval. A TV director is certainly no 'auteur', rather, as put by Cantor (ibid.: 80) 'merely a technician', less important than writers, actors and of course producers.

I only had the chance to interview one of the many directors who were at one time or another involved in the production of *Dynasty*. I talked to Curtis Harrington, who worked on *Dynasty* in 1983 and 1985, when the producers 'for reasons best known to themselves – sort of switched me to *The Colbys*', as he put it.

Harrington's background was impressively varied when he came to *Dynasty*. Educated at the University of Southern California, he directed avant-garde and surrealist films in the 1950s. He also lived in Paris for a while in the early 1950s. He wrote criticism for *Sight and Sound* and *Cahiers du Cinéma*, covered European film festivals for *Theatre Arts* and had a monograph on Josef von Sternberg published by the British Film Institute. On his return to Los Angeles, he started doing, among other things, horror films, 'low budget exploitation movies', at American International Pictures. The first was *Night Tide* (1960), with Dennis Hopper as the leading character. His most critically acclaimed feature film seems to be *What's the Matter with Helen?* (United Artists, 1971), with Shelley Winters and Debbie Reynolds. He also directed quite successful TV movies in the 1970s, mostly for ABC. The best remembered of these is probably *The Killer Bees*, with Gloria Swanson.

Harrington was quite happy with his work on *Dynasty*. First of all, the serial was shot on film and produced like any feature film technically. He said he hated video productions because of their poorer photographic quality and the inevitable sloppiness of the TV studio's three-camera editing (really careful framing is more or less impossible, cuts at the precisely right moment likewise). Second, the serial reminded him of the 'big, glossy films' from MGM and 20th Century Fox that he remembered so well from growing up in a small California town, 'pictures with people like Joan Crawford and Lana Turner in their heyday'. The nostalgic pleasures of recreating something like these films made up for much of the pressures of directing within a very strict schedule. The high quality of *Dynasty* was 'in the costumes and the sets, the incidentals, it's not in the shooting time at all'. 'The producers are more concerned than anything else with having the show brought in on time. [. . .] They want it to be good, but on time, rather than better and not on time.'

Harrington saw this absolute strictness about the schedule as understandable, since it had to do with the financial interests of the producers. They 'only get so much from the network to pay for each episode, so if it goes over that money, the producers have to make it up themselves, and that cuts into their profits'. And since 'all the people in power' in television as well as in the rest of the motion picture industry are 'business men, that's their primary concern'.

The scripts contained nothing about camera angles or movements. These were left for the director to decide. An experienced director like Harrington would know what was expected and normally do just that. But one of the reasons why he enjoyed working on *Dynasty* was that he had sometimes had certain directorial ideas accepted which he thought would be rejected when the producers did their final editing of the episode. One example may illustrate how the space for the director's creativity might be slightly stretched at certain times.

In one episode, Adam was to arrive home late at night, and Blake would suddenly appear in the hall, briskly ordering Adam to come to the library for a serious talk, '*now!*' This was what the script said. Harrington explains:

> So I thought, that would be very easy. [. . .] We begin with Adam coming through the door and pan over, and when you get to a certain spot, you see clear down the hallway and you see the father emerge. That would be the simple and obvious way of doing it. But I wanted to create a suspense, and *ambience*. Now this was my directorial choice. I began with the clock in the hallway, striking late, you know. Now the camera begins to slide and the camera glides past the empty hall, and you see that whole long expanse of emptiness, and it glides past there and it ends up facing the front door. And then you hear the key in the lock and Adam comes in [. . .] and then the father suddenly appears.

After the long pan, the late-night, quiet 'ambience shot', Blake's appearance would be 'doubly startling'. Harrington was free to do as he chose on the set, but he was certain that the producers would 'cut the whole pan out', cut to where Adam has the key in the door, 'because that would be the standard way of doing it'. This expectation was based on other experiences in the industry. But the producers in this case 'loved it', and kept the whole thing; this made Harrington very happy.

46

The space for directorial influence is still normally so small that it is almost impossible to distinguish between the 'styles' of different directors. Harrington claimed to be able to see differences, but mostly only between those very good and those particularly bad, for instance directors who would sometimes let the camera wander seemingly at random, zooming for no good reason and so on. He described his own style as 'classical', and said: 'Whatever flaws my work has, I think I can say it's *correct* most of the time.' Still, Harrington's pride and pleasure when talking about his ambience shot was obvious. It testified not just to his knowledge of what was 'correct', but also to his artistic sensibility. His story was moving on a human plane, since he had obviously so often had his choices refused by people with less feeling for the medium, both in film and in television. Not on *Dynasty*, though: he had never been upset by anything the producers had done in their final editing, even if they had taken out entire scenes – their reasons could be either the need for precise timing of commercial breaks or anything else.

> But I have been the victim of many arbitrary cutting decisions. The continuity of many of my films is expressly constructed with the use of dissolves. It's a whole way of expressing yourself, to dissolve from one image to another, not a direct cut. So one of my producers says 'I don't like dissolves.' And he cut out all my dissolves! And so all these beautiful, slow, elegant transitions are just cuts! That's because he just, you know, 'I don't like dissolves'! [. . .] That's the way all kinds of producers are in Hollywood. They are not creative people, they're businessmen, and yet, thrust into that position, they're constantly making, they're making . . . I'll never forget, the worst producer I ever worked with, who is a prized asshole, of all time. One day he called me into his office, and he said 'I am a creative producer!' I mean, he's about as creative as an ant, on the ground. But he had these pretensions, you know, and there's nothing worse than pretensions without any talent behind it, you know, and unfortunately that's true of a great many producers in Hollywood.

This last outburst can be seen to tell a whole story of what submission to often arbitrary decisions made by the business elite may cost an artist in terms of hurt feelings, self-esteem and so on.

Yet Harrington, in my interview with him, also demonstrated how much the logic of the industry had become part of his way of thinking about his work, part of his professional *habitus*, to use Pierre Bourdieu's concept. Hollywood directors of feature films very rarely have the right to final cut, and after the financial disaster of Michael Cimino's *Heaven's Gate* (1980) this right became even harder to get. Harrington had many times suggested – though it was never granted – that in a case of disagreement between the director and the producer about particular scenes one should show the film, in the director's cut, to a test audience and let their reactions decide whether anything should be changed or not. To a European director, mostly used to the privilege of having the final say on a film's shape on artistic terms, letting a simulation of market response decide will probably appear outrageous. Hollywood artists can never hope to escape the pressures of going for box-office success, and they have, to a large degree, made it part of their artistic identity.

DESIGNING A 'ROLLS ROYCE OF A PRIMETIME SOAPER': CONTI, MILLER, CRAMER

Dynasty would not have become what it was if it had not been for its luscious, luxurious, super-abundant appearance. Some very important people in the creation of this appearance have not yet been mentioned: Bill Conti, Nolan Miller and Douglas Cramer.

Bill Conti, a very experienced and competent Hollywood composer, created *Dynasty*'s slightly pompous musical theme (after discussing it with the Shapiros) and also different themes, 'leitmotifs', that would follow each of the principal characters. As long as he was with the show, it probably had the most meticulously constructed score of all prime-time shows at that time. (I will return to the music and its later development in detail in Chapter 4.) According to Gail Williams of the industry journal *Hollywood Reporter* (13 November 1981), the 'handsome production values' contributed by various members of the production staff were nice enough, 'but it's Bill Conti's lush theme, more than anything, that sets the superior tone of this Rolls Royce of a primetime soaper'.

Nolan Miller was once costume designer for Joan Crawford, and he was early on given up to $25,000 per episode to play with when dressing up the cast in the extravagant manner that came to be seen as one of the show's central characteristics. Alexis in particular was dressed in a way that would remind people of Crawford's conspicuous but carefully composed elegance. Esther Shapiro is supposed to have come up with the idea that Alexis should wear hats, and it was also decided that no central character should ever use the same clothes twice.

With Miller doing the costumes, the show was already half-way into its extravagant image. But the decisive shift to a really lavish look, in every detail, was achieved by Douglas S. Cramer when he was brought in as a producer, also between the first and second season. This was when Alexis was introduced, and, most probably, when significant alterations were made in the *Dynasty* theme music. The whole set at Fox's Stage 8 was refurbished and refurnished; hyper-expensive food and cars would appear in every episode. *Dynasty* was to represent opulence in the extreme. 'Whatever *Dallas* has, *Dynasty* has more. Whenever *Dallas* has enough, *Dynasty* has an excess', Bob Wisehart commented in *Los Angeles Times* (25 November 1982). In other words, the 'look' of the show spilled over on to the meaning of its stories. Cramer's efforts further amplified the potential (already present in Miller's costumes) for viewers' perception of the mise-en-scène as excessive. A decisive contribution here was made by Joan Collins, who was introduced as Alexis at the same time as Cramer joined the producers. The show became, to many of its viewers, obviously 'too much'. It seemed to leave its initial degree of social realism, and invited at least some categories of viewers to understand it ironically, to perform what is called a *camping* of the show. Its stylishness for such viewers turned into stylization, i.e. the show seemed to demonstrate its awareness of itself as 'artificial', as at least in part a generic parody, a play with clichés and formulas. But 'the show' did of course not have an awareness of itself, was not 'self-reflexive', as current criticism's short-hand formulations often have it. A text cannot think. A producer such as Cramer, a major art collector in his private life, may have self-awareness, be self-reflexive and know what he is doing, though. The right kind of audience may pick up the clues and understand the text accordingly.

THE UNCERTAIN POWERS OF ACTORS

None of the people mentioned so far in my presentation of *Dynasty*'s production were visible to the serial's audience. But the star actors were, and their visibility makes them quite powerful in the creative process. According to Muriel G. Cantor, the stars of a TV show could even be regarded as, 'without comparison', the most powerful of all the 'creative people who work in TV' (Cantor 1981: 85). The stars of a successful show are seen by the industry as major factors behind its popularity, and this empowers the stars in the production process – and in the negotiation of their salaries. On *Dallas* for instance, cast salaries constituted 45 per cent of each episode's million-dollar budget in 1987 (*Los Angeles Times*, 15 May 1987), and there is no reason to believe that the situation was any different in *Dynasty*. This is also why reducing the cast through changes in storylines is one of the most efficient forms of cost reduction. At a time when *Falcon Crest* was financially troubled, the executive producer of that show, Jeff Freilich, said to *L.A. Times*: 'We're talking some deaths, we're talking some disappearances, we're talking some escapes. And we're talking some happy endings' (15 May 1987).

But as long as they are in the show, the major stars are so important that they may influence its developments, particularly when it comes to the shaping of their characters. John Forsythe, who played Blake Carrington, was for instance not happy with Blake being such a hard, almost brutal man, and wanted to make him 'more human'. His wishes were approved by the producers. (Forsythe specifically mentions that Richard Shapiro agreed (Klein 1985: 36).) Interestingly, most of the female actors were, according to Klein, more inclined to make their characters bitchier than they were first written, the actresses playing Alexis and Fallon in particular.

The actors may not only suggest changes in the scripts – for instance changes of certain lines – in order to adjust their characters. They may also more subtly get around the original intentions of the producers and writers simply by, for instance, saying certain lines in a tone of voice which differs from the one intended. Joan Collins mentioned in an interview with the German magazine *Der Spiegel* (no. 9, 24 February 1986, 248) that she sometimes would find a line much too hard and aggressive. She would then take away some of the edge by using a slightly weaker voice or a slightly humorous tone, and thus make even 'I hate you' sound a bit lighter.

Joan Collins obviously contributed greatly to the particular appeal of her character. Her excessive, stylized acting added an ironic, humorous sense not only to the Alexis character, but also to the serial itself. In fact, Alexis was just about the only character to provide an *intended* comic element. John Forsythe's character did change towards something a bit more mellow than the bullying and violent autocrat he was in the beginning. Stars may in other words consciously influence the show in ways other than the inevitable – through their physical appearance. Still, since the actors are there basically to realize the finished script, since the shooting time is much more strictly limited than in a feature film, and since characters may be written out of the show if they do not perform as required in some way or other, it is hard to see that Muriel Cantor's placing of the stars in a uniquely powerful position can be justified – except perhaps when salaries are decided. If we look at what may be called middle-range stars, they will typically be less inclined than the leading actors to feel they have any influence. Ken Howard, who played Garrett Boydston for a while (in *Dynasty* and in *The Colbys*) said in *TV Guide* of 21 February 1987 that 'with a series, unless you're Bill Cosby, you have no creative control. . . . At the risk of oversimplification, there are three categories of people in this line of work: the creative types, the sales people who run the town, and the glamorous, gorgeous attractive meat. When you're an actor, you're part of the meat.'

Howard says that both the shows he played in 'felt like factory jobs. People put makeup on me and paid me a lot of money to learn some lines and be a product' (ibid.). The conditions of acting and their effects on the actual performance are described as follows:

> I don't think many actors who feel they have substantial ability would actually *choose* to do a series. For one thing, you don't have much time to do your scenes. You have to be ready in two takes. That can be an incredible burden. I think many good feature-film actors would be crushed on TV. They wouldn't have a chance, without the benefit of time. On the other hand, I've been doing television for a long time. Instinctively, I grew to think, 'What's the *simplest* way to get the scene done?' This is a business of big crews, overtime and high costs. Being able to work quickly and easily makes you a hero. But what about the value of the creative process?
>
> (ibid.)

What Howard is saying here is that TV acting in a serial or series requires a specific talent: that of being able to decide quickly on a simple, straightforward way to do a scene. In an interview on NRK-TV (25 January 1984), Al Corley, who played Steven Carrington for two years, compared acting on *Dynasty* to asking an artist to produce a painting in one minute. This may not at all result in 'bad acting' by all conceivable standards, but it certainly reduces the 'value of the creative process' for the actors. They are, as a rule, deprived of the sense of control or mastery which comes with time spent on rehearsals and adjustments of expressions, movements, intonations, etc. With the exception of the influence major stars may have on their characters over time, actors as a rule are mainly 'meat' to fill the narrative functions decided by the script.

PATTERNS AND PEOPLE IN THE PROCESS OF PRODUCTION

It is now time to try to get a little perspective on the above presentation of various structures, procedures and professionals involved in the production of *Dynasty* before I end the chapter by looking at the apparatus for the distribution of the serial.

An analysis of the production of television drama can be done in a number of ways. My largely descriptive analysis has so far tried to combine a chronicling of the process, placed in a certain institutional context, with both attention to more or less anecdotal specificities of this particular production (*Dynasty*) and the quite general problematic of creativity and its constraints in the culture industry. The intention has been to try to trace the reasons why the *Dynasty* text came to be constructed the way it appeared on US and foreign screens. I have tried to chart some of the major sources of influence, both institutional and personal. The problem is now, first, to establish the main pattern in the production process, a more or less synchronous overview of structure(s) and agents within them. Second, there is the more clearly theoretical challenge to establish the plausibility of significant links between the process of production and the process of reception. Few, if any, studies of television production have in fact dealt explicitly with this latter problematic, and it is about time someone tried. This part of the problem then includes the questions of the nature and role of 'authorship' in televised communication.

Starting with the overall pattern, it seems clear that the basic premises for the production of TV drama are presented by the commercial nature of US television. But the specific structure of the industry – the division between formally independent production companies and the networks – is not produced by capital alone. It is also shaped by political intervention, i.e. legally induced limitations on direct vertical integration in the industry. The role of television as seller of audiences for advertisements largely explains the mechanical nature of scheduling and programme formats. Programmes last for either one hour or a half-hour (sometimes ninety minutes or two hours) and must be constructed so as to allow for commercial breaks at certain intervals. All of this obviously imposes very definite premises for temporal features of programme forms, such as length and rhythm, and thus also limits and influences the dramaturgy, the forms of narration and characterization that may be

51

employed. A demonstration of this will be a main point in my analysis of the *Dynasty* text. The demands of the schedule, the need for precise control of production time and costs, determine the rigours of production schedules and to a large extent also the need for the executive producers' centralized control in a complex, collective production process.

The networks' programming schedule is furthermore divided into segments which traditionally have addressed different audiences or mixes of audiences. The daytime serial drama – the 'soap opera' proper – has, for instance, been conceived as addressing mainly housewives, while prime-time episodic series (sit-coms, detective shows, etc.) have normally been aimed at a mixed family audience – in which fathers are traditionally expected to be in command of channel choices. *Dallas* was the first attempt to shift the serial format from its traditional daytime position to a place in prime-time programming. This was, in fact, perhaps the really ground-breaking venture in our context, since its generic mixture implied a new kind of audience address in prime-time television form. It simply acknowledged the existence of women as a significant part of the prime-time audience. This was definitely something new, even if it was a *recombinant* form of creativity (cf. Gitlin 1985: 75–85) and developed in a haphazard way (cf. p. 36). It combined the narrative form and some ('domestic') thematic preoccupations of daytime serials and added elements of suspense, relatively explicit sex and other traditionally male-oriented themes and motifs.

Dynasty could build on the success of its predecessor, and a prime-time *serial* was what ABC wanted the Shapiros to come up with. The initiative was, in other words, that of the network: the Shapiros' fantasizing on a beach in Hawaii after having watched *I, Claudius* on British TV was not the kind of 'free creativity' associated with 'authorship' since romanticism. *Dallas* had already transgressed a few taboos, and *Dynasty* could be thought of as going even further in doing 'what you're not supposed to do on television'. In other words, *Dynasty*, another show about an oil-rich family, was in so many ways a clone, destined for a one-hour prime-time spot, that it may seem hard to speak even of recombinatory 'inventiveness' when it comes to certain basic features of the show, especially in its first season.

But within the confines of what was in many ways intended as a clone, the Shapiros brought together various televisual, literary and filmic impulses with a view both to their own fascinations (with wealth, power, old mansions, old films, Victorian literature, etc.) and – also important – to the suspected preferences of the middle-aged, male, network executives. In the midst of this, they could also draw on their experience with the production of 'socially relevant' material, as instanced in their placing of a homosexual son in the story. They could even let Claudia Blaisdel recite poems by Emily Dickinson in an early episode, not only to make her interesting but also to add a touch of cultural class to the show. Furthermore, in an interview with Carol A. Crotta of the *Los Angeles Herald Examiner* (4 February 1985), Esther Shapiro talked about the fascinating stories

52

she had heard when growing up, the daughter of an Italian and a Turkish immigrant:

> The stories I heard from my aunts would put 'Hollywood Wives' to shame [. . .]. They were racy – they dealt with suicide, all sorts of Eastern drugs, bizarre love relationships, multiple marriages or multiple mates. Some were real, some projected. All that goes into your head.

It is not my intention to say that *Dynasty* may be seen as the result of Esther Shapiro's growing up in a slightly exotic family full of gifted story-tellers. The point is that within the limitations of the industry and its formats, those who produce storylines and characters are individuals with particular backgrounds, particular interests, inclinations and talents, all of which are mobilized when the hole in the schedule, reserved for a particular format, is to be filled.

While all functions involved in the production of a drama series or serial play a role in the appearance of the finished product, at least in this case it seems quite obvious that the combined roles of executive producers and executive writers were absolutely paramount in the outcome. These were the people who could claim some degree of 'creative freedom', and as Ed Buscombe once pointed out, the question of creative freedom in television production is a question of power: 'It is a question not only of the freedom from interference from above, but also the "freedom" to control those below' (Buscombe 1980: 16). Aaron Spelling seems mostly to have acted as someone with a production company which enjoyed the network's trust, i.e. primarily dealing with the purer business dimensions of production. He may of course also have been important in securing the show's adherence to his successful, simplistic narrative techniques. His most vital contribution to *Dynasty*'s development, though, was probably the hiring of the Pollocks (and possibly also Douglas S. Cramer). Robert and Eileen Pollock soon acquired the producer-writer combination of roles when they came in after the first season with their solid daytime TV experiences. With the introduction of Alexis and more clever plotting they quite definitely changed the show and lifted it from a poor rating to the very top. Douglas S. Cramer, who is also known as a major art collector specializing in modern and contemporary works, brought a new degree of extravagance to the set and all kinds of props, thus adding the almost hysterical quality to the show's display of wealth. Nolan Miller was already, as mentioned, involved in costume design, working in much the same direction, drawing on his long-term experience in the film-making business.

While the industry's organization and functions may be said to provide a basic tendency toward the *sameness* of texts (forms, formulas, recurrent 'proven' themes, etc.), the vital *difference* between texts in the same genre, their *specificity*, can only be fully accounted for with regard to the actual people involved in leading roles in the production process. The individuals who produced the main specific features of *Dynasty* could most probably not have been replaced by just anybody else with some experience in the industry without altering the shape of the show. The making of cultural artefacts, of texts, can never be completely industrialized, completely emptied of preindustrial, more or less individual 'handicraft'.

This is one important point where Adorno may, at least in some of his texts, be said to have been mistaken in his analysis of the culture industry and its products. In, for instance, his analysis of popular music (Adorno 1941) he may rightly be accused of having 'ignored the inherent differences between text and functional artifact' (Gendron 1986: 27). These differences stem from the simple fact that each industrially produced non-artistic object is supposed to be identical to a prototype, while each more or less artistic artefact, a text, must be similar in some respects and different in others to an imagined 'prototype', a representative instance of a genre (cf. also Neale 1980: 52f.). The song is produced differently from the vinyl disc which is used for its reproduction; similarly the original 'negative' copy of a film or a *Dynasty* episode is produced in other ways than the tapes later distributed. The latter production is a totally standardized industrial production of identical copies, the former is a mode of production which may be rationalized in ways that imitate industrial production but still retain an element of difference, of uniqueness, however minimal, which stems from the individual human agencies involved in the various stages or elements of the process. (Cf. Gendron 1986 for a lucid and thorough version of this argument.)

Adorno's mistake here is in a way repeated in a very different theoretical context, in structuralist and/or semiotic critiques of the idea of 'creativity' tied to individual agents, particularly in collective media production. Ed Buscombe has, for instance, in a discussion of 'creativity' in television, argued that the search for 'a single, originating, creative source' is 'more an ideological project than a genuine quest for knowledge'. He claims that

> terms such as 'authorship' and 'creativity' can be misleading not only because the end product was the result of a collaboration between writers, producers, directors, script editors, actors, and others. They are misleading also because they necessarily obscure the way in which what finally turns up on the screen is produced by the intersection of a complex of pre-existing ideological constructs.
>
> (Buscombe 1980: 12f.)

The latter formulation evidences, in my view, how Buscombe's project here is, in his own words, 'more an ideological project than a genuine quest for knowledge'. The point is that the intersection of a complex of pre-existing ideological constructs did not come about by itself, and that intersections of ideological constructs cannot make anything appear on any television screen. Any such 'intersection' is a specific one, in some sense created out of many possibilities by way of specific selections and more or less idiosyncratic additions which mark the specificity of a particular text. Buscombe even says that 'the end product was the result of a collaboration' between specific people involved in the production. He has also previously said that the main character of a series is a result of a particular combination of 'source material', and that 'the actual things he [this leading character] says in the scripts are certainly attributable to the individuals who wrote the series' (ibid.: 12). The importance of individual human agency then disappears in the following sentences, most probably because for ideological reasons he is tempted to do what he has said he would not do: 'yet another demolition job on the auteur theory' (ibid.).

IMAGES OF AUDIENCES IN PRODUCTION

Films or television texts clearly result from collective processes. This may in fact be seen as something which helps to explain why successful movies or TV shows normally can attract far wider and more complex audiences than even the best-selling novel. Such a view can be deduced from an article by Herbert J. Gans, 'The Creator-Audience Relationship in the Mass Media: An Analysis of Movie Making' (1957), which I will devote some attention to in the following.

Gans is interested in how the audience for a movie may be said to play an active role 'within the movie-making process itself' (ibid.: 315). What Gans is thinking of is the 'creators'' image(s) of the audience, even if in his article he sometimes slides into talking about real or actual audiences. The distinction between actual audiences or readers and the 'implied' or 'model' readers whom one may deduce from an analysis of the text is vital to current empirical reception research in media studies which draws on semiotic and phenomen-ological theories such as those of Umberto Eco (1984) and Wolfgang Iser (1978). What Gans tries to find out, one might say, is how the implied audience(s) of movies are constructed in the empirical production process of individual films. Particular genres may in a sense have a general, gendered and generational implied audience always-already inscribed in them, but the point is both that even this textual structure must be reproduced in every individual film by way of concrete decisions and practices, and that every individual film also may have a more specific implied audience, related to the specific production process behind that particular film.

Gans states initially that every 'creator' (meaning all those 'whose decisions and actions create the movie' (1957: 315)) is 'creating *something* for *somebody*', and this 'somebody may be the creator himself, other people or even a non-existent stereotype, but it becomes an *image* of an audience which the creator develops as part of every creative process' (ibid.: 316). Gans holds that this audience image functions as 'an external observer-judge' which plays an important, if mostly unconscious, role in the creative process, which Gans regards as a series of choices between different alternatives. While the 'requirements of the product' (generic, for instance) are obviously also important here, Gans argues that particularly in the mass media, the expectations of the audience image are often more important. Gans further develops the notion of 'audience image' as follows:

The audience image is not a unified concept, but a set of numerous impressions, many of which are latent and contradictory. These impressions deal primarily with how people live, and how they look at, and respond to the roles, personalities, relationships and objects that movies portray. These impressions develop and accumulate in the mind of the creator in his contacts with potential audiences. The experienced movie-maker must have some image of the audience response to all of the innumerable situations and characters he is apt to work into different movies. As he begins to work on a specific picture, what probably happens is that he pulls together a group of more or less consistent impressions which will evolve into his audience image for *that* movie. This image is broad enough to permit him to communicate with many of the publics who will come to see the picture, although one rarely can reach all publics. Also, his image changes somewhat from movie to movie, but it can do so only within limits which are imposed on his sensitivity and skill by the familiarity he has with the social, cultural and psychological experiences of the total audience.

(ibid.: 316f.)

The variable and often contradictory, many-sided, more or less impression-istic audience image is thus shaped by the 'creator's' background, tastes, knowledge and way of life. Gans also mentions the role played by reference groups such as colleagues, superiors and critics. These may sometimes broaden and diversify the audience image, at other times they may conflict with the anticipated demands of the 'ticket-buyers', and they may then remind the 'creator' of his 'role conflicts', i.e. the differences between himself or herself as an artist and his/her presumed audiences. Still, in Gans's account, the primacy of the audience image as a guide or judge in the decision making of the creative process remains.

It is well worth noting that the focus on the 'ticket-buyers' which Gans assumes to be more important than the opinions of colleagues and superiors may be most typical of a thoroughly commercial production culture such as that of Hollywood. Philip Elliott (1972) demonstrated, in a study of the making of a documentary series for Britain's (commercial) Independent Television Authority, how the opinions of colleagues within the TV-producing community can be clearly more important than any considerations for the audience 'out there'. This must be understood as resulting from a professional culture in which, parallel to or inspired from the fine arts, only 'internal', artistic or professional criteria of judgement are regarded as valid. In Gans's terms, this means that their audience image is quite narrow – consisting mainly of impressions of their own socio-cultural and professional group.

Curtis Harrington's suggested solution for disputes between producers and directors on the 'final cut' – the use of audience previews – demonstrates, as noted above, just how engrained the idea of the primacy of the audience 'out there' is with Hollywood personnel. This is probably a key element in an understanding of why so many American audio-visual products are more successful than European productions, often even in the latter's home markets. There has been a tendency in Europe, to put it bluntly, for film and television producers to make films or TV programmes for themselves, their colleagues and socio-culturally related groups, not for the people who most frequently visit cinemas or watch television. Ian Connell has argued that 'market forces *do* impel commercial broadcasters to be responsive to publics that the BBC and its supporters have regarded principally as the targets of their reforming cultural zeal' (1983: 76), and even suggested a view of market research as a 'tool' useful to broadcasting practitioners who

> are not always of the cultures with which connections have to be made. [. . .] For all its faults and limitations, this kind of 'action research' has added other voices to the decisions made about production, and has rendered it, in this sector [the commercial], very often more socially responsive and accountable than in the BBC or even in the more radical regions of the public sector.
>
> (ibid.: 77)

The constant attention to how this or that element or scene will 'work' for an anticipated audience marks Hollywood's production culture in a variety of ways. Precisely because it is so integral to the culture, it may not even be explicated by writer-producers like Shapiro or the Pollocks. With the latter, the attention to audience response is a basic part of their knowledge of formal principles: they know from experience what 'works' with a serial's audiences and what doesn't. With Shapiro, one could also point to the way the general profile of *Dynasty* was conceived as a transgression of a number of 'no-no's' in the industry, i.e. that the show was intended to draw attention by a degree of shock effect. And since there was so little for women on prime time, she concluded that half the audience would welcome a female fantasy show. After the first season, Shapiro had, probably from a variety of sources, got the distinct impression that the oil-worker saga was less interesting to the majority of the audience than the internal family matters of the Carrington mansion. So be it! Her extensive reading of magazines and newspapers was obviously also important when deciding which 'climate' *Dynasty* was to be presented in. Last but not least, both the Shapiros and particularly the Pollocks are people whose tastes are, to a large degree, 'mainstream' and consequently not far off the tastes of a majority of audiences 'out there'. I asked the Pollocks about their favourite literature, and he said suspense, she said biographies. Their expressed preferences in film were what may be called 'quality mainstream': one of their favourite films was Nicholas Roeg's *Don't Look Now* (1973), a mystery-suspense story with supernatural ingredients. Esther Shapiro mentioned classical Hollywood films from the 1940s, thus marking a slightly different inclination towards the *cinéaste* category, but still not very far off the preferences of people of her generation outside the Hollywood community.

These producers, consequently, seem to resemble the kind of 'creator' Gans says 'shares enough of the characteristics of an actual audience so that by creating for himself, that is, for his self-image, he is also communicating to a larger audience'. This would otherwise particularly describe 'the folk artist in pre-urban societies, whose audiences were relatively homogeneous' (Gans 1957: 317). In the modern cultural industry, the heterogeneity of the audiences are on the other hand matched by the collectivity of production, and hence a degree of heterogeneity of audience images involved:

> The making of the picture itself can be viewed as a decision-making process. As each creator applies his audience image in the decisions that have to be made, he is 'representing' some of the publics who will eventually see the movie. The completed picture is a combination of the decisions made by its creators, and also a compromise or perhaps more correctly, a 'negotiated synthesis' of their individual audience images. However, this synthesis takes place within a power structure, and the final decisions are often made by studio executives who point the compromise in a direction that seems to assure the largest box office. Thus, the final product has some of the characteristics of a political party platform, seeking to please as many as possible.
>
> (ibid.: 318)

The hierarchical power structure in the production of *Dynasty* (and other shows) should have been made sufficiently clear in the preceding pages, and it is the existence of this hierarchy which may to some extent justify my limited attention to other than the top-rank producers. There is, however, one type of research which time did not allow but which I would have liked to have included, and that is participant observation at various stages of the production. The findings of Paul Espinosa (1982) in his study, precisely by way of participant observation, of a series of story conferences on the *Lou Grant* series of the late 1970s clearly support the above main points, though.

Espinosa identified four major 'rules or text-building practices' (ibid.: 79) at these story conferences. The first was '*engage the audience*'. A main element here was the effort to construct characters that (presumed) audiences could relate to and in some way or other identify with. But this was only part of the over-arching ambition to create *entertainment*, i.e. never to bore the audience. This entailed for instance, in an episode which centred on an act of terrorism, to create a sub-plot where the show's leading hero bought a new sofa – since, as one of the participants in the story conferences put it, nobody would watch a whole hour of terrorism. The second principle was to '*consider the audience's knowledge about the world*'. This included not only determining what the audience could be expected to know about the topic of the show (in this case, terrorism). It not least also included considering the audience's knowledge of television and its programmes. This was so important because it had to do with the show's image or profile in relation to other, competing series, and *Lou Grant* had a quality, minimum-violence image to maintain. Espinosa's third principle is basically an extension of the second, '*meet the audience's expectations for the show*'. This entailed specifically including the lead characters in as many scenes as possible, since they were considered extremely important for the series' drawing power, and also attaching positive moral characteristics to these characters in the various situations they were placed in. The fourth and last principle was '*don't divide the audience*', and this meant shunning plots and scenes which were about highly controversial matters, because they would allegedly only result in the audience debating these issues instead of paying attention to the story itself. A divided audience is a reduced audience, and the loss of ratings points is extremely expensive.

Espinosa explicitly wanted to study the ways in which the producers perceived the audience. What his study reveals is that images of the audience play a decisive role in the development of a series episode. At the same time, the considerations of how people in front of the screens would react blended in the discussions seamlessly with the intuitions and feelings of the writers and producers themselves. What 'felt right' and 'worked' for them was presumed to appear the same way to the audience.

My conclusion is, then, that the collective which decided the main features of *Dynasty* (within the parameters set by the television institution) had: (1) long-term experience with the demands and formal characteristics of US television fiction; (2) personal tastes and cultural profiles that were not very far off the mainstream of predominantly white, middle-class television audiences. Both of these points made it possible for them to trust themselves and their own intuitions when deciding about the construction of the text. This would not, however, provide much help in explaining the specificities of *Dynasty*, only its adherence to basic principles of US television serialized drama. But the executive producers and writers of *Dynasty* also represented a specific mix of competencies and orientations which clearly can contribute to an explanation of the show's specific character.

First, there were two highly competent women very centrally located in the team: Esther Shapiro and Eileen Pollock. This was in itself quite unusual, at least for a prime-time show. The feminist inclinations of the former were coupled with the latter's intimate, largely non-critical knowledge of feminine popular culture. The more or less realist, 'socially relevant' track record of the Shapiros was coupled with the Pollocks' solid experience with pop-culture fantasy productions. Shapiro, in my interview with her, claimed that the Pollocks really '*are* larger than life', thus indicating how closely she thought they identified with traditional Hollywood aesthetics. If we then add the extravagant contributions to the show's style from Nolan Miller, with his previous work for Joan Crawford, and Douglas S. Cramer, with his private collection of modern art, we also add the elements which helped to bring into the serial's total audience certain groups who saw its main attraction in its deliberate play with camp art(ificiality). Slightly in the background, but still at

59

the top, was Aaron Spelling, making sure that the synthesis of the diverse 'audience images' involved aimed for maximum ratings. He did this, not least, by hiring people who precisely would add new 'audience images' since they had backgrounds distinct from that of the Shapiros (Pollocks, Cramer), and he was thus of crucial importance to the show's development. In Gans's terms, the changes made after the first season amounted to an adjustment of the show's total audience image, after its first run had demonstrated that the audiences reached were especially interested in particular dimensions of the original concept. For feature films, the closest thing to such an adjustment would be the re-editing of a film after its first release, or a rewriting of all publicity material in accordance with the impressions from the film's first encounters with real audiences (cf. Gans 1957: 319).

Gans's idea of 'audience images' influencing the production of texts is, to my mind, a useful way to think about how the textual properties known as 'inscribed readers', the 'reader in the text' or the 'spectator in the text' are tied to the empirical circumstances of the production process. *Dynasty* could not have been produced outside the US television industry, and it could not have been made in the same way by just any team of industry professionals. The specific producers involved in a particular production process resulted in a text which offered a number of quite different 'readers' positions', but not an unlimited number. The audience positions were limited and organized in such a way as to give the show its particular profile, its difference from other shows, in both the same and in other genres.

ON NOTIONS OF AUTHORSHIP AND SUBJECTIVITY

The title of this section refers to some of the most central debates, on fundamental issues, in all kinds of textual and cultural studies since (at least) the early 1970s. I have already touched on them at the beginning of this chapter, and more indirectly along the way. What I will do here is not an impossible attempt at recounting all the important points and positions in this debate. Rather, I will try to comment on a few major issues, chosen with a view to the overall argument of this chapter and book.

The above picture of the creative processes behind the *Dynasty* text clearly differs from the romantic notion of creativity, which basically is about an individual creating something out of nothing (which God supposedly did when he created the earth), i.e. creating something wholly original, something never seen (or heard, read) before. Todd Gitlin, as mentioned on p. 52, talks about 'creativity' in US television production as being a 'recombinatory' form, i.e. a form of recycling of previously known ideas and forms. In one way or another, this will, however, probably be the case for most kinds of writing or other forms of textual creativity, and it has even been made into more or less a definition of 'postmodern' art and architecture. This is basically so because nothing is created outside a cultural context; all kinds of cultural production take place under various material and semiotic or cultural (such as pre-existing codes) constraints. As put by Steve Neale, 'no artist – and, indeed, no audience, no individual spectator – is free, and this applies equally to the abstract expressionist painter, to the lyric poet working in his/her own home or studio, to the experimental filmmaker working only in 8 mm and to the Hollywood director' (1983: 10). But Neale adds the very important point that precisely because of the universality of constraint, of pressures on production, 'it becomes important, indeed essential, to differentiate between the various modalities of pressure involved, and to relate them to the various modalities of the political, ideological and economic conditions in which they function and take effect' (ibid.). The difference between different forms of creativity in terms of their respective cultural and material constraints must also be expected to have consequences for the texts produced – in the specificity of various kinds of 'recombinations', and in the degree to which some really new, original or provocative element is added or emerges in the process.

In the case of *Dynasty*, it seems to me that the genre of 'prime-time soap opera' established by *Dallas* was a (re)combination of genres which brought something decidedly new to US television, first and foremost in terms of gender address. *Dallas* also made the break with the previous 'taboo' on the super-rich as main characters, even if the Ewings were made to look much like any middle-class family. *Dynasty* could build on this, and demonstrated its specificity, particularly from the second season on, not least by the marked presence of a strong feminine antagonist (or, for some, protagonist), hence a feminine thematic (Krystle vs Alexis as melodramatically opposed images of femininity). Further-more, the opulence of sets and costume design, the stylization of acting, the outrageous exaggerations of certain plotlines, all of which could be seen as quotations from previous forms of filmic melodrama, brought a new metatex-tual quality to prime-time drama, providing the show's invitation to a 'camp' reading, and thus to camp-oriented audiences.

It may still be debatable, but to me this will pass as 'creativity', if that concept rids itself of its theological connotations. *Dynasty* was definitely different, and also quite narrowly tied to its historical context. It could not have been developed in the early 1970s, and it died out as the 1980s and the Reagan era closed. The show came out of a particular historical 'moment', in which a specific combination of talents and competencies was brought together for the first – and probably last – time.

To me, all of this indicates that 'the author' is not dead. Authorship just needs to be thought of in a way which differs from traditional notions of it in the art forms of predominantly individual production. André Bazin once commented on the 'auteur policy', admitting that there was room for 'creative freedom' even within Hollywood film production, 'where restrictions of production are heavier than anywhere else'. The strong institutional pressures and genre codifications of American cinema made it 'classical art'. But, Bazin continued, 'why not then admire in it what is most admirable, i.e. not only the talent of this or that filmmaker, but the genius of the system' (Bazin 1968: 154, quoted in Schatz 1981: 3). To me, the system is not so much admirable as it is impressive, but the main point here is, that while the system provides certain basic conditions, procedures, formulas, etc., it does not eliminate the importance of differences between the individual agents within it. From this point, one may proceed to have another look at the ideas about the disappearance or dissolution of authorship which I talked about at the beginning of this chapter.

Roland Barthes's influential little article 'The Death of the Author' must be understood in the light of its specific context and the particular polemic it engages in. When he argues that 'writing is the destruction of every voice, of every point of origin' (1982: 142), this is not only a theoretical point, drawn from Lacan's conception of subjectivity and Althusser's use of that conception in his now classical piece on ideology (1971). Barthes's article also specifically opposes a traditional form of biographically oriented hermeneutic:

> The *author* still reigns in histories of literature, biographies of writers, interviews, magazines, as in the very consciousness of men of letters anxious to unite their person and their work through diaries and memoirs. The image of literature to be found in ordinary culture is tyrannically centred on the author, his person, his life, his tastes, his passions, while criticism still consists for the most part in saying that Baudelaire's work is the failure of Baudelaire the man, Van Gogh's his madness, Tchaikovsky's his vice. The *explanation* of a work is always sought in the man or woman who produced it, as if it were always in the end, through the more or less transparent allegory of fiction, the voice of a single person, the *author* 'confiding' in us.
>
> (Barthes 1982: 143)

I, and most other contemporary scholars of criticism, have no problem in joining Barthes here. His critique is in line with what every semiotically informed critic has said at least since the 1960s. It was actually both pre-shadowed and formed by critical 'schools' such as Russian formalism and the Prague structuralism of Jan Mukarovsky and his colleagues. The romanticist notion of an individual author as the sole originator of a text, a perspective in which the text is seen as the uniquely individual author ' "confiding" in us', was strong in most countries in the 1960s, often tied to forms of literary scholarship in which the existing canon was regarded as a near sacred expression of, say, the nation or (the only) cultural tradition. These political implications were the main reasons why the author-centred criticism was an important target for critique. But it is now hardly alive any more in serious criticism, even if it still lives on in the media and in schools.

Barthes's total eradication of any concrete agency in writing ('it is language which speaks' (ibid.)) may now be considered as a position which, at least in part, was produced by specific pragmatic/polemic circumstances. It obviously deserves critical discussion and modification. For instance, 'language speaks', but it only does so through the work of specific individuals, who are gendered and socially positioned in a number of other ways, influencing the way in which 'language speaks' 'through' them, and what it says. The idea that 'language speaks' cannot, as pointed out by Graham Murdock, 'explain why specific writers write as they do or why their work differs from that of other writers' (Murdock 1993: 131). Murdock then makes the following striking comment:

> It is particularly ironic that Barthes, who insisted so forcefully on the death of the author, should have taken so much care to develop a voice that is instantly recognisable as his. While this is entirely understandable in the context of Parisian intellectual life, where style is a decisive weapon in the struggle for ascendancy, it hardly squares with his stress on the relative autonomy of textual codes. If Barthes served a life sentence in the prison-house of language, his works strive remarkably hard to give the impression that he is out on parole.
>
> (ibid.)

It is consequently no surprise that a modification of the total denial of authorship ('anti-authorship orthodoxy') is finally called for, for instance in a relatively recent article in *Screen* (no. 2, 1991) about homosexuality and authorship. The author (!) of that article, Andy Medhurst, talks about the British film *Brief Encounter* (1945), which was written by Noel Coward and directed by David Lean. It is well known that Coward was gay, and Medhurst says he 'would insist on the centrality of Noel Coward's sexuality to the patterns of meaning' that he sees in the film (1991: 201). A writer's sexual orientation would, according to the pure anti-authorship position, be among the clearly irrelevant biographical mystifications of how 'language speaks'.

As I mentioned above, the form of romantic hermeneutic which Barthes is confronting in his article lost ground long before poststructuralist theory developed. The 'linguistic turn' in criticism, based on Saussure, Hjelmslev and other contributors to structural linguistics, radically questioned the centrality of the subject in the cultural realm, and psychoanalysis demonstrated how older notions of a unified subject were illusory. Sigmund Freud (not Lacan, not 'postmodernism') introduced the idea that the (modern) subject was/is fundamentally divided, and more or less internally incoherent or contradictory. (Writers such as R.L. Stevenson had done it before him outside theory – take another look at *Dr. Jekyll and Mr. Hyde* (1886).) According to Freud (his second 'topology', not the first, where he distinguished between the conscious, the preconscious and the unconscious), subjectivity was/is constructed as an intersection of three dimensions, an unconscious with certain basic, shared features ('the id'), a conscious ('ego') and a set of internalized social norms (the 'superego'). He thus dissolved notions of a 'unified subject' and left little space for absolute individuality. As Barthes points out in his article, the cult of the author is historically tied to 'the prestige of the individual' (1982: 143), but this cult/prestige developed precisely as the modern, split subjectivity actually came into being. The unified, unique subject was an ideal which became ideologically important in romanticism precisely because the experience of modernity early on contradicted it.

However, the modern image of the split subject, with a largely collective unconscious and social norms internalized in its 'superego', does not entail a total dismissal of every idea of individuality. Since every human being is a social being, he or she is also always a product of specific social circumstances and experiences, endlessly varied for every infant growing up. Simply put, while all of the elements that make up a particular individual may be of a social, hence non-individual, nature, including what count as hereditary features of various kinds, the specific blend of these elements is specific to each individual. Consequently, it is still meaningful to speak of 'the individual' and then also, in appropriate cases, to speak of something (like a text) as marked by the individual who was responsible for the actual, empirical production of it. This is so even if every element (which an analysis may discern) that went into the 'thing' (or the text) can be traced 'back' to other 'things' (or texts). Just as the individual's individuality lies in his or her specific configuration of social elements, so the originality of the individual text lies in what it does to elements which existed before its production. It may occasionally even be that an individual or a text contains elements which are previously unseen or unheard, by accident or by intent.

The adjustments of the well-known or the introduction of historically new elements or dimensions in a certain text need not, for all purposes, be traced to the individual who produced them. The producer is quite concretely separated from his or her product both in terms of time and space. Media audiences meet texts, not producers. This is why it may be perfectly acceptable, for the purposes of interpretation or textual analysis, to forget about the author/producer and his or her specific situation. Both as critics and as ordinary members of audiences, it is the text we are trying to understand and/or enjoy.

The position of media researchers may be somewhat different. To the extent that they are trying to grasp how a text came to be the way it is, i.e. trying to explain the text and its specific features socially and historically, then the individuality of the author(s)/producer(s) and the specificities of their context(s) are highly relevant. The distinction between 'interpretation' and 'explanation' I am trying to employ here (drawing a bit irresponsibly on the classical German distinction between 'Verstehen' and 'Erklärung') is clearly problematic, but may still be made meaningful if taken as referring to different ways of investigating different dimensions of the phenomenon under scrutiny. The interpretation of a text is an attempt to grasp its synchronically available meaning(s) for whoever is perceiving it. The explanation of a text is the diachronical, more or less analytical socio-historical description of how it achieved its specific shape. 'Explanation' will always rest on interpretation of a variety of data; the difference between explanatory and interpretational activities proposed here thus pertains only to the difference between the different kinds of knowledge sought for in relation to the text – a difference in knowledge interests. These interests may well – and should be – combined, as suggested by Max Weber, for instance, in the area of sociology (cf. the introduction to this book).

The area of criticism is traditionally that of interpretation of texts, and critics may therefore put authors/producers 'in brackets' for their purposes. But if one is interested not only in the meaning(s) of the text, but also the meanings of the whole communicative process as a social phenomenon, the role of authors/ producers becomes highly relevant. If one is not only interested in what one may find of meaning(s) or, for that matter, *jouissance* (Barthes) in a text, but is also interested in the empirical, actual 'readings' of a text by audiences outside the community of culturally informed criticism, because they are suspected to have certain social implications, then all the social determinations of such readings acquire relevance, including those that stem from the text's production. In fact, it needs pointing out that the conditions of production may be ultimately relevant for any sensible interpretation of a text. My placing of Roland Barthes's article in a particular polemical situation in the late 1960s could be one example of this. I would still hold that synchronic, text-focused interpreta- tion is fully legitimate and valuable as an attempt to answer the question 'what does this text mean (or do) to me, or "us"?' Ideally, though, even such inter- pretations should entail and include a form of self-reflection which necessarily has to deal with the differences between the stance of production and the stance of reception. For instance, in what ways are my reading of this or that American film influenced by the historical dominance of the American cultural industries?

CREATIVITY, CULTURE-INDUSTRY DETERMINATIONS, AUDIENCES

The kind of creativity, of authorship, involved in the production of *Dynasty* is fundamentally determined by the demands of the television industry. It can be seen as restricted to the 'filling of forms': it does not at all challenge the industry's basic requirements for hour-long, advertising-interspersed, prime- time serial drama. The rhythms of scenes, sequences, episodes and plotlines are thus predetermined and well known to at least American audiences. The techniques of plotting, the types of characters and forms of characterizations are likewise generally known beforehand. It is not the content but the persistence of the foreseeable, basic pattern which is the main target in Adorno and Horkheimer's merciless attack on the culture industry, and it is also this formal trait in practically all of its products, in all media, which remains hardest to understand as anything but a tool for conformist integration of audiences. As Bernard Gendron puts it in the above-quoted article about popular music:

> Perhaps nothing is as resistant to consumer reinterpretation as the standardized forms, sounds, and verbal devices operating at the conven- tionalized core of the popular song. Because of their intimate association

with constant repetition, plugging and self-advertisement, these standard-ized components probably evoke the entrenched codes of the dominant culture much more powerfully than do the non-standardized components.

(Gendron 1986: 35)

While every culture industry text is 'recontextualized' at the point of recep-tion, it is nevertheless a question worth discussing whether this recontextualiza-tion or 'appropriation' by audiences and their specific sub-cultures actually transcends or challenges the meanings inherent in the very structure of these texts. A final quote from Gendron signals a problematic which will be central in Chapter 4 of this book:

> There is in sum a constant struggle at the meeting point of production and consumption between the evocation of entrenched codes and the insinua-tion of alternative meanings. The tendency of the music industry is to employ in the production of musical texts devices, like standardization, that automatically call the dominant codes into play. Recent writers who have focused on reception in popular music have been insufficiently attentive to the power of these devices, and thus have tended to exaggerate the semantic creativity of the consuming subcultures. I believe that a reappraisal of Adorno's work can contribute significantly to these theo-retical deficiencies. To further our understanding of the complex political stances of rock 'n' roll, we must now engage Adorno's productivist approach in a constructive dialogue with the more recent and fashionable reception approaches.
>
> (ibid.: 35f.)

The problem is, in other words, to decide the specific meanings and impor-tance of the standardized (industry-determined) elements of culture-industry texts like *Dynasty*, in relation to the non- or less-standardized ('authorial') elements. These two dimensions of the text may work in the same or in different directions, the one may dominate the other. A combination of textual and reception analysis is required in order to reach a conclusion.

DISTRIBUTION AND MARKETING

Dynasty was not only produced in Hollywood, its distribution was also managed from there. The distributional apparatus is controlled by the producers, and it is part of the means by which they influence reception. I will close this chapter by briefly sketching the way the industry handled the show's marketing and how the media structure at the other end, in Norway, proved very helpful in the process.

Dynasty's distribution was for years handled by Metro Media, which hired the PR company Creative Services Group, later known as Parish-Segal Com-munications, to do various kinds of marketing and support work for the serial. The following account is largely based on a telephone interview I did with Rebecca Segal, then head of international affairs at Creative Services Group (11 November 1985).

Metro Media would inform CSG about when and to whom the serial was sold. CSG would then supply the customer – a broadcaster or a video distributor – with various kinds of support material, such as star biographies and photos. Such material would also be offered to individual journalists and directly to selected magazines and weeklies, particularly 'TV and women's magazines'. In the selection of print media, the PR company would prefer what Segal referred to as 'better magazines', i.e. publications not too remote from the show's desired high-class image. At the same time, presumably as a sort of check on just how 'good' these magazines could be, they would have to have a readership among 'those who watch *Dynasty*', as Segal put it.

CSG had sixteen representatives around the world who monthly received material whose usefulness in their respective areas they themselves would judge. Such material would include, for instance, copies of articles which had appeared in American magazines and newspapers, interviews and background stories of different kinds. (The interview article by Joe Klein which I have quoted from above is an example.) Cultural variations around the globe necessitated a certain tailoring of PR, but this is only one reason for this decentralized form of work. Another is the problem of keeping track, from Los Angeles, of just how far the serial had come in each country. According to Segal, in the autumn of 1985 the BBC was in the middle of the fifth season, while Malaysia was just about to start the third. Still, the CSG in L.A. would at times, either on their own or asked by Metro Media, decide to 'activate the press' in certain countries, for example when a major star was about to visit. Important women's magazines in England were thus 'activated' when Diahann Carroll went there.

CSG also developed different kinds of advertisements for print media, as well as radio and TV spots to be used by stations which bought the show. These spots were almost exclusively used in the US, while the printed material could more easily be transferred to other countries.

CSG was not the only agency doing PR for *Dynasty*. All the stars had their own people working for them. These were the ones making and distributing all off-the-set photographs, which were bought by press agencies very eager to get them. According to Segal, an off-set picture of Linda Evans was just about the hottest thing for these agencies in 1985.

In the autumn of 1985, CSG had run its successful 'Champagne Campaign', intended particularly to promote syndication in the US independents market for two years. The cost of the campaign was estimated in August of that year at $2 million (*Daily Variety*, 30 August 1985). A main element was a photo of central cast members in tuxedos and formal dresses, drinking champagne toasts. A campaign kit would contain specially produced champagne glasses. Interestingly, the basic idea of the campaign was to play on the serial's luxury image, rather than on the idea that it was 'an older women's fantasy'. Esther Shapiro supervised the PR campaign personally, and was extremely careful in maintaining what Segal referred to as the serial's image as a 'fantasy show', where fantasy was tied to the main characters' wealth, ultra-upper-class status and power. All photos were for instance to look like 'fashion spreads', and in production stills no character would ever wear casual, everyday clothes. Rebecca Segal still thought that audiences would experience the serial's characters as 'real people with some very real problems'. But most of the PR for the show obviously shunned all mention both of these problems and the feminist ideas which were supposedly behind its production.

A very important part of the marketing of the series, particularly in the US, was the multi-million-dollar merchandising operation initiated by Esther Shapiro. The idea was that audiences, through buying towels, clothes, jewellery and fragrances tied to the show and its stars, could buy into the fantasy, take part in its aura of immense wealth and luxury. The merchandise and the advertising campaigns for it would, of course, work as advertising for the show, increasing its visibility and consequently (hopefully) further improving its ratings.

The first of several merchandising deals was publicly presented in January 1984 as a deal between 20th Century Fox Licensing Corporation and the Charles of the Ritz Group. It was said to be 'the first exclusive affiliation between a major Hollywood studio and a leading cosmetic and fragrance company for the development of products inspired by a television series'. The whole package of merchandising deals was called 'the most expensive worldwide line of products ever inspired by a tv show'. The bulk of the products was to be introduced in the autumn. Deals were negotiated with thirteen clothing companies, producers of luggage, linens, jewellery, optical ware and home furnishings. The products would mostly be sold in boutiques in department stores, and the name of the show or one of the characters would be identified on each of them. Similar 'retail programs' were also 'underway' in France, the UK, West Germany, Canada, Australia and Italy. But since *Dynasty* at that point was being shown in sixty-four countries, the possibilities for further expansion were obviously very good (*Daily Variety*, 19 January 1984).

Merchandising was not a new idea. Fox was already merchandising products linked to *MASH* and *Star Wars*. What was new was the 'level' of *Dynasty* merchandise, i.e. the kinds of products and their prices. There were no T-shirts or plastic toys. It is an indication of the merchandising operation's success as part of the creation of an image for the show that *Newsweek* (3 December 1984) covered the presentation of *Dynasty* clothing at Bloomingdale's (not Macy's or K-mart) in New York in a large illustrated article. At the same time, the merchandise was of course supposed to appeal to a wide selection of middle-class customers – not the poor and not the rich. The advertising campaign for the perfume Forever Krystle consisted first of a TV spot, shown only on ABC (other networks would not take it since it also promoted ABC's show) during its daytime soaps and during *Hotel*, which followed *Dynasty* on Wednesday evenings and had plenty of *Dynasty* viewers in its audience. The spot was described like this in the *New York Times* (6 November 1984):

> In the Krystle commercial, Miss Evans, wearing a fetching white negligee, admires the perfume's bottle before applying some of the scent, while her unseen but adoring 'husband' reads the text of the note that accompanied this gift. The note explains how it was created especially for Krystle.

Full-page, four-colour ads in the magazines *Vogue, Cosmopolitan, Good Housekeeping* and *People* showed the bottle, a framed photograph of the couple and the note which Blake/John Forsythe read on TV. The audience profiles of the magazines mentioned indicate the anticipated market reach of the product. It was mainly targeted at women belonging to the middle and lower-middle social classes. But, according to Jane Feuer (1989: 454), who refers to a report in the *Wall Street Journal* of 23 January 1986, 'the big-ticket items were taken off the market' in 1986; only the less expensive products, such as the perfumes, were financial successes for their manufacturers, at least in the domestic market. 'Apparently, *Dynasty*'s mass audience had the power to desire the items but not to purchase them', Feuer comments (1989: 454), thereby in effect indicating that the 'mass audience' was probably not the (presumably more or less) upscale readers of *Vogue* and *Cosmopolitan*.

The merchandising brought the total marketing efforts for *Dynasty* to a level far beyond that of any other show, while simultaneously creating profits of its own, at least for the show's producers. The custom among *Dynasty* fans (at least in the US, according to various US media) of 'dressing up' to view their favourite show most probably did not occur or at least did not catch on until after the merchandising had started. The producers could thus be seen as the ones who suggested the various 'taking part in the fantasy' practices which were to become associated with *Dynasty*, and which have been seen as signs of how active and playful audiences were/are. Even if these practices and the attitudes associated with them were not initiated by the producers, it is at any rate clear that they would encourage them rather than oppose them in any way. They served the producers' interests perfectly: the culture industry could really live up to its name.

DYNASTY PR THROUGH PUBLIC SERVICE MONOPOLY

Dynasty merchandising to my knowledge never reached Norway except in newspaper reports. Not only may cultural factors have contributed to lesser market appeal for the products in question, but the marketing of the serial could also be done much more easily in a one-channel television environment.

The leader of the the Film and Series Department of NRK-TV, Rigmor Hansson Rodin, told me in a telephone interview in the autumn of 1983 that Norwegian papers and weeklies received a lot of free material from *Dynasty*'s producers. This was an important reason why so much was written about the show that the NRK eventually 'had to' buy it. In Rodin's view, the NRK had, so to speak, been a victim of an aggressive alliance between the Hollywood producers/sellers and Norwegian commercial print media, partners in an attack on the cultural responsibility she and the NRK represented.

Since Rebecca Segal in my later interview with her talked about how CSG could 'activate the press' in various countries, I wrote to the editors of five major weeklies in November 1986 to ask how they acquired their plentiful material about the show. The three replies I received all denied that any particular attention had been paid to them by CSG or anyone else in Los Angeles. In fact, only one weekly (*Hjemmet*) had ever been in contact with 'the Segal Company', at a television market in Cannes (the MIP) 'where one of our employees asked for material about *Dynasty* and got it' (letter from Knut Olav Jakobsen, 11 November 1986). With this exception, the material these weeklies used was either bought from press agencies, produced by themselves (star interviews in Hollywood, for instance) or given to them for free by the NRK after they had bought the serial. For newspapers, the NRK was the almost totally dominant source of information about the show, just before it was broadcast and during its run. The material the NRK provided to the Norwegian print media was of course mostly what CSG had sent them since they bought the show.

In other words, before *Dynasty* was bought, there had been little or no specific coverage of the serial in weeklies or newspapers, except for ordinary news and press agency material about its success abroad, and editorial writing about the need to import either *Dallas* (in particular) or *Dynasty*. No particular attention was paid to Norwegian print media by *Dynasty*'s distributors or their PR people. After the NRK had bought the show, the broadcasting monopoly itself became the dominant source of material, and that material was provided from Hollywood by CSG.

I will return to the content of this material and other coverage of the show in the Norwegian print media in later chapters. The point here is simply that through the NRK and through press agencies the producers and distributors in Hollywood to a large degree controlled the way *Dynasty* was presented to Norwegian audiences just before its introduction and during its run. The centralized structure of a media system in which there was only one television channel was in other words very helpful to the producers; marketing efforts could be reduced to an absolute minimum and still be enormously effective. The same PR pieces appeared in a variety of different print media, with only very minor differences. Stephen Carrington was, for instance, presented as 'thoughtful, courageous, sensitive' in a Christian Oslo daily (*Vårt Land*, 5 May 1983), as 'thoughtful, courageous and very sensitive' in the NRK's own magazine (*Programbladet*, no. 19, 7–13 May 1983), and as 'a very sensitive, thoughtful and intelligent young man' in the major West Coast newspaper (*Bergens Tidende*, 7 May 1983).

As things developed, however, the show came to be given an extraordinary amount of public attention, in a heated debate where the producers could not exert much direct control.

2

'THE CULTURAL DEBATE OF THE AGES':

History, culture and media politics in public reception

'Who watches programs about the inside of the brain on Wednesday nights? [We want] television for those who watch it!'
(Freddy Andersen, chairman, 'Friends of *Dynasty*')

THE IMPORTANCE OF GEOGRAPHY

Transnational television productions are inserted in a very wide variety of specific cultural and political contexts all over the globe. There is, consequently, a definite need to consider the specificities of these contexts if one wants to understand the different receptions of these productions. I would like to give just one example before I present my own research. Yahia Mahamdi (1988) has, in a very interesting study, demonstrated how the reception of *Dallas* in Algeria was shaped by, first, the particularly central place of television as a source of entertainment in that country, especially for women, who had in the preceding years been, so to speak, pushed out of cinemas and into their homes. Second, *Dallas* was, to begin with, extremely popular, according to Mahamdi, because it represented a widespread dream of affluence among frustrated, poverty-stricken Algerians. But then, in the second season, its popularity dropped drastically because of the perceived severe immorality of its characters. In both phases, the serial was interpreted as a representation of real conditions in the US, and compared to the Algerian situation. According to Mahamdi, Algerians concluded that western modernity and affluence were not worth their price in moral decay.

The political and social situation in Norway when *Dynasty* was broadcast was radically different, but that country's historically produced cultural and political specificities also 'framed' the viewing experience in a principally similar, yet qualitatively different, manner.

Contrary to reported popular belief in the USA, Norway is not a refrigerator, even if an American refrigerator was once named after it (Norge). It is a mountainous country, facing the North Atlantic, with just over 4 million inhabitants who have a lot of space to share, statistically speaking. Its name

71

indicates that its coastline was early on known as the way to go north, and it does reach far north of the Arctic circle. It is still more or less habitable even in the far north, because of the Gulf Stream. Apart from the economic and socio-cultural difference between its northern and its more populous southern part, a major dividing line has historically been drawn between the east and west in southern Norway. A mountain range in the interior divides the dramatic 'fjord' landscapes of the west coast with its North Atlantic climate, from the more open valleys and plains of the east, with its forests, inland climate and relatively densely populated urban areas, particularly around Oslo, the capital.

These geographical observations are meant, first, to indicate that Norway is situated slightly off-centre, to say the least, compared with the major metro-politan areas of continental Europe. But it has been far from isolated: due to its natural resources it was early on involved in the international economy. Second, geographical factors explain some of its social and cultural peculiarities. In order to understand the meaning(s) of the *Dynasty* event in Norway, one has to understand the country's broadcasting traditions, which are tied to the wider socio-cultural and political history. A very brief historical outline is therefore necessary if we want to grasp the relations between general and particular issues here. This chapter is, then, devoted to a descriptive analysis of the most clearly media-political dimensions of the public reception of *Dynasty*. The main point is to show how it was possible for a Hollywood television serial to become both a sign of a historical shift in broadcasting and cultural traditions and also an instrument for such change. The *Dynasty* experience may be said to have brought about change, on the one hand, in the way Norwegians relate to television and, to some extent, popular culture in general, and, on the other hand, in the way the public service broadcasting institution conceives of, and tries to fulfil, its functions in a new media environment. The introduction of regular audience measurements and new ideas about programming and scheduling are among the most obvious signs in the latter category.

This chapter is, then, the one where specifically Norwegian circumstances will have to be given some attention. To an international readership, some passages or references may seem unusually 'local', uninteresting or even exotic. It is worth pointing out, however, that non-Anglo-American students in all media and cultural studies, at least in the western world, have had to familiarize themselves with 'local' and 'exotic' American and British phenomena for decades. The chapter could then be seen as a practical lesson in what non-American and non-British students and scholars have to go through if they want to follow scholarly writing in 'international' media and cultural studies. Bear with me, and I promise to make the rest of this book more immediately accessible.

NORWAY: A CRASH COURSE

In 1980, the Norwegian Broadcasting Corporation (Norsk Rikskringkasting, NRK) operated the single public service radio channel and the single television channel available to most inhabitants. Though 25 per cent of the people (all of them living in the eastern part of the country) could receive Swedish (public service) radio and television, it is on the whole correct to say that Norway was one of the very last remaining one-channel countries in Europe at this time. The comparison with Albania was made by some participants in the public discussions on an expansion of television services.

The 1980s then brought a revolution in the field of broadcasting in general and television in particular. A second national public radio channel was followed by a multitude of local commercial stations. At present (1993/4) there are four national radio channels, one of which is commercially financed. Norway got its second terrestrial TV channel on 5 September 1991, commercially financed but with an obligation to a public service profile. It now reaches about 90 per cent of the population. Two other commercial Norwegian-language channels, one of them transmitting from London, are accessible only by way of satellite and cable. About 40 per cent of all households now either receive cable or have satellite dishes, and thus have up to forty foreign channels to choose from.

In order to understand just how dramatic these changes have been, they must be seen in the light of the country's particular history, sociology and culture. Single-channel broadcasting was in accordance with fundamental features of Norwegian society, which has been described as not only homogeneous (in terms of ethnicity, culture and language) but also as 'singularistic' (Galtung and Gleditsch 1975). The latter term refers to the level of social institutions, where 'pluralistic' has indeed been a foreign word. More than 90 per cent of the population are formally members of the same official/public Lutheran church; 99.5 per cent of all children go to public schools with very minor pedagogical differences between them; at high school level (16–18 year olds) 95 per cent go to schools within the same public system. In other words, Norwegians are not used to institutional alternatives.

The relative ethnic and cultural homogeneity of the country (with the exception of the relatively small Sámi (Lapp) population mainly based in the far north) is of course one reason for this. Another is the fact that Norway has been too small and lacking in resources for the development of, say, a system of private schools alongside the public system. Also important, though, is an egalitarian tradition related both to the social structure and to the historically dominating cultural and ideological formations: Norway was never really feudal and has lacked both an aristocracy and later a bourgeoisie comparable to those of other, more populous countries. Conservatives have historically used this fact to reassure themselves that the danger of a revolutionary uprising was quite small, and left-wing socialists have at times complained that the only bourge-oisie in Norway worth mentioning was the *petite* part of it. This is not to say that Norway has been without class divisions and class struggles – between the world wars its labour movement was more radical than those of most other western European countries. This shows how a relatively low degree of class difference

73

in terms of income, lifestyle, etc. has been an operative factor in the country's social, political and cultural development – not least by way of an ideological agreement that this feature is something quite unique to Norwegian society.

The impression made on foreign observers may have been like that of Elihu Katz, who once said to me that 'the country was so peaceful you had to find something to fight about'. He was thinking of the century-long struggles over the language issue. This has its roots in the fact that Norway was a part of Denmark for 400 years until 1814, when it was handed over to Sweden after the Napoleonic wars. In the vacuum of the transitional period, the country got its (for the time) remarkably democratic Constitution, and a parliament. Even if the Constitution stated that all laws should be written in Norwegian, the only written Norwegian at the time was pure Danish. Two strategies developed on this issue. One aimed at a gradual 'Norwegianization' of written Danish by bringing it closer to the Norwegian spoken by the educated upper class. The result was the now dominant form of written Norwegian, which is close to spoken Norwegian particularly in the east and in major urban areas. The other strategy aimed at a 'New Norse', developed in the mid-nineteenth century from studies of popular dialects seen as being close to the Old Norse of the Middle Ages, i.e. dialects in rural areas, predominantly in the west and in the mountain regions. The language question became a central dividing issue for more than a century primarily because it was tied to socio-cultural differences and conflicts of interest between geographical areas (east/west) and, more generally, between centre and periphery (city/countryside). The fact that the 'periphery's alternative', New Norse, both survived and achieved quite a strong position is in itself an indication of the relatively strong political and cultural position of regionalism and various popular movements (cf. Gripsrud 1994).

A parliamentary system of government was introduced in 1884, and in 1905 the union with Sweden was abolished. Norway thus has a relatively short history as an independent country, and this may be part of the reason why concerns with nationality have played a more important role in Norwegian cultural politics than for instance in Denmark or Sweden. The Constitution, from the beginning, granted considerable influence to farmers/peasants and other non-bourgeois groups, and the parliament early on installed a system of local democratic rule that provided further opportunities for political influence to farmers in the predominantly agrarian society of that period. In the struggle for a parliamentary system (against the power of the Swedish king), a nationalist and democratic/populist alliance between liberal representatives of the urban bourgeoisie and representatives of farmers and rural areas developed into a political party. This party/alliance was important in two ways in our context. It represented the socio-cultural periphery of the country in important issues, exemplified in support for the New Norse language. It also provided political opportunities for the growing industrial working class (universal suffrage was granted to men in 1898, to women in 1913) as well as a basis for the later development of a relatively stable social democracy, a 'welfare state' supported by a high degree of cross-political consensus. Last but not least, it gave 'nationalism' ties to progressive, democratic social and cultural politics. This is important to keep in mind when a 'national' rhetoric is used in public debates on, say, transnational popular culture.

Parties that later emerged from the above-mentioned party/alliance also provided the political basis for the establishment of the NRK (the Norwegian Broadcasting Corporation) as a broadcasting monopoly, financed by licence fee, in 1933. These parties were the social democratic labour party, the liberal party (the remains of the original alliance) and the agrarian party. This political constellation reflected a social and cultural alliance between the working class and its organizations on the one hand and various rural-based classes and cultural organizations on the other which until recently played a major role in a number of political issues and situations (such as the struggles over EC membership). Both were opposed to the powers and expressed interests of the urban bourgeoisie and the conservative party. The in many ways quite reactionary agrarian party helped the social democrats to form their first government in 1935 (two weeks in 1928 do not really count), and the social democrats remained in power until the mid-1960s. (See also Rokkan 1966, 1967 for classical accounts of the above features of Norwegian politics.)

THE BBC VS THE NRK: EXCLUSIVE VS INCLUSIVE OFFICIAL CULTURE

Like its British counterpart and ideal, the BBC, the NRK was expressly devoted to a programming policy intended to serve popular/public enlightenment purposes in a variety of ways. But, as the above historical sketch is supposed to indicate, the form, tone and character of the enlightenment orientations of the two corporations were from the beginning somewhat different. A key element in the British version of public service broadcasting was, according to Raymond Williams (1975: 33), that

> a dominant version of the national culture had already been established, in an unusually compact ruling-class, so that public service could be effectively understood and administered as a service according to the values of an existing public definition, with an effective paternalist definition of both service and responsibility.

Consequently, in the British context, enlightenment in the tradition associated with Lord Reith could be described as a 'top-down project, based on the shared cultural assumptions of the aristocracy and the metropolitan bourgeoisie with their emphasis on art and high culture' (Syvertsen 1992: 95). In Norway, both the labour movement and a complex of rural-based socio-cultural and political organizations (particularly those tied to the New Norse language) significantly influenced the composition and overall profile of programming. Various enlightenment elements were of a practical type, and the cultural programming

75

reflected both a rural, 'national' folk culture, urban high culture and the mainly, but not only, distributional cultural policies of the labour movement.

This meant that the NRK was always quite open to certain forms of folk and popular culture, forms that were acceptable to the intellectuals who represented the major socio-cultural and political forces in the public sphere. Both the NRK and the BBC relied on the standards that were held by their respective national establishments in cultural affairs. Their differences stem from the differences between these establishments. The NRK was clearly also paternalistic in its attitude towards its audiences: 'the emphasis was on *raising* rather than *reflecting* popular taste and standards' (Syvertsen 1992: 95). There was definitely the same emphasis in the cultural politics of the major mass movements (Gripsrud 1981, 1990). But the allegiance of certain intellectual elites to 'folk' and 'progressive' cultural forms may be said to have kept the domain of 'official culture' more complex and inclusive, and less stable, than in most other European countries, particularly outside Scandinavia.

A concrete manifestation of this can be seen in the existence of two National Theatres in Oslo: one historically a cultural centre for the urban elites, playing the preferred repertoire of these groups, and one tied to movement(s) for the New Norse language, supported in the capital by politicians, university professors, writers and other intellectuals with rural backgrounds and nationalist and populist inclinations. This latter theatre was opened in the presence of the king and prime minister in 1913 and has existed ever since, receiving increasing public financial support like other theatres, with a repertoire mixing popular genres (folk comedy, musicals), mainstream classics and various 'avant-garde' pieces. Its degree of national-popular cultural 'opposition' or difference was in other words blessed by the state from the beginning.

SOCIAL-DEMOCRATIC BROADCASTING

In the first 30–35 years after World War II, then, Norway was a one-channel, social-democratic country (even if 'bourgeois' coalitions formed governments at times after the mid-1960s), with an official culture relatively open to certain popular cultural forms. But the various factions of the cultural elite – urban-conservative, New-Norse national-populist and socialist alike – were united in their continuing rejection of the transnational, more or less industrial forms of popular culture that had been enjoyed by 'ordinary people' at least since the second half of the nineteenth century. To the nationally produced 'pulp' literature were added imported western, detective and romance novels. Film was installed as the major popular form of public entertainment in urban areas from about 1905, and represented a significant contribution to the 'Americanization' of Norwegian popular culture. 'American action films were popular in Norway in early 1914', when the capital alone had twenty cinemas (Thompson 1985: 38). In 1915, half of the films that passed through the state censor's office were American (Evensmo 1967), and in the late 1920s, US films constituted between 63 and 70 per cent of the total footage screened in Norway (Thompson 1985: 129). The syncopated music known as jazz was played both on gramophone records and by Norwegian orchestras from the mid-1920s on. Apart from occasional films and very few crime novels, none of this was accepted as 'quality' culture by the cultural elites until the late 1960s. It was not national, it was not progressive, it was not art. It was only popular because it appealed to all the 'lowest' dispositions in people.

The resistance of the cultural elites to transnational – modern – popular culture was part of the reason why Norway was among the very last countries in Europe to introduce a regular television service, in August 1960. Intellectuals reported from abroad in the early 1950s that the new medium had devastating effects on national cultures and education, and a nationally acclaimed writer said that if television was introduced, Norway might as well forget about its written language(s): it would all be 'jazz and boxing' anyway (cf. Dahl 1981: 65). But since both leading politicians and most of the people wanted television anyway, for different reasons, technical preparations and experimental transmissions took place throughout the decade up to the official opening.

As previously with radio, heavy investment in technical facilities for the distribution of signals all over the large, sparsely populated and mountainous country was given priority over the expansion of programming. Equal opportunities for all citizens to enjoy broadcasting services was a central social-democratic goal, in keeping both with regionalism and widespread egalitarian ideals. In 1967, television reached the northernmost county (Finnmark). At that time several hundred thousand people living in the shadows of various mountains still could not receive signals or had only poor reception. But it is still fair to say that in the late 1960s TV sets were to be found in most of the country's households. Colour was gradually introduced from about the same time.

In its first years, NRK-TV transmitted only a couple of hours of programmes per day, more at weekends. According to statistics, it was up to 3.8 hours daily in April 1967, and 6.8 hours in February ten years later (Østbye 1982: 288). Still, television almost immediately managed to position itself as the very centre of the public sphere, both as mediator and as originator of public debates – and as a subject for day-to-day talk between people.

In the 1960s, two topics dominated in discussions on programming: explicit sex and 'incomprehensible' modern drama (Beckett and Pinter, for instance). In fact, both subjects were in particular tied to domestic and Nordic drama productions. Nobody questioned the amount of nighttime educational programming (on natural sciences, religion, politics or various forms of 'high culture'), and the Friday night hour of American or British crime series (notably *Perry Mason* and *The Saint*) was clearly both tremendously popular and accepted by those who otherwise rejected transnational popular culture. The same goes for the Saturday night episodes of *Gunsmoke*. This show might have gained some extra popularity due to James Arness's Norwegian descent, but it was actually the comic character Festus who was most popular – he even had a particular brand of canned meatballs named after him. In retrospect, and with particular relevance to the *Dynasty* phenomenon, the general acceptance of these imported shows was probably not least related to the fact that they all represented typically male-oriented genres, even if adjusted to television's typical family audiences. Two very long-running British serials, *The Forsyte Saga* and (in the early 1970s) *Family at War*, were both extremely popular, while, for different reasons, also legitimate for the elites. The first had an aura of British literary culture, the second had, in addition to its focus on family problems, an aura of classic social realism and shared experiences of war and class differences.

British imports have always been important elements in NRK programming. The self-imposed limit on the proportion of imported programming was set at 50 per cent, but has normally been closer to 40. Typically, UK productions in 1977 constituted about one-third of the imported material, one-fifth came from other Nordic countries and a bit less than one-fifth were of US origin (Østbye 1982: 277). In 1983, total imports were down to 30 per cent, the UK supplying 32 per cent of this amount, the US 20 (Bakke 1986: 137). Most of the US imports have always been feature films, followed by occasional detective series and sitcoms. Norway and Denmark were in 1983 the only countries in Europe where most of the imported programme time came from the UK (Denmark, 27 per cent) (ibid.). British productions, both factual and fictional genres, have enjoyed both prestige and, in most cases, widespread popularity in Norway. But a certain popular form of British television was not imported: soap operas. In fact, no real soap opera from anywhere had ever been seen on Norwegian screens when *Dynasty* was bought. It is telling of the general profile of NRK programming that Norwegians encountered soap opera first through a parody of the genre: the US hit sitcom *Soap*.

Domestic and Nordic drama was still sometimes debated along traditional lines throughout the 1970s. But the typical debates of this decade centred on politics. The NRK was accused of being a leftist stronghold, with a more or less systematically biased coverage of both politics and culture. Even if these accusations were vastly exaggerated, there may have been at least some truth in them. The relatively much rarer and weaker claims that the opposite was the case could be seen as one indication of this. Nicholas Garnham has said that the BBC 'through the 1960's and 1970's betrayed public service broadcasting by progressively alienating the potential supporters of the public service ideal both among the audience and among broadcasters' (1990: 129). Apart from the corporation's London-based imposition of a political and cultural elite's 'tastes and views of the world', Garnham attributes most of the BBC's failure to its lack of positive response to 'the more democratic and participatory climate of the late 1960's and the early 1970's', which resulted in 'a situation where political progressives have increasingly come to see the BBC [. . .] as the major obstacle to reform and the main target for attack' (ibid.: 130). In Norway, 'political progressives' clearly perceived the NRK differently, as more complex and, in some areas, a potential ally, an institution in which there was significant support for a critical view on both international and national issues of the period. Still a relatively young and small institution, NRK-TV had many employees with generational and social ties to the socio-cultural conjuncture signified by '1968', and the strong social-democratic traditions of the NRK as a whole meant that the leftist tendencies within the social-democratic movement in general were also represented at various levels.

LIBERALIST MEDIA REVOLUTION AND THE *DYNASTY* DEBATE

All of the above old struggles over the NRK's programming dramatically lost importance in the 1980s. A whole new set of questions was brought to the fore, concerning the role of broadcasting media and public service broadcasting in particular, involving wide-reaching issues of socio-cultural values and interests in general. The number of television channels in Europe as a whole tripled between 1983 and 1986, and things were rapidly changing in Norway too. Satellite television, an explosive growth in the home video (and video rental) market, rapid expansion of cable services, etc., all happened more or less simultaneously.

The conservative party came to power in a minority government in 1981, and its minister of cultural affairs immediately started drafting and implementing a liberalist turn in media policies. This party had never very actively supported the NRK monopoly, but had on the other hand not been able or willing really to challenge it before, not least because the party's 'cultural' faction (as opposed to the 'industrial' one) saw the monopoly as the best way to secure cultural quality and moral standards in programming. Towards the end of the 1970s the balance between the two factions shifted, and so did the attitude to the NRK's monopoly. Action for change was now politically possible, first of all because the signs were obvious that complete national control over broadcasting was about to be made obsolete by technological developments. But a much more general ideological turn to the 'right', which the election of the conservative government (replaced by a 'non-socialist' coalition after only one-and-a-half years) itself represented, was also important. The conservative ministry of culture almost immediately authorized newspapers, voluntary associations of various sorts and cable companies to start local radio and television stations, and also to retransmit satellite television via cable (from Satellite Television Ltd, later known as Sky Channel). This change in policy was interestingly legitimated as a defence of Norwegian culture, since 'greater diversity and plurality' in the Norwegian output was necessary in the light of the 'threats' from the increasing availability of international television. Even if conservatives lost support in the elections throughout the 1980s, and the labour party was in (minority) government from 1986 to 1989, their offensive of the early 1980s to liberalize broadcasting laid the basic premises of later developments. In 1987 a new 'narrowcasting' Act was passed which allowed commercial local radio, and in 1988 a new Cable Act removed the licensing system for satellite retransmissions, so that 'anyone' (who had the financial resources necessary) could establish commercial television services – if only by satellite. (All of the above summary of developments draws on Syvertsen 1992: 202ff.)

The *Dynasty* event took place in the midst of these rapid and radical changes. It crystallized most of the wider cultural and ideological issues involved: notions of 'free choice', 'cultural quality', 'internationalization of culture', 'commercialization of the media', etc. The serial and the debate over it contributed to a decisive historical shift in the media and cultural domain.

An intricate complex of factors produced the new situation. International technological developments and telecommunications policies may have functioned as first movers, but several other economic, social, political and cultural forces also made significant contributions. It was precisely because the *Dynasty* phenomenon in Norway had so many determinants and implications that it could with quite a degree of justification be called 'the cultural debate of the ages' by a contemporary observer (Dahl 1983). The very heated public debate over the serial had many features in common with traditional cultural debates. However, three major elements created a decisive historical shift which marked the debate as unique: (a) the rapid, technologically induced changes in the field(s) of radio, television and video; (b) a general strengthening of 'commercialism' in all media, print included; and last but not least (c) the strong presence of 'ordinary people', speaking up for their cultural tastes and programming preferences.

The importance of the last element has, in my view, been underestimated in most of the critical scholarly discourse on the political implications of technological shifts in the distribution of audio-visual media and the concomitant crisis of public service broadcasting all over western Europe. This is what I attempt to argue in the following theoretical section.

TECHNOLOGY, CULTURE AND POLITICS IN THE BROADCASTING REVOLUTION

Researchers operating from a theoretical basis labelled 'political economy' have studied the political consequences of the rapidly developing video, satellite and cable technologies. They have pointed out how the economico-political struggles for de- and reregulation have served to secure profits for the transnational corporations most heavily involved in the field, and how all of this is part of a more comprehensive restructuring of the relationships between capital and the state and between capital, culture and the public sphere. The general, quite pessimistic perspective has been that which Philip Elliott once formulated: 'what we face is a continuation of the shift away from involving people in society as political citizens of nation states towards involving them as consumption units in a corporate world' (Elliott 1986: 106).

While this in my view is certainly a correct diagnosis of a major contemporary trend, prominent representatives of the 'political economy' group of scholars have tended to reduce developments to a mere expression of capital's ongoing quest for new exploits. As put by Nicholas Garnham, the proliferation of potential audio-visual channels 'is not a response to consumer demand but the result both of the search of multi-national hardware manufacturers for new markets, and of the industrial and economic strategies of various governments' (Garnham 1984: 2). This argument leaves out the fact that a quest for new markets ultimately relies on an *anticipated* consumer demand. Such anticipations will necessarily, since managers of transnational corporations are not stupid, at least not in financial matters, be based on some empirically grounded understanding of what consumers would like to have if it were available.

In other words, the enormous interest in developing viable domestic video products, in developing cable systems and satellite television, has been rationally founded in some knowledge of what people would want if it were offered: more popular entertainment of various kinds, twenty-four-hour services ('never-ending flow'), a wider spectrum of programme material available at any given time, etc. The sheer fascination with technological wonders which for instance enables us to see something going on at the very same moment on a different continent is also worth considering. Among my own very first memories of watching television is the direct transatlantic Telstar transmission of President Kennedy's speech in 1962. The meaning of this event, not least to a generation which was used to having Radio Luxembourg as a primary source of popular music, was that it promised an end to national parochialism, the opening up of greatly increased, exciting cultural opportunities, in short a significant new turn in the vastly expanded space for a number of wishes, demands and desires offered by modernity at least since the mid-nineteenth century.

In my view, this means it is time for another look also at Raymond Williams's now classic statement: '*It is not only that the supply of broadcasting facilities preceded the demand; it is that the means of communication preceded their content*' (Williams 1975: 25). While it is probably true that there was no strong or explicit demand for the specific forms of radio and television services that developed from 1920 on, the idea of direct transmissions of live images to people's homes preceded the actual development of the necessary technologies by several decades – just as the development of the film medium had been foreshadowed by the magic lantern and photography. It may be true that the definite contents of film or broadcasting media were not demanded or foreseen. But a series of drawings published in 1882 by the French artist Robida, in which moving pictures were transmitted on to the walls of people's living rooms, casts some doubt even on this:

81

One of the screens showed a teacher giving a mathematics lesson; another showed a dressmaker displaying his wares (a prediction of 'shopping by television' a century before it became reality); another had a ballet being performed; and yet another showed a full-scale desert war being fought, while viewers gazed in horror from their comfortable chairs.

(Wheen 1985: 11)

It seems to me that these drawings indicate the existence of not only ideas about moving images in private homes, but also quite specific anticipations of what such images would be about: education, art, commercial presentations and news/documentary. None of these forms of content were, of course, specific to television: the medium was, both in these imaginative drawings and in its actual development, mainly an apparatus for the distribution of pre-existing, external material and genres.

Robida was, importantly, not alone. In 1891, the major New Norse writer, Arne Garborg, published a novel in which a character, representing positivist optimism, envisaged a future in which people, in their own homes, had 'screens' by which they could choose to watch and listen to opera, ballet, circus, religious services, parliamentary debates or concerts. In the US, in the very same year, Edison proclaimed in newspapers that 'he was within a few months of achieving direct transmission of live events into the home', complete with sound and images, and similar ideas also circulated in popular books and magazines (Sklar 1976: 11). Even if a really functioning television technology still lay decades away, there is little doubt that widespread, quite specific visions of the medium indicated a vast potential market for it. It was simply in perfect keeping both with the 'mobile privatization' (Williams) characteristic of modernity, and wishes and desires shaped by the same social processes.

This historical detour is also relevant to an understanding of the developments of audio-visual technologies in the 1970s and 1980s. Corporations (and governments) worked intensely in this field with strictly economic (and military) motivations. This made for very rapid and dynamic developments, and certain essential premises for the use of these technologies were certainly not established out of concerns for a (more) democratic public sphere. But the corporations could at the same time be said to have worked with the support of potential customers among 'ordinary people' of various kinds. The increased imaginary mobility and real, if limited, freedom of choice that VCRs and satellite and cable television have made available to most people is in accordance with their deep-seated, historically shaped wishes, demands and desires.

It is absolutely necessary to come to terms with these wishes, demands and desires in some way, if critical intellectuals are to have any chance of establishing a dialogue with the majority of television audiences. This seems to have been realized by, for instance, Nicholas Garnham, who has talked about the need to change 'the contempt and lack of sympathy for popular tastes still all too prevalent among supposedly progressive cultural workers in the film and video field' (1990: 134). But the following paragraph may in my view also reveal a lack of understanding of the challenge:

> On the other hand we have also to accept that the steadily increasing privatization of cultural consumption makes the public itself resistant to participatory models of cultural production and consumption. That the UK at a time of deep recession was the fastest growing market in the world for video-recorders should give us pause for thought. It is clear therefore that much campaigning work needs to be done within the socialist movement to change deeply ingrained attitudes to cultural production and consumption before there is any hope of achieving concrete reforms.
>
> (Garnham 1990: 134)

Since this comes after Garnham has said that 'any socialist response to cable and satellite must be, so far as possible, to oppose expansion and face openly and coherently the inevitable charges of Luddism' (ibid.: 133), it seems to me that he intends to campaign against the widespread lust for a plenitude of television channels. Such an intention is reminiscent of the battles fought by socialist and communist parties before World War II against the 'individualism' and 'bourgeois immorality' of phenomena such as syncopated dance music and Hollywood movies. It was and is a totally futile project, because it is fundamentally at odds with the appeal of the phenomena in question to people whose desires and ideas of a better life are shaped by their situations, their actual lifeworlds, in modern or late modern capitalist societies. These desires and dreams will have to be recognized as they are, as an essential part of the basis on which progressive media and cultural policies must build. The question must then be raised if they are really adequately served by the existing or planned offerings. It is probable that quite a few of those eager to get as many channels as possible will sooner or later sing along with Bruce Springsteen about '57 channels and nothin' on'. That is when, if not sooner, a believable and attractive alternative, which is not simply a return to the good old days, should be ready for presentation.

My point here is, then, that if rapid, capital-driven technological developments presented entirely new premises for debates on broadcasting in the early 1980s, these premises also made for a release of popular wishes and desires for a different kind of broadcasting. These wishes and desires 'went public' in the debate over *Dynasty*, and Norwegian 'progressive' intellectuals had a hard time trying to deal with them. It is, finally, time to have a closer, concrete look at this debate.

PUBLIC PRESSURE ON PUBLIC TELEVISON: HOW *DYNASTY* GOT INTO THE SCHEDULE

The press played a leading role not only in the public debate on *Dynasty*, but also in a debate which led to the NRK's purchase of the serial. It is important here to note that a debate in the Norwegian press is something entirely different from a debate in, say, the US press. In fact, Norway is quite unique in the western world in terms of newspaper readership. In the year of the 'cultural debate of the ages', 1983, so-called 'lesser-educated' Norwegians (i.e. those with up to nine years' schooling) spent on average forty-two minutes per day reading newspapers. The more educated spent fifty-two minutes, according to the same survey (Høst 1983: 135). Norway has all in all about 160 papers published more or less daily for a population of 4.1 million. In 1991, 34 per cent of the population over 9 years of age read at least one paper per day, 30 per cent read two papers and 20 per cent claimed to read three or more papers (Central Bureau of Statistics, Report no. 12, 1992). In other words, a press debate in the Norwegian context is not something concerning only a minority with the equivalent of a college education, as it might be in the USA.

The newspapers, especially the nationally distributed Oslo tabloids, initially contributed to audience expectations about *Dynasty* by writing about the international success of its rival and generic predecessor, *Dallas* – and the NRK's attitude towards that show. The NRK had refused to buy *Dallas*, and the reason given was its 'low quality'. The tabloids created something almost amounting to a 'public outcry' about this, since Swedish public service TV started showing *Dallas* in the 1980–1 season. The chorus of course was 'why can't we take it if the Swedes can?' – a loaded question, given Norway's widespread national inferiority complex. (Sweden has twice as many inhabitants and, contrary to Norway, produces cars – Volvo and Saab.) Also important here is the fact that hundreds of thousands in the eastern parts of Norway could actually watch Swedish television, so other parts of the country suffered from geographically determined injustice. The fuss over the NRK's rejection of *Dallas*, and the fact that that show was already a tremendous international success, prompted a private video import company to buy the exclusive rights to distribute *Dallas* in Norway (thus making it impossible for the NRK to change its mind), even though they had to rely on video rentals since only one channel of broadcast TV existed. The NRK's decision to buy *Dynasty* was then made, indirectly as a result of the public pressure building mainly through the two tabloids, *Verdens Gang* (*VG*) and *Dagbladet* in the *Dallas* case. 'We *had* to buy it' (*Dynasty*), the then leader of NRK-TV's film and series department, Rigmor Hansson Rodin, told me in a telephone interview in the autumn of 1983.

The fact was that there were also internal struggles in the NRK leading up to the actual buying of the serial. The present head of the culture section, Stein Roger Bull, was at the time in charge of the entertainment department. He and associates in his department exploited the vagueness of the borders between the departments for film/series and entertainment by simply announcing that if film and series did not buy *Dynasty*, they would (taped interview, spring 1992). Bull and his colleagues also gained support from people in film and series who were more willing than their boss to listen to the 'demand' publicly expressed in the tabloids. The stubborn boss, Rigmor Hansson Rodin, then gave in, and bought the first episodes of *Dynasty*. Not surprisingly, her department presented the show officially as being of much higher quality than *Dallas* (see Chapter 3).

This story of how *Dynasty* came to be presented on Norwegian TV screens indicates how intimate the relations have been between the Oslo dailies – the two tabloids in particular – and the NRK. These relations have developed in the one-channel situation. The two tabloids have a combined national circulation of well above half a million copies per day, a huge figure in a small population. They are quite different from the tabloids of certain other countries, in that they have a reputation for quite solid reporting in certain fields: *Dagbladet* has, for instance, a tradition of being a central forum for liberal and radical intellectuals. Since their circulation is so large, this made (and makes) them not only powerful agents in the politico-cultural field, but also significant simply as barometers of widespread views, sentiments and opinions. The people in the NRK who wanted to buy *Dynasty* could use these papers to confirm their own feeling: that a certain puritan public service regime in programming was over, and that the survival of public service television depended on the corporation's ability to open up to the tastes of a now more vocal, less subservient audience.

In terms of internal politics, the advocates (and activists) for *Dynasty* could count on a growing support for their views at the executive level of the NRK. The corporation was at this point marked by a growing awareness of the fact that they were, willingly or not, facing a situation of real competition. Swedish television had been, as mentioned above, an alternative to parts of its audience, but it was no longer the only one. As of April 1982, Rupert Murdoch's Sky Channel was distributed by cable in central areas, and its blatantly commercial programming had become a topic of public debate. The number of VCRs increased rapidly, from 75,000 in 1979 to about 500,000 at the end of 1986. In Norway, significantly, these machines were mainly used to play rented tapes with films and series.

The total turnover in the video rental business increased from 240 million kroner (some £24 million, more than US $30 million) in 1982 to 850 million kroner in 1986 (NRK 1987: 9). A more comprehensive adjustment to a competitive market situation was already beginning, and the buying of *Dynasty* was part of a reorientation which was further developed as the debate about the serial went on. In short, the NRK itself took on many of the features traditionally associated with commercial broadcasting. I will return to this in a slightly more detailed way towards the end of this chapter.

PUBLIC DEBATE, POPULAR PARTICIPATION

The debate on *Dynasty* opened quite modestly in a small (if politically not insignificant) Christian Oslo daily and other local newspapers. The Christian paper asked a bishop and leaders of Christian organizations the key question for much later debate and research: 'Why do we watch that sort of thing?' (*Vårt Land*, 19 May 1983). The journalist pointed out that *Dynasty* was obviously something 'everybody' was watching while at the same time claiming that the show was 'meaningless, hopeless and spineless'. One of the Christian leaders did not 'conceal' that he had seen one of the two episodes broadcast at that time, and claimed that the serial 'glorifies a life of abundance, power and, in part, immorality'. But it was still mainly a 'waste of time'. Other leaders interviewed said that the show appealed to escapism, and noted its focus on wealth, family problems and sex. One of them, with a professional background in NRK-TV, also mentioned the high degree of professionalism in the production. In his judgement, the most problematic aspect of the serial, in moral terms, was the way it portrayed Blake Carrington: he was given sympathetic features in a way which could make his 'brutality in business' seem legitimate. The bishop basically said that he had no time for serials and that he preferred soccer and crime series on TV. In other words, after two episodes Christians had noted the strong appeal of *Dynasty*, but still had no strong negative opinion about it.

However, an interview in a local paper (*Fredrikstad Blad*, 21 May) could be seen as an indication both of what was about to come and of the degree of arrogant ignorance which marked much of the later criticism of the show: a female member of the government- and parliament-appointed Broadcasting Council, Liv Nordhaug, said that she had 'certainly not' watched *Dynasty* at all, but judging from the pre-showing presentation of it, she found it 'sad' that this was the kind of entertainment NRK had chosen to offer people on Saturday nights. It was obviously a purely speculative production about decadent life in the upper upper classes, and she would certainly enquire about the reasons for it being shown in the next council meeting.

Readers' letters in a social democratic paper published just outside Oslo (*Akershus Arbeiderblad*) also complained about *Dynasty* as a sign of increasing commercialization of NRK's programming (24 May 1983). But the public debate did not really get rolling until the show had been harshly attacked by a well-known marxist-leninist ('maoist') writer, Jon Michelet. He spoke in a meeting on 26 May 1983 of the Broadcasting Council, of which he was a member. According to newspaper reports the following day, Michelet said that *Dynasty* should be taken off the schedule as soon as possible, because it was 'non-culture from beginning to end'; it made '*Dallas* look like a piece by Shakespeare'; it demonstrated 'how decay marks current American acting'. The show was called a 'soap-stew'; the characters were 'made not of cardboard, but of ice'. All of this concerned the 'cultural quality' of the show. The other major thrust of his argument was that the serial was entirely irrelevant for Norwegian viewers, since the characters had a private park the size of the huge forests north of Oslo and a swimming pool the size of one of Norway's largest inland lakes: 'only one in a million of the world's population is interested in the problems dealt with in this serial'.

It is important to note here that Michelet owed most of his (macho) reputa-tion as a writer to his widely read novels, which attempt to use male-oriented popular genres (crime/detective fiction and thrillers) as vehicles for a 'progressive' political 'message'. This indicates that he did not react in this way out of contempt for popular culture or popular genres in general. Even if he himself was not aware of it, it was quite obviously not least what *Dynasty* had in common with popular *feminine* genres that disturbed him. In Norway this at the time meant literary (in books and weeklies) and filmic family sagas and romances, often set in aristocratic or very upper-class circles, texts very far from the officially preferred 'social realism' of Michelet and his political group. Michelet's attack on *Dynasty* is thus an early indication of the mostly implicit gender dimension to the struggle over the serial (cf. p. 95).

Two days later, Michelet was invited to a debate in the current affairs radio magazine *Ukeslutt* ('Weekend'), which the NRK then transmitted on both radio channels. He met with the editor of the most rapidly growing weekly, *Se og Hør* ('Look and listen'), a populist 'reportage' magazine which may be seen as a Norwegian version of the US *National Enquirer*. This editor did of course defend *Dynasty* as very popular entertainment, which deserved to continue for as long as audiences wanted it, while Michelet repeated his attacks. Shortly after the (live) discussion between the two had started, the switchboard at NRK almost melted as hundreds of people called in from all over the country (at one moment, 300 incoming calls were registered simultaneously) (*Aftenposten*, 30 May). The majority opinion in these calls was not only massively in favour of the show, it was massively aggressive in its attitude to Michelet ('dictator', 'worse than Hitler') and what he was seen to represent – the cultural elites who had prevented the screening of programmes like *Dynasty* for decades.

This spontaneous 'telephone storm' was followed up by the tabloid *Dagbladet* over the weekend. The paper invited its readers to phone in and have their say on the issue. Over two full pages, then, the paper could declare (31 May) that *Dynasty* was 'dividing Norway'. A selection of twenty-four callers, identified by full name, address and profession, were quoted. Negative and positive opinions about the show were more or less equally represented, as were women and men in both camps.

Such newspaper-organized phone-ins became a staple element of the public discussion, which went on in waves for about a year, reaching peak levels each time the NRK was running out of episodes and had to decide whether to buy more. A stunning crescendo took place in June 1984, when the NRK had finally decided to end *Dynasty* (if only for a while, as it later turned out). The phone-ins were of course not only pseudo-polls but also staged pseudo-debates, in the sense that none of the callers ever confronted any of the others, and what was printed was of course always the journalists' rendering of the callers' views. Nevertheless, these multi-interviews with dozens of ordinary people were very effective in forming the impression that *Dynasty* was the central topic of debate in the public sphere, and that the sentiments involved were extremely strong.

A somewhat peculiar indication of the scale of engagement in the debates occurred in October 1983, when the organization 'Friends of *Dynasty*' was formed in response to NRK threats to take *Dynasty* off the schedule. The man behind it was Freddy Andersen (the English first name connoting lower-class tastes), a driving instructor in an urban area on the west coast reputed for its enthusiasm for American culture. He advertised in the national populist tabloid *VG* that he was starting this organization, which soon gained hundreds of members from all over the country. In interviews on radio and in a number of papers he invited anyone supporting the demand for 'television for those who watch it', not just for 'those who work in the NRK' or other minorities, to join in (*Stavanger Aftenblad*, 25 October 1983). Andersen was popular with journalists (and presumably also readers) because he so bluntly stated his preferences and phrased his anger at NRK traditions so entertainingly: 'Who watches programs about the inside of the brain on Wednesday nights? And who needs a whole series about psychiatry which only makes you go nutty?' (ibid.). In one interview he said that the programme on the 'inside of the brain' should be transmitted either before children's TV at 6 p.m. or at 3 a.m.; in another interview he suggested that it should be distributed on video cassettes to 'doctors who don't remember their lessons' (*Haugesunds Avis*, 1 November.) Children's TV should consist of imported cartoons and comedies, not 'a Norwegian lady reading from a book'. The rest of an ideal TV night would contain news, a Norwegian soft-news magazine, *Dynasty* and a James Bond film. All of this would cost almost nothing compared to the Norwegian mini-series *Jenny* (based on a novel about a young female writer living in Italy around the turn of the century), which was getting on Andersen's nerves, not least because he estimated the production cost at 25 million Norwegian kroner (approximately US $3.5 million).

Freddy Andersen was in other words totally at odds with every 'responsible' principle of broadcasting, and this is part of the reason why his initiative attracted so much attention. Such views were previously only heard in conversations among 'ordinary people', in bars, among neighbours, at work. They were well known, but had hardly ever before been promoted so eagerly and openly in the public sphere. Even if 'Friends of *Dynasty*' never had more than 1,000 members, it was not insignificant as a sign of the accumulated frustrations the *Dynasty* debate released in large parts of the NRK's audience. The opinions dominating in the newspaper phone-ins confirmed the impression that Mr Andersen was a true 'voice of the people'.

The phone-ins were supplemented by interviews with all kinds of celebrities and people in various more or less powerful positions. Only a few weeks after Michelet's first attack on the serial, it seemed as if all such people on both local and national levels had given their opinion. The more serious part of the discussion took the traditional form of relatively long, more or less polemical newspaper articles, two of which early on presented more comprehensive, model arguments.

DYNASTY AS THE FUTURE OF TELEVISION

In *Dagbladet* on 4 June 1983, Rolv Wesenlund, a very popular comedy actor, pointed to the company Michelet attracted when he attacked *Dynasty*: Christians 'who hate to see divorce, nude swimming, hash and alcohol consumption with ice-cubes, the extreme Right which does not approve of the serial format, plus the leftist intellectual elite which actually doesn't like TV at all. *And* popular enlighteners who are against entertainment as a phenomenon.' All of these united to keep the soap opera off Norwegian TV screens – 'at least until the satellites arrive, and they will do so in multitudes'. Wesenlund maintained that 'broadcasting diversity can today only be countered by coercive means and prohibition of antennas'. He claimed to represent a 'silent majority' who had had to live with the total dominance of 'narrow' programming for much too long, and complained that those who enjoyed these 'narrow' programmes now showed a total lack of democratic tolerance of majority preferences when demanding that *Dynasty* be removed. He looked forward to the near future where systematic ratings would govern TV output, and raised the thought that TV possibly '*is* an entertainment machine with news'.

Wesenlund thus made *Dynasty* a (positive) symbol of the future of the medium, a technologically sustained future in which Christian moralism and left and right cultural snobbism would no longer dictate programming and hinder the dominance of the majority's preferred stuff: entertainment. His rhetorical appeal to democracy did not, however, include consideration for the rights of minorities. His idea of broadcasting 'diversity' amounted only to a whole-hearted welcome to a time where 'entertainment with news' would sum up the contents of television.

Jon Michelet answered a few days later (8 June). He pointed to the fact that he had received a lot of support from all political corners and all social groups for his attack on *Dynasty*. Consequently, he doubted the existence of a compact, uniform 'silent majority'. He stressed that he was not interested in censorship, he had only said that *Dynasty* should be taken off as soon as possible, and it was evidently not possible at that moment. He expressed his delight in the way thousands of people in the ongoing debate made use of their right to free expression of opinions. 'An open debate is better than polls and ratings as a source of advice for the NRK', he said, stressing at the same time the editorial independence and responsibility of the corporation itself. The importance of the *Dynasty* debate he had started was that it provided the NRK with lots of policy advice 'in an epoch where TV2 is on its way and satellites hang in the sky'. He admitted that the NRK had to compete and provide an answer to the 'wave of good and bad' stuff which was coming, but the question was whether the answer should be to turn 'yellow' and accept all kinds of speculation, 'buy the worst non-culture, cultivate all the cheapest tricks'. 'The big battle about to come' would be about the possibility for survival of Norwegian culture and 'our Norwegian character [*egenart*]'. More money for Norwegian television entertainment was necessary, according to Michelet, who also claimed to have support for this view in 'popular demand'. He suggested moving *Dynasty* from its spot on Saturday night prime time (the major television night in Norway), and finally declared:

> If I have contributed to an *increase* in the interest in the Denver-clan and its backstage managers, it is my comfort that we now have a *critical* interest in them. Maybe *Dynasty* should run for even more than the 14 episodes hitherto bought, as a lasting stimulus for the will among Norwegian TV-viewers and politicians to take a stand on the future of television in this small country with only one channel but with a lot of media worms in the ground and a big sky up above?

For both Michelet and Wesenlund, then, the ongoing and anticipated inter-nationalization and commercialization of television was a central part of the framework in which *Dynasty* was understood. *Dynasty* played the same role in Norway as *Dallas* elsewhere in Europe; it came to represent a future of television that seemed terrible to almost anyone with some sort of position or stake in official culture. As signalled by Michelet, the show itself was less important than its alleged referent: a TV universe completely dominated by TV entertainment of its kind. This is in fact a first and very important dimension of the meaning(s) of *Dynasty* (and *Dallas* elsewhere), not only in public debates, but also in house-holds, for individual members of the audience. These two prime-time shows came at a time when they acquired enormous 'metatextual' importance not least because of concurrent developments and debates over broadcasting, media and cultural policies. Had they (or something like them) hypothetically arrived in the early 1970s or in the late 1980s, they might well have been very popular, but they would hardly have drawn the same enormous attention, hardly been regarded with such extraordinary excitement, for or against.

THE 1980S: CHANGING CULTURAL VALUES

Pressure on traditional broadcasting policies was not the only factor that made the early 1980s a suitable moment for 'daring' prime-time soaps about the super-rich. The change in western political and cultural conjunctures during the second half of the 1970s also prepared the ground for them. This conjunctural shift, a widespread 'right turn' after a decade where various 'left' forces had been on the offensive, was no doubt tied in various ways to the international recession after the 1973 oil crisis. In Norway, this recession was experienced very differently from many other countries, because the 1970s were also the decade when the North Sea oil adventure really took off. The social-democratic government helped to postpone the effects of the recession by spending money from the North Sea in advance, so to speak. There was little unemployment, and a steady increase in wages. Norway continued its social-democratic tradi-tion of giving priority to public spending. Hans Magnus Enzensberger in an essay on the Norwegian 'offbeat' situation (first published in 1984) sums up his impressions like this:

> It is not private wealth but the wealth of society that counts. Consequently, citizens may with satisfaction observe that the number of employees in the [public] health system has doubled since 1970, and that the social security funds today spend three times as much money as they did before the oil-age began. The public sector has grown immensely. The redistribution of wealth is a demanding work that costs a lot of money. Local administration alone has increased its staff by 74 per cent in less than ten years, a nice growth in the number of jobs. [. . .] It has also been expensive for Norwegians that they wish to maintain the existing pattern of habitation in the country. [. . .] 'Where there are people there should be schools and hospitals, and buses and ferries should go there.' This infrastructure devours resources: 49 airports with regular departures are more expensive than two or three. [. . .] Private extravagance is regarded with suspicion, public luxury with patriotic pride. In a small place in Østfold [county] I saw an old American film with twelve other people in the audience. It was shown in a municipal cinema with 1200 exquisitely upholstered seats. The airconditioned, mosaic-decorated town halls I have visited in the most remote areas of the country were simply monumental.
>
> (Enzensberger 1987: 179)

Enzensberger lived in Norway for a few years in the 1960s, and the passage quoted was probably also influenced by what he had experienced then. What he did not see or at least emphasize in his report from 1983/4 was the change taking place at precisely that time in the views on the traditional balance between the private and the public sectors and in socio-cultural values. Oil had brought a sector with extraordinarily high wages and profits and a hectic, Klondyke-like atmosphere to both industry and financial businesses. It was a sign of the times that, in Stavanger, the country's oil capital, one of the many nouveaux riches entrepreneurs called his luxury boat *Black Money* (yes, in English).

From the mid-1970s, the leftist political orientations previously on the offensive, not least in connection with the broad popular resistance against EC membership, lost support. A generational shift gradually took place in high schools and later in universities, whereby the dominance of politically radical students, interested in theory, was replaced by a wave of much more pragmatic, apolitical or conservative students seeking careers in marketing and similar areas. Not only did Norway get its fair share of yuppies, the climate from 1980 on was, on the whole, perfectly in tune with the ideological melodies being played elsewhere in western Europe and in the US. The conservative government installed after the election in 1981 was a sign of the times, even if it may be said to have represented a form of conservatism resembling middle-of-the-road social democracy, compared with Reagan and Thatcher. It challenged the traditional strength of the public sector with arguments taken both from liberalist economics and from liberalist ideological thinking. The force of these arguments can be seen in the social-democratic party's internal discussions on the concept of 'freedom' and support for a campaign for a more 'open society', e.g. the liberalization of laws and regulations concerning opening hours (working hours) in the service sector. A financial boom was in a very visible way accompanied by booms in other sectors in the early and mid-1980s: spurred also by liberalized alcohol regulations, the total number of restaurant seats in the city of Bergen alone rose by 300 per cent in about three years.

The *Dynasty* debate was consequently also fuelled by all of these parallel shifts in cultural values. The show's focus on business, wealth, conspicuous consumption and individualized power struggles was in tune with dominant discourses on politics and culture at the time. Small houses on the prairie and British miners were definitely 'out', tycoons and champagne were 'in', at least in terms of their ability to kindle the imagination of large and vocal audience groups. *Dynasty* was showing what seemed to fascinate most people most deeply at the time: unlimited consumption and the lifestyles of the rich and famous.

CHRISTIAN CONCERNS AND GRASSROOTS FASCINATION

The debate branched out in various ways. A Christian organization monitoring broadcasting supported Michelet's critique of the series in their own way:

> From a Christian point of view, we have serious objections to the ideas about life which are presented in *Dynasty*. Divorce, infidelity, alcohol abuse, sex and intrigue – all is presented as a sweet and good life. Many of those in our own country who have been through some of this 'sweet' life know what despair and human tragedy can result from it. We read about it in the papers every day. The NRK should buy or produce series about normal people who live together in true love for each other. It is our duty as Christians to point out that life as God wants us to lead it, is the life that best protects human beings and society.
>
> (Statement printed in several papers, 30 and 31 May 1983)

This Christian, moral rejection of the serial was repeated again and again in the debate. Officially, Christian people were not supposed to watch *Dynasty* at all – it would be harmful to their moral standards, especially those of younger people. Still, the show remained popular also with the religiously active: in the spring of 1984, it was front-page news in Christian papers that since *Dynasty* was moved from Saturdays to Wednesdays in autumn 1983 it had proved destructive to organized Christian activities like Bible groups, choir practices, etc. People simply preferred watching *Dynasty* to these meetings and activities. When this story was presented in the national tabloid *Dagbladet* on 4 April 1984, the heading was 'KRYSTLE BEATS CHRIST'.

This split between the active Christian grassroots and their clerical and lay leaders was unique. 'Ordinary Christian people' would previously have shunned programmes that were declared immoral by their leaders. This time instead they adjusted the schedules of their Christian activities and flocked in front of their screens, even if the moral condemnation of the serial was reiterated by non-Christian groups. The episode transmitted immediately after the radio debate between Michelet and the *Se og Hør* editor fuelled such moral objections outside Christian circles as well. A social-democratic paper published near Oslo said in its editorial on 31 May 1983:

> The most recent episode of *Dynasty* fully demonstrates just how far American companies are willing to go in order to entertain us. In this episode we witness how two of the spoiled rich kids get high on marihuana before throwing themselves naked into daddy's swimming pool. Will the next be that we are to be entertained by watching the spoiled kids – in order to maintain the excitement – give us a lesson in how to take cocaine or possibly heroin?
>
> (*Akershus Arbeiderblad*, 31 May 1983)

Stuff like this would normally have infuriated every organized Christian if it had been Nordic TV drama. With *Dynasty*, the reaction was largely different. According to many in the audience who talked about the moral quality of the show, in newspaper phone-ins or in letters to the NRK, *Dynasty* very clearly represented a contrast to all the sex, swearing, drunkenness and general filth that marked the (stereo)typical Nordic social-realist drama productions they had seen. In other words, it seems that a number of textual characteristics were able to balance the portrayal of morally condemnable behaviour, in such a way as to maintain the overall respectability of the serial in the eyes of very many 'ordinary' people, active Christians or not.

WRITERS AND (OTHER) INTELLECTUALS

In another part of the cultural spectrum, literary people and other intellectuals also discussed *Dynasty*. Jon Michelet's total rejection of the serial was widely supported in these circles, but the reaction was more nuanced in some quarters. In order to understand this section of the public debate, it is necessary to know why a revolutionary maoist (hence in principle Stalinist) writer could be a member of the official Broadcasting Council. This advisory council has twenty-five members, fourteen appointed by parliament, eleven by the government, and is supposed to deal primarily with programming issues.

In the 1970s Norway's New Left was marked by the peculiar strength of its maoist faction, organized in the communist party AKP(M-L) from 1973. The party's members and sympathizers were extremely active in a number of 'front' organizations in various political fields. The total commitment of the 'M-L' movement's members, their strong rhetoric, uncompromising fighting spirit and roots in the 1960s student movement also brought them a surprisingly large following among artists of various kinds. They were active in the introduction of quite aggressive and successful trade-union politics in artists' organizations. A number of the most talented writers and visual artists joined the 'M-L' movement around 1970, Michelet among them. Their artistic productions in various media (literature, visual arts, film) were marked by their party's official support for the classic 'social realism' doctrine, even if most of them (luckily, many would say) had problems in ridding themselves of all the modernism that had formed their artistic identities and ambitions in the 1960s. Certain novelists and visual artists belonging to the movement were quite successful in terms of critical acclaim and popularity with the educated middle class. Their party never reached more than extremely minimal support in elections, but their cultural and political importance in non-parliamentary fields was considerable. They managed in the 1970s to establish the only maoist daily in Europe outside Albania, *Klassekampen* ('The class struggle'), which is now generally recognized for its reporting particularly in business/economics and politics. The appointment of Jon Michelet to the Broadcasting Council represented a recognition of the cultural strength of the maoist group and also of Michelet's success as a writer of 'political' thrillers and crime novels.

Socialist writers and intellectuals who rejected Stalinism and social realism were forced to define themselves in relation to the maoist group. Many of these have been labelled 'social modernists' because of their interest in further developing socially critical modernist traditions in the arts. Not least in literature, this 'social modernism' was marked by an open attitude towards and an engagement with transnational popular culture in various forms: jazz, rock and pop music; detective, crime and Western genres in film and literature. This acknowledgement of significant elements in popular culture was in stark contrast to the maoist rejection in the mid-1970s of the electric guitar as an 'imperialist instrument'. Even if never made official policy, the rejection of this instrument and the music associated with it was indicative of a quite strong nationalist element in the cultural ideology of the maoist group.

While these two leftist groups – social realists and social modernists – were clearly on the offensive in the 1970s, the arts were certainly far from totally dominated by them. More traditional, liberal and conservative artists and critics, both in aesthetic and political terms, were of course still active and held important positions in the various institutions of art. In the public debate over *Dynasty*, people belonging to these non-socialist circles of various kinds were all very clear in their condemnation of the serial's (lack of) quality, thus maintaining the traditional resistance to transnational popular culture.

The only category of intellectuals that might have presented a different, more nuanced perspective was the one I have loosely labelled 'social modernists'. Some of these are/were critics with a background or basis in academia, others were professional artists. A surprising move by the then editor of the most prestigious literary journal, *Vinduet* ('The window'), Janneken Øverland, revealed an interesting split in this non-maoist, more or less radical group. In her editorial in the journal's first issue in 1984, which had Krystle Carrington's face all over the front cover, Øverland wrote:

> Whatever one may think of 'ladies' novels', Krystle, or crime fiction, there is one thing the professional writers of literary series, TV scripts and crime stories know how to do: create viewer and reader involvement. They are able to force people to return to the kiosk or the screen or the paperback to get to know more. They reach their audience by creating a need they themselves then set out to satisfy.
>
> [. . .] This is not to be read as a call for Norwegian authors to write more 'simple', more 'understandable', 'trivial' books – it is rather meant as an appeal to individual writers and a milieu which seen from the sideline now seems more dead than it has been for a long time. [. . .] Write as excitingly as Krystle is beautiful, scare us as seriously as Alexis is evil, and seduce us just as openly to read good literature as the tabloids seduce buyers with celebrity weddings and royal visits. Let yourself at least be provoked and stimulated by the enormous need for fantasy, for fairy tales and adventure which the preoccupation with popular culture reveals.

The liberal tabloid *Dagbladet*, with its historical reputation as a forum for literary and intellectual debate, interviewed some authors about Øverland's challenge. The most celebrated and probably intellectually dominant of the 'social modernists', Kjartan Fløgstad, said that these were not new ideas, and that Norwegian literature over the last ten years – including his own writing – had employed elements of various forms of popular culture to a much greater extent than had the literature of neighbouring countries. He now rather feared that the increasing commercialization of the public sphere would turn writers and other artists into media clowns, and in that perspective it was increasingly important to 'stick to the seriousness of literature'. Two other authors, one female and one male, both representatives of slightly more traditionalist writing, rejected Øverland's idea. While they stressed that certain forms of popular culture could be inspiring and that writing 'good entertainment' could be perfectly respectable, they saw a writing governed by a commercial orientation as being fundamentally at odds with the basic principles of serious writing.

The most interesting element in this little literary debate is that which is missing, both in Øverland's editorial and in the invited responses in *Dagbladet*: reflections on the gendered character of popular culture. Both *Vinduet* and other serious literary journals had previously, in the 1970s, had issues devoted to various forms of popular literature and popular culture. But they were all about male-oriented genres. Nobody mentioned the fact that *Dynasty*, as a form of soap opera, in its focus on 'domestic' problems and by way of the prominent role of women both in the serial and in its production, must be seen in the light of feminine traditions in popular culture. This is particularly surprising in Øverland's case, since she, both as a scholar and in various other literary capacities, had been associated with feminism in general and feminist criticism in particular. The issue of *Vinduet* in which this editorial appeared was devoted to popular genres, and contained articles about contemporary hospital romances and nineteenth-century popular romances – articles which for the first time in a leading journal took these genres seriously. Nevertheless, the gender issue was not dealt with directly in the editorial at all.

This blind spot marks the public debate as a whole. One of the reasons is of course that the show also offered so many male-oriented elements that it exerted a major draw on male audiences, too. Still, many of the pejorative metaphors used by those who were against the serial obviously referred to traits it shared with traditional feminine genres (and certain constructions of femininity) – it was 'sickly sweet', 'sentimental', 'slow', 'soapy', 'glossy', etc. One of the very few people to present a more sympathetic, reflective interpretation of the serial in the press was a woman (Berit Hoff, in *Dagbladet*, 12 July 1984). She pointed to *Dynasty*'s melodramatic structures and devices, but she did not mention the historical gendering of this aesthetic or attempt more specifically to criticize the gender bias in the aesthetic condemnations. Such a bias would in fact seem particularly obvious since the attitude towards male-oriented genres had for quite some time been generally positive within the 'social modernist camp'.

COMMODIFIED DEBATE IN A CHANGING PUBLIC SPHERE

The picture of the debate provided so far is of course not in any way complete. I have for instance not talked about a number of longer contributed articles in different newspapers, in which the serial was analysed as a sign of the times, either in the US or in Norway or both places. The main point in these (often quite sensible) contributions was not to condemn the show, but rather to understand what it was saying and why it seemed so fascinating to so many. A few papers also had some of their more intelligent journalists write articles about the international market for television material, and the US dominance in that market. It is an interesting fact that the latter kind of articles never appeared in the two national tabloids; they were mainly done in the larger regional papers, such as *Stavanger Aftenblad*. The national tabloids concentrated almost exclusively on the 'popular opinion about *Dynasty*' angle. Politically, this was important in that it influenced NRK's decisions concerning the prolongation or ending of *Dynasty*'s run. But this influential part of the press did not spend any resources to speak of on a more far-reaching, systematic presentation of information on what actually went on in the international TV business, the world's 'information order' or other such issues.

Part of my initial interest in the total coverage of *Dynasty* in the Norwegian media was its exemplary relevance to Jürgen Habermas's theory of the 'structural transformation' of the public sphere (1971). Habermas describes a historical process through which the 'space' or 'sphere' for 'disinterested', truth-seeking debate over political, social and cultural issues tends to be crushed between state interventionism on the one hand and private interests of various kinds on the other. The latter category of interests are also represented by political parties, organizing people according to their class positions in the 'private' sphere of production, so that the downfall of the classic bourgeois public sphere was actually accelerated by parties which entered the public sphere in order to represent the 'private' interests of the working class, rather than seek the truth in dialogue with other disinterested participants. But this is only one element in the 'invasion' of private interests; perhaps more important (and more in line with other Frankfurt School ideas) is Habermas's perspective on the increasing importance of private economic interests in the very foundations of the public sphere: the media. When the media themselves become predominantly means for making profit, the public debate is turned into a commodity which the public then consume rather than participate in (1971: 149).

The problem then is not that the public debate dies out. On the contrary, it flourishes as never before, since it is 'guaranteed thoughtful care' in a plurality of organized, carefully arranged ways. The problem is that the commodification of debates alters their logic, their form and function. They become spectacle, staged entertainment: 'position and counter position are, in advance, committed to certain rules of entertainment', Habermas says, and 'when conflicts are brought into the public discussion, they are immediately displaced to the plane of personal friction' (ibid.: 152).

The Norwegian *Dynasty* event can clearly be used as an illustration of such developments. It really took off after the radio 'duel' between Michelet and the *Se og Hør* editor, and was further developed through the printed 'duel' between Michelet and Wesenlund. In both instances, the tone of the debates was quite personal. The phone-ins organized by the tabloids (predominantly) functioned first to build their corporate images as 'servants of the people', second to provide quite entertaining material with hardly any substantial arguments to support the opinions expressed. All the interviews with all kinds of more or less prominent people, in all kinds of newspapers, similarly amounted to little more than a *simulation* of a debate: a collection of opinions, not sustained arguments. Along with most of the journalistic coverage of the *Dynasty* event, the duels, phone-ins and interviews altogether clearly display the characteristics of a commodified debate.

Some of the 'letters to the editor', certain longer articles submitted to some of the papers and some of the journalistic coverage can on the other hand be regarded as contributions to a serious debate on both the serial itself and the wider perspectives of the whole incident. But such contributions were rarely aimed at providing concrete advice on whether *Dynasty* should continue or not, or on any other specific, politico-practical issue. In that sense they were politically impotent, since the 'effect' of their argumentation on the international trade in television fiction or the symptomatic meanings of *Dynasty* can hardly be 'measured' in any way at all.

It seems, then, as if the most clearly 'commodified' part of the debate was the part of it that was politically most effective, in the sense that it really did influence the NRK's programming. It worked to construct an impression of *Dynasty* as immensely popular with an otherwise 'silent majority'. While one may with Habermas lament the lack of substantial arguments in a debate transformed into spectacle, it is still quite obvious that the spectacle (in this case, at least) was a representation of some very real desires and sentiments in large audience groups who normally would not participate in a 'responsible' public debate. Various surveys confirmed this impression, both by showing how vast an audience *Dynasty* drew to the screens every week, and by indicating a solid majority for the continuation of the serial. A national survey with 1,003 respondents, reported in *Aftenposten*, 27 July 1983, showed that 22 per cent had watched all the episodes so far and 48 per cent had watched 'some' of them; 61 per cent of all respondents would watch the serial if it continued. In the following year, the audience seemed to grow rather than shrink. The NRK was again and again 'forced' to continue the serial, in spite of pressures from, for example, the Broadcasting Council to do the opposite.

After the first thirteen episodes (counted as fourteen in Norway, since the first was shown in two parts), twenty-two more were bought, with explicit reference made to the 'wishes of the audience'. In fact, it was noted that the Director of NRK-TV, Otto Nes, in a TV interview of 20 June 1983, referred to the audience as the NRK's 'customers' (*Aftenposten*, 21 June). This was the first time this term was used by NRK executives, indicating how *Dynasty* became a turning point in the way NRK-TV conceived of its relations with the audience. When the NRK ran out of episodes again, towards the end of October, they decided to go against the advice of the television sub-committee of the Broadcasting Council, and bought more episodes, again pointing to the wishes of the majority of its 'customers'. The show was moved from Saturdays to Wednesdays though, and in that sense it was somewhat 'downgraded'. Even if 25 April 1984 was then set as the absolute final date of *Dynasty* in Norway, the serial's run was again prolonged, until it finally ended in cascades of newspaper coverage on 11 July 1984.

Though it may be hard to accept in some circles, it seems one has to conclude that the 'commercialization' of both television and print media actually, in this case, contributed to a form of cultural democratization. 'Television for those who watch it' had been much too limited thus far, and the international commercial success shows that *Dynasty* was recognized as 'our kind of entertainment' by large groups. The commodified forms of (pseudo-)debate formed a pressure which could not be neglected.

On the other hand, it also remains a fact that the larger political, cultural and social issues underlying the debate were hardly clarified in its tabloid, 'spectacularized', commodified forms. Serious, enlightening contributions were almost drowned, i.e. overlooked, in the noise of sensationalist media. This fact does not engender optimism with regard to the future of the public sphere, if commercialization and commodification are to rule more or less unrestrained. The Norwegian *Dynasty* debate demonstrates, however, that commercial media may serve to remind intellectuals of the social exclusions which historically have followed the characteristic forms of serious, enlightened discourse in the 'bourgeois' public sphere. The challenge consists in negotiating between the need for a democratic representation of views and interests and the need for a non-manipulative, true exchange of arguments (cf. also Gripsrud 1991).

THE ROLE OF RESEARCH – AND THE RESEARCHER

As mentioned in the introduction to this book, my own project was immediately picked up in some media as a contribution to the *Dynasty* debate. The fact that research was going on was met with a positive curiosity in some papers where the show was celebrated, and with scorn among those who were against the serial. At a later stage someone ironically suggested, in a letter to the major newspaper of Norway's second-largest city, *Bergens Tidende*, that a whole team of researchers should immediately be put to the task of explaining the popularity and deeper meanings of *Falcon Crest*. In other words, the use of tax-payers' money for such a ridiculous project was implicitly opposed. For years after 1984 I was interviewed about my *Dynasty* research by a number of newspapers, regional and national, and by local and national radio. I gave various kinds of talks, not least to groups of teachers, primarily at high school (sixth-form) level. All of this never made me a celebrity (I was never on TV), but it was once used against me in a newspaper debate on police brutality in which I was more or less accidentally involved: I was called a 'soap opera researcher' (and consequently not to be taken seriously).

It was, in other words, quite clear that research on *Dynasty* could not be politically innocent or neutral, at least not in Norway. The attention gathered by my project reveals the immediate 'political' nature of any media research that addresses issues central to public and popular concerns. At a more specific level it is probably telling of the differences between the social positions and roles of researchers and other intellectuals in different national contexts. A research associate or Ph.D. student doing something along the lines of my work would probably not receive the same kind of public/media attention in most larger western countries, and particularly not in the US. The immediate involvement of research such as mine in the public debate and in various professional or further education events presents the researcher with a pressing need to reflect on the political implications of his or her work, theory, methodology, hypotheses and overarching hermeneutical perspectives. Journalists and the public expect clear answers to all sorts of value-laden and complicated questions, not cryptic remarks about theoretical problems or methodological technicalities, not strictly academic talk about the postmodern condition; and they want the answers right away, not in three years. It is not so easy, then, in a country like Norway, to achieve the kind of splendid isolation that also marks certain interesting and, in many ways, advanced academic discourses in the media and cultural studies field(s), and I have at times deplored this. But when it actually seems to *matter* what researchers say, when people in media institutions and the general public take an interest, one's work takes on a different meaning, that of social action, of some kind of practical political responsibility, beyond the often more or less inconsequential battles within academia.

In my case, I tried to convey three kinds of 'messages' in my various encounters with the media and the public. First, I tried to sketch the various overarching perspectives that made the *Dynasty* phenomenon interesting to me: the historical changes in our media environment, the historical opposition between high and low culture and its gendered dimensions, the questions of cultural identity in an increasingly internationalized media culture, the role of public broadcasting. I tried to say that there were more questions than definite answers here, but also that there was less ground for pessimism than many representatives of official culture seemed to think. Second, I took the opportunities I had to relate some factual knowledge about both the American TV industry and the textual traditions in the light of which *Dynasty* should be seen, these being primarily the daytime soap opera and melodrama. I also often pointed out the particular interest shown in the serial (according to surveys) by women. Third, I tried to balance respectful support for those in the audience who were most seriously engaged in the show with a slightly more ironic or playful attitude which was definitely closer to my own personal feelings about the serial. This latter point also allowed for a certain display of irony in relation to my own work, letting me show that I did not regard myself and my work in the somewhat pompous, complacent manner of the traditional academic.

I realize, then, that my voice in the public debate was basically heard as one advocating acceptance of the show; indirectly, because I, a university person, took it seriously without joining those who condemned it; directly, because I defended the right to enjoy it and also suggested ways of coming to terms with it for those who had problems either accepting their own fascination or simply understanding why anyone would find anything of interest, at all, in the serial. I remember more or less instructing, in private circumstances, an academic friend on how to '*camp*' the show, i.e. focus on and appreciate its elements of irony and wilful 'bad taste', and thus have a good time watching it. This was also – less explicitly – part of the talks/teaching I gave about the show to audiences such as teachers. At times, members of the audience – particularly women – would thank me for confirming that they were not so silly even if they had long been watching the serial with a mixture of keen interest and self-conscious irony, the latter tied also to a feeling of being guilty of bad taste.

Not that it had much to do with my work, but the public discourse about *Dynasty* throughout the 1980s developed largely in the direction of ironic acceptance. Its first run ended in the summer of 1984, but it returned twice in the second half of the 1980s. TV critics increasingly took to a humorous, ironic but still often enthusiastic tone when writing about the show. Headings

100

such as 'Oh – these lovely bubbles', 'Marvellous Krystle last night', 'Bye-bye in a blood-bath' all appeared in *Dagbladet* in 1987 and 1988. This shift in tone indicates how *Dynasty* may have functioned as a training in 'camp' attitudes to television, particularly in the educated middle classes. As I suggested in Chapter 1 above, the product, in Marx's abstract terms, demanded a parti- cular 'manner of consumption', and thus also produced a certain, adequate consumer subject.

Before closing this chapter, I will first briefly sketch *Dynasty*'s fate in Norway after its initial, first-year run and then finally sum up some of the event's consequences for the NRK and broadcasting policies.

DYNASTY'S GRADUALLY FADING APPEAL

When *Dynasty* ended on the NRK in July 1984, it was picked up by a video import and distribution company, DMD-International. They immediately advertised twenty-seven episodes for rental at a package price of 490 Norwegian kroner, i.e. about £45, less than US $70. The price was close to the total licence fee then paid for a year of NRK services. The ads claimed that '80,000 Norwegian families have said "We wish to continue following *Dynasty* on video" – and so can you!' This made it sound as if 80,000 families had already bought the video package but it seems that this figure only or at best referred to an estimate made on the basis of market research. At the beginning of August, a representative of DMD-International said more than 40,000 had bought the rental series ('The Dynasty Ticket') (*Bergens Tidende*, 3 August), while his boss claimed that 50,000 'tickets' had been sold, and that he expected a total sale of 80,000 (*Bergens Tidende*, 6 August). These figures were doubted by some observers, since the total number of VCRs in Norway at the time was about 200,000, many of which were owned by companies, schools and other institu- tions. Still, even if only 40,000 'tickets' were sold, at the price mentioned, it is an indication of the strength of the determination in the show's core audiences to go on watching for as long as possible.

As *Dynasty* left the NRK, it also left the public sphere almost completely for a while. Its replacement, *Falcon Crest*, did not create anything like either the public enthusiasm or the anger associated with its predecessor. The NRK still claimed to have audience figures from weekly surveys which indicated that it was 'very popular' and 'normally high' in its attendance. Other signs of interest among viewers were coverage in the popular weeklies and quite a few angry phone calls to the NRK when the show was skipped one Wednesday before Christmas. But the temperature was definitely lower. When asked to explain this, Janneken Øverland, the editor of the literary journal *Vinduet*, said:

> *Dynasty* managed in a relatively intelligent way to play with some fantasies which were more provoking than those in this serial. In some way or other, *Falcon Crest*'s temperature is too low. It does not follow its themes far

enough, sensations are more dispersed, and there's a lot of repetitions. It's as if it's not as grandiose and vulgar as *Dynasty.* There is something they have not achieved within the same format.

(*Bergens Tidende,* 6 February 1985)

Even if Øverland also pointed to the fact that *Dynasty* came first, and added that 'professional culture-debaters' are not really interested in such shows at all, this general characterization of the differences between the two serials indicates that the *Dynasty* debate cannot be seen as resulting almost exclusively from more or less contextual and accidental factors. The *Dynasty* text simply had particular dimensions and properties, such as those mentioned by Øverland in the above quote, which created very strong emotional engagement both for and against it. Its role as a point of crystallization for a complex set of issues could not have been played by just any never-ending American show. This is an important part of the reason why I insist on the centrality of the text in the process of communication, and, consequently, on the centrality of textual analysis in communication research of all kinds.

Dynasty continued to fascinate a very large audience when it was back on NRK-TV after DMD-International's video rights expired in the summer of 1986. Except for a few weeks' break around Christmas, it ran without interruptions in its Wednesday spot until 23 September 1987. By then the energy of its fans must have weakened, since it was replaced by *Falcon Crest* without any protest to speak of. The third and final run started on 18 May 1988, and ended on 14 December that year. I had a survey done by a local market research company in the city of Bergen in December 1988 (cf. Chapter 3 for results of an earlier survey and methodological comments). In what was still largely a one-channel situation, total audience figures were still very high: 63% of the women interviewed and 57% of the men claimed to have seen at least part of the serial in its last run. But the interest was significantly lower than in 1984: 44% of the women and 30% of the men estimated they had watched more than 75% of the episodes in 1988; in my 1984 survey the corresponding figures were 62% for women and 37% for men. The differences between educational levels became more pronounced. In 1984, 59% of those with less than nine years of school, and 39% of those with more than fifteen years, claimed to have watched more than 75% of the episodes. In 1988, the result was practically the same (60%) for the lowest educated, while only 10% of those in the most educated group now said they had watched more than 75% of the episodes broadcast that autumn. Interestingly, the drop in viewer interest seemed to be most marked in areas of the city where cable TV had now become widespread. *Dynasty* was not alone in the category of transnational fictional entertainment any more.

After 145 episodes, an NRK executive could say he was disappointed by the serial's quality over the last six months and that the NRK would now like some variation in the menu (*VG,* 14 December 1988) – without provoking any uproar

102

among audiences. It was not so much that the serial was no longer watched by so many: it was more that it had lost some of their strong interest, their emotional investment. Both the very strong initial fascination that *Dynasty* exerted and the gradual weakening of its hold on audiences are important heuristic pointers for the textual analysis in Chapters 4, 5 and 6 of this book.

THE WORLD'S VIEWERS PREFER INDIGENOUS PROGRAMMES

Certain Norwegian newspapers had surveys done during *Dynasty*'s first run, in 1983–4, which seemed to yield contradictory results, since high audience attendance was coupled with low scores in terms of evaluation ('did you like the programme?'). This could of course be related to the fact that audiences knew that *Dynasty* was regarded as a 'low-quality' show by the cultural elites, and that watching it was regarded as slightly 'immoral' since it was just 'superficial entertainment' (cf. Alasuutari 1992). But audiences were, in fact, generally not afraid to 'admit' that they had watched *Dynasty*, even if some, particularly those well educated, may have understated their attendance. A better explanation is simply that Norwegian audiences, like those of just about any other country of the world, prefer domestically produced fictional programmes to foreign ones, including those from the US, particularly if they are of a certain professional standard. This is convincingly documented in the UNESCO report *Import/Export: International Flow of Television Fiction* (Larsen 1990). A series of national and regional surveys (Africa, Asia, Europe, Latin America, North America) shows that indigenous productions get the highest ratings, suggesting that they provide audiences with a different, 'fuller' and more satisfactory experience than even the most popular of US shows.

This finding has been further elaborated and convincingly documented in a number of empirical, qualitative reception studies in several European countries in recent years. Anne Hjorth (1984) compared Danish women's reception of *Dallas* and the Danish serial (more precisely, feuilleton – it had an ending), *Daughters of War*, using loosely structured interviews with women of different social classes. She concluded as follows:

> The fascination *Dallas* offers is stronger than that of most other programmes, because it so directly appeals to the ambivalent (and unconscious) emotional and psychic conflicts in viewers, and because it provides an aesthetic bombardment of the senses. It gives primarily a 'here-and-now' experience. The viewer is kept in front of the screen – and her ambivalences maintained – and this results in a feeling of frustration and emptiness. *Daughters of War* is also fascinating, but it also has a greater use-value, because it is closer to women's everyday experiences and leaves more space for the conscious co-creation of the the text through relating it to viewers' own experiences. It therefore provides an experience which can be brought

103

out of the viewing experience itself –'you can take it home with you' – into life, one's own!

(Hjorth 1984: 358)

This conclusion has later been largely confirmed in similar studies by, for instance, Birgitta Höijer in Sweden (1992), who compared the reception of *Falcon Crest* to that of the Swedish serial (feuilleton) *Three Loves*; and, in Belgium, Daniel Biltereyst (1991). Biltereyst compared the reception of a US sitcom (*She's the Sheriff*) with that of an indigenous (Flemish) sitcom (*De Kollega's*), and found, even for this genre, that the domestic programme was both more liked and understood in a more complex way since it required the application of local cultural codes. As a result, '[i]t is safe to say that the indigenous drama functioned as a forum for introspection to consider themes of identity and current political, cultural and social issues, while in the responses to the US programme such issues hardly arose' (Biltereyst 1991: 489).

This is not, however, to say that US programmes are not really wanted by audiences across the globe. They are popular for a number of reasons, particularly their high professional standards, their tempo and their glamour, their references to the US as a kind of modernity's concrete utopia. But, even if they, as the following chapter will show, are sometimes able strongly to engage viewers who partly recognize themselves in their fictional worlds, US shows do not deliver what viewers treasure most: strong, many-sided, meaningful experiential relations to their own lives and conditions.

CONSEQUENCES FOR PUBLIC SERVICE TELEVISION

'In order to create something like the *Dynasty* debate now, we would have to programme soft-porn, something like *Playboy Late Night*', Stein Roger Bull, present head of NRK-TV's section for culture, told me in my interview with him in 1992. It did not sound as if the idea was too far out to be considered.

Bull was throughout the 1980s a pioneering spirit for a revision of NRK programming in view of the increasing competition from other channels, foreign at first and later also domestic. He was not only, as noted above (p. 84), instrumental in bringing *Dynasty* to the NRK in 1983. In early 1985, he engineered a 3.5-hour entertainment programme on Saturday nights which was designed as an imitation of commercial television's 'flow', including advertisements for various non-commercial organizations and generally accepted 'causes' (health, road safety, etc.). When interviewed about the programme, Bull referred to the audience as 'customers', and mentioned a single ambition behind the programme and its design: 'We wish to prevent people switching to Swedish TV or Sky Channel' (*Dagbladet*, 15 January 1985). Such an openly and exclusively competitive legitimation of a programme, completely empty in terms of (other) intended meanings and ideas concerning the show's qualitative dimensions, had never been heard before in Norway.

In autumn 1984, after *Dynasty* 'went rental', another entertainment pro-gramme in the variety format also signalled the introduction of a modernized form of TV in NRK, obviously created to imitate commercial television's typically very segmented and flashy visual style: *Lørdagssirkus* ('Saturday circus'). This programme's link to commercialism was also clear at other levels – from its logo/trademark being repeated a dozen times throughout the show to its thematic preoccupation with fashion and the fashionable, and its 'non-commercial' marketing of cultural products such as LPs, books, theatre performances and Oslo cafés.

Even if *Lørdagssirkus* was marked by its ties to openly commercial television and often seemed extremely superficial and yuppie-affected, it also represented a renewal of NRK-television in important ways. The show's producer, Per Selstrøm, said it was the first time he had made an entertainment programme with his own generation in mind, not that of his parents. He was then about 40.

Bull and Selstrøm supported *Dynasty* and the shift it represented towards a new relation with the audience for the NRK. The tabloid-mediated pressure from the audience that resulted in the buying and repeated continuations of that serial also reminded the NRK that they simply needed to know more of what their audiences were thinking. 'We must also get better at using these reports when we're making programmes', NRK-TV's Programme Director Otto Nes said, pointing to a shelf full of reports from the corporation's audience research (*Aftenposten*, 28 December 1985). The NRK had until then only surveyed their audience once a year. A highly significant consequence of the *Dynasty* experience was that it revealed the need for much more frequent and detailed monitoring of the audience and its reactions. The NRK started buying audience surveys on a weekly basis after or during the *Dynasty* experi-ence, and they now finance (along with the major commercial channels) a people-meter system operating according to current American principles, complete with overnight ratings and shares.

It is my conclusion, then, that *Dynasty* was both a *sign* of a historical shift in Norwegian broadcasting and, particularly by way of the public debate about it, also an *instrument* for change. It revealed that a rather rigid traditionalism and narrowness of taste in public service broadcasting had been overtaken, and it opened the eyes of NRK executives, politicians and various kinds of intellectuals to the realities of competition in the airwaves.

Programme Director Otto Nes said in 1985 that 'Pure entertainment will have more room as competition for viewers increases, and we have not so far been good enough at meeting the new challenge' (*Aftenposten*, 28 December 1985). But transnational entertainment has definitely not filled the NRK's prime time. Apart from finally broadcasting a British soap, *EastEnders*, in a late afternoon/early evening spot (for a while), the most striking change in the NRK's programming has been a rearrangement of the schedule to include a broadly popular programme, domestic or imported, every evening in the slot immediately after the 7.30 (now 7.00) news programme. Other adjustments include a solid strengthening of regional production (mostly for the national channel), emphasis on domestic entertainment (particularly for Saturday nights), extended sports coverage, maintenance and renewal of the traditionally strong production for children and teenagers. Important steps have, finally, also been taken to increase expenditure on drama, in several genres. Certain categories of cultural programming (such as classical music) have less space, but on the whole one can hardly say that the NRK has given up on its public service obligations. It has generally attempted to secure its position by maintaining broad support in the audiences. The one-channel system made such support relatively easy to obtain, and also of less importance. Increased dependency on audience support holds a number of problems, but it is hard to see that it in itself implies a weakening of democratic influence on public television. Just as Brecht once pointed out that people could 'vote with their feet' when fleeing oppression, TV audiences vote directly on the quality of programmes by pushing the buttons of the remote control.

3

DIMENSIONS OF DOMESTIC RECEPTION

> There are three kinds of readers: one, who enjoys without judgement, a
> third, who judges without enjoyment, and the middle one, who judges
> enjoyingly and enjoys judgingly; this one actually reproduces a work of art
> anew.
>
> J.W. Goethe quoted in Jauss 1977: 64)

INTRODUCTION

A basic idea in this book is that the reception of a transnational success like
Dynasty cannot simply be understood in terms of autonomous viewers exercising
a more or less total freedom of meaning- and pleasure-production in front of
their television screens. I argue that the encounter between viewers and the
television text cannot be studied in isolation, without taking into account
determinations and influences on the reception process springing from a
number of factors:

1 the structures and elements of the text, which are closely related to
2 the production process and the many-sided power of the US television
  industry
3 the broadcasting structures and wider cultural and political situation in the
  country or area of reception in which
4 other media, class structures and specific cultural practices and relations, etc.
  provide contextual inputs contributing to the reception.

Partly implicated in all this, and partly forming an overarching 'bridge' between
all the moments of the total process of communication, run currents of shared
social and cultural conditions, conventions, power relations, value systems,
textual traditions, etc. Every viewer is imbricated in these highly complex
networks of material and discursive structures.

I have so far presented my analysis of the production process (Chapter 1) and
the specific socio-cultural and political situation in which *Dynasty* was 'inserted'
and provoked such intense attention (Chapter 2). While the previous chapter
dealt mainly with the public dimension of the serial's reception, this chapter will

focus more directly on the less visible but also in a sense more central question of domestic reception. Television is watched mainly in the privacy of people's homes, and it was of course this 'primary' reception which was the object of the public debate on whether *Dynasty* was worth allocating time to in a single channel system, was worth watching or not, was important or not, had harmful effects or not.

Establishing reliable knowledge about domestic reception is, however, very difficult. Not only is it impossible for researchers to be present in all households when *Dynasty* is on – or even in a statistically representative sample of them – it is also a simple fact that the production of meaning and pleasure takes place inside people's heads and therefore cannot be directly observed in any way. The moment of perception, the immediate impression and 'processing' of sounds and images can actually never be studied. We will always have to rely on external observations and *post-factum* verbal reports from viewers. What goes on at that crucial moment of perception – when 'a synchronous search-movement in all the audiovisual and non-verbal systems of codes' takes place – can only be inferred, not least from an analysis of the text itself (cf. Rasmussen 1988: 35f.).

However, people think about what they see while watching, pick up 'clues' to the story lines, try to make connections, experience and take note of their own emotions, etc. All of this work may stay in their minds after the immediate experience, they may think and speak about it later, even much later. While the immediate perceptive experience is certainly important, the more or less delayed mental work on this experience, during and after viewing – the making sense of it – is at least equally important. The English language does not have the very useful distinction in Germanic languages between *Erlebung* (the momentary experience) and *Erfahrung* (the result of a reflection on the momentary experience), but the process of reception must be thought of as encompassing both. A number of contextual factors contribute both to the immediate decoding of the televisual signs (*Erlebung*) and to the less time-bound process of making sense (*Erfahrung*).

The purpose of this chapter, then, is twofold. On the one hand I want to discuss theoretical and methodological problems relating to the study of TV reception. On the other, I want to analyse various kinds of data in order to reach for an understanding of the reception of *Dynasty* in Norway. The idea is, as mentioned in the introduction to this book, that the use of specific, concrete exemplary material will help to illustrate the implications of more general issues and thus emphasize the heuristic role of theoretical and methodological work. I would in fact like to say a bit more about the role of theory in reception research before dealing with the more specifically methodological issues.

THE ROLE OF THEORY

Even if television is watched in people's homes, research on this activity never starts in the sitting-room or the den, or wherever the set is. It starts in the researcher's head, with a theoretical reflection which defines an area of interest, a problem, and a perspective, an angle from which the area or problem is to be seen. This theoretical reflection may point to, for instance, the sitting-room as a privileged place for investigating a theoretically formulated problem (cf. Morley 1992). The data produced by a method such as participant observation may, on the one hand, serve as specifications and examples, may offer opportunities for refinement of arguments, or simply add 'flesh and blood', substance, to otherwise anaemic academic writing. On the other hand, ethnographic studies of audiences may also lead to the discovery of unforeseen phenomena and problems, challenges to existing theories. This is absolutely central in any kind of empirical research, be it textual analysis or audience studies: the researcher must be willing to risk his or her theoretical preconceptions, allow for surprises and discoveries that may lead to reformulations of theory (cf. Doane 1990: 57). But such discoveries will always be in need of theorization, and theorization means 'translation', a more or less daring leap into a terrain of generalizations produced by interpretation.

If theory is given priority in research along these lines, it also means that research is regarded as basically a hermeneutic, interpretive activity, in all of its components, including the empirical. Such a conception of what research is draws attention to the importance of prescientific or prescholarly factors in the production of knowledge. Critical scholars can never ground their interest in 'critique' and 'critical theory' in purely scientific criteria. This specific knowledge-interest is personal and political, it is based in what may be termed an ethical choice, which may again be shaped by various social, cultural and personal background factors. The ethical choice then guides the selection of theoretical perspectives which privilege certain methodologies and empirical domains. It is important to note here, however, that such a selection is never a completely 'free', individual one; it is always a choice among more or less institutionalized, conventionalized options within historically produced scholarly traditions.

The above actually helps to explain why critical scholars so often are those in any research community who are most interested in 'high theory'. Theory's relative separation or autonomy, in relation to empirical facts, is what enables the production of ideas about alternatives to given conditions, something which primarily interests those who in some way or other feel that what exists is in need of change. A critical research interest in alternatives always implies a theoretically based understanding of social life, which is directed towards pointing out existing possibilities that social or cultural forms or conditions could be other than those now dominating. Theory, not empirical observations in themselves, is able to prefigure alternatives, to provide a more or less solid intellectual basis for social imagination – the solidity of which is based, not least, on how well it is empirically informed. In this sense, critical theory always has a 'utopian' element.

Furthermore, since theory is related to ethics, it is also a basis for evaluating not only society or culture as it is, but also alternatives, existing or just imaginable. Alternative social forms, cultures or identities are not necessarily acceptable or worth promoting just because they are 'alternative', or just because they are thought up or produced by, for instance, 'subordinate groups' in opposition to 'hegemony'. The historical example of fascism should have taught us that much, and various racist and right-wing populist movements and cultural forms in today's world actualize this historical lesson. Terrorist action and soccer hooliganism may be both anti-hegemonic and subordinate, but I am still not willing to defend them as interesting 'alternative practices'.

Linking 'micro' observations to 'macro' issues in research and analysis is not a simple, mechanical task. It is a problem, a problem which is linked to that of relating theory to the empirical. Ethnographic methodology has been advocated because of its sensitivity to specificity and concreteness. But its advocates often fail to specify, more precisely, how particular ethnographic 'micro' findings can be convincingly related to the necessarily general level of theory. There is no easy, general solution to this problem, primarily because theory is not simply derived from accumulated empirical data, even if it is informed by them. It is (also) constructed by researchers within a relatively independent, more or less philosophical discourse, which deals with the (meaning of) the 'whole' (e.g. society, culture, gender), not directly the innumerable parts that go into that whole.

My own suggestion here would be, first, that there is a need for empirical work at a level which in terms of abstraction and degree of generalization is somewhere 'between' the particular ethnographic finding and the 'totalizing' level of theory. The notion of 'grounded theory', originally proposed by Glaser and Strauss (1967), is useful here, even if it certainly does not present any definite solution to these problems. It refers to a construction of theory through analysis which is to stay 'close to the data', but still rely on 'sensitizing concepts' such as 'culture', 'institution' and 'social structure', and has been discussed and further developed by several social scientists involved in qualitative research (cf. Jankowski and Wester 1991: 67ff.). Critical scholars also ought, in my view, to consider once again what quantitative methodology might provide in relation to the mostly qualitative data gathered in ethnographic work.

Second, I would stress a couple of points concerning the relation between theory and empirical data. First, all forms of data are in a certain sense 'produced' by theoretical perspectives, data are never 'raw', always already 'cooked'. (Some data are no doubt also 'rotten', the third category in Claude Lévi-Strauss's (1966) culinary triangle.) Second, though data are always already 'processed', they are still analytically separable from theory itself. This point has actually been nicely put by the rock group 'Talking Heads': 'Facts always come with a point of view, facts don't do what you want them to.' A fundamental gap or difference between theory and empirical data should thus be regarded as a premise for relating the two aspects of research. A possible analogy could be that of translation between languages, which as we know always has an element

110

of 'treason' to it. As mentioned in the introduction to this book, when Lazarsfeld wanted Adorno to 'translate' his theoretical ideas on the sociology of music to survey categories, Adorno felt that he had been asked to 'square the circle'.

Since a fundamental difference or gap exists between the empirical and the theoretical, the one cannot be deduced or smoothly developed from the other. Their relation to each other, in research practice, should be thought of as a highly necessary confrontation, which is in a sense 'administered' in an interpretive process, a dialectical and hermeneutic 'thinking together' of heterogeneous elements. In this process, theory will be the dominant moment, since it guides the empirical investigations. An improved, or revised, theory will also be an important goal of scholarly work, not only very specific knowledge of very specific conditions.

The kind of theory which forms the basis of my work in this book is not a theory in the sense of a complete, coherent system of propositions. It is rather a set of perspectives which (to me and others) seem more or less related. Some are drawn from marxism and related theories of society, which combine an interest in material conditions and a notion of structurally determined conflicts of interests with a profound historical orientation and some notion of dialectics. Others are drawn from semiotic theories of texts and cultures, from psychoanalysis and from feminist discourses in various fields. I suspect that the text of this book has already indicated that I speak from such a position. Or, to put it less academically, if the reader has by now not figured out that something like the above forms a kind of basis for my interests and argumentation, then one of us has failed!

A NOTE ON THE USE OF QUANTITATIVE METHODOLOGY

If our general, theoretical conception of society is one in which various social divisions and conflicts are seen as being of fundamental importance, research aimed at understanding the reception of certain television texts should start by determining who, which kinds of people, constitute the audience or audiences. This remains a question best answered by traditional, quantitative methods. Research using such methods has already contributed significantly to the construction of a 'socio-cultural map' of western societies, by establishing certain consistent patterns of cultural preferences and practices relating to various social categories. Such patterns should be regarded as what they are: constructed simplifications. All kinds of modifications and exceptions can, of course, be found in the real world, among real people. Still, the generalized, simplified patterns can provide information as to how *Dynasty* or any other media text relates to general characteristics of the previous cultural experiences of various audience groups.

Current media research is characterized by a new interest in 'qualitative' audience research, i.e. a preference for participant observation and depth interviews. 'Critical' scholars often dismiss traditional audience surveys as 'empiricist' or 'positivist', as reifying the audience, as 'administrative' information gathering, etc. And, indeed, this critique has often been well founded. (Good examples are Gitlin 1978, and Allen 1985: Chapter 2.) The main problem with empiricism is its lack of emphasis on theory and the fundamental importance of interpretation. As Todd Gitlin has said of 'the dominant paradigm' in media sociology:

> It has tended to seek 'hard data', often enough with results so mixed as to satisfy anyone and no one, when it might have more fruitfully sought hard questions. By studying only the 'effects' that could be 'measured' experimentally or in surveys, it has put the methodological cart ahead of the theoretical horse. Or rather: it has procured a horse that could pull its particular cart.

(Gitlin 1978: 206)

However, the shortcomings of empiricism do not reside in the particular methods favoured by traditional, mainstream 'quantitative' research, but the uses to which these methods are put, and the value attributed to them. Bourdieu (1984: 18) has aptly phrased a fundamental reminder: 'One has explained nothing and understood nothing by establishing the existence of a correlation between an "independent" variable and a "dependent" variable.' The task of researchers is precisely to explain and provide understanding. Statistical correlations need to be made meaningful by the researcher, who may be tempted by 'positivist laziness' (ibid.: 94) to let correlations be the end-product of research. Bourdieu's work provides excellent examples of how quantitative data can be used to generate questions. Survey methodology may document large-scale regularities representing social forms that encompass the innumerable idiosyncrasies encountered in small-scale qualitative research. If, for instance, fifty years of research on the composition of soap-opera audiences show that this form of serialized fiction is consistently more popular with women than with men, and more popular with the less educated than the more educated, these regularities need to be explained, neither taken for granted as final 'facts' nor dismissed as 'empiricist' constructions that lack any significance.

AN AUDIENCE SURVEY IN MAY 1984 AND ITS LIMITATIONS

In May 1984, after *Dynasty* had been running for a year (about fifty episodes broadcast), a representative sample of 200 respondents in Bergen (Norway's second largest city with about 220,000 inhabitants), were asked nine questions about the serial. I formulated the questions in cooperation with a local market research company, who did the research and also the primary processing of data. This was done primarily to establish a rudimentary impression of what might be called 'the social distribution of fascination with *Dynasty*'. As I explained in Chapter 2, Norway had no regular TV ratings at the time. The NRK restricted its audience surveys to a minimum, once a year until 1983, two to three times a year after that, then weekly surveys until a market research company introduced 'people-meters' in 1992.

Even if certain newspapers and weeklies had surveys done on *Dynasty* now and then during its first run, I felt that I needed a simple overview and appreciated the opportunity to have a few of my own questions asked to a representative sample. The use of survey methodology was also intended as an experiment in methodology. The question was, not least, whether the results of a survey could be meaningfully interpreted as part of a wider set of data on the reception of the series. I chose to let a market research company do the 'technical' part of the work for me, for several practical reasons. I have only rudimentary training in quantitative research techniques; I had little time to spare; the company could do it quite cheaply and fast.

The survey was far from perfect in terms of statistical accuracy. (I am indebted to my colleague, Professor Helge Østbye, for the following critical comments on the quality of the company's procedures.) The sample ought to have been doubled if one wanted to make really 'safe' generalizations for the population the sample is supposed to represent. As it is, a margin of error of approximately +/− 7 per cent must be assumed. Where less than the full sample form the basis for percentages, the margin of error will rapidly approach +/− 10 per cent. The 200 respondents were drawn from the telephone directory, and that is not entirely unproblematic either, even if more than 90 per cent of all households have telephones in Bergen. Interviews were done by telephone. The advantages of this are that it is relatively easy to try again if a respondent is not in at the first attempt, and that it is likely to

Table 3.1 Audience pattern, May 1984

	Watched more than 50% of episodes	Watched more than 75% of episodes
Gender		
Male	60%	37%
Female	80%	62%
Education		
Up to 9 yrs	85%	59%
10–12 yrs	75%	59%
13–15 yrs	65%	40%
Over 15 yrs	59%	39%
Age		
18–29 yrs	61%	46%
30–44 yrs	78%	50%
45–59 yrs	74%	67%
Over 60 yrs	80%	40%
Total	70%	50%

Note: All figures have been rounded to the nearest whole.

encourage both participation and frankness of answers when the interviewer is not physically present in the respondent's home.

All of this means that the overall results and particularly the specific figures of the survey must be taken with more than just a grain of salt. A whole lump would probably be more appropriate from a strict, statistical point of view. However, the survey reveals tendencies so clear that it seems highly probable that they indicate patterns in the population as a whole. If treated with some care, they provide useful information. The degree of strict statistical reliability (and validity) in the survey is also less important to the extent that it is used here as an experiment, to illustrate a methodological point.

The audience pattern found was consistent with all other findings on the composition of soap opera audiences. The pattern can be seen in Table 3.1. The table shows that *Dynasty* was clearly more popular with women than men, and more popular with less educated groups than with those more educated. At the same time, it obviously attracted huge portions of viewers from all social categories. The figures seem to indicate that the show was more popular with older people than younger, but most probably this mainly reflects the fact that older people (particularly those over 60) tend to be heavier viewers, i.e. many watch (in some way or other) just about every programme every day. Age was important also in another way. In the autumn of 1983, the NRK moved *Dynasty* from its slot on Saturday night to Wednesday evening. Since Saturday night is the major TV night in Norway in terms of audience attendance, it was expected that the size of *Dynasty*'s audience would drop. The audience actually grew, and the survey indicated the reason: a majority of those between 18 and 29 said they would watch more often after the move to Wednesdays, and 25 per cent of those between 30 and 44 said the same. In other words, those who more often spend Saturday night out or at parties now had a better chance to watch the serial regularly.

The audience pattern found means that even if *Dynasty*, more than most other programmes, could (in a single-channel television system) attract people of all kinds, the systematic differences in viewing between gender and social groups as defined by education remain. Since there are great cultural differences between, say, an 18-year-old woman with nine years of education and a 65-year-old male professor, it is highly unlikely that they experienced or understood *Dynasty* in the same way. And why are some social groups more likely to be attracted by *Dynasty* than others? The problem is both to find out more specifically what characterized these experiences or readings, and to link the differences to more general social and cultural factors. After the audience pattern is established, the real work begins.

A couple of the questions asked in the survey were intended to register to what extent the *Dynasty* experience was a social one, something shared with others. Three-quarters (77%) of those who had watched had done so in the company of others above 12 years of age. A few also said they had been watching with children younger than 12. Television is indeed predominantly a family or household medium. The watching of *Dynasty* was largely a collective activity, clearly involving commentaries of various kinds from viewers. Another question asked, which also relates to the degree of collectivity in reception, was whether the show had been the subject of conversations at work or among friends: 57% of all respondents answered that *Dynasty* had been talked about 'often' or 'sometimes', 33% said 'rarely', and 10% 'never'. A very interesting result here was that there was hardly any difference at all between those with most and those with least education: 50 and 53% respectively answered that there had been talk about *Dynasty* 'often' or 'sometimes'.

Since the difference between these groups was so pronounced in terms of viewing, it is worth reflecting on why there was no difference in the amount of talk about the show. Of course, those most educated could have watched more frequently than they claimed. But it still seems as if the educational category that watched most faithfully did least talking about the show among themselves: 85% of them said they had watched more than half of the episodes, while only 53% of them said there had been talk about the serial at work or among friends. If these figures are to some extent reliable, about one-third of the audience in this group rarely or never talked about their viewing experiences (outside the family or household). In other words, they did their faithful viewing in relative isolation. Some of them may be old, others unemployed. But that could also be the case for the other categories.

The difference between social categories was also explored in other ways. I had noted a quite clear difference in the way weeklies and newspapers covered the serial after it had been introduced, and not least after the 'cultural debate of the ages' had started. I will return to this later, but the main impression was that while daily newspapers would often report about the show in an ironic or outright negative tone (or, sometimes, present the serial as if it was portraying the real lives of an extreme upper class in the US), weeklies concentrated on stars and characters, in such a way as to blend the two and present these mixed constructions as 'ordinary human beings', basically very similar to their Norwegian audience. This difference was the reason why the respondents were asked where they had read the most about the serial, in weeklies or daily papers. About 19% said weeklies, 40% daily newspapers, some 16% that they had read about as much in both kinds of media, 26% claimed not to have read anything anywhere. These total figures are less interesting than the ones for particular categories: 28% of the women had read most in weeklies, 9% of the men; 26% of those with the least education, 11% of those with the most. This pattern is parallel to the social variations in viewing frequency, and it is the well-documented social pattern of weeklies' readership which is reflected: the groups that make up a core audience for weeklies also were likely to be heavy *Dynasty* viewers.

Instead of asking simply if the respondents liked the serial or not, I decided to try another, more indirect question, on the verge of being 'leading': 'If you were to be critical, is there anything about the serial you find negative?' Respondents were here free to mention whatever came into their head, and the market research company grouped the answers in a number of categories which were recurrent: 31% of the women and 19% of the men, 41% of those with up to nine years of education and 21% of those with more than fifteen years saw nothing worth criticizing. In other words, the groups that watched most frequently also clearly were least critical (cf. also Herzog (1941: 67), who reports that 57% of her respondents 'could not mention any incident in the stories listened to which they had disliked in any way'). A bit more than 20% of both men and women felt the show was a bit slow or boring, and an equal proportion of each gender group thought it was unrealistic or artificial. Only about 6% mentioned 'morally bad'. In addition to these criticisms, 'all the intrigues', 'a lot of sentimentality' [kliss = stickiness] and 'superficial' were also mentioned by some.

In an open question like this, it would clearly have been interesting to have the complete conversation between interviewer and interviewee available for analysis. But even in the condensed version I have described, the answers are interesting, in combination with the answers given to other questions. For instance, the least educated watch the most, talk the least and find least reason to criticize anything at all. Probably the most interesting result was that only one-fifth of all respondents mentioned that the show was 'unrealistic' and/or 'artificial'. Even if those who said 'superficial' are added to this group, more than 75% of all viewers interviewed either found a lack of realism unobjectionable or did not agree at all that there was such a lack. It seems likely that some sort of recognition or experienced proximity between the serial's world and the world of the audience, at some level, was the reason for this.

Keeping this first indication of recognition or proximity in mind, I would claim that the study can illustrate how survey results may well point to the necessity of other forms of knowledge, thus functioning as a productive element in an empirical, though basically hermeneutic, research process. I also approached the issue of recognition or proximity in another question. Respondents were asked to rank three aspects of the text in terms of their ability to motivate interest in *Dynasty* viewing: (1) the characters and the relations between them; (2) the storyline(s); (3) the beauty of the people and milieu presented in the serial. These alternatives were constructed from opinions expressed by many viewers both in newspapers and personal communication with me at work and in my neighbourhood. 41% ranked the first alternative as most important to them, 27% the second and 12% the third. However one interprets the answers given to an admittedly awkward question, they indicate that an interest in 'psychology' and/or 'human relations' was given as a prime motivating factor. When asked in another question to name characters with 'personality traits' the respondents knew or knew of from their own lives, most of them came up with several names. Jeff Colby seemed to be a fairly common kind of guy in Bergen, since he was the most frequently mentioned (by 19% of all). Krystle (16%) and Blake (13%) also stood out as recognizable. An interesting difference between age groups is worth mentioning here: Krystle was recognized by 38% of those above 60, while the other groups varied between 12 and 15%. Blake was mentioned by 29% of the oldest respondents, but only by 6% of those between 30 and 44. Jeff Colby was on the other hand more frequently mentioned by the younger viewers. (If we let all statistical care go, it was interesting to note that while Alexis and Sammy Jo were not much recognized, they seemed familiar to twice as many men as women.) A fairly reasonable conclusion drawn from the answers to these questions would be that most viewers experienced some proximity between the fictional universe and their own lives: they were able to 'relate to' characters and plotline(s).

This made the answers to another question interesting. When asked if the problems or conflicts between the characters in the series resembled conflicts known from their own lives or the lives of people they know, 68% denied such resemblance. Of those with less than nine years of education, where 85% claimed to have watched more than half of the episodes, 79% denied any resemblance between conflicts they knew or knew of and those in the series.

The widespread denial of proximity between fiction and reality on this point is interesting because it directly contradicts the answers given to other questions I have mentioned. Respondents claim to be interested in the 'psychology' and 'human relations' of characters who resemble people they know from real life – but the conflicts that constitute these characters and the relations between them are supposedly unfamiliar. This contradiction suggests that the respondents are not willing to acknowledge these conflicts as familiar, either because they do not want to admit to them in an interview, or because these conflicts are not a conscious part of viewers' fascination with the serial.

The survey thus indicated the limits of the kind of knowledge this particular kind of survey methodology is able to produce. Certain essential dimensions of the viewers' reception – those that are either experienced as very private or must be regarded as unconscious – are probably generally inaccessible through a survey. Nevertheless the use of surveys may help us to discover the existence of such dimensions.

Before presenting other kinds of reception data, I would like to conclude this section by summing up some of what I think are the survey's most significant results and merits as a methodological tool.

1 The survey indicates the approximate size of the total audience, and the effect on this of the move from a Saturday to a Wednesday slot. More importantly, it provides an overview of the social patterning of audience attendance to *Dynasty*. This helps to 'open' the reception process as a social phenomenon to social and cultural conditions at large. It draws our attention to the importance of structured social differences in reception.

2 The survey indicates (in a quite loose manner) the existence of a number of gender-, education- and age-related differences in the 'readings' of the show, concerning such dimensions as the degree of critical attitude or ability, and

the degree of proximity experienced between the 'real' and the diegetic world. It also suggests that these differences are in some way related to the types of print media in which the respondents claim to have read the most about the serial. The coverage in the print media should consequently be examined in order to get a better understanding of the different readings. One might say the survey points to the necessity of other kinds of data and knowledge.

3 The contradiction between (a) the experienced proximity between the world of the audience and that of the serial expressed in the answers to some questions, and (b) the denial of such proximity in the answers to the question about the familiarity of the serial's 'conflicts', points to the limits of survey methodology itself. Possibly, it points to the limits of 'factual' knowledge. At some point, we may have to leave the terrain of facts we can all more or less easily agree on in order to reach for a fuller understanding of what is going on. This may involve us in 'speculation', but speculation can be more or less qualified, 'good' or 'bad'.

QUALITATIVE METHODOLOGY INVOLVES TEXTUAL ANALYSIS

Two main approaches to these dimensions are available: qualitative methodology in audience research and textual analysis of the serial itself. Qualitative methodology in audience research must also include textual analysis in some form – inspired by semiotic, psychoanalytic or other forms of textual theory. With 'deep', loosely structured interviews this is especially obvious; transcripts of interviews may fill 1,000 pages or more. These texts have to be read symptomatically, in some sense, in order to portray the kinds of consciousness embedded in them. This is a very different task from the 'counting of expressed opinions' involved in some simple forms of survey research. Ien Ang (1985) studied *Dallas* viewers by way of letters sent to her, and she has formulated this point as follows:

> It would, however, be wrong to regard the letters as a direct and unproblematic reflection of the reasons why the writers love or hate *Dallas*. What people say or write about their experiences, preferences, habits, etc., cannot be taken entirely at face value, for in the routine of daily life they do not demand rational consciousness; they go unnoticed, as it were. They are commonsensical, self-evident; they require no further explanations. This means that we cannot let the letters speak for themselves, but that they should be read 'symptomatically': we must search for what is behind the explicitly written, for the presuppositions and accepted attitudes concealed within them. In other words, the letters must be regarded as texts, as discourses people produce when they want to express or have to account for their own preference for, or aversion to, a highly controversial piece of popular culture like *Dallas*.

(Ang 1985: 11)

118

Participant observation requires the researcher not only to interpret his or her own notes but also to make sense of both verbal and non-verbal behaviour, something which is homologous to the act of critical, interpretive reading. This point is well exemplified by Janice Radway in her *Reading the Romance* (1984). Radway found that the act of reading itself was of great importance to her informants, who were devoted fans of romances. To read (a romance) was a way to inform the family that mum was not available, a way for these women to create a space for themselves. This finding is in itself not new, as many enthusiastic comments to Radway's work seem to imply. A Swedish study in the late 1960s (Lundberg and Hultén 1968) of 'the functional specialities of the respective media' reported that, '[a] retreat from the immediate environment and its demands – probably mainly by the act of reading itself – was character-istic of audience usages of weekly magazines' (cited in Katz, Blumler and Gurevitch 1974: 26). What separates Radway's study from the previous Swedish one can be seen in the following conclusion:

> Therefore, while the act of romance reading is used by women as a means of partial protest against the role prescribed for them by the culture, the discourse itself actively insists on the desirability, naturalness, and benefits of that role by portraying it not as the imposed necessity that it is but as a freely designed, personally controlled, individual choice.
>
> (Radway 1984: 208)

The seemingly neutral 'retreat from the immediate environment and its demands' has become 'partial protest against the role prescribed for them by the culture', and hence a contradiction arises between the meaning of the act of reading and the meaning found in the texts read. This conclusion is not taken directly from the romance readers' accounts of what they are doing and thinking when they read their romances. It is produced through a critical interpretation of two categories of texts: the romances, on the one hand, and the texts produced by readers in interviews, on the other. The hermeneutic of suspicion involved here is based in a critically informed stance towards basic features of the present social system, shaped through the discourses of socially critical scholarship.

Thus, Radway does more than demonstrate the decisive role of textual analysis in this sort of work. Possibly surprising to some of those currently involved in audience or reception studies, the conclusion cited above may also be said to confirm implicitly the importance of the text as a carrier of meaning. The fact that Radway's readers of romances are not feminists, even if they may be said to protest against basic features of their condition when picking up another romance, may have something to do with the material they read. Other forms of literature might have had a different influence on how they understand their own lives. Radway's bold statement about the undivided ideological insistence of the romance discourse is especially pertinent at a time when much so-called critical media theory tends to reduce the text to a

119

mere collection of 'narrative forms/devices that engender particular kinds of purchase within the decoder's cultural parameters' (Wren-Lewis 1983: 196).

Radway's authoritative treatment of the qualitative data provided by both kinds of texts demonstrates quite clearly the importance of the interpreter's relation to her or his object of research. Attempts to make sense of widely different kinds of reception data within a framework of international and national socio-cultural structures of power and meaning will perhaps further clarify the centrality of the researcher's position to the outcome of the research process.

THE ROLE OF THE RESEARCHER IN THE CONSTRUCTION OF KNOWLEDGE

A multidimensional, critical understanding of reception as a social phenomenon can only be attained through the reflective process known as interpretation, a process where the relations between highly heterogeneous pieces of information may be established. Interpretation implies a distance between the interpreter and that which is being interpreted. In reception research, this means that there is a fundamental distance and difference between the researcher and the audiences whose reception is studied. This distance not only arises logically from the interpretive activity itself, it is also an inescapable social distance since researchers rarely study their own social group. Within our field, Ellen Seiter has usefully pointed out how differences in class, gender and race may interfere with both interviews and the interpretation of these interviews (Seiter 1990: 69). In other fields and disciplines, this is common sense. However, much current research on popular culture audiences has tended to forget or bracket this point. John Fiske, whose position I will return to in a moment, seems to believe that since he also enjoys many forms of popular culture, he can regard himself and his often ironic pleasures as 'typical of the people in general' (Fiske 1989a: 178f.). A prominent representative of the 'ethnographic' approach in this field, James Lull, recently published a collection of his (in many ways valuable) articles without devoting this issue any attention at all, either in the introductory chapter where the 'emerging tradition' of this approach is presented, or in any of the articles included, one of which presents Lull's research in China (Lull 1990).

The impetus behind much qualitative research on reception and audiences – not least that belonging to the British cultural studies tradition – has been a determination to view cultural consumption from the side of the consumers. The intention has been to demonstrate that audiences are not mindless, passive, totally subsumed victims of the cultural industries, but conscious, active, critical people, often resisting the ideologically repressive messages of mass media texts. John Fiske (e.g. 1987, 1989a, 1989b) has argued repeatedly that socially subordinate audiences enjoy particular popular texts *because* they are able to read them in an oppositional way. Popular texts are, in other words, those which in some way can confirm a pre-existing oppositional disposition in their audiences. For instance, when discussing the ideological function of Madonna, Fiske argues:

> But, if her fans are not 'cultural dupes', but actively choose to watch, listen to, and imitate her rather than anyone else, there must be some gaps or spaces in her image that escape ideological control and allow her audiences to make meanings that connect with *their* social experience. For many of her audiences, this social experience is one of powerlessness and subordination, and if Madonna as a site of meaning is not to naturalize this, she must offer opportunities for resisting it.
>
> (Fiske 1987: 273f.)

But why should we assume that there *must be* something non-ideological or oppositional in this process of appreciation? Instead of assuming the existence of some extra-ideological authenticity forming the basis for resistance, an interpretation of Madonna's appeal to identity-seeking young fans might focus on how Madonna's image represents a basic and well-known tension *within* the ideology of capitalist societies, between individualism and socialization. Such a perspective might even lead to a better understanding of why there are so many world pop stars with rebel images around, also in times (such as the 1980s) when signs of social rebellion are hard to find.

I see Fiske's argument as an example of an important problem in some of the so-called ethnographic studies in our field(s): the tendency of researchers to over-identify with the audiences they study. In Fiske's case, it takes the form represented by the above example, where a critical consciousness in audiences parallel to that of the researcher is simply taken for granted. Fiske has, in another paper, made use of postmodern notions of subjectivity when claiming to be 'a different television "audience" when watching my football team from when watching *The A-Team* with my son or *Days of our Lives* with my wife' (1989c: 56). When elsewhere talking about his relationship to 'the people' and popular pleasures, he reasons as follows:

> I am 50 years old, and I have spent large amounts of my leisure time participating in popular culture. I enjoy watching television, I love the sensational tabloid press, I read trashy popular novels and enjoy popular blockbuster movies. I have spent many happy hours in Disneyworld, shopping malls, Graceland, and on the Universal Studios tour – and despite all this, I do not think I am the dupe of the capitalist system because I can find great pleasure within it; in fact, *my* pleasures typically have an edge of difference to them, an awareness that they are *my* pleasures that I reproduce for myself out of *their* resources, and that in some way I am, from their point of view, misusing their resources for my pleasure. My laughter occurs at moments they might not have chosen as risible; it contains a cynical bite they might not welcome. And in this I believe I

am typical of the people in general, that my experience of popular pleasure is not special or privileged because I am also an academic with a variety of theoretical perspectives that are not part of everyday life.

(Fiske 1989a: 178f.)

Fiske here seems to believe that he can leave behind his academic training and the political socialization that went with it when he enters Disneyworld or other spheres of popular culture, as if he could switch at will between the disparate elements of his 'postmodern' subjectivity. Good old idealism is the result – the belief that social structures and their influence on subjectivities can easily be transcended, if one decides to identify with 'the people'. If Fiske's position were acceptable, empirical audience studies could largely be replaced by introspection.

A similar confusion in the research the audiences studied appears in Ang's (1985) argument about the functions of watching *Dallas*. The conclusion drawn from her analysis of the serial and letters from viewers is that for female viewers the pleasure of watching *Dallas* mainly lies in identification with positions of powerlessness, a 'tragic structure of feeling':

At the level of fantasy we can occupy those positions without having to experience their actual consequences. [. . .] The politics of representation does matter. But the fact that we can identify with these positions and solutions when we watch *Dallas* or women's weepies and experience pleasure from them is a completely different issue: it need not imply that we are also bound to take up these positions and solutions in our relations to our loved ones and friends, our work, our political ideals, and so on.

(Ang 1985: 135)

The confusion here lies in the rhetorical use of the all-embracing pronoun, 'we'. Ang does not distinguish between herself (and other academically educated, critical, self-supporting women) and the millions of devoted female *Dallas* fans in less resourced positions, to whom the distance between fictional and real powerlessness may be less obvious. Ang's whole book is, in fact, evidence of the power of the distanciated, critical discourse which is rooted in scholarly training and which sets her apart from the general audience.

In order to reach for an adequate understanding of the socio-cultural distance between the researcher and the people he or she studies in their capacities as audiences, we need to rethink how knowledge is established in sociological research. Bourdieu (1979) defines three 'modes of theoretical knowledge' about the social world. The first, *phenomenological* (which he also calls the 'ethnomethodological'),

sets out to make explicit the truth of primary experience of the social world, i.e. all that is inscribed in the relationship of *familiarity* with the familiar environment, the unquestioning apprehension of the social world which, by definition, does not reflect on itself and excludes the question of the conditions of its own possibility.

(Bourdieu 1979: 3)

This mode of knowledge, then, is the systematic description of the kind of commonsensical, doxic, 'practical' knowledge of the world which Ang (1985: 11) thought it necessary to interpret 'symptomatically' when encountered in texts gathered in audience studies.

The second mode of knowledge, termed *objectivist*, 'constructs the objective relations (e.g. economic or linguistic) which structure practice and representations of practice' (ibid.). By asking the question 'which the doxic experience of the social world excludes by definition – the question of the (particular) conditions making that experience possible', objectivist knowledge 'can establish both the structures of the social world and the objective truth of primary experience as experience denied *explicit* knowledge of those structures' (Bourdieu 1979: 3). 'Objectivist' knowledge is, in other words, knowledge of abstract social structures and forces that form the conditions of the commonsensical, doxic experience of the social world.

But 'adequate knowledge' not only presupposes a break with the doxic 'primary experience' of the social world, it also requires a second critical break: an 'inquiry into the conditions of possibility, and thereby, into the limits of the objective and objectifying standpoint which grasps practices from outside' (ibid.). An investigation of the social conditions for establishing 'objectivist' knowledge of abstract social structures and forces (i.e. the social conditions of academic institutions) is, in other words, a prerequisite for understanding how doxic, commonsensical knowledge actualizes and reproduces its own social conditions. Scholars' own 'doxa' and practices tend to reproduce their own social conditions of existence, in much the same way as the commonsensical, unquestioned beliefs of other social categories tend to reproduce theirs.

The three modes of knowledge have to be dialectically understood as moments of one process, where knowledge is established, so that the 'final' moment is one of simultaneous synthesis of the first two moments and self-reflection on the limits of this synthesis. While trying to integrate 'ethno-methodological' knowledge of audience experience (as rendered in interviews, letters, observations, etc.) and 'objectivist' knowledge (of the social structures and forces forming the basis of this 'spontaneous' experience), the researcher has to reflect on her/his relations to her/his own social conditions and to the phenomena studied.

Considering reception research in these terms, we need to interpret the 'doxic' nature of the texts gathered from informants in relation to the objective social structures in which they are, so to speak, 'embedded'. This means, for instance, understanding the reception of *Dynasty* in Norway as, in a sense, framed by the American 'low culture' hegemony in cultural production on the one hand, and the kind of 'high culture' hegemony represented by the

123

NRK on the other. It also means understanding the reception of the show by people in particular social categories as related to their particular social positions and their socio-economic and cultural resources.

Bourdieu's perspective stresses the necessity for researchers to question their own position in relation to dominant social structures. But this does not lead to total relativization of the knowledge established in this process. The distinguishing characteristic of what he calls the scientific form of knowledge is precisely its self-reflective, theoretical nature: its ability to distance itself from itself, to defamiliarize itself and its foundations. This is a prerequisite for a socially critical form of research, one which transcends the doxa dominating the various forms of practical consciousness. Bourdieu's concluding remark, in his preface to the English-language edition of *Distinction*, has frequently been overlooked in the often populist academic reception of his work in Anglo-American media and communication studies:

> At all events, there is nothing more universal than the project of objectifying the mental structures associated with the particularity of a social structure. Because it presupposes an epistemological break which is also a social break, a sort of estrangement from the familiar, domestic, native world, the critique (in the Kantian sense) of culture invites each reader, through the 'making strange' beloved of the Russian formalists, to reproduce on his or her own behalf the critical break of which it is the product. For this reason it is perhaps the only rational basis for a truly universal culture.
>
> (Bourdieu 1984: xiv)

The ability to perform this kind of theoretically informed, distanciating self-reflection is produced in researchers through their training within the academic field. The education leading to research practice leaves none untouched. Researchers have all been socialized into more or less self-reflective, intellectually distanciating subjects, whether this is consciously recognized or not. This inescapably sets people like us apart from 'general audiences' of all other sorts; we can never 'completely' reproduce, either in our heads or on paper, the 'ordinary' experience of, for instance, television fiction. In view of what has been said about the possibilities for critical reflection inherent in the researcher's position, this should not be lamented, but consciously and actively regarded as a fundamental resource.

This also implies a renewed look at the distinction between 'high' and 'low' culture, or more specifically, in Bourdieu's terms, between 'barbaric' and 'pure' taste. Our enjoyment of 'barbaric' cultural products will always differ from that of normal 'barbarians' of various sorts: we are paid to produce papers and books about these products, using our acquired analytical skills to produce a better understanding of the artefacts in question and their social functions. Such an understanding presupposes the type of distanciated relation to text and context which, according to Bourdieu, defines the 'pure' taste (Bourdieu

1984: 30ff.). As the present generation of media researchers (not only John Fiske) have experienced, this need not exclude the possibilities for enjoyment of 'barbaric' products: to a certain extent it leaves us with a more or less conscious choice between cultural forms and forms of reception, a choice which is not available to the greater part of 'general audiences'. Intellectuals now have access to both high and low culture, they are 'double access' audiences; the majority of 'ordinary people' have only access to 'low' or popular culture. Our double access is a class privilege, a benefit of education, from which we cannot escape (cf. Gripsrud 1989a).

METATEXTS AND CONTEXTS: INCLUSION, NOT CONFUSION

How socio-cultural structures influence reception may be seen if the reception of a particular text is situated within a larger pattern of media consumption. Most Norwegian viewers had read something about *Dynasty* before they actually watched their first episode, and newspapers and weeklies gave extensive coverage of the show throughout its run, particularly the first year. I start by making this point because the role of various forms of PR and media coverage of serials such as *Dynasty* and *Dallas* has been largely neglected in previous research on the reception of these prime-time soaps. As mentioned in Chapter 1, David Buckingham's study of *EastEnders* (1987) is a rare exception to the rule. In the otherwise meticulously researched book by Liebes and Katz on *Dallas* (1990), no attention at all is paid to how their focus groups may have had at least some of their perspectives on the show shaped by the media coverage of it. In Ien Ang's study of a part of the Dutch reception of *Dallas*, the existence of 'the commercial machinery that has to sell *Dallas*' (1985: 15) is at least commented on. But its importance for an understanding of the show's reception is, in my view, far too easily dismissed:

> It would be naïve to suppose that the marketing practices of the commercial culture industry have no effect whatever on the involvement of the viewers. How great and what that effect is cannot be established here, however. On the other hand it would be far too easy to ascribe the popularity of *Dallas* totally to advertising. We must make a distinction between the programme itself as it can be seen week by week on television, and the advertising practices surrounding it.
>
> (Ang 1985: 15)

To the producers, the primary purpose of publicity for the show is surely just to attract viewers. But to reception research, the interesting issue is how all of the metatextual material affects the meanings and pleasures audiences derive from the programme text. The very distinction between 'the programme itself' and the various texts about the programme is, as will be demonstrated in the following, actually not at all unproblematic to make.

125

Jane Feuer (1989) is among the very few internationally published researchers of prime-time soaps (other than myself, Gripsrud 1989) who has dealt with this issue at any length. She asks how we are to 'constitute the text of *Dynasty*' as an object of analysis, and raises questions which concern four areas where the borders of the *Dynasty* text seem hard to find. First, there is the border between *Dynasty* and the flow it is presented as part of – consisting of other shows, commercials, newsbreaks, station breaks, promos, etc. Second, there is the border between the show and all the various texts and objects that have been produced in connection with it (articles presenting critical research are missing from Feuer's list). Third, there is the issue of defining the extension of the text for critical purposes: how many episodes do we have to include? Fourth, the question is raised whether a videotaped *Dynasty* is the same text as a broadcast *Dynasty* (Feuer 1989: 444f.). I will return to the two latter questions in a later chapter, and concentrate on the first two here.

Feuer argues that 'the text of *Dynasty*' must include all 'surrounding' material, on and off TV, which is/was about the serial, as well as a number of objects and socio-cultural practices related to the show. This position challenges the very possibility of comparative research on television programmes that cross national borders. If 'the text of *Dynasty*' is to include its specific context in US commercial television and its specific coverage in US print media, then *Dynasty* never left the US. What we saw in Europe was something else. While a basic idea of this book is to analyse the 'whole' *Dynasty* phenomenon or event in Norway, study it as a 'text', if you will, I still want to insist on the elementary analytical distinction between the serial's text and the 'text' of the event.

Insisting on the importance of such elementary distinctions seems more necessary than simply banal these days, because poststructuralist influences in media studies have tended to produce 'deconstructions' of all kinds of basic analytical tools. John Fiske has for instance published an article where he suggests that, 'There is no text, there is no audience, there are only the processes of viewing – that variety of cultural practices that take place in front of the screen which constitute the object of study that I am proposing' (Fiske 1989b: 57). More or less commonsensically, it seems quite obvious that a study of the 'processes of viewing' presupposes the factual existence and methodological acknowledgement of audiences and texts as distinct categories. One would think it is their encounter we are to study. But Jane Feuer makes use of Tony Bennett's (1983) notion of 'reading formations' – defined as 'a set of intersecting discourses that productively activate a given body of texts and the relations between them in a specific way' (quoted in Feuer 1989: 459, n.3) – to conclude that

> in the case of *Dynasty*, the reading formation *is* the text. Thus *Dynasty*'s interpretive communities never merely interpret – they enact, they are counted as demographics, they consume not just a fictional text but a whole range of other products as well. Not only would I posit that the

interpretive community *is* the text, it also *produces* the text and in addition is produced *by* the text.

(Feuer 1989: 458)

It is worth noting here, how 'reading formations' is confused with Stanley Fish's notion of 'interpretive communities' (cf. the Introduction to this book), and both are then said not only to *be* the text, but also to *produce* the text and to be *produced by* the text. The conceptual confusion is, in other words, practically total.

Feuer also draws on Tony Bennett's (1983) use of Pierre Macherey's notion of a text's 'encrustations'. In Macherey's use of this metaphor (in an interview in the journal *Red Letters*) it refers to way shells can cling to a stone on a beach, and the idea is that certain metatexts and contexts may cling as tightly to a text as shells to such a stone. Bennett maintains the difference, if barely, between the text and these contexts, which he calls 'hermeneutic activators', but Feuer (1989: 446) argues 'that the "hermeneutic activators" themselves constitute part of the text of *Dynasty*'. Such a contamination of categories is of course contradicted by the metaphor itself, since stones and shells are chemically different, and may well be separated.

The theoretical origins of Feuer's near-total confusion of text and context and of text and reader(s) can be traced in the appearance of the reader as a central figure in the most influential literary theories of this century. Since this is such a fundamental and complicated theoretical issue, and because an awareness of the history of current theoretical positions and problems is important, I will deal with it at some length here, even if it may seem like a detour for many readers. The point of the following section is that Feuer's position is different from that of previous reception- or reader-oriented theories in textual studies.

READER ORIENTATION AND THE RELATIVIZATION OF THE TEXT IN LITERARY THEORY

Russian formalism was preoccupied with the structures of literary texts, applying linguistics to the understanding of literature. But it also brought the role of the reader into the picture in a new way. Viktor Shklovsky, in his seminal essay 'Art as Technique' (1917), defined literary art by its ability to 'defamiliarize' language, and hence by breaking the 'automatism' of everyday speech and perceptions make the reader see the 'world' anew. Yurij Tynjanov later argued that since ordinary language would tend to absorb and 'normalize' the estrangement first produced by literary art, 'literariness' would have to vary according to the particular time and place in which it worked. 'Literariness' would thus not be guaranteed for ever, and would ultimately be decided by literature's relation to the reader and his or her 'ordinary language'. The Prague structuralists, such as Jan Mukarovsky (1970) and Felix Vodička (1976) continued this line of thinking in the 1930s and 1940s, inspired by Saussure's semiology. They differentiated between the literary work as a material artefact and as an aesthetic object. The latter is produced in the heads of readers, through the act of reading, and could consequently be regarded as a changing entity, changing with the historical and socio-cultural conditions of the reader. Mukarovsky also regarded aesthetic norms and values as related to social norms, values and class hierarchies, not as something entirely intrinsic to the object.

All of this is to indicate that, in the kind of textual theory which is influenced by or based in linguistics and semiology/semiotics there is a long tradition of focusing on the reader and the act of reading as an absolutely central dimension in literary studies, and hence of a degree of socio-cultural and historical relativization of the meanings of texts. Parallel to this tradition, similar ideas have been developed in phenomenological and hermeneutical literary theory. The phenomenologically based theory of Roman Ingarden (*The Literary Work of Art* (1973)) acknowledged the importance of the reader in producing the meaning of a literary work: its 'concretization' is produced by the reader, from the 'skeleton' of 'schemata' presented by the text itself. Wolfgang Iser (1974, 1978) may be said to have continued along the phenomenological lines suggested by Ingarden, with his notion of reading as 'gap-filling' and his theorization of 'the implied reader'. Hans Robert Jauss (1974, 1975) drew on the hermeneutic tradition in German philosophy, and the work of Hans-Georg Gadamer (1960) in particular, when he developed his idea of a literary history which would centre on the readers and their receptions of literature, rather than on the authors or on the texts themselves, treated in isolation from their specific historical contexts.

All of these contributions have subverted previous ideas of authorial intention as the only source of meaning in a text, and all have (at least since the 1930s) distinguished between the text as a potential of meaning (artefact, 'skeleton', etc.) and the text as actualized or realized meaning (aesthetic object, concretization, reception). A railway on which no trains run is a railway only potentially, as Marx put it in *Grundrisse*. Both semiotic and hermeneutic theories have also pointed out how each individual text is part of much larger networks of texts, ultimately part of a whole (or several) culture(s). They have argued that the meanings readers produce out of a particular text are necessarily related, in many and complex ways, to these readers' acquaintance with other texts. The very act of writing or producing any individual text does, of course, imply that elements are taken both from other individual, specific texts (direct and indirect quotes and references) and from the general semiotic resources of language. The completely 'autonomous text' is thus dead and buried in these perspectives. Still, none of the above-mentioned theories or theorists has ever questioned the existence of individual texts as separate entities, as specific objects of reading, analysis and interpretation.

'LAYERS' OF METATEXTS, HORIZONS OF EXPECTATIONS

It is, in other words, hard to see that anything is gained by regarding the serial itself and everything that openly refers to it as parts of one and the same 'text of *Dynasty*'. On the contrary, it reduces our chances for analytical insights. Why, for instance, should one only include the various texts ostensibly about *Dynasty* in the *Dynasty* text? A number of other texts are clearly also very relevant contexts. For example, in her article Feuer is particularly preoccupied with 'camp' readings of *Dynasty*. Such readings are obviously related to a whole cultural tradition of texts, readings and practices. Furthermore, 'camp' as a cultural tradition or formation is related to a complex social situation in which homosexuality has been and is repressed in various ways, and in which other categories of people, such as heterosexual intellectuals of certain kinds, have come to appreciate camp tastes and pleasures. All those who 'camped' *Dynasty* obviously made connections between the show and a practically unlimited number of other texts, objects and practices – the melodramatic tradition in film and popular literature, folk and fairy tales, previous films in which the stars had appeared, childhood play with dolls, genres of reporting in popular magazines, fashion advertising, etc. To include publicity articles, advertisements, fashions, etc. in the *Dynasty* text itself is thus in a sense a more arbitrary way to delineate 'the text' than sticking to the traditional and commonsensical definition of the text as the artefact, the particular set of signifiers, images and sounds, observable in or on every TV set where *Dynasty* appeared. If one wants – as I do in this book – to study the whole *Dynasty* event or phenomenon, one may well regard it as a text, since it is to be 'read' or interpreted as a sign consisting of signs. But the limits to this socio-cultural phenomenon-text can then not be drawn where Feuer proposes. The phenomenon must – as in this book – be studied in much wider contexts. Analytical distinctions between various levels or layers within the phenomenon, between interrelations among different elements in the situation in which it occurred, then become a pressing necessity, as does a minimum of focus. Ultimately, the focus must be the text itself, as it appeared on television screens all over the world.

In his *Television Culture* (1987), John Fiske has suggested a set of distinctions between the various 'layers' involved in the reception process, which is clearly more analytically helpful than the blurring of elementary boundaries which Feuer (and he himself, later (1989), cf. above) proposed. Starting with the notion of intertextuality – 'that any one text is necessarily read in relationship to others' – Fiske emphasizes how the study of a text's intertextual relations 'can provide us with valuable clues to the readings that a particular culture or subculture is likely to produce from it' because 'intertextual knowledges pre-orient the reader to exploit television's polysemy by activating the text in certain ways'. He goes on to suggest the following categories of intertextuality:

> We can envisage these textual relations on two dimensions, the horizontal and the vertical. Horizontal relations are those between primary texts that

129

are more or less explicitly linked, usually along the axis of genre, character, or content. Vertical intertextuality is that between a primary text, such as a television program or series, and other texts of a different type that refer explicitly to it. These may be secondary texts such as studio publicity, journalistic features or criticism, or tertiary texts produced by the viewers themselves in the form of letters to the press, or, more importantly, of gossip and conversation.

(Fiske 1987: 108)

A fourth category of texts is missing here: the mass of texts I just referred to which is not directly 'about' the primary text in question, but which still may be very important for the decoding or understanding of it. Such a fourth contextual dimension may easily be added to the list, though (cf. below). The important thing here is that this kind of categorization maintains the centrality of the text proper ('the primary text') while acknowledging and assigning vital importance to the masses of surrounding texts, both 'horizontally' and 'vertically'. I also prefer such a perspective since it is one in which the importance of specific creative decisions made in the production process of an individual text is acknowledged. What producers do matters. It is furthermore helpful in that – contrary to Feuer's amorphous, all-embracing 'text of *Dynasty*' – it invites a crucial differentiation between the receptions of socially diverse groups of readers or audiences, according to which secondary, tertiary and 'quadriary' texts they have encountered, prior to the experience of the primary text. While all viewers of *Dynasty* watch the same primary text, their receptions may vary in relation to their differentiated exposure to often socio-culturally stratified material in other media. Fiske's hierarchy of texts is thus also more appropriate than Feuer's 'total' notion of 'the text' for a study which is interested in the role played by general social divisions (class, gender, race, ethnicity) in the reception process.

The need for a fourth contextual dimension arises from the fact that people watch television equipped not only with more or less promotional background material and gossip about the show in question at the back of their heads. They also bring their previous experiences of both television and other media. Moreover, their social experiences at large are importantly present, different as they are, in accordance with the criteria for social divisions in our societies. What we need, then, is a way to think all of these elements together, without losing sight of the distinctions between them. The point is to establish what Hans Robert Jauss has called the 'horizon of expectations' for different categories of 'readers', which would encompass secondary and tertiary texts as well as quite a lot more. Jauss originally introduced this concept as follows:

The analysis of the literary experience can thus avoid the pitfall of psychologism when the perception and effect of a work is described in the objectifiable system of relations of expectations which is given for each work in the moment of its appearance from the pre-understanding of genre, from the form and thematics of previously known works and from the opposition between poetical and practical language.

(Jauss 1974: 173f.)

Later critical discussion of the concept, also involving marxist scholars, made it clear that the 'horizon of expectations' was not to be understood as limited to the realm of aesthetic experiences, but should also include more general social experiences (cf. Jauss 1975). The concept is thus methodologically highly useful for reception studies intended to transcend individualizing 'psychologism' and approach reception as a socially significant process. The 'horizon' is to be constructed by the researcher on the basis of available knowledge about the particular previous socio-cultural experiences of specific audiences. Thus it combines aesthetic and more general, class- and gender-related social experiences and points to the necessity of understanding, for instance, the reception of television as preconditioned by and intertwined with the reception of other media texts.

THE TELEVISUAL CONTEXT: MEGATEXT, SUPERTEXT, PROGRAMME TEXT

If we now turn to what Fiske called 'horizontal' intertextuality, in our case *Dynasty*'s immediate environment on US television screens, how can we separate the serial from all the surrounding and intersticed material? Nick Browne (1984) has suggested a set of analytical concepts which are highly useful here (Feuer for some reason does not refer to them). Browne proposes a distinction between the televison *megatext*, the *supertext* and the '*program proper*'. The megatext simply 'consists of everything that has appeared on televison' (p. 177). Browne admits that 'this notion is unwieldy from a practical standpoint'. But the megatext is made methodologically available for analytical purposes if one accepts that the schedule represents it. Analysis of the megatext will thus in practice mean analysis of the 'history, logic and form' of the schedule. (For early examples of such analysis, see Williams 1975 and Paterson 1993.)

The supertext consists of 'the particular program and all the introductory and interstitial material – chiefly announcements and ads – considered in its specific position in the schedule' (Browne 1984: 176). An analysis of the supertext thus requires that a first distinction between the programme and the additional material that comes with it is already acknowledged. This may clearly be done, even if, as Browne puts it, 'the limits of the text "proper" and its formal unity – apt to be broken at any moment by an ad or a turn of the dial – is suspect' (ibid.: 176).

Jane Feuer points out that certain ads for cosmetics and perfume in *Dynasty* are 'so closely linked to the mise-en-scène and narrative of the parent program that only a knowledge of the conventions of television flow permit us to distinguish them' (Feuer 1989: 448). I, for my part, would guess that knowledge

131

of these conventions is among the most common knowledge in the United States of America – there is hardly any 'information gap' in this particular field. Feuer still argues that ads for Ultress hair-care and the perfume Forever Krystle, in which Linda Evans appears, 'are easily read diegetically', since the perfume ad 'merely continues the development of the perfect relationship betweeen Blake and Krystle'. If the ad seems to mark a rather quick reconciliation between the two whose marriage was about to break up in the actual episode in which it is inserted, Feuer holds that this will be accepted simply as another instance of the narrative discontinuity experienced as fundamental to the plot construction of the show (ibid.: 449).

This remains a quite bold hypothesis about empirical readings, with no other empirical support than the observed similarities between the ads and the programme itself. I find it very hard to believe that American viewers will not, more or less immediately, recognize the ad as an ad. These similarities are clearly constructed so that the fantasy of unlimited affluence which is integral to the show will be metonymically represented by the consumer goods in question. But this is only a particular instance of a mechanism which operates in all 'supertexts' of US television. As formulated by Browne, 'program and ad are linked formally as question and answer, and psychologically as lack and liquidation' (1984: 180). The answer to the questions produced by the programme is the product advertised. In light of this, the Ultress and Forever Krystle ads in the *Dynasty* supertext are simply particularly clear – or heavy-handed – examples of a normal, formal interrelatedness between ads and programme. It is highly improbable that any viewer of *Dynasty* will mistake them for parts of the programme – unless the 'viewer' is someone who just catches a glimpse of the screen in passing.

The extreme discontinuity of televisual discourse in the US in itself works on an unconscious level to promote consumption, as argued by Beverle Houston (1984). Television promises the endless, always available flow of imaginary wholeness, but never delivers. It breaks the imaginary promise 'by separating the text into saleable parts, breaking up the promise of coherence and wholeness into short sessions'; the institution of television 'reproduces the imaginary in discrete, regulated entities – small, discontinuous, easily consumable, like the bits of information on a computer screen, like the items in the supermarket' (Houston 1984: 185). Television, according to Houston, promotes consumption (in general) 'by shattering the imaginary possibility over and over, repeatedly reopening the gap of desire' (ibid.: 184).

Both Houston and Browne have thus suggested ways of understanding the specific textual regime of the US supertext. In their perspectives, the elementary pragmatic and analytical distinction between the programme and the ads is not erased. It is precisely the nature, and the specific functions, of this distinction which is under scrutiny, because this is what the whole of the American institution of television is based on.

Two other arguments for the necessity of separating the programme-text

132

from the supertext are simpler, but hardly less important. First, in print media, fictional or factual stories may be interspersed with ads of many sorts, illustrations, comics, etc. It may of course be useful for specific purposes to analyse magazines like *Cosmopolitan* or *Playboy* as 'supertexts', containing both journalistic reportage, interviews, fiction and ads, in order to understand the publication, or particular elements in it, as a whole. But still, the individual items may also be discerned and selected for closer examination. This latter possibility is particularly useful if a certain article from one of the magazines mentioned – possibly about *Dynasty* – appears reprinted in, say, a Norwegian magazine or newspaper. The Norwegian editors in such a case have had no problems in discerning the text from the supertext.

The second simple argument for the necessity of this distinction is then related to the fact that American TV shows are often exported without all the additional material with which they are presented in the US. In some countries other ads will be included; in countries like the Scandinavian ones, the show may appear without commercial interruptions. This obviously does away with the original supertext, but not the text, the 'program proper'. Since the construction of the supertext in US television is, as indicated above, vital to the way television functions in American society, this means that the 'total' social meaning and possible 'effect' of the complete supertext may be presumed different from that of the programme-text alone. Still, the programme-text will remain the same in the two settings, and will be decoded as a separate entity by most viewers. Both general audiences and media researchers in the US and elsewhere will be relating to the same set of characters, the same plotlines, the same music, etc. The addition of subtitles in some countries (such as the Scandinavian ones and the Netherlands) normally represents a minimal divergence from the original, while the practice of dubbing (in countries like France and Germany) seems more drastic. In both cases, though, the forms of translation will on the whole be so precise and so 'natural' for the audiences, that they can hardly be thought of as making, for instance, *Dynasty* something other than *Dynasty*.

An analysis of the programme-text may thus have relevance for audiences and researchers of both the exporting and the importing countries, even if 'something is missing' and 'added' in the latter. Thus, I and many others benefited greatly from reading Jane Feuer's 1984 article in *Screen* about melodrama and the prime-time soaps, *Dynasty* in particular, in which there was no mentioning of the ads that went with *Dynasty* in its American presentation. And if social meaning is what the researcher is interested in, then the supertext is not wide enough a context: in that case, the whole institution of television in its local specificity is of interest, as well as culture and society in general. That is why Chapter 2 of this book had to include at least a brief sketch of the historical and social conditions that shaped the Norwegian broadcasting system and also otherwise provided a particular cultural framework in which the primary programme text of *Dynasty* was received.

SECONDARY TEXTS: THE NEWSPAPERS

I mentioned briefly on p. 115 that the coverage of *Dynasty* in weeklies and newspapers differed significantly. The differences concerned both subject-matter and perspectives. In this section, I will deal with these differences in greater detail, not least because the social composition of the readerships of these print media differs. The following is the result of a qualitative analysis of a great number of clippings – a near total collection of the newspaper coverage of the serial during its first-year (1983–4) run, helpfully made available to me by a Christian organization monitoring broadcasting in Norway (see Chapter 2), and a more unsystematic but also quite voluminous personal collection of clippings from weekly magazines. The analysis performed basically consisted in registration and interpretation of recurrent themes and styles of presentation, seen as representing attitudes to and understandings of the serial.

The newspaper coverage has actually largely been presented in Chapter 2, so what I primarily need to do here is to sum up briefly what has been said already. The newspapers, particularly the nationally circulated Oslo tabloids, first worked as a marketing agent for the serial, since they both voiced a demand for *Dallas* which eventually led to the NRK's buying *Dynasty*, and then printed information about *Dynasty* which was more or less directly supplied by the producers/distributors. The stories printed about the show before the first episode was broadcast mainly consisted of sensationalist paraphrases of the plotlines, descriptions of central characters and generally not really reliable information about *Dynasty*'s incredible success in the US. Nothing was initially provided in the way of critical information, for instance about the genre, which was totally unfamiliar to an audience which had never seen a daytime soap, American or British.

The newspapers then staged the public discussion on *Dynasty*. This discussion inevitably endowed the serial with political significance, in several ways. First, the serial came to represent 'low culture' in the socially charged opposition between 'high' and 'low' – both in culture and in society at large. An important part of this was the discursive opposition established between the socio-cultural 'oligarchy' which attacked the show, on the one hand, and the 'populist alliance' which defended it, on the other. Second, the serial came to represent a certain form of programming which was advancing on an international scale, and which would sooner or later seriously threaten Norwegian national cultural identity. An important dimension here was the implication of *Dynasty* in discussions on broadcasting policies, making a 'yes' to the show a 'no' to the established popular enlightenment tradition of programming. Third, the very clear condemnation of the serial, on moral grounds, by various Christian leaders and organizations meant that watching *Dynasty* could easily acquire a sense of decadence or sinfulness, for those who otherwise usually would take notice of religious authorities.

As a result of all this, watching *Dynasty* – or deciding not to watch it – became a choice loaded with socio-cultural and political meaning; a choice one would have to be prepared to defend among friends, colleagues and neighbours – and for oneself. The awareness of this must also have been a factor in the act of viewing, for instance by sparking off comparisons between particular scenes and episodes and what was said about the show in general in the newspapers: 'Was this immoral?' 'Oh, well, it's superficial, all right.' 'At least it's better than the Swedish TV drama yesterday' (these lines are not quotes, but do not lack empirical grounding, as I will later demonstrate).

The debate went on, in waves, throughout most of 1983–4. But the newspapers also covered the serial in other ways during its first and subsequent runs. On the one hand, the tabloids in particular supplied gossip and PR material about the stars. For example, *Dagbladet* of 10 April 1984 carried a title on the front page which said 'ALEXIS SCARED STIFF BY HERPES'. The title referred to a full-page report inside the paper from an interview Joan Collins did with *Playboy*. On the other hand, the same newspaper could take any opportunity to preach against the show. In the same issue that ran the 'herpes story' about Alexis, there is a story about the Forever Krystle perfume, illustrated with a photo of Linda Evans as Krystle. The readers are also informed in this piece that 'Linda has also lent her name to a new soft-drink, Crystal light'. And the paper adds: 'Even if we risk challenging the very spirit of the Norwegian people, we are tempted to compare it [the soft drink] to the TV-serial: it sparkles and shines, but contains nothing but water and additives. It lacks calories and other nutrition completely' (*Dagbladet*, 10 April 1984, p. 7).

This particular issue of *Dagbladet* is quite typical of a double, more or less hypocritical, attitude taken in newspapers, again particularly (but far from exclusively) the tabloids. By covering the serial, even on its front pages, the press acknowledged that it was of great interest to a large portion of their readership(s), and indirectly it then also confirmed that the show was worth this interest. But at the same time, it is stated (in the passage just quoted) that *Dynasty* is completely stupid and without cultural value. The only way these two attitudes can go together is one of irony: 'we watch it with a certain pleasure, but we know it's actually idiotic'. The newspapers reflected, and significantly promoted, the enormous interest in the show, in a coverage which reached an unparalleled level of hysteria when it was finally to be taken off the schedule, in the early summer of 1984. Many newspapers then printed several pages of paraphrases of future developments in the serial, illustrated with huge photos, accompanied by interviews and 'phone-ins' on audience reactions.

But the ironic tone also lasted, even if a shift eventually took place in the way the newspapers' TV critics wrote about *Dynasty* in its subsequent runs. While, during its first run, it had predominantly been reviewed in a condescending or otherwise negative ironic tone, critics increasingly took to a 'camp' perspective, ironically celebrating the show's formulaic and excessive features. Under the title 'Oh – these lovely soap bubbles', a female journalist in *Dagbladet* (16 July 1987) wrote:

We had to wait for a whole week to find out what happened after The Kiss. Only last night could we learn that Daniel (Rock Hudson) Reece had been waiting for this since adolescence in Dayton. We, on our part, are only waiting for the continuation. The eternal continuation. Of *Dynasty, Lace, North and South* and of *Eastenders*. It is great times for us soap opera lovers. The NRK has generously seen to us in particular this summer, and offers continuing oil struggles in Denver, Manhattan girls with family problems and American Civil War nostalgia. In addition to British kitchen-sink drama twice a week, plus reruns. [. . .] Wednesdays are probably the ultimate, particularly for those of us who can get Swedish television, since right after *Dynasty* we can switch to TV1's *Falcon Crest*.

The journalist continued this piece with a brief overview of the success of domestic soap operas around the world, and a note on the history and fascination of the genre (on the latter theme, she quoted a British producer, Bill Smethurst, saying that the main secret of soaps' appeal is that they make the audience wait).

This sort of critical commentary in a nationally distributed newspaper, which has traditionally been favoured by many radical and liberal intellectuals, represented a shift in the attitude to *Dynasty* and the soap opera genre since the days of the great debate in 1983–4, a shift which was most probably not limited to the editorial staff of this or other newspapers. On 15 March 1986 the same paper interviewed the present researcher and reported from a conference at the University of Oslo (at which the Danish researcher Kim Schrøder also participated) in a full-page article with the title 'Soap opera approved by the cultural elite'. Nobody protested. When *Dynasty*'s second run ended in September 1987 with the Moldava massacre episode, another female journalist gave an ironic, joking commentary in which she said that 'we who have followed *Dynasty* all these years' had done so because 'it gives such a wonderful opportunity to laugh in all the wrong places' (*Dagbladet*, 24 September 1987). In its third and final run, a male journalist in the same paper commented on one episode, saying that '*Dynasty* was wonderful yesterday, when Linda Evans played out both her facial expressions to the full. One of them at home with Blake (the copy) and the other with the sinister doctor (the real Krystle)' (11 August 1988). These and other signs clearly indicate that the more or less educated middle class – here represented by journalists – had learned how to cope with and/or enjoy a prime-time soap without risking being regarded as stupid. They 'camped' it.

The newspaper coverage, particularly during *Dynasty*'s first run, can be seen as resulting from the social differences between journalists and significant parts of their readership. Newspapers are read every day, in all social groups in Norway (see Chapter 2), making their readership far more heterogeneous in social terms than their producers. Journalists are predominantly male and normally have 12–15 (sometimes more) years of education. That their coverage of *Dynasty* was gendered can be seen in at least two ways. First, their interest in Alexis was clearly a lot greater than their interest in Krystle. The tabloid *VG* had *Dynasty* on the front page at least twice in autumn 1983, and both times they had titillating photographs of Alexis as illustrations (15 October and 1 November). This is not to say that women were not interested in Alexis, it is to say that Alexis was easier to present as a slightly daring sex symbol. The pictures of her chosen for presentation tended to be ones in which she was scantily dressed or sported a 'come-on' look. Perhaps more important is the contrast with the 'family-oriented' weeklies, which have more female journalists and women as the bulk of their customers. These concentrated entirely on Krystle or Linda Evans in their choices of cover photos relating to the serial and in their selection of PR material, interviews and reportage.

Newspapers in their coverage also suggested a reading of the serial which was never really presented by the women/family-oriented weeklies: that *Dynasty* was a more or less realistic depiction of life in the extreme upper class in the USA. This suggestion emerged, interestingly, not least through the increased, repeated use of the word 'dynasty' in reports about Norwegian businesses and rich families. That multimillionaire shipowners' families were called 'dynasties' was probably not new, but this particular word clearly became more frequent in such contexts, and worked as a reference to the show. A journalist's quite serious investigative book about one of these families was called *The Bergesen Dynasty*, and the publisher ran an advertisement in newspapers (not weeklies) which said that,

> This is the story of a real Norwegian dynasty, the Bergesen dynasty, one of Norway's richest and most powerful families, a clan with roots in Stavanger – not Denver, Colorado – but which has had both its Blake, its Stephen [*sic*], its Alexises and its Fallons.

An advertisement is not part of a paper as a journalistic product. But it works in relation to the journalism presented. This advertisement simply followed up on the many journalistic references to parallels between the fictional world of the Carringtons and the real world of super-rich families like the Bergesens.

Newspapers thus ended up saying to their readers, on the one hand, that *Dynasty* was lowbrow, unrealistic trash one might kill time with or enjoy for its sex and its ludicrousness, and on the other, that it was, in a sense, a realistic depiction of life among extremely rich people in the US. The 'documentary' realist reading of *Dynasty* was openly suggested in an issue of *Verdens Gang* (28 April 1984) which devoted all of page 27 to a story about 'THE REAL BLAKE CARRINGTON': an oil billionaire in Denver, Colorado, whose position, life history and Washington connections clearly resembled those of the fictional tycoon. But on the opposite page, two unemployed citizens of Denver were interviewed under the title 'THE REAL DENVER, COLORADO'. They said that the Denver of *Dynasty* did not at all resemble the Denver they knew. They did watch the serial, though. Readers were not informed as to whether the tycoon did. The conclusion to be drawn from these two stories would be that an immense gap between rich and poor exists in the US. It was consequently not unreasonable to suspect that the rich could live like the Carringtons. If that was the case, then *Dynasty* was not only a kind of realist drama, it also appealed to the social voyeurism that the TV show *Lifestyles of the Rich and Famous* and its print media equivalents thrive on.

My analysis of the secondary texts provided by newspapers concludes, then, that these contexts and metatexts made three major contributions to the reception of *Dynasty* in Norway. First, they politicized the act of viewing by attributing various extra-textual socio-cultural and political meanings to the serial. Second, they suggested an ironic reading, at first of an openly condescending kind, later more clearly camp-oriented. Third, they suggested what one may call a voyeuristic 'realist' perspective, possibly functioning as some kind of 'rational' legitimation of an interest in the show, not least for male viewers. All of these three contributions can be said to have encouraged distanciated forms of reception, where 'uncritical' emotional involvement in characters and plotlines would be restricted.

SECONDARY TEXTS: THE WEEKLIES

Norwegian weeklies, those intended for adults, come in four major categories: 'family-oriented', news/reportage, women's and men's magazines. The 'family-oriented' category is in practice also basically women-oriented, even if male family members may also read (certain parts) of them. This category also dominates in terms of total circulation. However, the single most successful magazine of the 1980s (and 1990s) belonged to the news/reportage category, where the audience address, in terms of gender, is clearly more mixed. In the following, 'weeklies' will refer to family-oriented magazines, unless otherwise specified. The reading of all categories of weeklies is generally, according to all available cultural statistics, clearly more popular with women than with men, and more popular with lower-educated people than it is with those who have university degrees.

The weeklies in contrast to the newspapers mostly promoted proximity between viewers and the fictional world of *Dynasty*. This was done by way of a more or less exclusive focus on the stars of the show, which were 'Norwegianized' in two steps. First, the features of the characters and those of the actors were blended in the coverage. Second, these mixed constructions were tied to elementary and hence common emotions, moral qualities and character traits, and to everyday practices and experiences.

This is particularly striking in the material on Krystle/Linda Evans. Krystle, as the classic suffering protagonist, was obviously central to many, particularly female, viewers of the serial (cf. Herzog 1941: 70–5 especially, the sections 'A Chance to Cry', 'If I'm blue it makes me feel better' and 'The Union of Sufferers'). While Linda Evans was often ridiculed in the newspapers for what they claimed was lack of acting skills ('both her facial expressions', p. 136), her image was uniformly positive in the weeklies.

Neither Linda Evans nor any other star of the show had an established star persona in Norway before *Dynasty* appeared. This made the construction of star images based on the fictional character both 'natural' and easy. The character had to be the starting point, since no other reference was available to the audience. As early as 24 May 1983 – a fortnight after the show premiered on NRK – 'The TV-star Linda Evans' declared on the cover of *Norsk Ukeblad* that 'I play myself'. The heading inside the magazine, on pages 24–5, was: 'I have everything – except a child'. As then known to viewers, this was also a central desire in Krystle Carrington's life in that early phase of the story. The weeklies followed up on that theme in numerous articles. Readers were informed that the house Linda Evans lives in is almost as grand and luxurious as that of Krystle Carrington. Still Linda/Krystle is just like one of us. Not only does she want a baby, readers were also presented with pictures of Linda in her kitchen, preparing vegetables for a meal, as well as of a room with a small dining table. The captions which accompanied these pictures informed readers that 'Linda loves cooking' and 'Linda serves her meals in this cosy dining room.' Almost a year later (13 March 1984), another weekly, *Hjemmet*, invited, on the cover, its readers to 'knit Krystle's sweater'. The sweater in question was, to my knowledge, never worn by Krystle in the serial, but Linda Evans wore it on the cover of that issue of the magazine. The two names were, here as elsewhere, interchangeable. Since knitwear in Norway is considered a national speciality, this particular item indicates also how Krystle was 'Norwegianized'. Her Norwegianization really took off when it was discovered that 'Evans' was derived from the Norwegian name 'Evenstad', and that Linda/Krystle had relatives in Norway. This increased the attention Krystle/Linda was given in these magazines, and also obviously contributed to strengthening the invitation to positive identification with Krystle among Norwegian female viewers.

The construction of Krystle/Linda Evans in the weeklies focused only on a few aspects of her life history and her 'real life situation'. Readers were not much informed about Ms Evans's previous work in film or other pre-*Dynasty* activities. The family- and female-oriented weeklies never mentioned her three known marriages/cohabitation relationships or other romantic affairs. (These were only mentioned in an article in a 'reportage' weekly, *NÅ* (no. 15/16, 1984), which addresses both men and women. The article announced that Linda Evans was to marry Richard Chamberlain in Malibu on Easter Sunday.) Her feminine ordinariness and her desire to become a mother were pushed forward in the articles, enhancing viewers' sympathetic identification with her (this latter term is taken from Hans Robert Jauss (1977), and I will return to his categories of identification in the analysis of the serial's text). The most recent evidence of Krystle's popularity was that she came back on the cover of *Norsk Ukeblad* in autumn 1991 (12 November) when the magazine carried a story about the mini-series *Dynasty: The Reunion* which was never shown in Norway.

The construction of Alexis/Joan Collins also had to start from scratch. A couple of her previous films – namely *The Stud* (1978) and *The Bitch* (1979) – became available in video rental stores after *Dynasty* had been on TV for a while. They could then only serve to reinforce an already established image: that of the ultimate bitch. The family- and female-oriented weeklies therefore, not surprisingly, relegated her to columns for showbiz gossip. I have not found a single article on or interview with Ms Collins in these magazines.

But, as I have mentioned, there are also weeklies that are more (if not at all exclusively) male-oriented. These presented Alexis/Joan Collins in a way which also erased the distinction between actress and character. A particular issue of *NÅ* (7 December 1983) is exemplary. The cover had photos of several of the characters from *Dynasty* in a montage with the following words in capital letters: 'DESPERATE, NASTY, UNFAITHFUL, HAPPY'. 'Unfaithful' was written in bright yellow. Each star photograph also had a word or two tied directly to it: 'Wedding' (Jeff Colby), 'Childless and bitter' (Krystle), 'Immoral' (Dr Toscanni). Next to a photo of Joan Collins, it said 'Become nasty like Alexis'. This cover is clearly related to the sensationalist, sex-focused presentation of *Dynasty* in this magazine before the show was broadcast for the first time (see the end of Chapter 2). But it is also clear that none of the emotions, events or conditions indicated are unknown in Norway. Except for the text tied to Joan Collins, there was no irony in this cover – it basically seemed to spell out what *Dynasty* was all about: emotions, events and problems in anybody's personal life.

Inside this issue, on page 3, there was a full-page picture of Joan Collins, pornographic in posture and style. She is looking at the camera, with lips parted, thighs wide open, wearing a negligée with one shoulder strap fallen down to her elbow. The following text accompanied this picture:

> The superbitch in person, Joan Collins. She is scheming and nasty towards anyone who gets in her way. A new book teaches you all the tricks you need to be a bitch. A really nasty one. It is not necessarily something you are born with. It may very well be learned.

The use of Joan Collins's name instead of Alexis gives deeper meaning to the notion of 'typecasting': complete psychological identity between actress and character is assumed.

The article which accompanied this, signed by a male journalist, was actually a presentation of an American book by Dianne Row, called, in the magazine's Norwegian translation, *The Perfect Bitch*. It seems from the article that in this book Joan Collins was compared to other 'PBs', such as Indira Gandhi, Jane Fonda, Julie Andrews (!), Nancy Reagan, Germaine Greer and a number of other women whose only common denominators could be that they are out-standing in some field and known to be more or less independent in relation to (their) men. The book's author is quoted as saying that 'It takes time, talent and class to become a PB, but when you have reached the top, it's alway you who manipulates. A PB is never manipulated.' The article is most probably a rewritten version of some American material on the book in question. The book seems related to *Dynasty* to the extent that it is about the 'bitch' character type which Alexis represented. The article is placed up front in the magazine for two reasons, first because *Dynasty* was attracting so much attention at the time, and, second, because it gave the magazine the opportunity to present the soft-porn photograph of Joan Collins (which may be a publicity still from *The Bitch*).

This particular issue of the weekly *NÅ* is representative of the way Alexis and Joan Collins was/were presented to the Norwegian audience, in both news-papers and weeklies. The star image of Joan Alexis Collins was constructed around her ruthless power lust – and her unabashed sexuality, which was also a potential instrument in her struggle for power. As with Linda Evans, particular elements of Joan Collins's real life story were left out of her star image. Even if Joan Collins may also cook now and then, she was never shown cutting carrots. Collins's relationship to her daughter, once a victim of a severe traffic accident, was to my knowledge not picked up by Norwegian media at all, even if a book was published about the struggle for her rehabilitation. Adding Collins's capacity as a mother would have made her image more complex, confusing her role as man-eating bitch. As mentioned in Chapter 1, Alexis's undivided love for her children was supposed by her creators, the Pollocks, to be her only mitigating feature. In spite of the obvious possibility of tying Alexis to Joan Collins in this too, the star image remained quite simple, even more one-sided than the fictional character.

The star images presented by the weeklies can thus be seen as hermeneutic pointers which simplified the comprehension of the primary text by reducing the antagonism between the most important female characters to a well-known conflict between 'mythical' female stereotypes: the madonna vs the whore, the mother vs the 'phallic' bitch. This stereotypical conflict is to be sure also very clear in the primary text (as my analysis will demonstrate), but the point is that the secondary texts did not add to the possibilities for ambiguities to be found in the primary text. *They did not expand the range of possible interpretations; rather they narrowed it.* And, given the social distribution of weeklies' readership, it seems likely that they contributed to a certain social pattern of reception.

This contradicts the conclusion of David Buckingham's analysis of print media coverage of *EastEnders* (Buckingham 1987: Chapter 3). Buckingham ends his chapter on the public debates and print coverage by stating that 'the sheer amount and diversity of this material' means that its 'influence is likely to be variable and, in certain cases, contradictory. Far from generating uniformity, it may well produce a greater variety and flexibility in the ways in which audiences respond to the programme' (ibid.: 152). But Buckingham does not really consider the socially differentiated readership of different print media, and differentiated audience survey data for the serial are not presented. It is thus hardly surprising that, in effect, Buckingham ends by throwing his hands in the air and saying that viewers respond to the programme in unpredictable, infinitely variable, 'selective' and 'critical' ways, whatever they read in the papers and in magazines. While I do not deny that there is an infinity of individual variations, the analysis of secondary texts is in my view particularly important to a charting of socially differentiated types of readings.

The distanciated reception of *Dynasty* mostly suggested by the Norwegian newspapers (largely ironic, with the voyeurist 'realism' version as a secondary option) was particularly appropriate for people who to some degree share the distanciated 'pure taste' (Bourdieu 1984) of the social classes with some amounts of cultural capital, i.e. internalized knowledge of legitimate culture, acquired through education or primary socialization. The kind of reception suggested by the weeklies was one of proximity, where the show and its stars were directly tied to basic moral values and character types which were known from people's everyday lives (and their imaginaries); i.e. it was particularly appropriate for people with what Bourdieu calls 'barbarian taste', which insists on treating 'art' as a part of everyday life rather than as a sphere which demands distanciated, specialized attitudes and norms.

'MULTITUDES OF MEANINGS' AS CULTURE INDUSTRY STRATEGY

The simple pure/barbaric taste pattern is of course a construction, which is not nearly as clear-cut in reality, among actual viewers. Newspapers are very widely read in Norway, and those who in Bourdieu's perspective are expected to represent 'pure taste' will in many cases and some contexts, behave as fully fledged barbarians. I am in other words speaking of tendencies, of the relative dominance of basic types of reception in particular social groups. A main point remains, though, that the number of readings of *Dynasty* are limited on a 'typological' level. The 'multitudes of meanings' so often celebrated in writings within the kind of cultural studies most heavily influenced by poststructuralism and postmodernism are not incalculable. It is only when we get to the individual viewers that the meanings produced in the encounter with a text may multiply in ways that are more or less impossible to chart. This point is parallel to the distinction in semiotic theory between connotations and associations: the first are culturally codified meanings tied to a particular sign, the latter are personal meanings that the sign 'produces' in the individual. A stylized drawing of a lion's head may connote 'power', while I may (also) associate it with a particular professor's face.

There are, however, also good reasons for questioning the idea of 'multiplicity' of readings at the individual level, the 'association'-like receptions of the text. Or rather, there are reasons to question the autonomy of all the individual varieties one may encounter among real viewers. If they can be seen as resulting from culture industry strategies, it will at least be harder to regard idiosyncratic readings of a text as significantly 'aberrant' or 'oppositional'.

All the secondary texts in effect work as parts of the culture industry's promotion of a particular television text, whether or not directly produced or controlled by its producers. They highlight particular elements of the primary text, be it certain stars, plotlines, themes or whatever. The primary text itself is constructed, not least in a case like *Dynasty*, so as to facilitate the isolation of particular elements in promotional material and in viewers' reception. All the divergent aesthetic and ideological inputs from the people who took part in the show's production, the multiple plotlines and the highly segmented narrative form, all of these provide a number of possibilities for a variety of focuses in individual viewers' attention. This is what Adorno (1991: 26–52) regarded as a result of the commodification of cultural products: a reification and fetishization of particular elements serving to obscure, not critically expose or oppose, the impoverished whole. The culture industry's products are constructed for a form of reception which is 'deconcentrated' or 'distracted'. Concentrated reception will become 'unbearable', i.e. unbearably boring. Speaking of the commercial music of his time (late 1930s), Adorno says that '[t]he usual commercial jazz can only carry out its function because it is not attended to except during conversation and, above all, as an accompaniment to dancing. Again and again one encounters the judgement that it is fine for dancing but dreadful for listening' (ibid.: 43).

It is important to note here that Adorno also found fetishization resulting from commodification and the parallel 'regressive' forms of reception in the 'high' or 'serious' cultural realm, which was increasingly being penetrated by capital. The 'star system' was, as pointed out by, for instance, Richard Sennett (1986: 287ff.), first developed in 'serious' music – cf. the role of artists such as Pavarotti and Nigel Kennedy in today's classical music scene. The main point here, though, is that this perspective differs significantly from one which regards the 'selective' readings of popular texts as 'poaching raids' in which readers/ viewers/audiences demonstrate their social opposition in 'resisting or at least evading the ideology and social meanings structured into the text' (Fiske 1989a: 144). If 'a multitude' of 'selective' readings are already intended or calculated by the industry, 'the individual's manipulation of commodity discourses may not testify to his/her autonomy and ability to react to the system, but to the achieved strategies of these discourses' (Klinger 1991: 132). As pointed out by Barbara Klinger, speaking of the role of secondary, promotional texts in relation to the reception of feature films,

> the industry which creates these commercial epiphenomena is not primarily concerned with producing coherent interpretations of a film. Rather, the goal of promotion is to produce multiple avenues of access to the text that will make the film resonate as extensively as possible in the social sphere, to maximize its audience. Promotional categories will then often tend to diversify the text by addressing several of its elements, including [. . .] subject matter, stars, and style.

(ibid.: 125f.)

My own additions to Klinger's argument here are that: (a) it is not the (primary) text which is diversified, it is its potential for 'personalized' meanings; and (b) the 'avenues of access' to the text are not multiplied in an unlimited way. As I have tried to show above, the secondary texts on *Dynasty* which appeared in Norwegian print media suggested a limited set of 'avenues of access', thus contributing to a structuration of reception which cannot be regarded as challenged by innumerable idiosyncratic, 'associative' readings. The stereotyped star images of the leading female actors/characters were open to numerous understandings and uses in the concrete contexts of individual viewers, but remained stereotypical, allowing, for instance, only a very limited number of evaluative options: one could identify and sympathize with Krystle (the madonna) or Alexis (the bitch) or both at different times.

TERTIARY TEXTS: VIEWERS' LETTERS TO THE NRK

The NRK received, according to the film and series department's archive, about 200 letters from viewers about *Dynasty* during the serial's first run, 1983–4. Copies of them were sent to me in four parcels, of which I opened three at random to study in detail the 144 letters contained in them. The letters varied a lot in length and style, from postcards to lengthy essays on *Dynasty* and related issues, from well-mannered argumentation to rude name-calling or artistically illustrated pieces of paper designed to attract attention. Most of them were handwritten personal letters, though, written in a style which varied between the personal and the semi-official prose of 'letters-to-the-editor' in regional newspapers. Female viewers were massively overrepresented among the authors. Of the letters I picked, 103 were written by women or girls, twenty by men, seven were co-authored by men and women and fourteen could not be clearly placed in either gender category. Names were erased from the copies of the letters that the NRK supplied, but gender was indicated as well as the postal code where known. Children were for the most part the only authors who explicitly mentioned their age, but an approximate age could very often be seen from the handwriting and linguistic/grammatical indicators. Forty-seven letters were from children under 20, thirty-nine from people between 20 and 50, and forty from people over 50. It seems, in other words, that children and young people were overrepresented, otherwise all age groups were fairly reasonably represented. (Children would often claim to represent their parents: 'And mum agrees completely!') In social terms, lower-class people were clearly over-represented, as revealed by orthography, grammar and other socio-linguistic markers.

The social composition of my sample of letters is related both to the composition of the audience as a whole, as evidenced in my survey, and to the social status of the act of writing to the NRK at all. It is definitely not the kind of thing intellectuals or people in high-income groups would tend to do. Writing to the NRK expresses a kind of socio-cultural naïveté, a belief in personal communication with the people in powerful positions which disregards the kind of political games at play in decisions about programming.

Upper social groups would rather write an article in a newspaper or dismiss the whole issue as being without serious interest. However, naïve people are often right, and in this case the 'flow' of letters to the NRK demanding 'more *Dynasty*' had an effect, since it could be used rhetorically as an indication of popular opinion by those in favour of the serial's continuance. Only sixteen of my 144 letters argued that the serial's run should be ended.

The letters do not provide direct insight into the way people experienced *Dynasty*, since they are to a large extent designed to be rhetorical pieces drawing on common sense or other sources of legitimation. The echoes of the public debate on the serial are consequently loud and clear. Most pro-*Dynasty* writers argue in a vaguely populist fashion against the powerful elitist and/or leftist people who want them to watch dreadful Scandinavian or European programming instead of 'the best we have ever seen on television, and we have had a set since 1961' (letter no. 34, female, 45). Letters from the far north and other areas outside the central Oslo region argue that their choice of television programming is far more restricted than that available to people living close to Sweden, and that *Dynasty* represents a kind of programming they have missed for years: 'I hear you down there won't take on any more of the *Dynasty* serial and I think like many others in the north that this is simply unfair' (letter no. 17, female, 50).

Interestingly, the tone of this and other letters of the same kind still testifies to an experienced closeness between these viewers and the NRK institution. They have missed a certain kind of programming for a number of years, but they still in a way regard the NRK as their broadcasting institution, governed by people who should feel obliged to listen to them, whom they have a right to talk to. Indirectly, this indicates that the NRK in spite of its 'elitist' programming had managed to keep quite close ties to its audiences. It seems probable that this is due to the fact that significant parts of the NRK's programming had not been seen as elitist: non-fiction domestic entertainment shows in both radio and television, children's programming and a number of feature, music and talk programmes in both broadcasting media had produced the feeling of rights, of belonging, that forms the implicit basis of very many letters and their personal, direct style.

The perception of *Dynasty* in relation to other forms of programming – the *Norwegian* 'supertext' – is in fact one of the major dimensions of the show's reception which these letters document more clearly than did the public debate, in which it was also present. It is, for instance, very clear from these letters that a major quality of *Dynasty*, in the eyes of very many viewers, was that it was not offensive in any way. It is contrasted to a wide selection of programming which obviously is regarded as disturbing in one way or another:

1 Scandinavian and continental television drama:

> *Dynasty* is *good* entertainment with superb acting, good music and a professional set of characters [*sic*]. So what do these intellectual snobs expect? Maybe something like the play in the TV theatre last Tuesday. A story

which takes place between two lovers in a railway compartment, where nearly every dialogue was stuffed with swearing and dirty talk?

(No. 28, male, 45?)

The programme-committee of the broadcasting council now wants to stop *Dynasty*, and I can only deplore that. We rarely get such good entertainment by first-class actors. When one thinks of all the incredibly dreary Finnish and East European films shown by the NRK, well, one ends up switching off the set. Can't Michelet & co. use that button for one hour each week? Also, the Swedish film last Tuesday, about the couple that travelled from Munich to Athens, really disgusting is what it was, stuffed with swearing and yelling. What is the honourable committee's purpose in airing such rubbish? I also switched off the TV yesterday, Tuesday, during the Italian TV drama *It's So Quiet Tonight*. The disgusting stuff was there already at the beginning – a man wakes up and goes to the toilet, where he is urinating for a very long time. Then I had had enough, and called on my neighbours. They had switched off, too.

(No. 39, female, 50s)

2 Certain British social-realist serials and 'intellectual comedy':

What happens in *Dynasty* is not further removed from real life than what goes on in the miserable serials from nineteenth-century England where they argue and fight and don't earn a bare living. And we're also thoroughly fed up with war and the dangers of the atomic bomb which you love to feed us with.

(No. 88, female, 20s/30s)

If the choice is between *Dynasty* and some serial about social problems or for instance mine workers, then let us ordinary people keep *Dynasty*, because that is a *relaxing* serial, and that's what we need.

(No. 125, female, 55?)

Put *Dynasty* on earlier on Saturday nights. Place instead *[Yes,] Minister* and the other *shit* late.

(No. 70, female, 10?)

3 News and current affairs:

What I am asking is that we are allowed to keep *Dynasty* because it is a wonderful serial which brightens things after all the sad news on *Dagsrevyen* [main newscast]. I am thinking of one example in *Dagsrevyen* of 22 October 1983, where we were shown corpses in decay. Unfortunately, my daughter was in front of the screen and no one was prepared for what we could see. Keep *Dynasty* which is worth watching.

(No. 35, female, 20's)

We can't be governed by a group of marxist-leninists who probably would prefer that we only watch politics, debates plus documentary programs from Nicaragua!

(No. 33, female, early 20s)

Use rather the [broadcasting] council where it is needed, make them stop all the reality, all the sad stuff because I think that has negative effects, people get broken down and nervous from watching all the sad and cruel [material].

(No. 142, female, 30s)

4 Crime/detective series:

Why do you show the series *SK917 Has Just Landed*, with two murders in a row during prime time? And there is also the crime series every Friday. Scary stuff which has nothing to do with entertainment. There are enough murders on TV. Far too many! Therefore, let *Dynasty* have a better time slot.

(No. 41, female, 50s?)

5 Sports:

Those of us who don't like sports still have to accept *hours* each week of various sportscasts, and then we are even denied forty-five minutes every week of *Dynasty*!

(No. 142, female, 30s)

The male audience can get a lot of entertainment from the numerous sportscasts or films with clown-comedy, but the female – at least the middle-aged and elderly – audience are pleased to watch beautiful surroundings/interiors even if those involved are possessed by all sorts of devilry.

(No. 125, female, 55?)

In addition to the above genres, writers mention as contrasts to *Dynasty* 'opera and string concerts', jazz, (noisy) rock and documentaries about old-fashioned, rural cultural practices. This last addition to the list was given by a (very) young female, and suggests that *Dynasty* also represented modernity and internationalism to some viewers. The list of genres selected for negative comments amounts to a characterization of the viewing experience among devoted *Dynasty* fans: the show was seen as non-provocative, non-offensive, easily understandable and relaxing. It is worth remembering here that the weekly magazines aimed at a female/family audience focused mainly on Krystle/Linda Evans as the show's icon, not Alexis. The Krystle character was hardly threatening to 'family values'.

But this is not the whole truth. As can be seen in particular, explicitly, when women contrast *Dynasty* to sportscasts, it is also a non-masculine programme.

147

Since social realism, news, current affairs, crime series and sports are all male genre preferences, and only in part ('arty' drama) marked as 'intellectual', *Dynasty* stood out as 'the only thing for women' in the context of NRK programming at the time. Very few letter-writers made the 'femininity' of *Dynasty* an explicit argument, though, even if it was clearly an underlying factor. This parallels the lack of attention to the gender factor in the public debate. If some of the intellectuals who took part in the public debate had made this an issue, they might have furnished quite a few of these letter-writers both with arguments for their letters and a possible seed of a feminist consciousness.

Many of the female letter-writers instead took the show's 'morally and aesthetically positive' image to the extreme, almost carried away by their own rhetoric:

Thank you for *Dallas* [*sic*] and *Dynasty.* If I could only describe my joy at watching everything and everybody there! The Light, the Love, *all of it!* It is life itself they show! / You people in Oslo have more than enough theatre and film. Throughout the country we are so poor in this respect! / Don't take *Dynasty* away! / It *is* a *great joy* when it is finally there! And painful that it is a week until next time. We come to love the people there! We get to see so much ex- and interiors! / I think these two films send light, yes, love into so many hearts! / Isn't that what we need just now? To balance all the dark and incomprehensible reality of our days?

(No. 47, female, 30?)

It is again worth noting how *Dynasty* is perceived as a 'balance' to a reality which is not only dark and sad, but also incomprehensible. This writer does not suggest that the broadcasting council should 'stop all the reality' (cf. p. 147), but she certainly wants to get away from reality as often and for as long as possible, and *Dynasty* offers the desired kind of escape.

Very many letters describe the particular pleasures involved in watching beautiful people in beautiful surroundings. One letter, with touchingly hopeless orthography etc., combines this and other arguments as follows:

It [*Dynasty*] is the only bright spot in life to many who only have television to take to. It is a shame to treat viewers like this [threatening to stop the serial]. It is after all they who pay for it. But we do understand you Southerners, because you have so many opportunities we in the periphery do not have. [. . .] No, you think only about yourself because there's always something for you who sit at the wheel. The rest of us must tolerate all the dirt which is shown on TV with bawling and crazy youngsters who demand everything. [. . .] Much of what is shown is just rubbish which teaches them all sorts of tricks for burglary and devilry. Take away all dirt with bad people with bad manners and ugly poor clothing. It is wonderful to watch good-looking people with clothes they can really carry. Let's have well-mannered people on the screen and things one can understand and not the kind of thing one has to think about what is behind it. I think we have a right to that since we are plagued by taxes in all directions.

(No. 115, female?, 60s)

Dynasty's visual gloss and its portrayal of an extreme upper-class lifestyle was clearly appealing to very many viewers. To most people it seems, enjoying *Dynasty* was harmless, decent family fun. According to Esther Shapiro, the show was intended to be 'like a glass of champagne among friends' (see Chapter 1), and many letters to the NRK indicate that her description was not at all inaccurate. A 12-year-old girl from the Oslo area gives a description of how watching *Dynasty* became a weekly family ritual:

The serial has become the high point of the week. On Wednesdays mother prepares a little cosy meal and the whole family gets together in front of the TV screen to meet Krystle, Blake and Alexis once again. And on Thursdays everyone talks about *Dynasty*. What will Adam be doing next week? Will Fallon marry Blake in the end? And what about Jeff, will he die? We'll never know, because this summer it will all be over.

(No. 7, female, 12)

The speculation about incest between Fallon and Blake does not seem to have bothered anyone or undermined the family ritual. *Dynasty* remained a decent family show to most fans, and only a few Christians and conservatives were worried about its moral 'messages'. Other negative comments were that the show was unrealistic, of poor artistic quality, or that it was 'cold' and like 'plastic'. Some of the most vigorous complaints about the show were, interestingly, not so much about its lack of qualities as about the disastrous effects its popularity had on social life:

Some people get so dependent on watching every episode and that is very destructive. Example 1: We were at a fortieth birthday at my sister-in-law's. Suddenly some of the guests disappeared from the party. They went to a neighbour's house to watch *Dynasty*, and then they returned to the party later in the evening. Example 2: Our son is not interested in such an unrealistic and 'sticky' [sentimental] programme. One Saturday he had invited some youngsters home for pizza and a cake he had worked hard to cook by himself. They [his guests] were very clear: we'll watch *Dynasty* or we'll go home! Only two remained after 10.30.

(No. 65, female, 30s)

The feeling that no episode could be missed, which explains the behaviour reported here, was not simply related to a fascination with the serial. It should also be understood as a result of Norwegian viewers' lack of experience with the open-ended format. If viewers watched *Dynasty* with expectations based on previous experiences of serials with an ending, it becomes more understandable that not missing anything was so all-important. And very many letters

149

explicitly demonstrate that a significant part of the audience were not aware that no ending to the serial was actually intended. The serial could not be taken off now, people continued to argue throughout its first-year run, because: 'we have got to get a proper ending' (No. 43, female, 14); 'If we can't get all the episodes, there was no point in showing any of them' (No. 45, female, 10?); 'I work [. . .] every night, Friday and Saturday are the only nights I can watch television and I look forward to *Dynasty* all the time and I find it very disappointing to have it cut off like this. Regards from a housewife! [*sic*] who does not think you are right in changing this serial so drastically in the middle of it' (No. 82, female, 55?); 'One may ask what the point is in starting a series when we are not allowed to see how it all ends' (No. 99, female, 20?); 'Can a serial really be ended without you showing all episodes completely?' (No. 114, male, 70?).

The expectation of narrative closure seems to have strengthened the show's powerful draw on many in the audience. Quite a few letters are from people who, because of work or choir practices or whatever, were unable to watch *Dynasty* when it was moved to Wednesdays, and they beg the NRK to rethink their schedule. This devotion to the serial reaches touching proportions in letters from old and disabled people who say that *Dynasty* is their only real pleasure in life. One of the strongest declarations of loving dependence on a weekly dose of *Dynasty*, however, comes from a female teenager:

> So instead of going to a discotheque (which I would have done otherwise), I watch *Dynasty*. I'll never be able to do without that film. It is the world's best film. I wildly protest that we in Norway are not to be allowed to watch the whole serial. [. . .] / From Al Corley's [Steven Carrington's] visit to Norway, he said in a weekly that he didn't understand us Norwegians who don't buy all the episodes, because it's toward the end that it gets really exciting. So there! If I had met the people who decided that we are not to see all of *Dynasty*, I'd spit in their faces. ([Deleted only by a thin pencil line; other deletions scribbled:] I'll commit suicide if *Dynasty* ends.) *Dynasty* is absolutely fantastic. [. . .] Things have started to happen already. So you MUST understand that nobody likes not to be able to see how it continues. Now I am almost crying, too, just because I'm thinking about when *Dynasty* ends.
>
> (No. 125, female, 16)

The conclusions so far to be drawn from these letters are that they (those from *Dynasty*'s fans) portray the show as being:

1 inoffensive (beautiful, morally sound, family-oriented);
2 easy to follow (compared to much European TV drama and non-fiction);
3 non-masculine/feminine (in relation to most other programming);
4 highly engaging and entertaining, with very strong emotional appeal (compared to other available programming).

The overwhelming majority of the letters were (a) in favour of *Dynasty* and (b) written by females of all ages. As noted earlier, the social background of the letter-writers can only be loosely deduced from the letters' orthography, grammar, phrasing, and direct statements about lifestyle or profession. Judging from such features, it seems clear that most of the letters (something like 75–90 per cent) came from people with lower-class or lower middle-class backgrounds. In other words, these letters were written by people who belonged to *Dynasty*'s core audiences, according to my survey. The letters have, in my opinion, proved valuable as a set of data on reception, since many of them are so direct and personal in their style that something more than just echoes of the public debate are heard in them. Still, they do not reveal anything which can really explain the fourth conclusion in the above list: the (in some cases very) strong involvement in the text.

Some letters say that the serial is 'thrilling' or 'exciting'. This may in part be tied to the activity some of them (like the one about the family viewing ritual) described, where viewers were busy trying to guess or make inferences about future developments, based on clues in each episode. Similar activities also take place during and immediately after viewing, when audience members try to fit various new pieces of story information into the picture. Schröder (1988), who interviewed twenty-five American and sixteen Danish regular viewers of *Dynasty*, has emphasized the importance of these cognitive, often collective activities. Commenting on an excerpt from an interview with a Danish working-class couple, Schröder says:

> When they follow the serial, these two people are engaged in a continuous fictional jigsaw puzzle, constantly on the look-out for new pieces, imagining what they will look like, tentatively fitting them into gaps in the narrative structure or character relations, and experiencing triumphant gratification when they succeed. Among all the aesthetic magnets built into *Dynasty* the game of fictional puzzle is one of the strongest, rewarding viewers for imaginative skill with a feeling of 'competence' and 'ingenuity'. For the regular viewer, watching *Dynasty* becomes the weekly reconstruction of self-confidence.
>
> (Schröder 1988: 63)

The centrality of this aspect of the viewing experience should not come as a surprise, if one considers how the text is constructed with particular attention to such pleasures. A steady flow of new characters and relationships, familial, professional and/or erotic, is combined with the children's theatre technique Aaron Spelling is supposedly very keen on, in which the audience is always better informed than the characters (see Chapter 1). The more interesting questions are (a) for what social reasons such a pseudo-'reconstruction of self-confidence' seems to be so important and (b) how the puzzle activities work, in relation to other dimensions of reception. Schröder himself mentions, at the end of the article quoted, that 'concentration on the unravelling of plot obscurities takes attention away from less prominent ideological strands', such as '*Dynasty*'s overall feeling of existential meaninglessness', which 'never surfaces as a compelling experience in the interviews' (ibid.: 80). The fact that Schröder wonders about this, because he thinks the meaninglessness is there in the text, is interesting, since he has also said that 'only "actual" readings count' and that 'traditional critical analysis of textual content [thus] loses any vestige of validity' (ibid.: 63). I for my part at least agree with Schröder that the puzzle activities are both important as an overt part of reception, a kind of pastime, and as a kind of diversion from less obvious, more or less unspeakable psychological forces at play on a different, 'deeper' plane.

This concerns the level of emotional and more or less unconscious involvement in characters and narrative which we call identification. My survey ended in a paradox, where the stated interest in psychological relations and 'human problems' was contradicted by the respondents' refusal to acknowledge any familiarity with the basic conflicts or problems in the serial. The kind of deep emotional interest in the show, which can be read out of so many letters to the NRK, cannot be explained in a satisfactory manner by the puzzle activities alone. And the letters themselves can only supply a few pointers in addition to those relating to *Dynasty*'s position in the Norwegian supertext as 'feminine', 'non-offensive', etc. Analysis of the serial's text is obviously needed here.

Only a few of the letters from those who were negative about the show repeat the argument in the public debate that the serial was 'unrealistic'. A female teacher, probably in her thirties, demanded: '*Let's have something which could have happened in reality!*' (No. 64). But most of those who wanted the show ended argued otherwise, on more moral grounds – infidelity and other forms of immorality were not worth watching (Nos 72, 90) – or they argued that it was simply boring and stupid (No. 67). Those in favour of the show would in many cases argue that it was realistic in one of two ways. It was on the one hand a serial which was emotionally and morally realistic, since it 'shows us human characteristics in all nuances, from the good to the worst (most devilish), just like we human beings are and will recognize ourselves in many situations. It just seems so overwhelming here because it's all concentrated in one family circle' (No. 120, male, 35?). The same position was represented in the almost ecstatic letter, No. 47 from which I quoted above: 'It is life itself they show!' (Cf. Ien Ang's (1985: 41–7) notion of 'emotional realism'.) The other position encountered is that the show is called 'educational' (*lærerikt*) (!) since 'we can now see how most corporate wealthy people [*sic*] have problems and which problems they have [. . .] and why they have so many problems' (No. 127, male, 13). As put in another letter:

> Even if not everyone in *Norway* lives like that in the everyday, it may be that some do, and it's quite fun for us to watch something other than the ordinary everyday. In addition, one can also see that the rich don't have fun all the time, either.
>
> (No. 136, female, 14)

Even if these quotes are from letters written by young teenagers, it seems probable that they reflect attitudes in their family and/or wider surrounding milieu. Adults also write that the show was informative or educational (e.g. No. 55, male, 50s). As I pointed out in my discussion of the newspaper coverage, a 'voyeur'-realist reading (*Dynasty* is about the super-rich in the US) was also suggested by newspapers. Such a reading may be tied to the idea expressed by Esther Shapiro (see Chapter 1) that part of the pleasure of the show was to be the pleasure of watching 'the rich get it'. If this idea is to work, there must be a degree of realism in the depiction of the rich; the characters have to be believable or, at least, possible representatives of the class of super-rich and powerful people everyone knows in fact to exist.

The two claims for the serial's realism might also be combined. One letter said that *Dynasty* is 'not a sunshine story, it depicts the realities of life in a particular milieu' (No. 116, female, 35?). This seems to be the perspective most viewers shared during the serial's first year in Norway: the emotional and moral situations and problems in the serial were mostly recognized in one way or another from viewers' own lives, while the general setting and particular incidents, acts and characters could be seen as representing a real world of the super-rich in the US. Both of these could well be combined in a general perception of the serial as 'great entertainment', 'somewhat exaggerated', 'containings every element of drama' or whatever the phrases would be in statements about how the serial was not to be taken entirely seriously.

The fact is that the issue of realism was not very important for the majority of those who wrote to the NRK, either for or against *Dynasty*. This is why I suggest that both forms of realism mentioned and the more playful 'this is just entertainment' attitude could well coexist in one and the same recipient. As demonstrated by Liebes and Katz (1990: 53–4), in connection with *Dallas*, viewers 'commute' between fiction and real life, both in the course of watching and in conversations afterwards. They may treat fictional characters as if they were real people, using their own real-life experience in order to understand actions or situations ('attribution'), or they may apply story elements to their own lives ('referential decoding'). Such meaning-making practices do not, however, preclude the possibility that the same recipients may, at other times, take a more distanciated position and note for instance the mechanics of the genre at work.

The notion of 'commuting' between real life and fiction is only a description of how involvement in televisual fiction takes place in time. It does not explain the degree or more precise characteristics of the involvement. Many of the letters to the NRK demonstrate a considerable intensity in some viewers' involvement, but they explain little about why some people were so emotionally engaged. There are, for instance, very few remarks about specific characters or situations, except one about Krystle: 'we sympathize with Krysti [*sic*]' (No. 58, female, 20s). Other kinds of data are obviously needed in order to explore the undercurrents of involvement.

TERTIARY TEXTS: A PERSONAL MEMORY AND AN INTERVIEW

I did not myself do any interviews with *Dynasty* viewers. My resources – time, in particular – did not allow it. Studies like those of Liebes and Katz and Schröder on the reception of *Dallas* and *Dynasty* outside the USA, the comparative Tübingen soap opera project (Seiter *et al.* 1989) and that of Andrea Press (1991), who interviewed American women about their experience of both prime-time soaps and a wide range of other programming, have in my view demonstrated that very useful information can be gathered from deep, loosely structured interviews with viewers. Such interviews could also have been combined with participant observation in the homes of informants.

If such methods – now often referred to as 'ethnographic' methodology – are clearly useful, the uses they sometimes are put to may be problematic. As in, for instance, the cases of Liebes/Katz and Schröder, 'ethnographic methodology' tends more or less to replace an attention both to the text and to certain important contextual determinations (production processes and distribution practices, US cultural hegemony, media coverage, the programme's position in relation to the supertext of which it is a part, etc.). All of this is related to an image of the viewer as a sovereign individual, at the most a member of a small (family) group, who independently 'makes meaning' in front of the small screen. The methodological individualism so characteristic of uses and gratifications research has also characterized much of the recent 'ethnography of audiences'. Issues relating to cultural power and issues of aesthetic quality have thus often suffered from inadequate attention.

On the other hand, researchers such as Seiter *et al.* and Press have shown how the interview method may contribute to a more holistic and socially critical form of audience studies. Not least, their emphasis on class differences in the perception of television programming allows their studies to raise questions concerning the quality of TV texts and the medium's relations to overarching structures of power.

I want to present two examples to indicate how reception data other than those I myself compiled may fill in the picture. One of them is a letter, written in response to an invitation to write about any memories of film and television, which was printed in a Bergen newspaper, in connection with a national project on the reception history of moving images in Norway in 1990. The other is an interview with a (completely anonymous) married couple, conducted as part of a project on wife-battering among fundamentalist Christians, the transcript of which was kindly given to me by the researcher who did it, Eva Lundgren.

The letter was from a 60-year-old literate middle-class woman, who not only had vivid memories of movies she saw as a young girl and woman, but also willingly supplied reflections on her experiences, including those of television. (The letter is published in the report series from the project, *Levende Bilder*, No. 4, 1991.)

This woman often went to the cinema a lot before she married and had children. She and her husband bought a TV set in 1961, and she talks about her favourite programmes over the years. She was for instance 'enslaved' by the British serial *Family at War* in the 1970s, but she also enjoyed (and enjoys) crime fiction, newscasts, wildlife documentaries, opera – and rock concerts! In 1990 she had had multichannel television for a while, by cable or dish. She says her husband 'dominates' the only TV set they have, but she goes through the programme listings each week and 'orders' particular programmes (*Dynasty* was among them) before her husband makes his choices. It is over sports programmes that she and her husband really differ: she hates them, he loves them. She finds it hard to explain her particular fascination with rock concerts (not shared by her husband), but compares it to what she thinks her husband has felt when watching speed skating (also mysterious to her!). She then continues:

> It is easier to explain why I was so engaged in *Dynasty*. It has to do with this ability to unconsciously identify with someone, but it was hard to decide whether one wanted to be Krystle or Alexis. For me I guess it was Alexis, I seem to remember I was a bit fresh at the time *Dynasty* was shown. The clothes, the surroundings, it is just wonderful to watch, and the problems they have – they give you exactly that feeling of complacency that your own problems are a lot easier to overcome. And then it's also joyful with all these gorgeous men, who may not be so great after all . . . and then it's also fun to notice a touch of uncertainty in one's own man about what his wife is so fascinated by. It sometimes seems as if they think they're unchangeable even after 40 years. I at least admit that I like such 'detrimental' serials, while my husband, for instance, like others, may express condescension – but missing an episode? Unthinkable.

This middle-class woman is obviously also an intellectual (her profession is not mentioned, but she does say she retreats to books, music and her typewriter when her husband watches sports on various European channels). The way she openly talks about the problems of choosing between Alexis and Krystle as objects of identification reflects a relatively high degree of self-awareness in relation to her viewing pleasures, something which is not to be seen in any of the letters to the NRK, or to the newspapers for that matter. Her leaning towards Alexis is contrary to the suggestions of the women/family-oriented weeklies, and can be tied both to various signs of her intellectual and emotional independence and probably also to her social position more generally. The way she talks about the role of television in her marriage also provides a key to the way her insistence on watching *Dynasty* also was an element in a quiet, multilayered struggle between her and her husband. Her strong fascination or rather obvious (visible?) pleasure while watching evidently likewise fed into the tensions between the two. *Dynasty* thus, in this case, was turned into an instrument in a domestic battle as a marker of feminine cultural preferences. It was the text that allowed this, its focus on female leading characters and concerns. The husband was 'allowed' to watch with her. In spite of his expressed condescension, his interest in the serial implicitly represented an acknowledgement of her preferences, thus letting her feel on top of the situation.

If there was a quiet battle going on in the above marriage, the struggles in the marriage of another *Dynasty* fan would sometimes get violent. The wife is an intelligent bank employee in her thirties, with some professonal training; her husband has a bit more education, but (in my judgement, based on the transcript of a separate interview with him) far less intelligence. They belong to a fundamentalist Christian milieu, in which biblical passages about the leadership privileges of men are taken quite literally. The wife says that 'he's a man and he's the boss and . . . and . . . and . . . it's OK that he rules, it's in the Bible, so it's OK. But it's more like the way he – I mean, what is said about God giving wisdom to those He gives power, I'm actually not always certain that's really the case.' Some understatement: her husband regularly beats her and humiliates her in various other ways. Her whole life with this man is obviously unbelievably trying, since his insecurity and narcissism are also tied to a very strict religious regime in their everyday life. Sadistic physical abuse is a normal introduction to and a regular part of intercourse. When telling the interviewer about her sexual misery, the wife on her own initiative started talking about *Dynasty*.

INTERVIEWEE: You know . . . I'm quite romantic, you see. I know that. What I like to watch on television is *Dynasty* – Blake – Krystle . . . I can see that it borders on parody, of course. But it's this 'I love you' . . . ah . . . 'tender' [quotes in English] and all that. I for my part think it's good that I dream a little about that. And in the romances in weeklies. I know all that is just crap, you know, but I for my part do in a way think it's okay to read it. The hero who comes and is warm and caring and with flowers and everything. And then I've had a little sort of experience, that sort of . . . at work, then, you see, that you meet a guy who's really okay, who was sort of a bit like that . . . who came to the bank all the time with small presents, took me out to lunch and that kind of thing which you can do without anyone noticing. And . . . and met a few times in private. . . . It . . . it was very good to experience that, to be sort of paid attention to in that way. . . . It's the best I have ever experienced. Then I understood that there was in a way something more. . . . But . . . what I wanted to say was that . . . that . . . *Dynasty* is . . . it is so that I dream that I'd like some tenderness and compassion and all that. I can see that it may be a little sentimental, but that's also part of life, in my opinion. [. . .]

INTERVIEWER: But the guy who came to the bank, you started talking about him

156

in connection with *Dynasty* . . . so you've got to have some dreams . . .

INTERVIEWEE: Yeah, of course . . . but you know – in *Dynasty* everyone's having a relationship with everyone . . . so I guess there was some association there, too, but [laughter] . . . [. . .] But mostly it was that he represented in a way . . . yes . . . he cared about *me*, you see, I was at the centre of things, and we could talk and care about each other and receive small presents.

This interview is, I think, a simply moving text about how *Dynasty* could work in relation to a bright (if confused) lower middle-class woman in an extremely repressive marriage. This excerpt indicates, first, how the show was perceived as a parallel to the serialized romances in the women/family-oriented weeklies, the relationship between Blake and Krystle in particular. Her horizon of expectations is shaped in part by such reading material. Her choice of English in the 'quotes' from the serial is also interesting here, since it points to a familiarity with English as a 'romantic language' in pop songs and films. A televisual love story in Hungarian or German would have much less of a resonance with such previous cultural experiences. The excerpt also shows how the messages from the cultural elite, in the public debate about *Dynasty*, also informed her viewing experience: she knew, and seemingly agreed, that the serial was 'close to parody', or 'crap' in a sense. This added some element of distance to her experience, but it did not at all do away with her pleasures in watching, which she openly defends. It may even seem to be the case that this element of distance inspired and enhanced her reflection on her own fascination, prompted her asking why this show was, after all, so important to her.

The very good but often suffering Krystle was an obvious object of identification for this viewer, an identification most probably strengthened by the focus on Krystle/Linda Evans in the weeklies. This viewer found her dreams of a warm and caring relationship represented in Blake and Krystle. The more brutal sides to the Blake Carrington character seem to have been overlooked, or possibly made into an attractive 'manly strength' in his basically kind personality. This viewer also has an openly admitted fascination with strong men, a streak of masochism in her, which had led her into her miserable marriage.

But second, *Dynasty* also provided something which has – at least until recently – been very rare in the weeklies' romances: a sort of legitimation for illicit, extra-marital affairs. Everybody's having affairs with each other. Women like Alexis go for the men they fancy. The interviewee initially made an association from *Dynasty*'s 'immorality' to her own affair – and then associated the affair with the show's (partial) portrayal of Blake and Krystle's marriage as an ideal relationship. She could use both dimensions of the show, easily moving between identifications with Alexis, on the one hand, and Krystle, on the other.

I believe this interview takes us quite far into undercurrents of many women's experience of *Dynasty*, also women in 'normal' relationships – or single women for that matter. The serial clearly addressed fundamental contradictions in many women's lives, ideals and dreams. Krystle and Alexis were experienced as opposites, but opposites which at least secretly could be recognized as parts of each female viewer's own psychological make-up. Young intellectual women have told me that Krystle is a bore and that an hour of *Dynasty* was endurable only if the episode contained one of Alexis's stylish exits. Krystle was more like ordinariness incarnated. I have observed laughter of ambivalent relief at Alexis's actions when watching *Dynasty* with very mature housewives (in their sixties), but, if asked, they would only admit to identification with Krystle. Very few would, like the two women I have quoted in this section, readily talk about how they actually, in a sense, could identify with and feel partially represented by both Alexis and Krystle.

The interview with the battered woman bank employee demonstrates the possibilities of the depth interview method in reception studies. But it must be added that it is very hard to get an interview like this one. The interviewer was, first, a woman, and she managed to create a very friendly, intimate 'women's talk' atmosphere. Second, this atmosphere was created over quite some time: the informant had been interviewed by the same researcher about two years earlier. It would have been virtually impossible for me or any other male researcher to achieve anything so open, so based in trust, with female informants, at least after only a very brief acquaintance.

Finally, even if an analysis of the data presented in this section has, in my view, brought us closer to an understanding of central dimensions in the reception of *Dynasty*, it has not explained how, more specifically, the serial was able to do what it did for its fans, or how it allowed them to do what they did with it. Not just any text with a good blonde and a bad brunette and a selection of good-looking men can work as *Dynasty* did. And our understanding of what went on in the reception process can certainly be further 'deepened' or improved on various dimensions which even the most successfully intimate interview cannot cover. A reminder here is the following quote from a devoted female *Dynasty* fan in her sixties, interviewed in a local newspaper in southern Norway, after a small catastrophe hit her one Saturday evening:

> I was sitting comfortably in my chair with my two cats on Saturday night. The summary of last week's episode of *Dynasty* was on the screen. Suddenly, I'm sitting there in the dark, without Krystle, Blake and all the others in front of me. The power was out in the entire Lund area. *The disappointment I felt cannot be described*, says Elisabeth Tambs of Kristiansand, who is a faithful friend of *Dynasty*.
>
> (*Sørlandet*, 21 October 1983; emphasis added)

In other words, the pleasures of *Dynasty* did in part belong to the realm of the 'undescribable', or 'unspeakable', beyond the immediate reach of an interview.

Until now, I have only analysed the texts of recipients (and, in Chapter 1, of producers). An analysis of the serial itself is what remains to be done in our exploration of the various dimensions and determinations of reception.

TENTATIVE CONCLUSIONS

In this chapter, I have discussed theoretical and methodological issues which are central concerns for reception analysis. The basic methodological idea has been that different methods can do different things, and that only an overarching, theoretically founded and guided, holistically oriented hermeneutic approach can bring together the various pieces of information into a complex, but still patterned, picture of the reception process. In its empirical parts, I have attempted to construct the chapter so that it moves from the most abstract demographic patterns of the survey, via the inputs of secondary texts in print media and *Dynasty*'s position in the Norwegian television supertext, until it zooms in on a core issue: the reasons for the intensity of involvement in the text, which was clear in particular with women and less educated groups. Less educated women would then seem to be a kind of core audience in Norway, even if the show was popular with people of many social categories and both sexes.

The pattern which emerged from the survey was one of clear educational and gender-related differences, although total audience figures were very high in the absence of an alternative channel. These differences were to a considerable degree repeated and sustained in the secondary texts, which suggested different readings of *Dynasty* to their differently profiled audiences. Still, this did clearly not lead to completely separate 'interpretive communities', or anything approaching 'interpretive ghettos'. The public debate on the serial informed every viewer, as evidenced in the letters to the NRK and various responses in the debate itself (see Chapter 2). Moreover, the promotional material from the show's distributors reached practically all viewers, not least because of its dissemination through the NRK to newspapers and weeklies which address both gender groups. Last, but not least, all viewers were watching the same primary text, made in Hollywood.

It may seem as if different audience groups were partly targeted by, and partly picked up, different clues to an understanding of the serial. Except for those who, owing to their socio-cultural positioning, taste and political convictions, flatly refused to watch this kind of 'plastic', 'garbage', etc., the various print media suggested a limited set of approaches to the serial which could all lead to some minimal legitimacy and gratification in watching it. Newspapers suggested, besides rejection of the show, that *Dynasty* was either a realistic depiction of the lives of the super-rich in the US or 'harmless entertaining crap'. The latter attitude could eventually develop into a more fully fledged 'camp' approval. Weeklies with a mixed-gender address focused on the show's sensationalist features, on Alexis and sexual 'boldness'. Weeklies with a female- and family-oriented address concentrated on Krystle and the 'decent' aspects.

All of these four perspectives, singly or in varying combinations, were evidently picked up by viewers. Personal experiences and concrete life situations played into individuals' receptions in innumerable ways, but the individual 'concretizations' were still closely tied to the thematic and aesthetic premises of the text itself, and clearly within the combined field of approaches suggested by the print media. What this leads to is the conclusion that *nothing encountered in the analysis of reception, except the refusal to watch, seriously contradicts or otherwise challenges the ideas and intentions of the producers of the show.* Their complex, but still structured, audience image was obviously successful in capturing Norwegian audiences in some way or other. No convincingly 'subversive' or 'aberrant' readings were discovered.

NORWEGIAN AND US RECEPTION, BRIEFLY COMPARED

One striking difference between the Norwegian and the American reception of *Dynasty* seems to be the relatively weak and late reception of the show as camp. This is obviously related to the difference in media culture traditions in the two countries, not least the drastic difference in television systems and television history. I am tempted to say that Norwegians were simply used to taking television seriously. They were used to informative programming, domestic and 'homelike' variety entertainment, satirical comedy and realist or avant-garde television drama. The open-ended serial was new to them, as was stylized melodramatic acting and the mix of sentimentality and general immorality. *Dynasty* appealed to them, reminiscent as it was of certain forms of well-known popular literature and film, but it took time to develop the 'entertaining crap' attitude into something in the neighbourhood of a full-blown camp appreciation in parts of the audience.

It may well be, however, that, for instance, Jane Feuer (1989) is mistaken when she treats the American reception of *Dynasty* as if the notion of 'camp' could be said to cover it more or less completely. The empirical research conducted by Andrea Press (1991) and Ellen Seiter *et al.* (1989) presents a quite different picture. Press, for instance, sums up the parts of her interviews with women of different class backgrounds which were about prime-time soaps as follows:

> In contrast to the way many middle-class women react to these shows, these working-class women find them unrealistic and tend not to like them for this reason. Some middle-class women also found shows like *Dynasty* and *Dallas* to be unrealistic, but, for the most part, were not prevented by this perception from enjoying them and from using them in a personal way, nonetheless, by becoming affectively involved with the characters, their families and their relationships with one another.
>
> (Press 1991: 114f.)

In other words, working-class women were not likely to appreciate these shows at all, and certainly not in a 'camp' fashion. The latter was more of a possibility for middle-class women, who nevertheless also in part became involved in a 'serious' manner.

The importance of social class also emerges from the study conducted by Ellen Seiter and her German colleagues. They interviewed sixty-four people (fifteen of whom were men) with predominantly working-class backgrounds, in twenty-six group interviews. The interviews were about soap operas in general, but the interviewees would mostly prefer to talk about their daytime favourites, simply, it seems, because they did not like the prime-time serials very much:

> Another aspect of their generic competence was the informed and mostly negative opinion the majority of our interviewees expressed about prime-time soap operas. [. . .] Prime-time soap operas were judged as too glittery and expensive-looking; our informants complained that they don't deal with 'the normalcy of people'. Others resented the rich veneer of prime-time soaps, their 'mega-buck characters', especially the actress Joan Collins ('She makes more in a day than I've made in my whole life').
>
> (Seiter *et al.* 1989: 235)

In other words, there was no trace of a camp reading among these working-class viewers either. A central conclusion in this study was precisely that '[c]lass, among other factors, plays a major role in how our respondents make sense of the text', and that '[t]he class discrepancy between textual representation and their personal experience constituted the primary criticisms of the programmes' (ibid.: 241). Press's study indicates that this is not so with middle-class women. Camp readings are obviously primarily middle class, and Feuer's reading of *Dynasty* is an academic version of this type of reception.

If we now compare the results of these studies of American *Dynasty* audiences with those of my own research in Norway, it seems that Norwegian working-class viewers were in fact less strictly oriented towards realist values than their American counterparts, in spite of the dominance of realist drama (serialized or single plays) on Norwegian TV prior to *Dynasty*. 'In spite of' is, I would argue, probably not appropriate here: 'because of' may be more relevant. The previous lack of melodramatic, easily 'understandable' serialized drama dealing with 'basic human problems' must have been a major factor in the immediate appreciation of *Dynasty*. The most enthusiastic fans 'saw through' the insistent display of wealth (while enjoying its 'beauty') and concentrated on the 'emotional realism' of the serial. They may, it seems, be said to have acted as American middle-class (female) viewers in that respect.

But in the Norwegian case, cultural factors outside television, which do not apply in the US, were probably important. Not only are Norwegians used to being entertained by both fact and fiction about the basic 'normalcy' of royalty, upper upper-class people, politicians and all kinds of media personalities in their popular culture. They are also used to regarding American cultural products as marked by a 'larger-than-life' aesthetic, and are used to being charmed by this quality. They simply do not expect a true-to-life realism from any American

161

media text. Such texts are seen as being fantastic rather than realist (in the narrow, naturalist sense) by definition. Hollywood film realism has probably always been experienced as marked by a particularly attractive form and degree of fantastic or 'magic' realism. Social realism comes from Europe, and Hollywood is not supposed to serve that kind of stuff. American daytime soaps would have a hard time achieving any popularity worth mentioning – they can hardly qualify as 'social realism', at least in northern Europe, and they would fail to live up to the historically produced expectations of Hollywood magic. *Dynasty* succeeded, at least in part, on the latter account.

Most of those who enjoyed *Dynasty* in Norway had also enjoyed a number of Scandinavian and British productions, along with much of the domestic variety entertainment, news and current affairs – and continued to do so. In terms of genres and styles their television experiences were much more varied than those of the average American viewers – thanks to the institution of public service television. In terms of cultural politics, what most *Dynasty* fans expressed was a desire for a widening of the spectrum of textual formats on offer, and an improvement of the democratic profile of Norwegian television's megatext, through the inclusion in programming of a serial with several 'layers' and several avenues of entrance, which proved quite uniquely able to address deep-seated dreams and dilemmas.

Judging from the total collection of reception material presented in this chapter, most of *Dynasty*'s audiences in Norway may be said to qualify as 'readers' of the kind Goethe favoured in the triad of reading practices described in the epigraph to this chapter: they enjoyed judgingly and judged enjoyingly, and thus in a sense 'reproduced the work of art anew'. But Goethe's other two categories are also represented: those who judged without enjoying and those who enjoyed without judging. These two groups are likely to be located at different ends of the socio-cultural pyramid.

So *Dynasty* was a tremendous success in Norway. But was it *good*? The issue of textual *quality* – or, rather, qualities – can only be raised after the *Dynasty* text itself, the primary text, has been more closely examined. And what did this text mean, as C. Wright Mills might have put it, in the light of 'the historical trend in our times' – and 'in what direction does this main drift seem to be carrying us'? (Cf. the Introduction of this book.)

4

RECONSIDERING (PRIME-TIME) SOAP OPERA

What is experienced by the spectator must first be constructed in the work.
(Ricoeur 1985: I, 50)

DEFINING THE GENRE

The genre 'soap opera' originated in US commercial radio of the early 1930s, when it was referred to as 'daytime (dramatic) serials'. *Painted Dreams*, 'invented' by Irna Phillips, premiered on 20 October 1930, and is usually thought of as the first instance of the genre. It proved successful, and US daytime radio was soon filled with a great number of serials of a similar kind (cf. Allen 1985: Chapter 5). With the advent of television, the genre, as well as specific serials like *Guiding Light*, made the transition to the new medium, where it soon also became the main ingredient in daytime programming.

The term 'soap opera' probably appeared for the first time in the late 1930s, in the entertainment trade press (Allen 1985: 8). 'Soap' referred to the sponsors of these serials, producers of household cleaning products like Procter and Gamble and Colgate-Palmolive. 'Opera' is, on the one hand, obviously ironic, intended to highlight the extreme distance in terms of social status between opera proper and the cultural form in question. (This is Allen's interpretation (1985: 9).) On the other hand, 'opera' might also be seen to indicate perceived similarities between the two forms, such as their emphasis on emotions and 'matters of the heart', and a leaning towards hyperbole or the excessive. Last, but not least, the importance of music, already observable in the radio serials, might well have contributed to a perceived similarity with opera. This latter factor is, significantly, overlooked in all studies of the genre, historical or contemporary.

Allen lists four elements (1985: 137–8), 'the combination of which made any given text legible to its readers as soap opera':

1 'absolute resistance to [narrative] closure';
2 'contemporary setting and emphasis on what we might call "domestic concerns"';

3 'didacticism';
4 'produced for and consumed by women . . . most of whom spent their weekdays at home, managing households and taking care of children'.

The first two of these are clearly still defining elements of the genre, if 'domestic concerns' are taken to mean more or less intimate interpersonal relationships, particularly in a family setting. The orientation towards audiences mainly comprising women, both historically and in a contemporary view, is also a fundamental feature, even if the last ten or fifteen years (since around 1980) has brought considerable changes in both subject-matter and audience address. As late as 1981, 70 per cent of the audience for US daytime soaps were women (Cantor and Pingree 1983: 118). The only one of Allen's four criteria which no longer applies is 'didacticism', since the openly didactic character of the early soaps is gone. This is, however, not to say that their didactic function for the audience is gone. As Herta Herzog concluded her 1941 study of daytime serial listeners:

> The analysis of gratifications, which was the problem of this study, has shown that the stories have become an integral part of the lives of many listeners. They are not only successful means of temporary emotional release or escape from a disliked reality. To many listeners they seem to have become a model of reality by which one is to be taught how to think and how to act.
>
> (Herzog 1941: 91)

The didactic function is, in other words, not dependent on an overt didacticism in the programme. There is little doubt that the genre has changed on this account, though.

A genre is a class or category of texts that are similar in some way(s) or other. But not just any 'similarity' between two or more texts will justify the classification of them as a particular genre. Tzvetan Todorov (1990: 17) has usefully suggested that 'we agree to call genres only the classes of texts that have been historically perceived as such', i.e. that 'the *historical* existence of genres is signaled by discourse on genres', so-called 'metadiscursive discourse'. But genres are not just meta-discursive notions. The historical evidence of the existence of genres is the starting point for the study of genre, which has as its 'ultimate objective' the establishment of the *discursive* properties that constitute a particular genre. A genre is, then, according to Todorov 'nothing other than the codification of discursive properties' (ibid.: 18). These properties have, in a semiotic tradition which Todorov attributes to Charles Morris, been thought of as either *semantic* or *syntagmatic*. Rick Altman has, in a film studies context, presented this distinction, as it operates in different approaches to film genre, as follows:

> we can as a whole distinguish between generic definitions that depend on a list of common traits, attitudes, characters, shots, locations, sets, and the like

– thus stressing the semantic elements that make up the genre – and definitions that play up instead certain constitutive relationships between undesignated and variable placeholders – relationships that might be called the genre's fundamental syntax. The semantic approach thus stresses the genre's building blocks, while the syntactic view privileges the structures into which they are arranged.

(Altman 1986: 30)

Todorov adds a third discursive level or aspect to the semantic and the syntactic, which he calls the *verbal*, which is to 'encompass everything connected with the material manifestations of the signs themselves' (ibid.: 18). This is obviously useful to general media studies, particularly because they cover more than a single medium with distinctive material properties.

Soap opera is definitely a meta-discursive, historical genre, and Allen's list of defining discursive features, cited above, combines semantic and syntagmatic properties. It does, however, leave out the 'verbal' dimension. This omission is more of a rule than an exception in television criticism, which has tended to overlook the importance of certain dimensions of the material complexity of television's electronic signifiers – such as colours and music – for the total viewing experience. These are of course also elements in the semantic and syntactic dimensions, but their role there is based in their distinct material qualities as signifiers.

A genre is a codification of discursive properties, but it is of fundamental importance not to think of genres as completely fixed sets of 'rules'. Todorov talks about genres as 'principles of dynamic production' (1990: 20), and Steve Neale stresses that genres 'are not systems', they are 'processes of systematisation' (Neale 1980: 51). This is clearly related to their role as a link between producers and audiences, as codes or conventions regulating production and limiting the possibilities of reading (see p. 177). All genres change over time, changes that may also lead to the emergence of new genres. 'A new genre is always the transformation of an earlier one, or of several: by inversion, by displacement, by combination' (Todorov 1990: 15). The soap opera was, then, not born out of nothing, but represented a particular combination of features known from previous forms of women-oriented fiction (such as the 'domestic novel') adjusted to the requirements of commercial broadcasting. It has, in turn, contributed to new forms of fiction, primarily televisual – crime or cop series like *Hill Street Blues* and 'work-place soaps' such as *L.A. Law*, which is also, in part, drawing on the courtroom drama. Demographic changes in the audience(s) and increased competition over these audiences, related to technological developments (cable and VCRs), have spurred increased experimentation with the blurring and blending of genre categories in US television over the last fifteen years. The emergence of the sub-genre '*prime-time* soap opera' can be seen as related to these developments, and simultaneously illustrates the limits to generic innovations in US television: with extremely few possible exceptions

165

(such as *Twin Peaks*) they remain within the spectrum of genres already estab-lished, at most displaying an awareness of the fact that they are inescapably based in a commercially determined, very limited set of 'formal' options. (For a partly different view, see Caughie 1991: 149.)

The very term 'prime-time soap opera' indicates the meta-discursive exis-tence of a particular class of texts as a historical sub-genre. The texts belonging to this category are then still soap operas, but of a particular kind. They can be discursively separated from their daytime relatives, first, as their name indicates, by their scheduling in the evening, the peak viewing hours. It follows from this position in the US schedule that they also are marked by much bigger budgets (higher 'production values') and a more mixed audience address, particularly in terms of gender, than daytime soaps. Prime-time soaps come in weekly episodes, not daily, and take summer breaks, unlike daytime soaps. Moreover, the prime-time soaps that appeared from about 1980 were as a rule shot on film, not video, which made for higher-quality images, and they were about richer and more powerful people than those portrayed in daytime serials. In short, they differed from daytime soaps both in the semantic, syntactic and 'verbal' dimensions.

However, the fact that they are still called soap operas points to a perception of them as a variation within the genre, not a transcendence of it. The same goes for national or cultural variations of the genre. British soaps are clearly different on many accounts from their US counterparts (they are, not least, marked by a social realism which allows working-class milieux, less-than-pretty actors and political problems to appear in them). They are still recognizable as soap operas, just as prime-time soaps are. The reasons for this can be seen from the criteria listed by Allen above. Prime-time soaps are marked by 'absolute resistance' to narrative closure; they still concentrate on 'domestic concerns', i.e. intimate personal relations primarily in a family setting; and they obviously address women viewers in a particular way in their thematic preoccupations and by prominently featuring female stars. This is why, in spite of all the differences listed above, throughout this and the following chapters I generally refer to *Dynasty* as a soap opera and discuss it in the light of theories of (daytime) soap opera.

My choice here can be further legitimated if one regards the defining features of soap opera as hierarchically ordered in terms of importance. As Christine Gledhill has pointed out, the 'initially accidental but ultimately defining feature of soap opera is its endless seriality' (Gledhill 1992: 112). Gledhill also some-what self-contradictorily says that 'the dominance of dialogue over action' is 'equally important as seriality' in defining soap opera (ibid.: 114), but this is in my view not the case. While never-ending seriality is a fundamental defining characteristic, the 'dominance of dialogue over action' in soap opera – where 'action' must mean *physical* action (see below) – can of course also be found in the tradition of realist stage drama and hence in all the cinematic and televisual texts related to it. The same goes for the dominance in terms of subject-matter of 'personal' or 'domestic' affairs. While soap operas in both daytime and prime-time versions also have these two latter characteristics (in different degrees and ways), what separates them from all other kinds of narrative fiction in all media is their 'endless seriality'. This is why the major focus in the following chapters will be on the general implications of this ultimately defining feature, and its specific version in *Dynasty*.

My perspective on the genre and my analysis of *Dynasty* will in many ways differ from and be critical of much recent criticism in this field. I argue that the critical reappraisal of the 'soap opera' genre has not only made soap operas a legitimate object of serious study and convincingly demonstrated that earlier off-hand dismissals of the genre blocked an adequate understanding of it. This reappraisal has to a considerable extent also become an uncritical celebration of the genre and, by sometimes explicit extension, the commercial broadcasting institution which produced/produces it.

My 'negative' perspective on the genre will tend to dominate because of this discursive situation in the field. As noted in Chapter 2 above, my arguments when involved in the Norwegian public debate about *Dynasty* had a different emphasis, geared to support those in the audience who warmly welcomed this kind of entertainment in their struggle with representatives of the cultural elites. Outside that particular context, I find it important to keep in mind what Todorov, among others, has underlined:

> Like any other institution, genres bring to light the constitutive features of the society to which they belong. [. . .] [T]he existence of certain genres in one society, their absence in another, are revelatory of that [society's] ideology and allow us to establish it more or less confidently.
>
> (Todorov 1990: 19)

Dynasty's core audiences in Norway belonged to the less-privileged social categories in terms of class and gender. The socially and intellectually responsible critique of popular genres is not a critique of their audiences; it springs from the conviction that these audiences deserve better.

LIBERALIST RHETORIC IN THE REVALIDATION OF SOAP OPERA

Horace Newcomb was a pioneer in the new, less prejudiced television criticism which emerged in the 1970s. He generally advocated a shift to less snobbish, more open and positive perspectives on the medium and its possibilities. In the chapter on soap operas in his *T.V.: The Most Popular Art* (1974), he pointed out some ways in which he thought this genre was making the most of the aesthetic premises of the television medium. Its small screen suggested 'intimacy', and broadcasting continuity from day to day, week to week, etc., suggested serial form. The soap opera genre is thus, according to Newcomb, particularly well suited for treating character development and interpersonal relations over time, and because of this it could also produce greater 'audience involvement, a sense of becoming a part of the lives and actions of the characters they see' (Newcomb 1974: 253, quoted in Modleski 1982: 87).

The problem with this defence of soap opera is, however, that seriality as such (presentation of a narrative in several instalments) and 'intimacy', either in terms of subject-matter or visual style, are not specific to soap opera form. Both elements may be found in a number of other genres, within and outside television. It is consequently somewhat unclear what Newcomb meant precisely by the term 'soap opera' at this point. As late as 1983, he included narratively closed mini-series like *Roots* and *Rich Man, Poor Man* in the soap opera category, talking about 'mini-series soap opera' (Newcomb 1983: xxxi). To me, this is clearly an unhelpful confusion of generic categories.

Later in the 1983 article, however, Newcomb directly addresses soap opera proper, and suggests a politically significant validation of its particular narrative form. It is well worth noting in which decade he was writing: the 1980s, the decade of liberalism in economic and social politics and postmodernism in intellectual fashion. Newcomb says that prime-time and daytime never-ending serial narratives share 'the sense of openness, the rejection of inevitability and closure, of endings anticipated or already known', and, he adds, 'the triumph of the soap opera form is that it engages us in the sense of progressive unfolding, emergence, growth and change' (Newcomb 1983: xxxiii–iv). These very positive characterizations (note the optimistic and organic metaphors) are echoed in almost all later scholarly critical writing on soap opera. It is again and again argued, as I will show in later sections, that soap operas inherently, simply because they never end, are ideologically 'open' and thus work to support socio-cultural change. A main point in my own analysis and argument is therefore to demonstrate that narrative 'openness' in the sense of an always deferred ending, does *not* imply ideological or 'perspectival openness' (Allen 1985: 174). In line with Ellen Seiter (1981), I will argue that soap operas, including *Dynasty*, are 'closed' texts in Umberto Eco's (1984) sense, and that the best critics can do is to suggest 'possible ways that women can read soap operas subversively – ways that do not exclude or negate the widespread negative interpretation of soap opera viewing as escapist fantasy for women working in the home' (Seiter 1981, quoted in Allen 1983: 100).

Soap opera has from its very emergence as a genre been tied to commercial broadcasting, where programming basically serves to deliver audiences to advertisers. Since soaps historically are so clearly linked to the fundamental principles of commercial broadcasting, it might seem to follow that this latter institutional form must share their presumed virtues. While this is most often only an unsaid premise or implication in celebrations of the genre, it sometimes also surfaces in more direct ways. Sandy Flitterman-Lewis, for instance, once expressed the connection with the following selection of liberalist and post-modernist keywords, where, also typically, US commercial television in effect becomes confused with the medium's 'essence': 'Based on ambiguity and lack of closure, segmented both diegetically (within the narrative) and intertextually (the commercials, the different programs), the soap opera, as TV's own apotheosis, has openness, multiplicity, and plurality as its aims' (Flitterman-Lewis 1988: 120).

Flitterman-Lewis is an accomplished feminist film scholar. She is not the only feminist who has turned critical interest in a revalidation of a historically despised, woman-oriented genre into a celebration of the industry that produced and produces the genre. Martha Nochimson, who was herself involved in soap production for years before turning to academia, presents in her recent book her project as that of giving a voice to a repressed, marginalized group – soap opera producers. Nochimson's rhetoric is perhaps more politically 'correct' than politically liberalist, but her support for the industry and its products is equally clear:

> Unfortunately, the people who make soap operas do not themselves have easy access to language that allows them to conceptualize what they are doing. This is a situation common to all marginalized endeavors and peoples. People who do not fit the mainstream categories are 'stuck' trying to express their own desires and to organize their experience with a set of categories that pointedly exclude them. In the soap opera community, the result has been that the inordinate power of groundless mainstream ideas has riddled that community with cynicism and self-deprecation, obstructing self-knowledge among the majority of soap opera professionals, even those who are excellent at what they do.
>
> (Nochimson 1992: 4)

The starting point for the feminist reconsideration and revalidation of the soap opera was, however, quite differently ambiguous. The next section is a discussion of Tania Modleski's pioneering article, 'The Search for Tomorrow in Today's Soaps' (1982: 85ff.), which interestingly presents both a negative and a positive perspective on the genre. It was the negative one that got lost in soap criticism throughout the 1980s.

THE FEMINIST DILEMMA: TANIA MODLESKI'S TWO ARGUMENTS

Since soap operas were originally intended for an audience of women, and their audience, particularly for daytime versions, has remained overwhelmingly female, feminists have of course taken a special interest in the genre and provided much illuminating work in the fields of both textual analysis and audience studies. The feminist discourse on soap opera is interesting not least because it is profoundly marked by feminism's uneasy balance between its support of women as they are in patriarchal society and its desire to change the same 'ordinary' women, their conception of themselves and their socio-cultural position (cf. Brunsdon 1991, which thoughtfully discusses implications for feminist pedagogical strategies). The dilemma is in principle the same as that faced by any other theoretically informed emancipatory political movement, a fact which may make it less unique but hardly less important.

Tania Modleski's seminal article (1982: 85ff.) displays the dilemma in a quite exemplary manner. In the first part of the article, Modleski provides an incisive analysis of, first, 'the sense of powerlessness induced by soap operas' (ibid.: 91). She says the 'subject/spectator of soap operas' is 'constituted as a sort of ideal mother: a person who possesses greater wisdom than all her children, whose sympathy is large enough to encompass the conflicting claims of her family (she identifies with them all), and who has no demands or claims of her own (she identifies with no character exclusively)' (ibid.: 92). Modleski goes on to argue that soap opera narrative 'by placing ever more complex obstacles between desire and fulfillment makes anticipation of an end an end in itself'. Therefore, '[s]oap operas invest exquisite pleasure in the central condition of a woman's life: waiting – whether for her phone to ring, for the baby to take its nap, or for the family to be reunited shortly after the day's final soap opera has left *its* family still struggling against dissolution' (ibid.: 88). Soap operas 'constantly' present the desire for a 'just solution' as 'unrealizable, by showing that conclusions only lead to further tension and suffering. Thus soap operas convince women that their highest goal is to see their families united and happy, while consoling them for their inability to realize this ideal and bring about familial harmony' (ibid.: 92). And in connection with her analysis of the obligatory character of the villainess, she concludes:

> Since the spectator despises the villainess as the negative image of her ideal self, she not only watches the villainess act out her own hidden wishes, but simultaneously sides with the forces against fulfillment of those wishes. As a result of this 'internal contestation', the spectator comes to enjoy repetition for its own sake and takes her adequate pleasure in the building up and tearing down of the plot. In this way, perhaps, soap operas help reconcile her to the meaningless, repetitive nature of much of her life and work within the home.
>
> (ibid.: 97)

This uncompromising critique of how soap opera narratives may contribute to the perpetuation of women's repression is, however, followed by a very different argument in the second half of the article. Here Modleski argues that the never-ending soap opera opposes the dominant 'masculine' narrative form and 'may be in the vanguard not just of TV art but of all popular narrative art' (ibid.: 87). Soap opera form thus suddenly becomes inherently 'feminine' and 'avant-garde'. She refers favourably to Marsha Kinder, who in a review of Ingmar Bergman's *Scenes from a Marriage* suggested that the 'open-ended, slow-paced, multi-climaxed' structure of soap opera is 'in tune with patterns of female sexuality' (quoted in Modleski 1982: 98). The actual variations in the patterns of female sexuality aside, this clearly points to an untenable essentialist conception of narrative form. Via a clearly strained, very abstract and some-what cryptic reference to Luce Irigaray, Modleski then also sees the narrative structures of the soap opera as a model for future feminist art:

> Luce Irigaray, describing woman's 'rediscovery' of herself, writes, 'It is a sort of universe in expansion for which no limits could be fixed and which, for all that, would not be incoherence.' *The similarities between this description and soap opera as a form are striking.* They suggest the possibility that soap operas may not be an entirely negative influence on the viewer; they may also have the force of *negation*, a negation of the typical (and masculine) modes of pleasure in our society.
>
> (ibid.: 105; first emphasis mine)

Instead of concretely exploring this 'negation' any further, for instance in relation to the first part of her own article, Modleski then simply says that what Dennis Porter (1982: 124) has called soap opera's 'process without progression' is 'endorsed by many innovative women artists' (Modleski 1982: 106) and exemplifies this with a quote from a (female) critic's 'praise' of (Russian-born, French) author Nathalie Sarraute's work. The critic, Mary Ellmann, says that Sarraute is not 'interested in the explicit speed of which the novel is capable, only in the nuances which must tend to delay it', that Sarraute is 'entirely anti-progressive' and 'dislikes' the 'haste' of 'ordinary dialogue' (quoted in Modleski 1982: 106). Modleski concludes:

> Soap opera is *similarly antiprogressive.* Just as Sarraute's work is opposed to the traditional novel form, soap opera is opposed to the classic (male) film narrative, which, with maximum action and minimum, always pertinent dialogue, speeds its way to the restoration of order.
>
> (ibid.: 106; my emphasis)

If texts could really be charged with speeding, then Modleski's would obviously be in for a ticket. Nathalie Sarraute belongs to the group of French modernist writers associated with the term *nouveau roman*, the 'new novel', along with male authors such as Alain Robbe-Grillet. An article in which she speaks about her work and her understanding of literature can be used in any under-graduate class as an illustration of what a classic modernist conception of art is all about:

> I am convinced that the work of novelists precisely consists in research. And through this work of research they strive to uncover an unknown reality. [. . .] The newer the reality which is uncovered by the literary work is, the more unusual its form must be, and the greater strength it needs to penetrate the thick screen which protects our emotional habits against any disturbance. This protective screen is made of the illusions, the clichés, the conventional and prefabricated ideas which continuously place themselves between the reader and the new reality one shows to him, and

between the author and the reality he wants to uncover. [. . .] These clichés, these sanctioned emotions and these learned and serially fabricated sensual impressions push themselves on us everywhere, from everything we hear and from everything we see, from songs, films, advertising, press, radio, conversations and chatting, and from a rudimentary knowledge of psychology acquired through the reading of popular science books and literature without value.

(Sarraute 1966: 107f.)

There are, in other words, reasons to suspect that Sarraute would be amazed and (hopefully) amused by the idea that her form of writing is paralleled in soap operas. Her work is not only tied to the particular form of seemingly 'plotless' novels characteristic of the *nouveau roman*, which 'may seem as [. . .] exclusively consisting of objects described for their own sake, independent of any human presence' (Robbe-Grillet 1966: 113). It is also, explicitly, regarded as a continuation of a much longer and wider modernist tradition (J. Joyce, M. Proust, V. Woolf, etc.) of resistance to the traditional (nineteenth-century) novel and its dependence on plot, a resistance primarily expressed in texts directly or indirectly being 'about' narrative, playing with minuscule elements of plotting and readers' expectations of them. To say that soap opera and the *nouveau roman* are 'similarly anti-progressive' is consequently a remarkable jump to a clearly impossible conclusion based on an abstract, completely decontextualized and quite arbitrary similarity. Soaps are obviously not at all 'plotless'. As Modleski herself puts it, they 'appear to contain a ludicrous number of climaxes and actions: people are always getting blackmailed, having major operations, dying, conducting extramarital affairs which inevitably result in pregnancy, being kidnapped, going mad, and losing their memories' (1982: 106). This extreme plotting is a basic feature of soaps. Modleski tries instead to convince us that it 'only' serves, 'just as in real life', to 'provide convenient occasions for people to come together, confront one another, and explore intense emotions' (ibid.). If it is not essential to the genre, can one imagine a soap without it? Nathalie Sarraute does without it, but would soap audiences be able to? The cynicism or thoughtlessness of the remark that, say, death and psychiatric illness are in real life only convenient occasions for exploring interpersonal relationships and intense emotions is also worth noting in passing. This cynicism is that of the soap opera genre, not (hopefully) that of its audiences.

Importantly, I am not saying that there are no links between the aesthetic and philosophical concerns of modernist art and the modern 'everyday' concerns addressed by soap opera and other forms of popular narrative. They may well spring from common sources in the socio-cultural conditions of modernity. But the major differences in the ways these categories of texts address and work with these conditions need to be thoroughly considered before parallels are pointed out and particularly before near complete identity is asserted. Modleski's attempt to 'dignify' soap operas by assuming a partial formal identity between them and prestigious 'high art' textual forms is problematic in the same way as the far too easy talk about 'self-reflexivity', 'distanciation', etc. in much recent writing about popular culture. (Cf. John Caughie's (1991) discussion of problems involved in such a transference of terms from avant-garde aesthetics to television.) Such strategies for revaluation of popular culture tend not only to confirm unwittingly the existing textual hierarchies, which there may be some good reasons to do, but basically fail to identify and investigate the specificity of popular genres – what they can do which no other genres do, and what they do for some audiences that other genres do for other audiences.

The second problem with Modleski's argument is her short-hand gendering of narrative forms. Nathalie Sarraute is a woman, therefore it is implicitly assumed her way of writing is 'feminine'. The simple fact that the nineteenth-century, 'progressive' novel was to a very large extent written by women and primarily enjoyed by women readers disappears. The work of Agatha Christie, Patricia Highsmith, Dorothy L. Sayers and dozens or hundreds of other more or less prominent female writers of detective novels all over the western world must be seen as essentially 'masculine', and so must 99 per cent of whatever else women write and read. The same percentage would be an adequate estimate of the proportion of melodramatic, clearly plotted and quite fast-paced films among all those enjoyed by women of the world over the last ninety-five years. How slow and 'anti-progressive' is the world's largest-grossing picture, *Gone With the Wind*, or a classic woman's picture such as *Stella Dallas*? The idea that the 'classic (male) film narrative' always has 'maximum action' and 'minimum, always pertinent dialogue' is clearly a misunderstanding if one looks at hundreds of Hollywood romantic comedies with abundant chatting, or an often action-poor, ambience- and talk-rich category such as *film noir*. Turning to theatre, is the realist tradition there 'feminine' since there are few fist-fights and a lot of talk in plays by Chekhov, Ibsen or Bernard Shaw?

The quite paradoxical arguments of Modleski's very influential article are reflected in the divided reception of it. On the one hand, Modleski has been criticized for portraying the implied or model female viewer of soap operas as 'curiously passive and isolated', as 'distracted, lonely, unable to make judgements or to discriminate' (Geraghty 1991: 45). On the other, her article is invoked as a major source of inspiration by, for instance, Martha Nochimson (1992: 194) in her passionate advocacy of soap opera as a 'resistant feminine discourse' (ibid.: 2), based in an idea of a specifically 'feminine syntax' (ibid.: 193). This idea quite clearly derives from an essentialist conception of femininity, even if her argument on the issue of essentialism leaves it to the (natural) sciences to decide if gender is 'innately determined': 'We simply are not scientifically equipped to decide between essentialism and constructionism' (ibid.: 3). Nochimson is, however, not in the least doubt about the qualities of soap opera (Modleski's deep ambivalence is long gone): 'When things are working well, the daily soap opera is a triumph of fresh and unorthodox

173

narrative made possible by a marriage between technology and the spirit of the creative artist' (Nochimson 1992: 9).

ON BRITISH CONTRIBUTIONS: CHARLOTTE BRUNSDON AND CHRISTINE GERAGHTY

British work on soap opera tends to be much more careful in its appraisal of the genre's merits. Its 'femininity' is, for instance, in an early piece by Charlotte Brunsdon, tied to its demand on 'cultural knowledge of the socially acceptable codes and conventions for the conduct of personal life', so that its particular appeal to women is related to historically and culturally produced

> feminine competencies associated with the responsibility for 'managing' the sphere of personal life. It is the culturally constructed skills of femininity – sensitivity, perception, intuition and the necessary privileging of the concerns of personal life – which are both called on and practiced in the genre.
> (Brunsdon 1983: 80f.)

Essentialist conceptions of gender and the gendering of texts are explicitly countered both here and in other British contributions to the field. But also in British work one finds a preoccupation with the 'openness' of soap opera.

In tune with, for instance, Horace Newcomb, Christine Geraghty once made not just the lack of closure but 'the sense of a future' a defining characteristic of the continuous serial: 'The apparent multifariousness of the plots, their inextricability from each other, the everyday quality of narrative time and events, all encourage us to believe that this is a narrative whose future is not yet written' (Geraghty 1981: 11). More recently, in her useful comparative study of British and US prime-time soaps, Geraghty takes this view a step further, talking about the 'utopian possibilities' inherent in the never-ending serial's form. She says that 'soap's major contribution to women's fiction lies in its ability to handle change' (Geraghty 1991: 128). Particularly in view of the political scene of the 1980s, she says that

> in reflecting on a period, when public rhetoric took on a harsh and intolerant note, an eagerness to condemn and a refusal to deviate from a fixed position, we might be grateful that at least one form of popular culture in the eighties gave its audience the experience of accommodating and responding to the possibilities of change.
>
> (ibid.: 130)

This latter point simply seems to make soap opera's never-ending narrative structure a form of opposition against the rigid conservatism of Thatcher's and Reagan's decade. Such a conclusion is only possible if, fixated on the fact that soap narratives never end, one disregards features of these texts which work to contain the possible ideological instability of such a narrative form.

A FORGOTTEN GENERIC FEATURE: REPETITION

If we look again at Geraghty's first (1981) formulation of how the never-ending structure supposedly conveys a 'sense of a future', we notice how she talks about the *apparent* multifariousness of plots. The pervasive element of *repetition* in soap opera narratives, produced by the regularity of its scheduling and the never-ending, multiple-plot structure, is in fact the main focus in her 1981 article. She talks about how various strategies (such as the cliffhanger, moments of temporary resolution and the use of the serial's past) are employed to 'prevent a sense of complete repetition' (ibid.: 18). In the conclusion of her article she says the soap format allows 'sufficient flexibility to be able to present *apparently* different situations' (ibid.: 25; my emphasis).

It is striking – and actually symptomatic – that Geraghty ten years later devotes much less attention to the issues of repetition and the continuity of the fundamental structures in soap worlds. Chapter 7 of her book is about how soaps 'have attempted to articulate social change through issues of race, class and sexuality' (1991: 165), and deals explicitly with this problematic. But she is basically only able to show that 'social issues' are in different ways articulated in soaps, not that their narrative 'openness' actually allows these issues to be presented as disruptive or indeed subversive, either to the soap opera worlds or the world outside. Her book certainly reveals a greater awareness of this quite fundamental issue than more naïve writing about the genre. But the main impression is that repetition is now less regarded as an aesthetic and political problem than a source of politically innocent pleasure:

> It is easy to underestimate the pleasure of predictability but very often the repetition of plots, so tedious to the casual viewer, is part of a pattern based on the well-established character traits of particular individuals. To see Cliff Barnes embark on yet another ill-fated attempt to foil JR, or Angie in *EastEnders* begin another emotional and fraught battle with her husband, Den, is to set off on a roller coaster whose ups and downs are reassuringly predictable because the viewer has been gaining knowledge of them for years. Familiarity with the characters allows the viewer to bring meaning to the narrative rather than having to rely on what is shown in a particular episode. It is the viewer who brings richness and density to material which on the surface can look thin and unrewarding.
>
> (Geraghty 1991: 15)

This passage is to me clearly paradoxical. How can the 'casual viewer' find any repetition at all – if it is not constant? How can the impression of repetition be lessened if one has seen the same plot unfold several times before, and all ups and downs are 'reassuringly familiar'? And, finally, how can the experience that one is watching yet another repetition bring not just variation but 'richness and density' to the same 'thin and unrewarding' stuff?

It is in short as if Geraghty tries to avoid the conclusion which is so very close at hand, that a – possibly the – primary ingredient in the pleasure of watching soaps is the reassuring one of repetition of the already familiar. As already Herzog concluded from her interviews with fans of radio soaps, 'The desire to have things "go on" seems really a desire to have them continue in the expected way, along accepted patterns' (1941: 84). Even when Geraghty tries to balance the impression that repetition is a fundamental ingredient in soap opera by saying that soaps also invite the audience to 'relish change and disruption', she immediately adds that 'what happens may be predictable, but the interest lies in the many variations on how it will happen' (Geraghty 1991: 15), thus clearly modifying the degree of actual 'change' and 'disruption' involved. In short, little is provided which can counter the optimistically conformist summary of dozens of (radio) soaps given by the fans interviewed by Herta Herzog. They said the stories were all about '*getting into trouble and out again*' (Herzog 1941: 66). One is left wondering what Geraghty more precisely means by 'accommodating and responding to change', and one may notice that for instance 'realizing the need to initiate and organize lasting social change' is not mentioned as a significant ingredient or outcome of the soap opera experience.

Geraghty's reduced attention to the issue of repetition from 1981 to 1991 is on the whole indicative of a general tendency in that decade's critical revaluation of soap opera. Robert C. Allen (1985) dismisses the issue after briefly stating that the individual products of the cultural industries cannot be identical, as those of other industries can. Every episode of a soap opera must be 'the same, but different' (ibid.: 47). Jane Feuer (1984) does not mention repetition at all. She claims that since 'we know that every happy marriage is eventually headed for divorce' (ibid.: 13), it may be argued that soap operas 'offer a criticism of the bourgeois marriage' (ibid.: 14). But she does not consider the fact that soap characters keep (re)marrying all the time, thus maintaining marriage as a primary goal. In general, one may say that if repetition is mentioned, it is not considered a problem and quickly dropped as an issue except with regard to the regularity of viewing, which is seen as an enabling factor for the entire textual regime of soaps.

THE MEANINGS OF REPETITION

My intention here is certainly not to claim that repetition is uniquely characteristic of soap opera. On the contrary, repetition is in a general way pervasive in almost all cultural production, high and low. One may point to the music of J.S. Bach or Mozart, or the literary texts of acknowledged serious writers as diverse as Balzac and Borges: repetition is obviously a central element at some level or other. What remains an issue is what kinds of repetition we encounter in each different case, what is repeated and how repetitions affect the respective textual universes *in toto* and their possible socio-cultural functions. Adorno (see above, Chapter 1) claimed that the simple form of repetitiveness characteristic

of the 'standardized' products of the cultural industry was their totally dominating structural feature, geared towards producing conformity, influencing
audiences basically to accept their position in the world and the social system
at large. Ever since this allegation was put forward, it seems to me that a socially
and politically inflected analysis of any text or class of texts will have to consider
the specific function of structural repetitiveness in each case.

The notion of genre itself is defined by the repetition of certain textual
structures and elements from one text to another. Such repetitions never
exclude difference, since each individual text has to be perceived and appreciated in a double relationship of similarity and difference to other instances of
the genre. This 'difference in repetition' is why genres are always in a degree of
change, of process (cf. Neale 1983: 50f.). The limits to these changes exist in a
genre's pragmatic character, its status as a kind of agreement between producers
and audiences on how texts of a certain kind are to be constructed. Genres are
not only a set of texts which share certain discursive properties, they are also 'a
coherent and systematic set of expectations', and thus 'a means of containing
the possibilities of reading' (ibid.: 55) for the producers in question. The media
industries may try out variations and new genre formulas, constructed from
previously existing ones, and the response of audiences decides if they are
successful, i.e. are accepted, strike an acceptable balance between repetition
and innovation.

The pleasure in repetition is a pleasure of recognition. The audience of a
genre text 'continuously recover, point by point, what they already know, and
what they want to know again' (Eco 1985: 164). While such pleasures are well-
known features of both children's culture and preindustrial, oral folk cultures,
Umberto Eco has suggested a historical explanation for the obviously great
need for such pleasures among adults as well in modern, industrialized societies:
that 'the social change, the continuous rise of new behavioral standards, the
dissolution of tradition' in modern societies 'require a narrative based upon
redundancy', which appears as 'an indulgent invitation to repose, a chance of
relaxing' (ibid.: 165). This is also why, since romanticism, a constant transgression of 'the expected', of established genres, structures and devices, has been
regarded as a hallmark of 'authentic' art, and the reason why the repetitive
character of, say, episodic series, has been regarded with such suspicion by all
kinds of radical critics. The 'relaxation' offered by the recognition of familiar
patterns is likely to represent a comforting 'repose' in dominant ideologies,
and the constant repetitions of these patterns an effective pedagogical or
propagandistic practice of the brainwashing kind.

It is obvious that the never-ending soap opera form works in ways that
differ significantly from the episodic series. Adorno's paradigmatic critique of
early television episodic narratives appears inadequate and outmoded in
relation to serial form. His reasoning in the following passage in fact seems
to support those who view soap operas as marked by profound 'openness' and
'multiplicity':

The popular or semi-popular novels of the first half of the nineteenth century, published in large quantities and serving mass consumption, were supposed to arouse tension in the reader. Although victory for the good over the bad was generally provided for, the meandering and endless plots and subplots hardly allowed the readers of Sue and Dumas to be continuously aware of the moral. Readers could expect anything to happen. This no longer holds true. Every spectator of a television mystery knows with absolute certainty how it is going to end. Tension is but superficially maintained and is unlikely to have a serious effect any more. On the contrary, this longing for 'feeling on safe ground' – reflecting an infantile need for protection, rather than the desire for a thrill – is catered to. The element of excitement is preserved only with tongue in cheek. Such changes fall in line with the potential change from a freely competitive to a virtually 'closed' society into which one wants to be admitted or from which one fears to be rejected. Everything somehow appears 'predestined'.

(Adorno 1991: 138)

For what seem to be mostly rhetorical reasons, Adorno here emphasizes the degree of non-schematic 'innovation' in the nineteenth-century feuilleton novels of Sue and Dumas, much as contemporary critics emphasize that of soap operas. According to Adorno's reasoning here, these critics actually have a better case than him, since soaps, contrary to feuilletons, never end. In my view, both are wrong. According to Umberto Eco, 'the nineteenth-century feuilleton and contemporary mass media [only] use *different* devices for making the expected appear unexpected' – 'Eugène Sue pretended not to know in advance what her readers suspected' (Eco 1985: 165). The point is that both literary feuilletons and televisual soaps strive to make the expected *appear* unexpected, i.e. to cover up their repetitiousness. Adorno's critique of the episodic series can surely not be directly transferred to the never-ending serial, but his basic concerns in the piece quoted above may still apply. My arguments in this and the following chapters will be that soap operas and *Dynasty* in particular:

1 in fact both rely on the reassuring repetition in their scheduling and contain a high degree of narrative repetition of a few basic plots; and
2 that instead of providing 'safe ground' through final narrative closure, they provide it (a) by demonstrating that endings do not really matter because everything remains basically the same anyway; (b) by providing an experience of wholeness 'over' and 'across' the narrative(s) by various formal means; and, finally, (c) by offering various additional aesthetic devices which distract viewers' attention from the significance of the disturbing underlying premises of the narrative(s) which still work as 'bait', as sources of fascination.

These texts themselves claim to be ever ongoing, continuously changing as weeks, years and decades go by, never ending and never really repeating themselves. Criticism which more or less exclusively focuses on and celebrates the 'openness, multiplicity and plurality' of these texts not only repeats the claims of the texts themselves, but also provides a classic ideological cover-up for a cultural production which, particularly in the US TV institution, openly serves the at least slightly dubious main function of producing happy, obedient consumers.

In my analysis, then, I not only want to draw attention to fundamental elements of repetition in the narrative. In accordance with points 2 (b) and (c) above, I will also try to point out other ways in which 'perspectival openness', 'change' and 'disruption' are contained by rarely focused aesthetic means, registers of the text which are often overlooked by a hermeneutic fixated on the image and dialogue. I believe something like the 'erotics of art' once suggested by Susan Sontag (1966: 14), which was to deal with the wider register of sensual experience involved in the reception of art, is needed also if we are to understand the televisual experience in general and not least that of *Dynasty*. Seemingly 'non-meaningful' elements of the text definitely helped to make the show the ideologically safe 'glass of champagne among friends' (Esther Shapiro) it was intended to be, so that what was probably a majority of its Norwegian viewers could regard it as safe family entertainment. This is also why a whole section will focus on the use of music in film, television – and *Dynasty*.

But first, the following section will take a closer look at a particular attempt to elevate soap operas to the higher levels of cultural respectability, also in order to introduce a couple of analytical terms important to my own analysis.

THE QUESTION OF 'PARADIGMATIC COMPLEXITY'

In his otherwise well-informed and in many ways recommendable study of soap operas, Robert C. Allen (1985) unfortunately misunderstands a fundamental theoretical distinction between two dimensions of texts. The misunderstanding is important, because much of his attempt to build an aesthetic and political respectability for the genre hinges on it. Since the argument concerns absolutely central features of the soap opera genre, and the theoretical distinction in question also informs my own analysis in the sections that follow, I will discuss Allen's argument in some detail.

Allen starts out by briefly referring to the theoretical insight from structural linguistics that 'language and narrative are structured along two axes: a syntagmatic (combinatory) axis and a paradigmatic (associative) axis' (ibid.: 69). Allen goes on to point out correctly that the syntagmatic axis in soap operas is marked by the lack of ultimate narrative closure, but then also adds that an often overlooked feature of the genre is its 'paradigmatic complexity – a complexity that makes the soap opera unique among visual narratives and unmatched in literary narrative except for the most elaborate of epic novels' (ibid.). Complexity in a text is traditionally considered a central criterion of artistic quality. But Allen's bold claim for soap opera's unique complexity

179

immediately boils down to the trivial fact that these serials present a 'large community of interrelated characters' (ibid.). Equating a large number of characters with 'paradigmatic complexity' leads Allen astray when he uses this misunderstanding in an attempt to explain why viewers are able to tolerate what he terms 'inter-' and 'intraepisodic redundancy'. A rather long quote is needed in order to show how Allen's argument works – and fails:

> As an illustration of intraepisodic redundancy, let us presume that in scene one of a soap episode we learn from a conversation between Lucy and her friend Debbie that Lucy is pregnant with Rick's child. In scene three, Debbie tells her husband Chris of Lucy's pregnancy. In scene five, Chris warns his friend Billy against becoming too involved with Lucy.
>
> Such references to Lucy's pregnancy might continue for days or weeks without anything 'happening' to move this subplot closer to resolution. The same information – Lucy is pregnant with Rick's child – is passed along from character to character to character. In terms of the syntagmatic, or story, dimension of the soap, such exchanges *are* redundant, since the audience already knows that Lucy is pregnant and Rick is the father, and since such redundant dialogue scenes do not move the story forward at all. Paradigmatically, however, such exchanges are far from redundant. The experienced reader of the soap is able to read these exchanges as invokings of the paradigmatic network. It makes a difference that Lucy chose to confide in Debbie about her plight because Debbie was once married to Rick. Debbie's telling Chris of Lucy's revelation is read against the background of Debbie's inability to conceive a child and Chris's recurrent infidelity, and so forth. Reduced to its syntagmatic axis, the soap opera becomes an endless string of excruciatingly retarded subplots, related in episodes whose redundancy gives them an almost Sisyphean tiresomeness. To the experienced reader, however, soap opera's distinctive networks of character relationships open up major sources of signifying potential that are simply unreadable to the naive reader.
>
> (ibid.: 70f.)

Allen's very aptly invented example is of course about a string of events in which a particular piece of significant story information is passed on from character to character along the syntagmatic axis of the imagined serial. A syntagm is nothing but the actual sequence of an utterance such as this sentence, or, as in the above quote, sequences of conversations (accompanied by other sounds and images) in an audio-visual narrative. In other words, anything that takes place in time takes place on the syntagmatic axis, and the meaning of every element on this axis is in principle dependent on the elements that went before it – and those that follow. One cannot drop into a sentence or a chapter in the middle of a novel and expect to understand its meaning fully in the narrative context, and the same goes for a scene or an episode of a soap opera. But this fact has little to do with 'paradigmatic complexity'.

1 Opening shot: mountains appear

2 The city

3 The Carrington mansion

4 The title appears

5 Blake

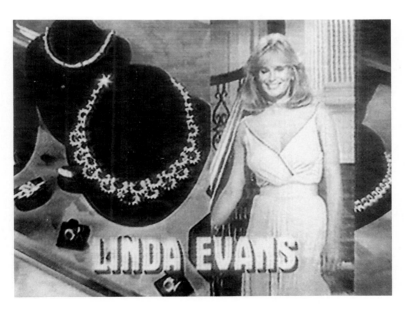

6 Krystle

7 Fallon

8 Claudia

9 Jeff

10 Adam

11 Kirby

12 Mark

13 Steven

14 Joseph

15 Alexis

16 Final shot of the Carrington mansion

The structuralist theory invoked by Allen stems from Saussure's distinction between the 'syntagmatic' and the 'associative' dimensions of language, which again largely corresponded to earlier distinctions between syntax and morphology. In his 'glossematics', the Danish linguist Hjelmslev distinguished between relations 'in absentia' and relations 'in praesentia'. The terms 'syntagm' and 'paradigm' were introduced by André Martinet in the 1950s. Roman Jakobson's classic article from 1956, 'Two Aspects of Language and Two Types of Aphasic Disturbances', introduced an argument about the homology (but not, importantly, identity) between the syntagm/paradigm distinction and that between the rhetorical terms metonymy/metaphor. Here, however, it is only necessary to keep in mind the simple definition of a paradigm, like the one provided by Christian Metz:

> The paradigms of language can contain 'members' distributed around a single semantic pole at varying distances (as in 'Warm/Hot/Boiling', or the general phenomenon of parasynonymi) and, equally well, terms grouped together because they are opposites ('Hot/Cold' and all antonyms); in either case, the language presents us with a delimited field within which we have to choose – this being the definition of the paradigm. Strictly speaking it is linked neither to resemblance nor to contrast, but to the existence of a *series of interchangeable items*, covering both configurations, which from this point of view are simply two sub-categories.
>
> (Metz 1982: 180)

A paradigm thus 'sets up several units in competition for a particular place in the syntagmatic chain' (ibid.: 181), and 'each realised unit (word, image, sound, etc.) acquires its meaning through a comparison with the others which could have appeared in the same place' (ibid.: 184).

'Paradigms' can thus be grammatical categories (nouns, adjectives, etc.), they can be technical categories (camera angles and other stylistic options in film/TV) or they can be cultural, connotative categories (the male/female (stereo)types available in a culture or in a certain genre). A text's paradigmatic structure is thus the key to its thematic dimension, i.e. what the text is 'about' and how its theme(s) are regarded and treated. The list of all characters in a soap opera is a list of choices made from (a) the generically specific paradigm of characters in soaps, which is again drawn from (b) the culturally specific paradigm of possible characters in the culture in question. The character paradigm of a soap opera is like that of any other genre marked not least by its exclusions. Consider this quite accurate description of the not-so-complex character paradigm of US soaps:

> Soap opera people belong for the most part to the socially and professionally successful. They are the well-groomed and cleanly limbed. They live in homes without visible mops or spray cans that yet wait shining and ready for every unexpected caller. At the same time, almost all of soap opera's

characters are drawn from the age group that spans the late teens into middle-age. They constitute what might be called the legitimately sexually active portion of the population. And the great majority come from the generation that reaches from the mid-twenties into the mid-forties. That is to say, they suggest a sexuality that has transcended the groping awkwardness of adolescence but that never goes beyond a commerce of bodies which are personable and smooth – even the older men are clean older men.

(Porter 1982: 126)

The exclusions made in the construction of such a character paradigm obviously contribute to the potential of meaning in the texts, and the differences between, for instance, British and US soaps become evident at this point. The character paradigm in US soaps may of course be seen to place them closer to fantasy than social realism, but a more interesting question is what kind of fantasy this is. It is not hard to see that, whatever else it is, a fantasy which only allows for conventionally handsome characters belonging to the 'legitimately sexually active portion of the population' is strikingly similar to the fantasy tailored for consumerist purposes in the commercials.

There are many problems in transferring the syntagm/paradigm distinction from the analysis of verbal language to that of audio-visual texts. There are for instance in paradigms of visual devices not clearly discrete alternatives to choose from but continuums of camera angles, foci, movements, lighting, etc. Still, the distinction is to me illuminating, in that it points to the performance of (a) 'authorial' choice behind every element of the observable syntagmatic chain and (b) that these choices are patterned so as to reveal a particular set of meaningful codes regulating which choices are made by producers, consciously or by way of cultural norms, myths or socio-psychological constitution. The notion of paradigms is thus for instance able to suggest meaningful cultural and thus also ideological reasons for 'pure incidents', by relating them to a limited set of alternatives available within the paradigmatic structure of a certain kind of narrative, a certain genre. Most genres may be defined at least as much by their particular paradigmatic structures as by their overall syntagmatic shape, and there is a close interdependence between the two dimensions.

Allen's equation of 'many characters' with 'paradigmatic complexity' thus must be said to represent a misunderstanding of what the paradigmatic dimension of a text is. 'Paradigmatic complexity' must, according to the above, mean a complexity in terms of codes at play and their aesthetic and thematic implications. Allen's misunderstanding of the term would lead to somewhat peculiar consequences if applied to, say, literary history. Samuel Beckett's play *Waiting for Godot* would be embarrassingly simple in paradigmatic terms, because only two people are involved on stage, and could hardly be saved from pure banality by its syntagmatic complexity. Even a film such as (Marguerite Duras and Alain Resnais's) *Hiroshima, mon amour* (1959), with basically two characters involved in an encounter with each other and their respective histories, would be strikingly barren in terms of what Allen suggests is its paradigmatic structure. And poems which are all about a single person, but still have both syntagmatic and paradigmatic axes, would be the simplest texts of all – paradigmatically speaking.

I stress this point to such a degree because it leads to a main argument of mine, which is to be sustained by the following more concrete analysis of *Dynasty*'s narrative. I propose that *Dynasty* is characterized by a quite limited, simple paradigmatic structure, both in terms of character types and in terms of themes. This implies that it is a narrative which is in fact rich in repetition and hence only seemingly marked by 'openness, multiplicity, and plurality'. What we need is not to avoid or counter the 'allegations' of repetitions and redundancy but confront them and ask, first, what gets repeated in which ways, and second, why paradigmatic simplicity and syntagmatic repetitiousness are able to fascinate so many viewers of so many (but only so many) kinds.

My hypothesis is, then, that *Dynasty* is constructed in a way which, on the one hand, minimizes the impression of pure repetition, and, on the other, makes repetition pleasurable. I also argue that the relative simplicity of *Dynasty*'s paradigmatic structure is a feature the serial shares with classic melodrama. The whole rationale of the melodrama was from the beginning to present narratives in which a simply structured moral (and later also psychic) universe was presented as a set of fundamental conditions for human life. But while classic melodrama always made morally compelling statements about the consequences of the melodramatic condition, *Dynasty* and other never-ending serials tend to reduce what was once a vision of the human condition to a set of audio-visual and narrative devices which arouse titillations and emotions which are not tied to *anagnorisis*, recognition of, insights into, or 'knowledge' about the conditions of human existence in today's world (cf. Chapter 6). Such an aesthetic diagnosis is capable of saving the sanity of those who endure with pleasure endless 'excruciatingly retarded subplots', while still allowing a critique of an aesthetic form which, as a matter of historical fact, was invented to promote the sale of consumer goods and consumerist conformism.

The final sections of this chapter will accordingly be devoted to an investigation of the aesthetics of *Dynasty*. I try to demonstrate how a range of elements work to conceal the syntagmatic repetitiousness and paradigmatic simplicity of the show. They work to make the actual repetitions pleasurable instead of unbearably boring, and, importantly, to cover up the potential unpleasantness of central thematic implications of the serial's paradigmatic structure. A main device here is the use of music.

THE RHETORIC OF MUSIC

The first little glimpse any viewer gets of a *Dynasty* episode is auditory, not visual: music starts before the first image in the title sequence appears on the screen. The title sequence of a television show is its self-presentation and self-promotion.

It is made with particular attention paid to its audible qualities, so that its particular music etc. can signal throughout viewers' homes that a particular show is about to start (cf. Ellis 1982: 128). The quite minimal musical themes are often extremely 'catchy', and may, particularly because they are repeated again and again, be remembered by viewers decades after a particular show is taken off. People in Norway still whistle or hum for humorous effect the theme of the British detective series *The Saint*; I for one still remember the fanfare of the daily newscasts from the 1960s. The theme of *Dynasty* is definitely one which is and will be remembered for a long time, and I will deal with that in some detail later in this section.

The musical themes of title sequences are repeated again and again throughout every episode of a series or serial. Since they are designed to identify a particular show, they will try to capture and express a particular affective mode which the producers wish to be associated with it. The affective 'meaning' of the theme from *The Saint* is clearly one of 'suspense', but also of 'mystery' or even 'sudden revelation'. This can in fact be seen in the ways in which this theme may still be playfully used in everyday life: baba-da-ba-daa-bee-daa may be sung if, for instance, someone has removed a pint of beer while the owner visits the men's room, or it may be hummed dramatically when one unexpectedly enters someone else's office.

Such use of music for a rather loose designation of an affect or affective mode was foreshadowed in the rhetorical theories of Ancient Greece. In the Middle Ages, grammar, rhetoric and music were formally regarded together as *artes dicendi*, 'the speaking arts'. A rhetorical perspective on music was further developed into fully fledged systems in the early eighteenth century. Publications both in Germany and France then proclaimed that music 'contained' certain 'affects' which it would also impose on its listeners. Particular keys (C major, F minor, etc.) were believed to have particular affective values, and the same was believed to apply to particular harmonies and melodic intervals. This kind of thinking was also used in various forms of musical theatre, including melodrama, and was early on picked up and systematically employed by cinema. Silent films were, as we now know, rarely silent. They were accompanied by music, which might for instance be chosen from catalogues which listed appropriate music for particular moods or affects, such as Sam Fox's *Moving Picture Music* (1913). And today, *Boosey & Hawkes. Recorded Music for Film, Radio & TV* comes with a catalogue which lists musical pieces according to genres and particular affects within them. The 'drama' category contains options such as 'ominous', 'modern, forceful' and 'noble, dignified', while the 'humorous' category features 'slightly tipsy', 'clumsy', 'frivolous', etc. (For all of the above, see Bjørkvold 1988: 15–28.)

There are two reasons why I give such a detailed historical overview here, apart from a general interest in promoting an awareness of the history of today's research subjects and problems. First, I think the role of music in film and television (and in modern mass communication in general, for that matter) has been overlooked to an embarrassing degree. I have only come across a single article which deals specifically with music in daytime soap operas (Silverman *et al.* 1983), and a passage in Finch (1986) is one of very few instances of actual analysis (not just a brief mention) of the music in prime-time soaps. Film scholars tend to treat films and televisual texts as if they contained only dialogue on the soundtrack. Film scholars have written interesting articles and books about music videos without really considering the fundamental role of the popular song in providing coherence and even verbal meaning to the confusing mass of visual signifiers (cf. Goodwin 1993: 46ff.). Similarly, Robert Allen's (1985) otherwise quite exhaustive analysis of soap opera form does not deal with the role of music at all, neither does Christine Geraghty in her perceptive study of British and American prime-time soaps (1991); in her incisive analysis of prime-time soaps, Jane Feuer (1984: 10) only in passing mentions that '[a]cting, editing, musical underscoring and the use of the zoom lens frequently conspire to create scenes of high (melo)drama'.

The second reason for paying particular attention to the theories and practices of musical affects is that they so perfectly illustrate what communication is all about, thus illuminating current debates: the affective 'meanings' of musical themes may of course be said to be produced by those who listen, the 'readers' or 'viewers' or 'audiences'. But it takes only minimal brain activity to 'decode' the music for someone familiar with western musical tradition. It may even be done without any conscious effort at all. The musical signifiers themselves are of course meaningless, objectively describable in the language of physics as they are. But they do *carry* meaning, from producers who put them there, in the text, for a reason. This meaning does not stem from inside the heads of producers or composers, but is derived from a shared, historically and culturally determined set of codes which have been deeply implanted in each and every one of us, even those who can't sing a single straight note. (Many psychologists, and the producers of muzak, in fact believe that many basic responses to sounds and music are physiologically determined (cf. Gorbman 1987: 61).) What the producers do is *select* what goes into the film, and the audience *responds* to that selection. It is of course possible that the audience may produce an 'oppositional reading' of the music ('this music is stupid, this scene is not funny at all'; 'we're supposed to cry, the violins go crazy again'), but they have still understood precisely what the music is 'saying'. 'Oppositional readings', a quite simplistic favourite term in early British cultural studies, now seemingly popular in both film and communication studies in the US (cf. Bobo 1988; Staiger 1992), are basically not about the comprehension of what the text is saying, but about evaluations of it which may be different from those desired by the producers. This distinction between 'decoding' and evaluation was actually implied, if not sufficiently clarified, in Dave Morley's (1980) original definition of 'oppositional reading':

> the decoder may recognize how the message has been contextually encoded, but may bring to bear an alternative frame of reference which sets

185

to one side the encoded framework and superimposes on the message an interpretation which works in a directly 'oppositional' way.

(quoted in Morley 1992: 89)

The total confusion of the two developed later. (See also Corner 1991: 8f. on this issue.)

In *Dynasty*, music is almost constant. Between 56 and 70 per cent of each episode's total time contains music (according to measurements of episodes 16 and 115 respectively, in Reitan 1987: 2). This seems to be much more than in other narrative television shows, even in the US. Each one-hour episode of, for instance, *In the Heat of the Night* contains 8–15 minutes of music (interview with composer Nan Schwartz Mishkin, *L.A. Times* 22 September 1993). If the time for commercials roughly equals that of a *Dynasty* episode (around fifteen minutes), this means that a maximum of 33 per cent of the actual narrative is accompanied by music in that series. So, what is it that music does to, or, rather, in audio-visual fiction?

Claudia Gorbman's *Unheard Melodies* (1987) is, to my knowledge, the most useful critical study of music in film so far. She lists a number of different reasons why music was used to accompany films already in the silent era (ibid.: 53), and then proceeds to ask why the use of music persisted into the narrative sound film, where non-diegetic music 'simply does not logically belong' (ibid.). Her answer is that non-diegetic, background music has two overarching roles, one 'semiotic' and one 'psychological' (ibid.). It functions semiotically as *anchorage*, Roland Barthes's term in 'The Rhetoric of the Image' (1977) for the semiotic function of linguistic texts attached to images which '*directs* the reader through the signifieds of the image, causing him to avoid some and receive others' (ibid.: 40), i.e. narrows down the multitude of potential meanings in the image alone. Peter Larsen (1988) has, however, convincingly argued that Barthes and, consequently, Gorbman, misleadingly simplify what actually happens when two sets of signifiers (visual/verbal or visual/musical) are combined in the same syntagm. Larsen (1988: 51) shows that

the music-image relationship within classical narrative film may be described as a process of *mutual anchorage* based on semantic *isotopy*: the chain of visual signifiers functions as a context for the musical chain, selecting and 'anchoring' identical or corresponding musical signifiers, and vice versa.

In other words, music does not unilaterally specify or add to the meaning of the images, the images also lend meaning to the music. The two are interpreted together. There are, however, instances where music operates as a more independent provider of a meaning which may, for instance, directly contradict the dialogue's suggested anchoring of the image. Gorbman does not mention it here, but in such cases the function of music approaches what Barthes called the *relay*, which is – like dialogue in film, according to Barthes – to function 'not simply as elucidation' but really to 'advance the action' by 'setting out [. . .] meanings that are not to be found in the image itself' (Barthes 1977: 41). This is the case when, in episode 43 of *Dynasty*, Blake looks just very serious as he stares in the direction of Alexis, and says he has seen something 'dangerous'. The music contradicts him: it is romantically sentimental, and says Blake is actually jealous (cf. below).

Music's second main function, according to Gorbman, is psychological. Music functions as *bonding*. It binds 'shot to shot, narrative event to meaning, spectator to narrative, spectator to audience' (Gorbman 1987). Film music works in part like functional music (such as muzak and other easy-listening background music) to relieve anxiety, not least by covering silence and preventing the anxiety that might have arisen from it, signifying basically 'general *pleasantness*' and aiming to 'lull the individual into being an *untroublesome* (less critical, less wary) *viewing subject*' (ibid.: 58). Film music 'helps to ward off displeasure' of two kinds: the 'displeasure of uncertain signification' (ibid.) (the anchorage function) and the potential 'loss of identification which filmic discourse constantly threatens, via the very means that carry the narrative (cutting, the frame, etc.)' (ibid.: 59). Music gives a 'for me-ness' to the soundtrack and the filmic narrative: 'I hear (not very consciously) this music which the characters don't hear, I exist in this bath or gel of affect; this is my story, my fantasy, unrolling before me and for me on the screen (and out of the loudspeakers)' (ibid.: 5). Gorbman sums up her argument thus:

> The bath or gel of affect in which music immerses the film narrative is like easy-listening music in that it rounds out the sharp edges, smooths roughnesses, masks contradictions, and masks spatial or temporal discontinuity with its own sonic and harmonic continuity. Film music lessens awareness of the frame, of discontinuity; it draws the spectator further into the diegetic illusion.
>
> (ibid.)

Television has a relatively small screen, it is watched in a domestic setting, and its mostly discursive texts (cf. Morse 1986) have accordingly been seen as constructed more for the 'glance' than the 'gaze' associated with cinema (cf. Ellis 1982: 163). This general point has often been made in an essentialist fashion, making the often strong audience involvement with both televised feature films and much serial drama appear as an anomaly. It is true that most television sets have, at least until recently, normally had loudspeakers of quite poor quality, in spite of the fact that sound generally has a more prominent role as a channel of information in television than in film. Even if the rendering of music will thus be significantly poorer on TV than in cinemas, music is also essential to all fictional forms on television – and increasingly in non-fiction formats too. This is so precisely because all the technical and social features of the medium which tend to make it less 'absorbing' than the cinema render the role of music even more crucial to its ability to draw and maintain the viewer's desired psychic involvement.

Roy M. Prendergast (1992: 276) points out three standard functional forms of music in television narratives – with historical roots in dramatic radio shows – the 'bridge', the 'act-ins' and the 'act-outs'. The 'bridge' is 'an aural seam', a piece of music which links two scenes, thereby carrying out precisely the 'masking of spatial and temporal discontinuity' which Gorbman mentioned. A musical bridge occurs at all transitions from one scene to another in *Dynasty.* According to Prendergast, composers for feature films try to avoid such bridges 'for fear of "sounding like TV" ' (ibid.), and those who compose for TV increasingly try to avoid them, in an effort to make the show in question 'different' – but:

> It is always amusing to attend a music spotting session for a television show [producer and composer pick segments in an episode which 'need' music] when the producer has announced that his show is 'different' and he doesn't want it to have a typical 'TV feel', and then proceeds to suggest music spotting that is identical to every other show on the air.
>
> (ibid.)

'Bridges' are consequently still an essential element of television fiction. The same goes for the 'act-ins', pieces of music leading the audience into a new act after a commercial break, and 'act-outs', which mark the end of an act. They normally do so by heavily emphasizing the high degree of drama which supposedly is to remain in the minds of viewers across the commercials, an effort, in other words, to diminish the disruptive effect of the commercial break. The rapid pace of television editing creates problems for the composer with all these three main forms of music: music simply needs time in order to 'express something' (Prendergast 1992: 276). This is in itself a reason for the repetitiveness of *Dynasty*'s music: bits and pieces of the *Dynasty* theme are used again and again, since it is so well known that its 'meaning' may be invoked in a couple of seconds. The leitmotif technique, where characters get their own little melodic motif, is also used, notably for Kirby, again making for easy recognition – and repetition. Both with 'bridges' and, in particular, 'act-outs', the composer

> looks for a point, however small or subtle, where the scene shifts slightly. This could be a change in the subject of the dialogue where one idea is complete and a new one begins, or one character finishes speaking and another begins. By introducing the music before the climactic moment a more subtle and tasteful effect is created since the music is already an element in the scene.
>
> (Prendergast 1992: 281)

The majority of scenes in *Dynasty* last less than three minutes (see the descriptions of episodes in the Appendix), and this is probably more or less representative of a US television standard. With the techniques described by

Prendergast, the use of the serial's theme and the leitmotif technique in mind, it is easy to see how television fiction will probably contain more music than the average feature film, and the music will tend to be much more mechanically applied. Quincy Jones once pointed out in an interview that there is much more music in television than in feature films: it is 'loaded with music'. And since with TV one does not have 'a captive audience' as in cinemas, there is little room for a subtlety which production schedules forbid anyway: 'In television you compete with a can of beer so you have to grab' (quoted in Skiles 1976: 230).

What I have argued in this section, then, is that music is an integral part of the soap opera text, which is highly important for the total meaning perceived and for the affective experience of the text. Since *Dynasty*, as mentioned, also uses music far beyond the three forms Prendergast discusses, the extremely high percentages cited above become understandable, and point to the corresponding extreme importance of the music's 'warding off displeasure' and 'lulling the spectator into being an *untroublesome* (less critical, less wary) viewing subject' in this serial.

In the following, final section of this chapter, I will first describe and suggest an interpretation of the visual signs of *Dynasty*'s title sequence, and then return to the specific functions of music in the show's self-presentation. I believe both parts of this analysis are able to tell us important things about the serial in general.

DYNASTY'S PRESENTATION OF *DYNASTY*: THE VISUALS OF THE TITLE SEQUENCE

The title sequence of *Dynasty* is a simple little text, lasting eighty-six seconds, clearly separable from the various episodes it introduces. Certain alterations were made during the serial's run, particularly in the section where the major characters are presented (see p. 197), but its structure and basic elements remained largely the same. It was organized as follows in episode 57, the third to last episode in the show's first run in Norway.

Visually, it is organized in three, clearly separate, main parts. The first part consists of shots establishing the geographical/spatial location of the series (this is an interpretation, see p. 190), the second presents the characters and actors in segments lasting approximately five seconds each, and the final part is a quite short, very high helicopter shot of the Carrington mansion. Only three of the five normally available channels of communication in film and television are employed: image, graphics and music. No dialogue or location sound is heard, while the music is continuous.

In greater detail, the following happens visually: narrow vertical strips of an image shoot upwards to the top of a black screen, eventually forming a pattern which looks like a stylized 'fountain'. The pattern disappears as the whole picture is revealed: a shot, from an airplane or a helicopter, of snow-covered mountains, where the camera moves towards the left. After only a couple of seconds of the complete picture, a new image shoots into it in the same pattern as that just described, eventually showing an overview of a big city with no particular features, zooming out until a cut to black. The next shot shoots up in another 'fountain' on a black screen: a helicopter shot of a large house, seen from the front, in luscious, green surroundings. The camera dips a little as the helicopter passes the balcony over the entrance, when strips of bright yellow start to shoot up in the now familiar pattern, eventually forming the capital letters of the word DYNASTY as they 'drop' and the camera passes the roof. The yellow letters disappear, and the camera catches a glimpse of a park-like garden on the other side of the house. There is a cut to black again, and the second part of the title sequence starts: the presentation of characters and actors.

These presentations all appear by way of the graphic pattern described above, and they are all constructed as vertically split-screen images of the actor juxtaposed with some other image, while the name of the actor appears in yellow capital letters across both images, thus graphically 'connecting' them. The images of the actors are not stills, but seemingly taken from episodes; all contain motion of some sort. The same is true for the images that accompany the actors – either in the picture, by camera movement/zooms or both/all. Instead of trying to describe each of these presentations of actors/characters, I refer the reader to the videoprints between pp. 180 and 181. It is worth noting, however, that the sequence starts with John Forsythe/Blake Carrington, who is followed by Linda Evans/Krystle Carrington. Both are absolutely central characters. Then a string of less central characters follows, some family members and some not. This is the part of the title sequence which varies according to which characters are currently involved in the show. The final actress/character is Joan Collins/Alexis Carrington Colby, with her cigarette and her low- and wide-angled shot of a Rolls Royce. The order of the presentations is, in other words, decided not from narrative importance alone, nor from a mere division between good and bad guys.

After this, there is a cut to the title sequence's third and final part: the bird's-eye view of the mansion, surrounded by rolling greenery on all sides.

I wish, first, to point out a couple of important syntagmatic features which one must suppose are perceived by practically any viewer, even if the importance attributed to them will vary considerably. The basic three-part structure is one of these. Included in the recognition of this structure is that the first three shots (mountains, city, mansion) will be understood as a three-part 'establishing shot', forming a zoom in on the 'location of action', not as unrelated, at least by anyone who has ever seen a film. The other very important point concerns the aesthetic dimension of editing. Principles of striking contrast and constant variety mark the construction and succession of shots and sequences, both in terms of character and camera movements (up/down, close/distant) and in terms of colours or tones (bright/dark). At the same time, one colour clearly stands out as dominant – blue – while white and black dominate in clothing.

Second, if we have a closer look at all the different elements which make up this whole syntagm, it is important to note how every sequence, particularly those with the split-screen effect, carries meanings of a simple connotative sort, likely to be very easily understood anywhere in the world, and of a slightly more specifically western sort, easily understood, consciously or unconsciously, almost anywhere. In other words, I believe practically any viewer anywhere will pick up and correctly 'process' very many of the characterizations of characters and the show as a whole implied in the split-screen part. A closer look at the various connotations involved will take us towards an area of interpretation where opinions might start to differ, but even here I suspect most viewers would agree with me, if they were asked.

The title sequence is rhetorically an announcement, more precisely a promise, of what the serial will offer in terms of 'content' and experiences. Even more than presenting individual character types, it constructs, by way of very simple signs and their practically universal connotations, an image of what the show is about. The elements in the syntagmatic chain are selected from a limited set of paradigms, and if categorized accordingly, they reveal the themes which the title sequence promises that the show will be about.

1) Affluence (power):
The building shown at the beginning and end is obviously the main location of the story to be told. No factories anywhere in the world look like this, no barns either. It could be some sort of hospital or school, but then none of the people presented appear to be teachers, pupils or nurses. So, if no sooner, by the last bird's-eye view of it, even the slowest viewer will suspect it is a home. And if so – home to very rich people. Clothing, jewellery, drinks, sports, car – almost every item shown represents affluence in a very direct manner, understandable any-where. The colour blue has the advantage of not only 'looking good' on TV, but also of being associated in many cultures with royalty and wealth, and the eternally good weather in rich people's playgrounds.

2) Clear, conventional gender differences:
All women are shown in very elegant and/or extravagant dresses, wearing more or less conspicuous jewellery and other accessories, and the framing is such that these attires are convincingly displayed: all except Alexis are shown standing, cut at or below the knees. Men are shown in medium or medium-close shots, cut at the waist or above, as is Alexis. They are all wearing formal evening clothes (a sign of affluence) and they are all busy with more or less expensive-looking drinks (more affluence). All the women except Krystle and Alexis are portrayed against scenes of nature – the cute little chapel in the woods gives a slight modification for Kirby. Krystle comes with jewellery, Alexis with a vertically dominated car grille and cigarette holder. Practically all the men are presented with vertical, man-made structures: skyscrapers (Blake, Jeff), oil derrick (Steven), leaning (75 degrees?) champagne bottle (Adam), lifted tennis racket (Mark). In other words, men are tied to towers of power, sport and expensive intoxication. Women are more clearly on display (framing, dresses,

jewellery) and tied to nature (pasture, lake, woods). The only clear, and therefore significant, exception here is Alexis, with her low- and wide-angle Rolls, cigarette and holder. Also, her black dress stands out: all the others are white, silvery, or, in Fallon's case, red. Colour symbolism varies around the world, but anywhere in western cultures, white will tend to be associated with innocence, red with passion and black with 'sin'. I am not saying that the systematic ordering of connotational gender attributes is necessarily consciously noted by audiences. I am only pointing out that it is there for anyone to see, and that it is completely in line with deeply entrenched ideas about gender in most of the world's cultures, particularly the western ones. A few plain women in business suits, pictured behind impressive desks or operating machinery, accompanied by scenes from a laboratory or tractor factory would, on the other hand, have been noticed, as obvious breaks with the familiar pattern, thereby confirming the pattern's existence as a more or less 'unconscious' code.

3) Sex:

All the characters portrayed will be recognized all over the world as more or less good looking, even if appealing to different tastes. The marked gender differences, including the contrast between the fully-dressed males in black and white and the women in low-cut, bare-backed dresses, openly inviting looks of admiration and desire, will certainly imply to viewers around the world that sexual situations will occur between these characters. This is unambiguously shown (promised) in the presentation of Mark, who is stroking a woman's leg, with part of her thigh visible. At a different, much more indirect level, it is not unreasonable to suspect that many, consciously or unconsciously, will grasp the possibility for viewing, for example, Adam's ejaculating champagne bottle as the effectively vulgar metaphor it is. If the sexual meaning is not understood in this way, the popping cork and the flow of foam will nonetheless join the mass of other signs of

4) 'High life' and general excitement:

The rapid pace, the insistent, rhythmic repetition of the graphic punctuation mark between each segment, bright colours, 'formal' contrasts and variety underscore the signifiers of wealth, partying, movement and expressive gestures (Fallon, Steven) – all suggesting a high level of consumption, visual pleasures, speed and emotional intensity in this fictional universe: an emotional/cognitive rollercoaster for those who get involved as viewers too.

5) Personal emotional conflicts:

This is most clearly signified by the aggressive gesture made by Steven, less obviously by Claudia's sullen look as she leans against the wall. All other characters have rather cool, calm postures and expressions, or they appear frankly happy and carefree, indicating the dominance of the '(desirable) affluence' theme over the theme of personal battles. (A 'glass of champagne among friends' cannot be spoiled by too much arguing and agony.) Again a special case, the presentation of Alexis indirectly suggests a threat. The almost ominous impressiveness of the low- and wide-angled close-up of the Rolls is combined with her cartoon-stereotype black dress and cigarette-with-holder. (Cf. for instance Cruella de Ville, in Disney's *One Hundred and One Dalmatians* (1961), who wanted to skin sweet little puppies to make herself a fur coat.) I strongly doubt that any viewer anywhere will miss the point in this presentation: this lady is *bad*, and she is going to cause serious trouble.

All of the above connotational 'clusters' or paradigms are, in my view, clearly available to all viewers anywhere. (Numbers 2 and 3 could probably be combined into one, but there are also reasons to keep them apart.) They bring to mind Richard Dyer's (1981: 177) argument, that 'light entertainment' presents, rather than re-presents, utopia, that is 'what utopia would feel like rather than how it would be organised'. Contrasting with everyday life, light entertainment offers abundance, energy, intensity of experience, transparency in human relations and the feeling of belonging to a community (ibid.: 183f.). The emphasis in *Dynasty*'s title sequence is clearly on the first three of these, but the series of portraits and the implied close relations between the people presented also promises a kind of community where relations might be 'transparent'.

A sixth connotative promise is available for a possibly more restricted group of viewers: that of

6) Humorous irony and camp:
Some viewers will laugh when they recognize Cruella de Ville (or someone like her) in Alexis, will see and be delightfully shocked by the ejaculating champagne bottle, and might even find further sexual innuendo in the way Blake's enormous skyscraper is immediately followed by the necklace, a shiny circle on a black background, representing Krystle. These people know the popularized catalogue of Freudian 'symbols', and can pick up such things without much effort. But the invitation to a 'camp' reading may also very well be picked up at a different level, by way of the hyperbolic presentation of Alexis as 'bad' or otherwise. There are hints available to most adult viewers here that the show is not necessarily to be taken completely seriously.

The 'Freudian' catalogue of symbols is certainly also known to the show's producers, including those who put the title sequence together. It is hardly reasonable to believe that most of the connotational meanings listed above were not quite deliberately intended by these producers. They made sure that the whole thing would be clearly 'legible' for most conceivable viewers above kindergarten level in age and intelligence. Every single element in it, imagery, editing, graphics, speaks of solid, clever craftsmanship. Subtlety is hardly invoked. A strong, almost aggressive announcement of quite clear-cut pleasures is what this is about. One may come to think of a differentiation D.W. Griffith once made between European and American films. The European film says to its audience 'Come and *see* an experience!' The American film says: 'Come and *have* an experience!' (Monaco 1981: 316). While this latter message will be universally recognized in *Dynasty*'s title sequence, it is, however, not guaranteed that the invitation will be accepted or whether/to which degree satisfaction will be experienced.

If we now look again at the whole syntagmatic structure of this text, it seems possible to say that its three-part structure is reminiscent of the structure of a story or fabula, a 'complete' narrative in the Aristotelian sense. It has a beginning (the three establishing shots 'zooming in' on the mansion), a middle (the presentations of actors/characters) and an end which returns to the starting point – with a difference (in angle, etc.). It is not really a story, though, since there is no narrative progress in the middle part, at most a signalling of a dramatic conflict between Blake and Krystle at one end, and Alexis at the other, with the rest of the characters stuck in between these main warring parties. Rather than a narrative, one might call the title sequence a 'poetic' syntagm in Roman Jakobson's sense:

> *The poetic function projects the principle of equivalence from the axis of selection into the axis of combination.* Equivalence is promoted to the constitutive device of the sequence.

> (Jakobson 1988: 39)

What I mean is that the repeated combinations in the syntagm of elements from originally different paradigms (those of characters, buildings, clothes, drinks, etc.) establish new equations, new paradigms if you like. The characters are equated with the objects and the surroundings in which they appear. And the point is to say, in precisely a compressed, 'thematic' way, what the episodes are supposed to say in a narrative form. That the title sequence thus is not really a narrative does not interfere with the fact that it, contrary to the serial itself, has a rounded, 'complete' or closed three-part form. To the degree that it is a promise of what is to follow, the sequence thus signals something the show delivers, not in its narrative but, as I intend to argue, in other registers of the text. On the other hand, the paradigms/themes identified in the title sequence are constantly rehearsed in all episodes. A closer look at the narrative level will, however, also show that far less attractive, if somehow fascinating, themes are constituted at a less immediately accessible level.

DYNASTY'S PRESENTATION OF *DYNASTY*: THE MUSIC OF THE TITLE SEQUENCE

From a production point of view, the title sequence is closed because it is constructed so as to fit the *music*. In principle, however, the soundtrack could have included both location sound and bits of dialogue. The result would have been a very chaotic montage of noises, since the footage used is taken from a wide variety of 'sonic environments'. That would have made the title sequence appear as some sort of disturbing, avant-garde piece about the chaos of modern urban life. Not surprisingly, then, the visual montage is instead equipped with a musical score which formally functions to contain and smooth the visual 'shocks' provided by the fast-paced montage of so many narratively incoherent images. The *Dynasty* theme, composed by the experienced craftsman Bill Conti, is very simply and highly conventionally structured in three parts: first a main melody or theme, then a contrasting middle section and finally a repeat of the main theme. While it is to function like an overture to a classical opera, its shape is closer to a narrative than that of most overtures, which tend to be a loosely structured compilation of themes from the opera introduced. Conti's piece is from a formal point of view actually closer to a sonata, which traditionally has a beginning ('home'), a middle ('away') and an end ('home again'), like a story. The 'poetic', repetitive/additive structure of the visuals is in other words made to appear more dynamic by the 'progressive', 'narrativized' and closed structure of the music. It is a very interesting fact that the music was changed early in the serial, most probably after the first season, when a number of other changes were also made (see Chapters 1 and 5). The original version had a melodically much less defined opening, a middle with relatively intricate shifts between solos and 'tutti', i.e. the whole orchestra, and an ending in dissonance which would precisely signal 'narrative openness', non-closure (Brincker 1985: 169–71). Obviously, a clear melodic 'statement' in the opening, a simplified instrumentation and an unambivalent closure were thought to be a more attractive signal to viewers.

Musicologists who have analysed this piece of music (Reitan 1987; Bjørkvold 1988) point to Conti's clever use of highly conventional, hence for most people, at least in western cultures, immediately 'understandable' devices. The main theme, particularly the first two bars, is constructed on quart-, quint- and octave intervals characteristic of military fanfares and (consequently) royal rituals and pompously heroic music, well known from thousands of films. (Incidentally, the piece is also in 4/4, the beat of marches – and most popular music.) These musical structures will carry these musical traditions as connotations (particularly because of the instrumentation, see below): they signify (glorified) *power*, royal and military. While these connotations may be specified in various ways around the globe (the cavalry in Western films in the US, royal ceremonies in the UK), the basic meaning will most likely be picked up anywhere. This is so particularly because the choice of main instrument in this section supports the structural meaning: the brass tone of a trumpet carries similar connotations. The old rhetoricians of music would also have said that the choice of key equally supports the melodic structure and the choice of instrument: it is C major which, according to the pre-semiotics tradition of musical rhetoric, is 'among the brightest and most extrovert of the major keys' (Bjørkvold 1988: 66). *Dynasty* could hardly have been presented in, say, F minor. Such a theme might have led audiences familiar with the present semantic codes of the western minor/major dichotomy to suspect that the serial was a moody story about the misfortunes of people with wealth and power, the frustrated emptiness of their lives, etc. The choice of C major emphasizes that the show is to be a glorification and celebration of power and wealth, and the use of a full symphony orchestra delivers impressive support here.

The contrasting middle part of the piece consists of rapid sequences by a solo cornet, which very clearly imitates the style found in baroque instrumental music. While this part appears less military, and even contains some chords in minor adding a touch of the melancholy, it represents a musical style clearly connoting 'high culture', 'fine art', 'refined taste' to audiences, at least in western countries, thus emphasizing connotations already available in the use of a symphony orchestra instead of, say, a rock band. Consequently, the middle part in no way contradicts the meanings of the main melodic part. It only adds a particular dimension which is slightly more mundane than pompous heroism, closer to well-known features of cultural sociology. The choice of a classical musical idiom and a symphony orchestra must not least be understood in the light of *Dallas*'s signature music, which consisted in a two-part, eight-bar theme repeated as long as the title sequence lasted, and with a beat and an instrumentation which connoted popular music styles, from 'disco' to 'country'.

A final connotation tied to this kind of music and particularly its orchestration is simply that of classical Hollywood films. Late romantic music was always the preferred style of Hollywood. But even if the stylistic model here is baroque, the fact that the music is 'classical' and played by a full symphony orchestra, will most probably ensure that it will be perceived as 'cinematic' and 'Hollywood-esque'. The music thus points to the many ways in which *Dynasty* is indebted to American films of the 1940s and 1950s. But it does more than just appeal to middle-aged people's nostalgia:

> Music, especially lushly scored late Romantic music, can trigger a response of 'epic feeling'. In tandem with the visual film narrative, it elevates the individuality of the represented characters to universal significance, makes them bigger than life, suggests transcendence, destiny.
>
> (Gorbman 1987: 81)

The music of the title sequence, and of course its repetitions and variations in the episodes, thus signals that *Dynasty* is to be viewed as a broad, slowly but relentlessly unfolding epic, involving characters and events loaded with symbolic, cultural significance.

Even more interesting than the basic structures and connotational meanings of the music is the way it functions 'formally' in relation to the visuals. Effectively and yet almost casually or effortlessly, it metaphorically 'follows' the visual structures and movements. Technically this is because the visuals have, of course, been edited to fit the music. Examples: the initial tremolos of the orchestra are heard as the first image gradually appears. Cuts generally appear in keeping with the beat of the music and/or melodic shifts. The tilt up Blake's skyscraper is accompanied by a 'rising' melodic line, the slightly downward pan right on Jeff's skyscrapers is accompanied by a 'downward' melodic line. Mark's tennis ball in the air (slow motion) is seen as the swirling strings of the orchestra build towards the reappearance of the trumpet in the final part. The trumpet's melody slows down to a halt exactly parallel to the movement of Alexis's white Rolls Royce, and the final, super-high, clear C accompanies the face of Alexis, the Rolls Royce grille – and the final, extreme bird's-eye view of the Carrington mansion. This impressively thorough orchestration of the whole audio-visual text speaks eloquently of the determination to move the viewers emotionally, to provide not just 'one hell of a story' (Robert Pollock), but also an experience of being 'carried away' into an exciting, dynamic world.

Parts of the title sequence changed visually several times during the serial's run. Krystle was initially presented with an airplane just after take-off, but this 'phallic' breach in the overall distribution of signs for 'femininity' and 'masculinity' was corrected after a couple of seasons. Alexis was at first represented by the dark interior of her garden studio, then by a pool and a palm tree among high-rise buildings, until her much more powerful Rolls Royce arrived. Presentations of supporting actors kept coming and going. There have been old cannons and a limousine on big-city streets before the final shot of the mansion. The music never changed after the early revision mentioned above (p. 195), however, and it kept doing its work: providing formal coherence, a degree of semantic clarification, and 'narrative' progress and closure to the quite disparate, 'poetic' visual montage, attempting to set or guide the overall mood of the viewing experience.

Bjørkvold (1988: 69ff.) reports relatively informal experiments he conducted with groups of students in diverse disciplines who were all familiar with *Dynasty*. (I was myself present at one of them.) Bjørkvold would replace Conti's theme with a piece of modernist 'electrophonic' music by the Norwegian composer Arne Nordheim (for the ballet *The Storm*). The part taken from Nordheim's work is described as 'simple and low key', as 'electronically produced sound-masses representing a grey ocean in monotonous, rhythmic movements' interspersed with flute-like sounds, imitating lonely seagulls. The students were asked to write down their immediate impressions of this new audio-visual combination. The almost unanimous response in all groups (less than 2 per cent are said to have reacted differently) was that something ominous was added. The implied threat could, however, be seen as signalling a variety of different genres, such as 'psycho-thriller', 'horror' or 'catastrophe' (for instance a natural or nuclear disaster). Many reported that the pace of the title sequence appeared slower than in the original (cf. Gorbman 1987: 25f., 38), that colours seemed altered and, not least, that the perception of the people portrayed changed considerably: they now appeared less significant, more lonely, empty, powerless in the face of a major threat. (Cf. above, p. 196, about the effect of 'lushly scored' music.)

This experiment is problematic in many ways, but it does illustrate how important music is to the total meaning, and, particularly, to the emotional/affective impact of the audio-visual experience as a whole. It is reminiscent of the classic experiment traditionally attributed to Kuleshov (which on closer inspection seems to have been neither a real experiment nor done by Kuleshov alone (see Hollander 1992)) where the same close-up of an actor's face was perceived as expressing radically different emotions when juxtaposed with shots of a plate of soup, a dead woman in a coffin and a little girl playing with a toy bear. Bjørkvold's experiment indicates the importance of keeping in mind the particular complexity of audio-visual texts, how combinations of physically different kinds of signifiers interfere with or modulate the processes of significa- tion. The musicologist Bjørkvold tends to overestimate the unilateral deter- mination of signification exerted by music, when saying that 'music alone is in other words still able to turn everything on its head' (1988: 71). We should rather understand what happens as more complex flows of connotational signifieds are tied to the various (kinds of) signifiers, visual and aural, merging or separating in different ways, none of them totally dominating, though possibly forming hierarchies of importance, possibly varying for different groups of recipients at different times (cf. Larsen 1988).

A BRIEF AND PRELIMINARY CONCLUSION

On the basis of the above analysis and theoretical points, my argument in the following analysis of single episodes and sequences of episodes is that the 'polysemy' of prime-time soap operas like *Dynasty* has tended to be overrated by researchers fixated on the large number of storylines, unexpected twists in character- and story developments, overt ideological ambiguities, the open- ended or rather never-ending format, etc. I am not saying that such features are not there or that they are unimportant. But I suspect that paradigmatic stability, syntagmatic repetitions and the unifying, coherence-producing func- tion of music observed in the title sequence also appear in the episodes, with significant support from other structural elements, all working to regulate and contain the show's reception, its social meanings.

5

THE NOT SO 'POLYSEMIC' *DYNASTY* TEXT

'We walk a fine line, just this side of camp.'

(Douglas S. Cramer, Executive Producer)

'Who remembers yesterday?'

(Blake Carrington, episode 40)

SELECTING A TEXTUAL CORPUS

I said in Chapter 3 that I would return to two of the problems raised by Jane Feuer (1989) concerning the 'object' of an analysis of the *Dynasty* text. One of them is whether watching *Dynasty* on videotape is the same as watching *Dynasty* as it is broadcast. My answer to this is that it is the same programme text, but with a different pragmatic setting, with a very different degree of viewer's control. Watching *Dynasty* on one's own VCR is a different experience from watching it on broadcast television, but it is still watching *Dynasty* (not *Rambo* or *Roots*). Reading at home a xeroxed version of one of Feuer's articles a year or two after its publication is a different experience from reading it in a journal at a library when it was brand new. I still believe I can work from the presupposition that Feuer's article is the same in both settings.

The other problem that Feuer points out is deciding how much of the serial one needs to have seen in order to be able to say with some confidence that 'I have seen *Dynasty*'. This is a question to which a definite answer is hard to find. In my research on the *Dynasty* phenomenon in Norway, I frequently encountered people who willingly expressed opinions about the serial after having seen one or two episodes, or in some cases even after no viewing of the actual text at all. The latter group formed their opinion solely on the basis of those additional texts to which Tony Bennett wanted to give 'methodological parity' in the study of reading (see Chapter 3). Since I, along with John Fiske, regard these texts as secondary or tertiary, I (not Bennett) have a reason to say that you must have seen at least some of the primary text in order to form a legitimate opinion about *Dynasty*.

But the question remains: how much? Robert C. Allen has demonstrated the practical impossibility of 'reading it all' before you utter anything about long-running daytime serials like *Guiding Light* (Allen 1985). *Guiding Light* is not yet a 'complete' text, even if it has been on the air since 1938. Allen calculated that only watching all the episodes broadcast on television (since 1952) would take him '233 days of non-stop viewing, during which time another 164 hours of text would have been produced' (ibid.: 13). This example is hypothetical also in the sense that all soaps were transmitted live until the mid-1960s, so that roughly thirteen years of storytelling are lost for ever. One can hardly think of a better legitimation for selecting a piece of a text to represent the whole thing; anything else is in practice out of the question.

One might think of a study of parts (specific episodes) representing the 'whole' as analogous to the Saussurean study of *langue* (the linguistic system) by way of *parole* (instances of speech/language in use). *Langue* consists of a set of elements and a set of rules for the combination of these elements. The point of such a study would be to construct the '*Dynasty* system' from a study of concrete *Dynasty* episodes, to specify the basic elements and rules from which new episodes can be constructed. Something like that is, as a matter of fact, one of the intentions of the following analysis – also because I think the '*Dynasty* system' has a lot in common with the 'soap opera system', so that *Dynasty* in a sense is an instance of *parole* in relation to the latter, more general *langue* of the genre. This analogy also implies, importantly, that the constructed 'system' would have to be revised if new instances of *parole*, i.e. other episodes than those studied, can be said to contradict it. In a less strict sense, this is what happens when someone delineates basic features of, say, the Western genre, without actually having seen every Western ever produced. The '*Dynasty* system' is, however, not my only interest in the following. I also study the episodes chosen (or parts of them) in their specificity, not only as examples of an 'underlying *Dynasty* system'. Similarly, *Dynasty* is of course also studied with a view to its specificity, and not simply as an example of the 'soap system'. Neither part of the analysis is rigorously (or rigidly) 'Saussurean', though.

Contrary to *Guiding Light* (so far), *Dynasty* had an ending, if only in the sense that its production was discontinued. (The two-part 'mini-series' *Dynasty: the Reunion* (1991) was a separate phenomenon, even if interestingly intended as a kind of ending to the serial.) Since *Dynasty* was shown in weekly episodes during a limited 'season', not the whole year round, it would take less than a year of continuous viewing to watch the whole thing. To me at least, this would definitely be too much. With serials this long, it simply cannot be demanded that one has 'seen it all' before an analysis is attempted or an opinion is formed. In fact, a single episode may be sufficient material for many conclusions on the basic construction of the serial. Most or all of the central characters can be observed, the multiple-plot structure can be identified, the elements of melo-dramatic aesthetics may be pointed out. One may in other words identify the fundamental textual strategies at work in the serial, the basic preconditions of meaning production that it presents to any reader.

But if a *Dynasty* episode is chosen at random, it might be the season finale episode about a certain wedding in Moldavia, which is atypical in many ways. The serial also changed drastically after the Pollocks' Alexis was introduced and Douglas Cramer gave the show its definitive super-abundant look. These changes, which occurred after the first thirteen episodes, were in other words what made *Dynasty* become *Dynasty* as we know it. Also, throughout the show's run certain parts stood out as more important than others, certain moments as more memorable than others. These may include the fight between Krystle and Alexis in the lily pond, the return of Steven with a new face, the Moldavia wedding massacre, the wild plotline involving two Krystles, etc. It should be noted here that all these are examples of *Dynasty* going 'over the top', displaying its ironical 'camp' character for many and possibly most viewers. (And the producers knew what they were doing: when I asked about the wedding massacre, Esther Shapiro laughingly said, 'Oh, that was *total* opera!')

In order to form an opinion about the show and its relations to various audiences – and audiences care little about the system, only about *parole* – at least some of these significant parts and moments should be included in the corpus chosen for closer examination. The point is that the material should at least approach the quantity and complexity required of the representative. Any such selection may be questioned, as with the selections of data made in other areas of textual, historical and social studies. An absolute rule, which for instance would quantify the number of episodes required, is unthinkable. I have chosen to concentrate on episodes broadcast during the serial's first run in Norway, not least since that is the period from which most of my reception data stem. Since this was just before I myself acquired a VCR, I had to order a limited number of episodes taped at my university after I started my project. I decided to tape one sequence of five mid-season episodes and three end-of-season episodes, 42–6 and 57–9 respectively. From a colleague at Bergen Pedagogical College (Jostein Saakvitne, thanks!) I also received a copy of episode 16, in which Alexis has recently been introduced. During one of my many moves of both office and home, the end-of-season episode (59) disappeared, so I am left with episodes 16, 42–6 and 57–8, eight in all. These form the central corpus I analyse, with particular attention paid to the middle five. In addition I also have some fifteen other, later episodes on tape, one of which is a season finale taped in Los Angeles in the spring of 1987. This additional material will serve mainly as a support reservoir of examples. Finally, the two-part *Reunion* series (given to me by John Ellis – thanks!) will be brought into the discussion here and there, even though it was never broadcast in Norway. The news of its production merely gave one of the family/female-oriented weeklies an opportunity to put Krystle back on the front page again.

I have placed relatively detailed descriptions of what goes on in the episodes chosen in the Appendix. For episodes 42–4 I have also included quite detailed descriptions of the music, as it appeared to my non-musicological ears. A more precise description would have required a training I do not have. In defence of my kind of description, it may be argued that most listeners also lack musico-logical training. They pick up the musical input in the viewing experience without normally noticing it very much. Simply for reasons of time and space, in the rest of the episodes described, music is only mentioned at points when it seemed particularly important or striking.

Returning finally to Jane Feuer's question as to whether *Dynasty* on video is the same text as *Dynasty* broadcast, I will briefly note that I watched *Dynasty* several times when it was broadcast, without taking notes, before I had decided to do research on it, thus watching as an 'ordinary viewer' of my gender, age and social category. I also watched it in the company of others, old and young, men and women, at very different educational levels. I am sure this very unsystematic 'participant observation' when *Dynasty* was being shown on about two-thirds of all TV screens in Norway also feeds into my analysis.

EPIC EXPECTATIONS: THE FIRST THIRTEEN EPISODES

Dynasty started with the wedding of self-made oil tycoon Blake Carrington and his secretary, Krystle Jennings. Blake had two children from a previous mar-riage, Fallon and her younger brother Steven. Fallon returned from Europe, Steven from New York, to attend the wedding. Shortly after her return, Fallon found out that Blake was having financial difficulties, and agreed to marry Jeff Colby, who had loved her unrequitedly since childhood, on condition that his uncle, Cecil Colby, bailed Blake out. The marriage was Cecil Colby's idea, and miserable from the start. Fallon had affairs, a major one with the family's chauffeur, and basically spent her time being nasty to Krystle, for instance by smoking pot and swimming naked in the pool during Krystle's first formal dinner party.

A former employee in Blake's Denver-Carrington oil company, Matthew Blaisdel, had had an affair with Krystle before she married Blake. Matthew was married at the time, but he was sort of excused since his wife, Claudia, spent a year and a half in a sanatorium after suffering a nervous breakdown. Matthew, returning home from a job he took in the Middle East to pay for his wife's sanatorium costs and to forget about Krystle, now 'struck out as a wildcatter', to quote Esther Shapiro's *Dynasty. The Authorized Biography of the Carringtons* (1984), i.e. he started his own drilling company, just as Blake had done twenty-five years earlier, the same source reminds us. Steven started working for Matthew, 'resentful of his father's demands', after returning from New York to attend his father's wedding. He had lived in a homosexual relationship in New York, but he started an affair with his boss's wife Claudia, as soon as she was out of the sanatorium. His lover from New York, Ted Dinard, came to Denver to renew the relationship after Steven had left Matthew's drilling company, gone to evening classes in business administration and started working at Denver-Carrington. As Ted and Steven had agreed it was over and were saying goodbye on friendly terms, Blake Carrington rushed in, misunderstood and pushed Ted Dinard so he fell, hit his head and died. Blake was tried and convicted of manslaughter (two years' probation). This trial not only brought Krystle back to her beloved husband's side after a minor crisis, and had her show brilliance when attending board meetings at Denver-Carrington in Blake's absence. The trial also had two major consequences for further developments: (1) Claudia testified that she had a relationship going with Steven at the time of the crime, so it was less likely Ted and Steven were at it again; her testimony made her husband Matthew so angry that he ran off to South America with their daughter Lindsay; (2) Alexis, Blake's first wife, the mother of Fallon and Steven, was brought in to testify to Blake's violent streak; she had spent the previous sixteen years out of the country, mainly in Acapulco, without ever trying to get in touch with her children.

The above is a summary of *Dynasty*'s first thirteen episodes. Many minor incidents have of course been left out, incidents which provided each episode with peaks of dramatic tension, scenes of show extravaganza or shock. The main impression remains, though, that there *is* a story being told, recounting the development of dramatic tensions between the characters presented at the initial event, Krystle and Blake's wedding. Apart from the veiled appearance of Blake's first wife at the trial in the final scene of episode 13, I believe Ted Dinard was the only significant character to be picked up from an unknown past, and Steven's relationship with him was known early on, or at least his homosexuality was known. Even if Fallon's marriage to Jeff and her escapades could be seen as sidetracks, they were clearly related to her love for her father and her resentment at his marriage to Krystle. The main narrative question remained whether this Cinderella marriage could work out, if they really could live happily ever after. Blake himself was the main obstacle to this happiness, with his total commitment to his business, his troubled relations with his children and his severe degree of brutality. Krystle was basically striving to make him change his ways. In other words, the story is clearly related to the well-established tradition of female popular fiction in which a woman's love 'humanizes' a man who is more or less violent or otherwise an insensitive brute, achieving 'the magic transformation of his cruelty and indifference into tender care' (Radway 1984: 147; see also Modleski 1982).

All the events to do with Matthew Blaisdel and Steven on the oilfields could be seen as serving to accentuate the difference between big and small business, corporate management and physical labour – traditional Hollywood representations of class differences and class conflicts – besides being about the flaws in Blake's character (see also Geraghty 1991: 155). Class was also an important element in the problems Krystle-the-secretary experienced in being accepted as mistress of the manor and learning how to fill this role. This touch of US-style social realism also allowed a degree of topicality, represented in particular by Steven's gayness. In the early episodes this issue was made political in a way which later disappeared. Consider this piece of dialogue from episode 2:

BLAKE: Steven, I'm about as Freudian as you could hope for in a capitalistic
          exploiter of the working classes. When I'm not busy grinding the faces
          of the poor, I even read a little. I understand about sublimation. I
          understand how you could try to hide sexual dysfunction behind
          hostility toward a father. I – I'm even prepared to say that I could
          find a little homosexual experimentation . . . acceptable – just as long
          as you didn't bring it home with you. Don't you see, son, I'm offering
          you a chance to straighten yourself out?

STEVEN: Straighten myself out? I'm not sure if I know what that means. I'm
          not sure I could if I wanted to. And I'm not sure I want to.

BLAKE [*sarcastic*]: Of course! I forgot the American Psychiatric Association has
          decided that it's no longer a disease. That's too bad. I could have
          endowed a foundation – the Steven Carrington Institute for the
          Treatment and Study of Faggotry. [*Angry*] Now if you'll excuse me,
          I've got to go and get married.

                                                      (quoted in Finch 1986: 31f.)

Mark Finch (1986) has tied this exchange to the 'liberal gay discourse' which,
he convincingly demonstrates, shaped the show's handling of 'the gay issue' in
general. 'Specifically, this is the gay movement at its most consumerist and
acceptable after Stonewall (1968) but before AIDS (1980), and its message is
that we are individuals, just like you' (ibid.: 31).

My point, however, is that both the degree of social realism, the degree of
real narrative progress throughout the first thirteen episodes and Steven's
gayness and the way it is handled in the show can be related to the particular
record or profile of the Shapiros as writers of 'socially relevant' material. The
liberal conception of social and political issues is of course institutionally
favoured, but it is also in line with the proclaimed political orientation of
Esther Shapiro – 'I'm still a liberal, a *conservative* liberal . . . and Richard.
We're pretty middle-class. We have middle-class values' (in Klein 1985: 32).
For me, the above dialogue between Blake and Steven also brought to mind
something Esther Shapiro ('I *am* Blake Carrington') said in my interview with
her. Talking (supportively) about one of her daughters being actively and
progressively engaged in the political struggle in Central America, she added
ironically: 'And here her parents are spreading capitalist propaganda!'

My second point, then, is that an audience unfamiliar with the never-ending
format of the soap opera was not particularly stupid to believe that the serial
was headed for a conclusion of some sort after these first thirteen episodes. The
role of music in suggesting a broad, larger-than-life epic (cf. the previous
chapter) comes in addition to the shape of narrative developments. What later
would more clearly be seen as storylines only loosely tied to one another could
in these first episodes easily appear rather as indications of epic scope, of a really
grand, many-faceted 'one hell of a story'. It would necessarily take a long time
to tell, but it would eventually reach a conclusion on a grand scale, yet parallel

to that of lesser romances. The uproar among enthusiastic viewers when a member of the Norwegian broadcasting council demanded that the serial be discontinued is perfectly understandable – at this point.

With Blake's trial and its immediate consequences, the show clearly changed. That is, it 'clearly' did so in hindsight. Ted Dinard was, as already mentioned, the first significant person to be pulled out of the past, from the times before Blake and Krystle's wedding, to bring about a major crisis – towards the end of the season. Alexis was the second to come as a surprise, out of a largely unknown past. The unlikeliness of her total disappearance for sixteen years (although she claimed strong motherly love for her children) indicated a significant shift in the balance of the serial's mode: from melodramatic with a degree of realism as its overall premise to a melodramatic mode in which a peculiar blend of fantasy and irony became much more prominent. This implied an increase in the apparent arbitrariness or unpredictability of story developments, since once the boundary of realist credibility had been resolutely transgressed, producers/writers were free to draw almost any rabbit out of their high hats at any time – if still within certain, reformulated generic limits. Krystle could not, for example, plausibly go to college, take sociology classes and become a marxist social worker in Philadelphia.

As this new freedom was exploited, the chances increased that an adequate understanding of the never-ending, multiple-plotline generic formula might dawn even on viewers who did not actually know that this is a characteristic of 'soap opera' serial drama. Judging from the letters to NRK-TV, however, this realization certainly took time for many viewers (cf. Chapter 3). It would possibly not occur to some until well into the second stretch of episodes, by which time they had also become acquainted with *Falcon Crest*. It is of course probable that newspapers or other sources provided this elementary knowledge of how the serial worked to quite a few. But the fact that so many believed in an ending for so long, in spite of newspapers eventually reporting the 'news' about the genre, suggests that direct, factual information had limited influence. An indication that the misunderstanding was over is the minimal open resistance of the type 'we need to know how it all ends' both when *Falcon Crest* was discontinued and at the second discontinuation of *Dynasty*. By then it seems most of the audience had learned about the genre – not necessarily by external information but the hard way, through viewer experience.

To summarize, most viewers initially believed in the serial's narrative cohesion and eventual resolution. A combination of external information and viewing experience then gradually taught a majority that these expectations were illusory. What appears to be a minority kept their illusion at least through the first fifty-eight episodes, possibly longer. Letters to the NRK and general knowledge of socio-cultural stratification suggest that this latter, stubborn group falls into what my survey indicated was *Dynasty*'s core audience: people with lower education, and women of this category in particular. They were in a sense tricked by the serial text and by secondary texts specifically geared towards them (i.e. women/family-oriented weeklies) into misinterpreting the show's construction.

'DYNASTY AS WE KNOW IT': A PATRIARCHAL SOAP

With Alexis's arrival, the fictional universe was restructured. Throughout the first thirteen episodes, Blake's mansion and his Denver-Carrington company had been placed in opposition mainly to the middle-class home of the Blaisdels and Matthew Blaisdel's 'wildcatter' company. This was a main axis in the show, even if Cecil Colby and his Colbyco were also around as a potential threat to the Carrington empire. The greater importance of the Blaisdels was for instance manifest in that their home was an important location, as was their site of business. To my memory, this was not, or only minimally, the case with Colby. With Matthew and Lindsay sent off to the jungle in Peru, the whole big vs small capital (rich vs middle-class and working-class people) opposition was out of the picture. The Pollocks told me in my interview with them that a primary objective of the developments after Alexis was introduced was to provide her with a 'power-base' from which she could challenge Blake Carrington. Immediately after the trial, she moved into a studio in the Carrington mansion's garden, so as to make her presence strongly felt in the family. She then proceeded to establish a relationship with Cecil Colby, who started having heart attacks as they made love. (A memorable scene was Cecil gasping in a painful attack while a scantily clad Alexis on top of him pounded his chest with both fists, shouting 'don't die on me!') Alexis married Cecil in the hospital just before he died, leaving her with half ownership of Colbyco. The other half was inherited by his nephew Jeff. *Voilà*: a power-base for the vindictive ex-wife.

This was the establishment of what I above called '*Dynasty* as we know it', a restructured fictional universe. The quite sensational story of Alexis's clever move to a position of financial power provided a degree of real narrative progress to this string of episodes. The parallel adventure involving Blake in the business of American football, where he was up against a mysterious mobster who turned out to be an alias of Cecil Colby, and in which Blake was temporarily blinded by a bomb intended to kill him, may have led some viewers to see (!) that events in this serial were not necessarily integrated in an overall drive towards resolution of some sort. But the story about Alexis was no doubt the main thing in this period, sustaining an impression of narrative progress which faded after she was installed at Colbyco.

'*Dynasty* as we know it' is then basically a large number of stories unfolding both simultaneously and in sequence within a fictional universe structured by the opposition between Blake Carrington's business and home on the one hand and Alexis Carrington Colby's business and home on the other. The four buildings in question totally dominate as locations of action, presented *ad nauseam* in a small sample of day and nighttime establishing shots. One might suspect, then, that the equal number of buildings on each side of this conflict axis would suggest a parallel equality in terms of power and centrality in the presentation of struggles. There is, however, an important fifth location: La Mirage, a hotel managed by Fallon, daughter of the two warring parties. Even if La Mirage thus works as 'neutral ground' to some extent, it is in fact owned by Blake Carrington, who has given Fallon her job without considering head-hunting for the best possible manager. What seems neutral consequently demonstrates Blake's upper hand, both in his relation to Alexis and in his general position in the serial.

Blake's position as not only head of the family but also head of the show is constructed in numerous ways:

1 It may not be consciously noted by the audience, but the establishing shots of the Colbyco and Denver-Carrington skyscrapers are consistently different in one symbolically important respect: the shots of Denver-Carrington always display the phallic grandeur of the high-rise, most often by tilting upwards, normally all the way to the distant top against the sky. The corresponding shots of Colbyco either go directly to a zoom of the entrance to the building or in some (rarer) cases move down-right across the building, from about halfway-up down to the groundfloor entrance. This difference is also under-lined in the music which accompanies these shots: while Denver-Carrington gets pompous extracts and versions of the triumphant *Dynasty* theme, Colbyco gets a variety of less defined 'dramatic' music.

2 Blake owns a forty-eight-room mansion surrounded by a huge park. A white marble swimming pool and the lily pond are major outside marks of absolute affluence. The mansion is the home of a varying but always large number of family members, and 'the library', 'the conservatory', the breakfast room, the kitchen and various king-size bedrooms with fireplaces are repeatedly used as mood-suggesting locations for various kinds of conversations between char-acters. Alexis lives in an apartment building. It may be a penthouse apart-ment, the furniture looks expensive, and her bathroom is at least once revealed as glamorous. But the living room where practically all conversa-tions take place, including those over a meal, remains the size of a sit-com dwelling. Alexis does not even have a separate study or home office. The Carrington kids could say that their father's house has many rooms, but certainly not their mother's. And even if the building is peach/pink-coloured and looks nice on the inside, it remains a high-rise which to Norwegian viewers looks much like any suburban cooperative housing block. It is defi-nitely not the natural main habitat of a mega-rich corporate owner-executive.

3 All storylines directly or indirectly involve or centre on Blake. Ultimately, he is the character the show is about. The first, very clear indication of this in my material is the 'last time, on *Dynasty*' summary introducing episode 16 (see the Appendix for a detailed description). The ten short segments from the previous episode seem to represent up to eight closely related but possibly separable storylines, defined as areas of conflict with semi-independent

developments: (1) Blake's trial; (2) Blake's problems in Denver-Carrington as a result of the trial; (3) Blake's love for Krystle and vice versa; (4) Blake's anger with wild daughter Fallon; (5) Blake's continued conflict with his homosexual son Steven; (6) Blake's struggle with Alexis; (7) Blake and Krystle having a baby; (8) Blake taking responsibility for Claudia. Even if this is extreme in that Blake is physically present in every segment, it is still representative of the serial as a whole in its concentration on him. All the storylines in a sense boil down to struggles for his love and recognition, his business, his power. Alexis does not in any way represent an alternative to the grand patriarch. She is more like a particularly irritating and persistent horsefly bugging the giant stallion. Her apartment can never be a family home, and her business dealings are all directed at making trouble for Blake, they do not have any other meaning or goal. Blake on the other hand has his often proclaimed national responsibility for securing oil supplies, and strives, in the episodes forming my material, to protect, develop and implement new technology for this purpose (the 'shale oil process'). He also talks about his responsibility for his thousands of employees, a consideration Alexis, to my knowledge, never makes.

The two poles of the *Dynasty* universe are thus imbalanced, so that Alexis is less a formidable challenge than a formidable nuisance. Her sometimes even physical fights with Krystle are catfights over a man they both seem to be deeply attached to. Episodes 42–6 contain a number of indications that the strength of the bonds between Alexis and Blake is the reason why she is so totally devoted to making trouble for him on all fronts (see for instance 42: 7 (i.e. episode 42, scene 7), 42: 15, 42: 17, 42: 19). Particularly noteworthy here is the meaning carried by the music in 43: 24, where Blake stops and stares as Alexis disappears into a hotel room with Congressman McVane at a point where the 'shale oil' story is approaching a climax. Blake says to Krystle he has seen something dangerous, but the music very clearly signals romantic melancholy and jealousy. Confrontations between the two also reveal a kind of mutual respect (e.g. 43: 31) which may be seen as signifying that this 'original couple' was the one which 'was meant to be' but could not happen. The many melodramatic Hollywood forerunners in this category of couples include Rhett Butler and Scarlett O'Hara in *Gone With the Wind* (Victor Fleming, 1939) and Lewt and Pearl in *Duel in the Sun* (King Vidor, 1946). The mythic cultural logic at work in these narratives asserts that women who are too 'strong', too 'wild' and hence too 'masculine' cannot fulfil the domesticating, civilizing or 'humanizing' function necessary finally to socialize, i.e. domesticate, the male, thus limiting (and productively channelling) his 'natural' tendency towards asocial transgression (violence, disorderly sexual conduct). Such women cannot adjust themselves to the submissive passivity of 'proper femininity', and the tremendously successful films just mentioned may owe a significant part of their popularity to their display of the strength and independence of their heroines. (Cf. Mulvey

1989 on the pleasures of *Duel in the Sun* for a female audience; Taylor 1989 and Kolbjørnsen 1993 on *Gone With the Wind*.) Their endings interestingly differ: while Pearl hyper-melodramatically dies after shooting and being shot by her 'wild' lover, thus demonstrating the tragedy of the cultural impossibility of this couple, *Gone With the Wind* ends with Scarlett, on her own again, optimistically saying 'after all, tomorrow is another day'. Both films thus in different ways, pessimistically and optimistically, make serious melodramatic 'statements' on the cultural norm in question, simultaneously acknowledging and deploring its existence. *Dynasty* can only play with this norm, forever reiterating the existing situation, the existing distribution of power. (See the section 'Meaning vs manipulation: melodrama vs melodramatic devices' in Chapter 6.)

Esther Shapiro once made another literary and film-historical reference when explaining the basic set-up of the show: 'It's the story of Daphne du Maurier's *Rebecca* retold with the wicked first wife still alive and kicking high and hard' (*Radio Times*, 21–27 July 1984, quoted in Finch 1986: 26). This categorization of Blake and Alexis also underlines the fact that Blake's relationship to Krystle is one of obvious inequality in terms of power. Krystle (the former poor secretary, who signed a premarital agreement) has nothing in particular going for her except (her looks and) her 'personality', i.e. the power of her love. This is how she is described in *Dynasty. The Authorized Biography of the Carringtons* (1984: 25):

> But even if the Carrington fortune is lost, Krystle is a woman who wants her husband more than anything else, for richer or for poorer.
> It pleases Krystle to [. . .] share the frustrations and challenges of Blake's life. She still greets each day with bright-eyed vitality and a zest for living. Her goodness and concern for others are stabilizing factors in the Carrington family, ones that have earned her the admiration and respect of all. Krystle Carrington is a tender, loving, feminine woman – a passionate romantic living the life of every girl's dream, but bringing to it common sense, compassion and cachet. She is truly a beautiful human being.

This quote is from a secondary text, supplied by producers to promote and support an intended reading of the primary text. To a feminist with a witty, cynical view of the serial, like the video artist Joan Braderman, Krystle is the most despicable of all the characters: she's a terrible 'Polyanna', who is 'constantly annoying everybody with dumb clichés' and makes Braderman 'want to throw up' (Braderman's video *Joan Does Dynasty* (1986), a truly remarkable piece of what she calls 'stand up theory'). Nevertheless, there are reasons to suspect that the Krystle character Braderman talks about with such unmitigated contempt fulfilled its intended narrative function:

> A bridge was needed to lead the audience from the real world to the fantasy world of the Carringtons. That bridge was, it turned out, felicitously easy to come by, she almost created herself.

Her name would be Krystle Grant Jennings, Blake's secretary, whom he would wed in the opening episode. An American Aphrodite, good as she is beautiful, Krystle maintains an abiding, charming – sometimes infuriating – disregard for Blake's wealth and a disconcerting propensity for keeping her head screwed on straight in spite of the opulence she has married into. She would epitomize everything women want to be and men want to love.

(Shapiro 1984: viii)

'Epitomize' is of course a key word here. It is relevant to just about all characters, in keeping with the serial's use of melodramatic devices. But the main points in this connection are that: (a) Krystle was intended as a 'bridge' for the audience between the real and the fantasy world of *Dynasty*, i.e. as object of identification; and (b) that this bridge 'almost created herself' as a carrier of a moral norm and common sense, i.e. she was a staple character of women-oriented popular fiction. While Shapiro only expresses a writer-producer's intent, the degree to which the producers succeeded in this respect can be seen from the reception data presented in Chapter 3 of this book: women writing and talking about *Dynasty* as bringing love and light into the world, how they 'suffer with Krystle', women's (family-oriented) weeklies constantly promoting Krystle as the icon of the show as a whole, obviously in keeping with how the show was perceived by its core audiences (and, incidentally, by my nine-year-old daughter, whose spontaneous drawing of 'watching *Dynasty*' had an enormous Krystle coming out of the TV set, practically filling the room with her kind smile and voluptuous chest). Krystle was extremely important to the show as a main provider of what Ien Ang (1985: 45) usefully termed *emotional realism*. While the world she inhabits is exotic and more or less 'unreal', the relations between characters, specific events and situations of conflict are recognized and experienced as very real. Without Krystle, this kind of 'reality-effect' would have been much harder to achieve.

Krystle is thus a key to an understanding of the show's particular appeal to women. She cannot alone account for this appeal, since the whole show is so clearly related to several traditions of 'mass-produced fantasies for women' (the subtitle of Modleski 1982), but she is definitely the 'bridge' that made the fantasy accessible and enjoyable to the vast majority of female viewers who did not feel like throwing up whenever she appeared. It could well be argued that the whole fictional universe and the various developments in it are seen from her point of view – most of the time. This is so on the one hand because there is basically so little doubt about what is right and what is wrong, good and bad, who deserves our sympathy, who does not, and when. It is evidently the good girl's moral sensibility which is reflected, also in the degree of motherly understanding provided for some transgressions. The modification 'most of the time' is necessary because there is also what I have called an authorial voice or point of view, most prominently represented by Alexis, termed 'the enunciator' by Mark Finch (1986: 38ff.) because of her ironical role on the borders of the diegesis, often coming close to addressing the viewers directly. This 'voice' delights in the ironical display of 'badness', adding a humorous, ironic tone to characters and events which from Krystle's point of view are deadly serious – such as Alexis herself and, for example, the fight in the lily pond. A clear-cut good-bad dichotomy is furthermore, as I will argue later, systematically under-cut by the never-ending narrative structure. This, in the long run, tends to render the distinction less significant than it is in truly melodramatic texts which emphasize lasting consequences of moral transgressions (see Chapter 6).

The other main indication of the importance of Krystle's point of view is that personal and family matters totally dominate as focuses of attention and motivation for action. What goes on in the offices of Colbyco and Denver-Carrington is largely the same as what goes on in the two homes and at La Mirage. Blake's business dealings and battles with various enemies are almost exclusively portrayed to the extent of their relevance to 'personal' or 'family matters'. (See below, p. 222, about the storyline concerning the government loan for the shale oil process.) This is a significant part of what makes *Dynasty* different from *Dallas*, where the 'most important conflict in the Ewing family is that of business interests', according to Gillian Swanson's analysis (1981: 33). The South Fork Ranch 'contains the domestic conflicts which are contingent on the action and relations set up by the Ewing business. The men come back in retreat from the business world and exert power over their women' (ibid.: 34). (It should be added here that later *Dallas* changed somewhat, giving women roles in the business world; see Geraghty 1991: 136.) Swanson's point must have been part of what Esther Shapiro had in mind when she said that whereas *Dallas* was rural and male, *Dynasty* was urban and female (Klein 1980: 37).

But in both *Dallas* and *Dynasty*, women 'can be seen as the moral centre of their families – Miss Ellie and Krystle Carrington. Certainly, these figures are crucial to the family set-up in that they act as a constant reminder to the men of the need for integrity, humanity and domestic harmony' (Geraghty 1991: 73). I would add that they remind not only men of these values, but certainly also a number of transgressive women at various times. They represent the moral standards of the audience, which condemn 'bitchy' women at least as much as men (cf. Modleski 1982: 94, 124 n.24). This is ideologically important. Christine Geraghty calls both *Dallas* and *Dynasty* 'patriarchal soaps':

> The male hero in US prime time soaps is engaged, then, in a continual struggle to keep control over the family, to bar entrance to unsuitable entrants and keep inside the family space those who belong there through birth or marriage. On his failure depends the continuance of the story since his absolute success would presage the lack of movement which signifies a happy ending.

> (1991: 69)

This is what separates the US prime-time soaps from their British counter-parts, which Geraghty calls 'matriarchal soaps'. Women tend to dominate not

211

only emotionally and morally in British soaps, but also practically and even financially. British soap families are also much more open than those of US prime-time soaps, thus both representing more of a community in themselves and an openness to the community outside the matriarchal, more or less extended family (ibid.: 69ff.).

Geraghty sees the continuing challenges to the patriarch's power in *Dallas* and *Dynasty* as a key to the pleasure women viewers find in them:

> It is the position of the hero which is at stake in US prime time soaps. The women may be the strongest figures but it is significant that their function is to offer the male characters alternatives, to challenge his control and to block his power. The pleasure for women viewers of patriarchal soaps is the demonstration that male power, challenged on the one hand by moral questioning and on the other by the women's refusal to be controlled, can never be fully or unproblematically asserted.
>
> (ibid.: 74)

I agree with this view. But there is one important addition to be made: while the patriarch's power is continually challenged, the genre makes it impossible for him to lose it. His position is just as permanent as the challenges to it. This is a basic premise for the serial, which makes the delight taken in, for instance, Alexis's attacks on Blake's power perfectly 'safe': they will never lead to profound, lasting changes.

The ludicrous 'ending' to the show provided in the two-part *Dynasty: the Reunion* has Blake reinstalled as the head of the family, reconciled not only with his mean son Adam (finally coupled with Kirby) and the gay Steven (in a stable gay relationship), but also with Alexis (still on her own) who gives a great speech about unbreakable family ties at the reunion dinner. Ironically, perhaps, this final clarification of ideals underlying the serial is actually far more subversive in its utterly unbelievable ideological 'closedness' than the ever-ongoing 'challenges' to the patriarch ever were.

This also brings to light how, in an era where 'family values' has been a primary slogan of the political right in the US, the *Dynasty* patriarch also all the time represented the US of A as a nation. The shale oil storyline in my material clearly underlined this, and the Britishness (i.e. foreignness, Europeanness) of Alexis was always clear to at least American viewers. She was also the one who in another storyline fraternized and plotted with evil Middle Eastern people. The meanest guy Fallon ever got involved with was also a foreigner (Peter de Vilbis). The unbearable aristocratic snobbishness and cruel terrorism found in 'Moldavia' (which, incidentally, in part was represented by footage from Øystese in Hardangerfjord, Norway) was among other tributes to American clichés about 'foreign countries', and the US as the only place for real democracy and unfailing morality in the world. Blake, though not perfect, even if made more mellow than he was in the beginning (cf. Chapter 1), represented US values not only as an incarnation of the American dream but also in a geopolitical context. The military connotations to the brass fanfares in the title sequence music were not accidental. None of the challenges to Blake's power in the serial ever cast the slightest shadow of doubt on this part of his role. The *Reunion* mini-series emphasized it to the nationalist and racist maximum by concentrating completely on a foreign 'syndicate''s brutal and clever attempt to take over the whole American economy, to control American society completely. The leader of this syndicate was European, but his two closest and meanest associates – one of them a black woman from Jamaica, the other an overweight East Asian – took over as he failed miserably (and idiotically) in the end. The battle would consequently still go on. It's good to have Blake back where he belongs. Where would Alexis, Krystle and the rest of the world be without him?

NARRATIVE TIME, THE DOMINANCE OF PLOTS AND THE ROLE OF DIALOGUE

The rhythmic regularity of the *Dynasty* experience is already one important element in its repetitiveness. *Dynasty* appeared in hour-long (in Norway, without the commercials, approximately 45–50-minute) weekly instalments. This immediately separates the serial from its close daytime relatives, which are broadcast daily. Contrary to daytime serials, *Dynasty* in the US also followed the seasons of other prime-time programming, going on 'hiatus' every summer. The importance of this for the narrative organization of the show is that the impression of immediate contemporaneity with viewers' lives is reduced. Still, the sheer weekly regularity of episodes in combination with the lack of closure creates much of the same effect: that life in the fictional world runs parallel to that of viewers. This notion underlies many formulations in the letters to the NRK, and can even be said to have been sustained by the way in which NRK announcers tended to introduce episodes: 'We are now going to Denver, Colorado' – implicitly or explicitly 'to see how the Carringtons are doing'.

Daytime writers will normally take care to keep the action of each episode within a twenty-four-hour frame, and their shows will also always reflect the time of year, marking seasonal phenomena such as Christmas and New Year (cf., for instance, a useful manual for daytime writers, Rouverol 1984: 41, 80). Though in many other ways they are quite different, this is also true of British soaps: in *EastEnders*, 'plastic daffodils are planted in the Square when filming takes place in early March to ensure that the flowers will be correctly in bloom in April when the episode is shown' (Geraghty 1991: 12). In *Dynasty*, seasonal changes are non-existent: the continuous sunshine and obviously comfortable temperature could be said to locate action in southern California, not Denver. But every episode adheres to the twenty-four-hour rule (see summaries of episodes in the Appendix), and the time lapse between episodes is normally, if not always, sufficiently unclear not to disrupt the feeling of simultaneity.

In following seasonal changes and imitating the twenty-four-hour span in each episode, the soap opera addresses a particular dimension of our sense of time: the circular dimension. This is no longer the socially dominant form of time in our modern societies, where linear time structures so much of our conception of selves, our practical realities and the way all kinds of institutions work. Circular time is still an important element in our everyday sense of time, and more so in some social settings than in others: not only farmers but also 'home-makers', and, for instance, long-term unemployed people may well experience circularity as a prominent feature of time. A third geometrical metaphor for the experience of time is the punctual form, where time is experienced basically as a succession of more or less disconnected moments, or moments related in an ebb-and-flow, pendulum rhythm. All of these forms of time may be seen to have counterparts in textual forms, in different kinds of textual syntax. A classical Hollywood film may be seen as representing linear or – in some cases, from some perspectives – circular time (to the extent that it returns to an identical situation). A variety show represents punctual time in its relative lack of causal or cumulative relations between its elements, making each act an 'island' which is appreciated in and for itself. It is also possible to relate these three forms of time to different kinds of societies, but the main point here is that all three exist in our culture even if the linear form is in many ways dominant, and that there are important tensions between them (cf. Johansen 1984).

Soaps mimic linear time in their intended impression of ongoing narrative progress and follow a circular time in their seasonal and twenty-four-hour rhythms. But punctual time tends to dominate not only by way of inserted show numbers (e.g. 43: 9) but, more importantly, by way of the ill-hidden repetitions of incidents and storylines which fail to make lasting marks on the characters or the basic structures of the fictional universe, and therefore appear strangely disconnected.

The effect of this partly 'faked' adherence to the experienced everyday time(s) of viewers is at least twofold: first, it obviously enhances viewer involvement by installing a feeling of close proximity to the fictional world and its characters, a reading of the story developments as 'real' even if they are of course known to be fictional. Second, its narratological consequence is that it affects the very construction of the narrative(s). Christine Geraghty has argued that '[i]nstead of narrative time being subordinate to the demands of the story, it dominates the narrative process and enables other formal structures to be brought into play. Time rather than action becomes the basis for organising the narrative' (Geraghty 1991: 11). This, particularly the latter sentence, is clearly problematic if it is taken to mean that there is narrative time without action (cf. the syntagm/paradigm discussion in Chapter 4). As Rouverol's writers' manual reminds its readers, *conflict* 'needs to be present or potential in almost every scene', though it does not have to be physical 'or even overt; sometimes it can exist in the most seemingly casual scene' (1984: 47). Rouverol goes on to list a large variety of human conflicts, and concludes that '*[t]here is conflict inherent in every human situation,* and it is the headwriter's task to recognize and make use of it. *Without conflict, there is no drama*' (ibid.: Rouverol's emphases).

What the soap opera narrative has to do, then, in daytime as well as prime-time versions, is to comply with two conflicting demands: its narrative time mimics real time, and yet 'almost every scene' must contain 'present or potential' dramatic conflict. The word 'dramatic' is worth stressing here, since there are limits to the triviality of conflicts one wishes to spend time watching. Even in the most scrupulously everyday-realist British soaps the conflicts portrayed are of a certain psychological or social significance. As pointed out by Michael James Intintoli (1984: 76), there are no dirty dishes, unmade beds or misbehaving children in American daytime soaps (and certainly not in *Dynasty*). The outcome of the collision between the kind of narrative time demanded by the genre and the demand for a continuous feed of conflict is, then, that the everyday of soap worlds of all kinds has a remarkably high degree of *drama*. And if this is so with daytime soaps, it is so to a considerably larger degree in prime-time serials.

Prime-time soaps are more spectacular in many ways not only because they also have to attract (male) breadwinners who traditionally would demand more physical action and more abrupt tension spans than a female audience of home-makers. They also must compensate for the relative lack of viewer involvement resulting from less frequent (not daily) encounters with the fictional world by employing stronger attractions in terms of heightened levels of tension, more spectacular scenes, more physical action and higher production values in general. Their ability to draw a demographically more complex audience than most daytime soaps had done up to about 1980, including males, younger and more educated groups, was probably one reason why daytime soaps made a similar change from about that time, and also achieved a demographic shift in their audience. (Cf. for instance Intintoli 1984: 84f., where a detailed overview of these changes in *Guiding Light* is given.)

In spite of the more pronounced reliance on the spectacular in prime-time serials such as *Dynasty*, the emphasis is still on intimate 'human relations', and most of the action consists in dialogues, just as in daytime shows. As I mentioned in Chapter 4, p. 166, Christine Gledhill has seen the dominance of talk over (physical) action as a defining feature of the soap opera genre. She ties it to the genre's origins in radio and the traditionally low budgets of soap opera production. The almost continuous chains of conversations in each episode are said to 'offer an arena for learning, for bringing things out into the open, talking problems over and working them through'. Soap opera thus 'constructs a feminine world of personal conversation, into which male characters are integrated' (Gledhill 1992: 114). This can obviously be tied to the point Christine Geraghty (1991: 124) makes (referring to Dyer 1981) about 'transparency' of human relations as one of the utopian ideals embodied in soap operas, the 'utopian possibilities of being open and honest in emotions without being hurt', and 'the capacity to speak out when necessary in defence of the truth', represented by Pam in *Dallas* and Krystle in *Dynasty*. The degree to which this aspect of the use of dialogue in soaps is specifically 'feminine' is debatable, however, since it is pervasive in so many other forms of drama (see Chapter 4, pp. 166 and 173) and also relates to a common belief in the therapeutic value of 'talk' in modern western culture. The question worth further examination would rather be what *kind* of talk fills soap operas, and whether it is different from or similar to the talk that fills other genres.

My impression of the dialogue in my material is that it varies considerably in style. This is no doubt related to the fact that so many different writers do the 'fleshing out' of episode scripts. The only pieces of dialogue that stick in my mind as really dense and dramatically both effective and interesting writing – excellently performed by the actor – are Nick Toscanni's rambling monologues as he saves Claudia from suicide in episode 16. Then there are a lot of well-placed cynicisms and witticisms, and not only from Alexis, though the humour in *Dynasty* (the intended part of it) is normally more tied to situations and physical acting than verbal comedy. A third category comprises the direct, unmitigated expressions of emotion at points of high tension or harmony, which is akin to the desire to 'say it all' characteristic of melodrama and the above-mentioned fantasy of 'transparency'. But finally, the quantitatively dominating category by far contains the simply functional and in themselves relatively boring (uninventive, cliché-ridden, without detectable self-awareness) exchanges of direct or indirect information about the characters, their relations and the things they do. This must be as a result of the time pressures of both the production process and the generic demand for a rapid succession of scenes. The functionality of dialogue is of course its role as conveyor of plotlines. Talk is (almost) all the action.

CHARACTER RELATIONS, STORYLINES AND THE PRINCIPLE OF ADDITION

Episode 16 was, as noted on pp. 207–8, introduced by a 'last week' resumé representing up to eight storylines, if this term is defined as an area of conflict with at least semi-independent developments. Such a definition is of course not very clear, on the other hand neither are the distinctions between storylines in the show. This is so mainly because the distinction between a storyline and a relationship between characters is impossible to make in an absolutely clear manner. (How to actually separate story- or plotlines is not addressed, and the very notion of 'storyline' or 'sub-plot' is not clearly defined anywhere in the scholarly soap literature.) Any relationship is potentially or manifestly disharmonious, or liable to produce conflict with some third party.

However, in all episodes there will be glimpses of relationships which for the time being seem stable. These glimpses have the important function of marking the continuous existence of the fictional universe as a whole. A full concentration on escalating conflicts would drastically reduce the feeling viewers have of observing a whole particular world and an unfolding, broad epic, a saga. The glimpses of relatively stable relationships thus work as a sort of glue or cement in the portrayal of the fictional universe, while also providing dramaturgically necessary spaces for 'breathing' or relaxation of tension within each episode. Closely linked to the latter function, they also add degrees of 'harmony' or even 'bliss' to the spectrum of emotional states offered by each episode (cf. the final section of this chapter, pp. 236–41).

One example of how this system works would be the story of Krystle's pregnancy. When Krystle discovers she is pregnant in episode 15, this seems to be a decisive development in the overall story of her marriage to Blake, where the issue of procreation was a recurring source of strong tensions throughout the first season of episodes. (Krystle secretly took birth control pills; Blake raped her when he found out in episode 7.) The pregnancy seems to close this area of conflict, and allows for scenes of blissful harmony, while it also provides the foundation for different stories – about Fallon's pregnancy and about Alexis organizing a riding accident for Krystle to make her miscarry. These are of course also stories within the story about Blake and Krystle but they still stand out as more or less separate chains of events. Similarly, the story of Blake's trial is obviously tied to his conflict with Steven, which is still a more general storyline with a number of sub-stories as the serial develops.

The organization of the plot structure is thus tied to relations between characters and resembles the hierarchical, upside-down 'tree' structure of IBM computer directories. Blake is the 'C' prompt, and not because his name is Carrington. As noted above (pp. 207–8), all storylines or areas of conflict are ultimately related to him, at least in this stretch of episodes. 'C' or 'Blake' contains 'directories' such as 'Blake:\Krystle', 'Blake:\Steven', 'Blake:\Fallon', etc. Each of these directories is in other words a comprehensive file for various sub-stories involving Blake and another major character. Since these other characters of course also interact, certain sub-stories will appear in more than one of the 'Blake:\' directories. The sub-story 'Fallon marries Jeff' is for instance part not only of the Blake:\Fallon and Blake:\Jeff directories, but also of the Blake:\Cecil Colby directory, since the marriage was part of Cecil's attempt to gain the upper hand in his competitive or adversarial relationship with his former friend Blake. Alexis complicates the system a little as early as episode 16. Her appearance immediately introduces the directory 'Blake:\Alexis', but also the sub-directory 'Blake:\Krystle\Alexis'. These directories will to a considerable degree contain the same sub-stories, since so many of Alexis's activities are directed towards destroying Blake's marriage to Krystle and putting Krystle down is part of this. But other of Alexis's projects as the serial develops are more or less limited to the realm of business, and thus belong more exclusively to the 'Blake:\Alexis' directory. This directory is also the file folder for sub-stories about Alexis and her children – Steven and Fallon, and later Adam and Amanda – since these stories are related to her struggle with Blake directly, not via Krystle. At the same time these sub-stories may be placed under the respective directories for Blake's relations to his children.

This computer directory metaphor of story organization illustrates the hierarchical ordering of conflicts and storylines, which is fundamental to the way each episode relates to the overall story and/or the fictional universe as a whole. A huge number of conflicting relationships are established, but most of these will be kept on the backburner or 'the hard disk' where they in that sense accumulate. Only very few (four to seven in my material) are 'pulled' to act as 'major' (one or two) or 'minor' storylines in each individual episode, while an additional few are merely hinted at without unfolding any further. Second, the metaphor is actually a possible tool for headwriters and story editors: they need such a system computerized or on paper, in order to keep track of relationships and developments. Closed files may be reopened, since they remain on the hard disk. Third, the computer metaphor emphasizes the degree of mechanics involved in the organization of the story/storylines.

Part of what I mean by mechanics here is that a simple *additive*, rather than dynamic and cumulative, principle underlies almost every significant new development in the serial. A new storyline does not really influence, at least not lastingly, characters or their relations, it is just added to the pile of previous stories. New storylines also regularly involve adding a new character, something which might be done in two ways.

The first one is, of course, having some new person appear from out of the past or outside the fictional universe established so far. Ted Dinard was one of these, and so was Alexis. After her (re)appearance, we were told that Blake had sent her away with $250,000 per year, on condition she stayed away from him and their children. Fallon and Steven were never told why mummy disappeared, and she never even sent them a postcard. In all the quarrels between the father and his children we witnessed in the first stretch of episodes, she was never mentioned. Of course, Blake and Alexis's long-lost children, Adam and Amanda, were never talked about either, until they appeared in the show. Other significant new characters in the episodes in my material include Nick Toscanni, Mark, Kirby, Congressman McVane, Dr Edwards from Montana and Steven's lawyer, Chris. Somewhere between episodes 46 and 57, Krystle's niece Sammy Jo was both introduced and temporarily sent away.

'A new character' might also be added by having an established character act 'out of character', for instance behaving much more stupidly or much worse than their initial presentation would seem to allow. A good example from my material would be big business executive Jeff's complete lack of intelligence when Adam has his office redecorated and he does not think of the new paint as the cause of his headaches and dizziness. Another example is Krystle's incredible lack of common sense when Mark says she is still not formally divorced from him. Or, when Kirby, the Sorbonne graduate, is not able to think of any way to terminate her pregnancy with Adam the rapist's child other than staging another riding accident. All of these storylines depend totally on an unbelievable change of character.

This latter technique is hardly separable from the use of a fundamental instability in characters introduced as 'double' in some way from the outset.

218

Sammy Jo, 'the valley-girl who escaped from the supermarket into the mansion' (Joan Braderman), is such a character. She is both a 'regular young woman', teenagerish but basically OK on the one hand, and a calculating bitch on the other. Kirby is another example, as sweetly innocent as her musical theme on the one hand, and a somewhat promiscuous, ambitiously scheming narcissist on the other. Claudia is a particular case, since her initial instability involved medically diagnosed psychosis. This makes her an ideal character in this kind of narrative regime: she can be made to do virtually anything and still remain in character. Most of the others are undiagnosed schizophrenics. Core characters like Blake, Fallon, Adam, Steven and 'good old smack-me-again Jeff' (Joan Braderman) are basically stable, but may either drop sixty points in their IQ score or suffer from amnesia or some other medical condition to allow wild storylines. In spite of her stupidity when the plotting so demands, Krystle is one of the most stable characters overall, for reasons discussed above (p. 209). The producers openly declared this a problem: 'I mean,' Esther Shapiro said, 'if she has to stay good, what do you have her *do*?' (Klein 1985: 36). The storyline where a bad, perfect *doppelgänger* is introduced, so two Krystles were in the show, was in fact conceived as a way to solve this problem. And in November 1986, Aaron Spelling declared at a press conference that the audience would soon see 'an Alexis you've never seen before' (*Los Angeles Herald Examiner*, 18 November 1986), i.e. Alexis would appear as a 'new character', meaning she would go soft and romantic on Blake.

All of this shows how the requirements of the *syuzhet* (cf. Bordwell 1985: 50) or plot (the specific arrangement of the story elements) dominates over the characters. Character 'serves a narrative structural function rather than being something which the narrative investigates', as put by Rosalind Coward (1986: 177). While it is important for writers to keep in mind what the audience already know about a character, so as to avoid all too obvious breaches in a believable, if not realistic, depiction of him or her, a character may, as noted above, still be stretched to the implausible if the plot requires it. The main objective of writers is always to maintain an optimum (not a maximum) of 'drama' in each episode (cf. 'The order of disorder', pp. 236–41). This is what makes the plot necessarily more dominant than character in the organization of the narrative. The need for a constant feed of 'new' conflicts leads to a steady feed of more or less 'new' characters, in one of the forms outlined above.

The second point of all this is that the successive developments in the serial are not determined from established character relations in a dynamic, continuous fashion. The various storylines develop on the basis of permanent tensions and conflicts in the basic set-up of characters and relations, which more often than not need 'new' characters to get going, even if Alexis or other baddies initiate them. Each new character adds a different touch to what basically, after the establishment of '*Dynasty* as we know it', are repeats. Krystle leaves Blake at least four times, and her troubles are not just related to the pendulum moods of the 'geriatric macho' (Braderman) Blake, they are also tied to the temptations of Matthew Blaisdel, Nick Toscanni, Mark Jennings and Daniel Reece. Alexis again and again uses her sexual charms – on Cecil Colby, Congressman McVane, Dex Dexter, etc. – in order to challenge Blake.

The impression of a family epic, a saga, has to be maintained, while the overall 'story' increasingly consists of an infinite chain of sub-stories which will tend to be sensational or shocking in some way, but, as noted above (p. 218), still fail to make any lasting impact on the characters. Just as characters appear out of the blue, they also disappear into the blue. Just a few examples from my material may illustrate this narrative amnesia.

Alexis is, from the start, doing her best to terrorize Krystle in any conceivable way. She is directly responsible for the riding accident which causes Krystle's miscarriage. In spite of this vicious act (and innumerable other stunts), Krystle is very surprised when Mark tells her that Alexis is behind his appearance at La Mirage in Denver, and there is often a humorous tone between these two women (notably 43: 9). Similarly, when the oil rig Steven works at explodes in episode 44, Blake says he 'feels closer to him than ever', and works desperately to find and bring back his beloved son. But shortly after Steven's return Blake is just as hostile towards him as he used to be. Adam tries to kill Jeff by having his office painted with an extremely poisonous compound (a main storyline in episodes 42–6). Eleven episodes later, Adam is not in jail, Jeff's brain is miraculously intact – and the relationship between the two is what it used to be. Even if Claudia was absolutely central to the serial and, indeed, to Steven's life, nobody says a word about her once she is placed in psychiatric care – until she is to be brought back.

The short and general conclusion practically any viewer will draw after a varying number of episodes is that *nobody ever really learns anything from their experiences* in this story. This is what makes for the intended or unintended irony in Blake's remark to Fallon in scene 14 of episode 42: 'Who remembers yesterday?' It is also why the spectacular changes of actors (Steven, Fallon) are relatively unproblematic. Rosalind Coward (1986) formulated the paradox: these serials which seem to demand so much of our memory demand at least as much of our ability to forget.

What all of this means is that a major part of all the information about a serial's developments, which faithful audiences accumulate, is in fact irrelevant or at least unnecessary. This significantly reduces the paramount importance recent soap critics have placed on extensive viewing. If (a) once important characters leave the show without leaving a trace, and the same goes for many experiences which would be deeply traumatic for real people; if (b) basic relationships remain the same, possibly swinging between two versions (harmony and conflict); and if (c) new characters (those with new names and faces) largely fill the narrative functions of characters who have left – then we have an explanation of why it is in fact so *easy* to return to a soap opera after a very long break. Bernard Timberg has recounted the following illustrating experience with daytime soaps:

220

Tuning into a soap opera I had once watched regularly but had not seen for a year and a half, I felt a shock of recognition. There they were – all my old friends and acquaintances from Port Charles (the mythical kingdom of *General Hospital*) just as they had been eighteen months before. It is true that several important events had occurred since I last tuned in, but people I had gotten to know [. . .] had not changed in any fundamental way, and more importantly, the soap opera rite itself was exactly the same. The same fluid camera movements took me into and out of each scene, making me feel somehow complicit in the ebb and flow of relationships and emotions in the soap world I had come to know so well. Because of my previous knowledge of the plot, characters, and conflicting moral principles in the soap opera, I was able to catch up – within a single day – on all the important developments. Almost immediately I settled into my customary patterns of booing and cheering, analyzing and second-guessing my favourite characters.

(Timberg 1982: 132)

This passage documents an actual reception, and it basically confirms the points I have tried to make above. There had been 'several important events' in the preceding eighteen months, but to Timberg nothing important had changed. The point is also expressed in the title of an article by Mary Cassata (1983): 'The More Things Change, The More They Are The Same [. . .]'. Moreover, the strikingly precise metaphor Timberg uses to describe the basic form of narrative development is 'ebb and flow', i.e. a pendular movement, back and forth, more than either linear or circular. Umberto Eco, speaking of the enormous, serialized nineteenth-century novel by Eugène Sue, *Les Mystères de Paris*, calls a similar phenomenon there a '*sinusoidal structure*' (1984: 132), which he says consists in an ever-ongoing switching between tension and (partial) resolution.

The soap opera narrative, here exemplified by *Dynasty*, is thus characterized across a large number of episodes by a specific configuration of weak forms of linear progress on the one hand and structurally dominating additive, pendular forms of repetition on the other. A variety of more or less dramatic events and more or less new characters serves to disguise the insistent repetitions of the same set of conflicts. The importance of these variations should not be disregarded, however, since they may provide a degree of topicality, for instance, a notable shift in narrative motifs: e.g. Steven's struggle with Blake remains the same, but the issue of gay parenting provides a new twist to it which helps to sustain interest in a conflict which would otherwise stand exposed as basically static and unbearably boring after some sixty episodes. Such twists, and dramatic events like fires, car crashes, attempted murders, fistfights, etc., may still after a while be perceived as what they functionally for the most part are: in the long run narratively inconsequential 'tricks' to provide pleasant bursts of emotion of one kind or another. When this is recognized, the narrative desire (cf. the following section) set in motion by earlier episodes, where a stronger sense of narrative progress prevailed, will necessarily be reduced. There is simply less motivation for investment when it is doomed to frustration. The options are then either to stop viewing, to continue in a more purely distanciated position, coolly observing the generic devices at work, or to swing between the two. The latter two alternatives, especially in the long run (when one knows the game really thoroughly), presuppose that there are very few other ways available to get the desired affective kicks and feeling of competence, and/or that the particular set of repeated relations and conflicts continues to exert a quite high degree of more or less unconscious fascination.

THE LACK OF ENDING AND NARRATIVE DESIRE

It follows from the organization of storylines charted above that every relationship is always in one of the four first stages or elements of a complete narrative identified by Todorov (1990: 29) who draws on a large number of theoretical and empirical studies from Aristotle on: (1) initial equilibrium; (2) the disruption of the equilibrium; (3) the state of disequilibrium; (4) the efforts to recreate equilibrium; and (5) the re-establishment of (a new) equilibrium. Todorov says any actual narrative may not include all of this cyclic structure; it may for instance leave out the first or the last two elements, but 'we sense that these [tales] would be two halves of the cycle, whereas here we have the cycle in full' (ibid.). With the exception of an occasional mini-story like Claudia's attempted suicide in episode 16, and scattered scenes of harmony (i.e. 'initial equilibrium'), the development and escalation of conflicts receive practically all the attention in *Dynasty*. I will give a couple of examples.

In many ways the most prominent storyline in episodes 42 and 43 is the one about Blake's struggle to get a loan in Washington which would allow a development of the 'shale oil process'. Blake is in severe financial difficulty if he does not get this loan: his whole empire is at stake, we are led to believe. This storyline seems to climax in episode 43, the party episode, where Alexis almost succeeds in getting Congressman McVane on her side, by rekindling an old sexual relationship between them. The most serious threat (as the story goes) to Blake's project is, in other words, introduced and handled successfully in the same episode, thus in a sense also creating a complete mini-story, like Claudia's suicide attempt in episode 16. But the story is not really over, Blake still has not got his loan. What is striking, then, is that the actual negotiations in Washington, and the following landmark political victory for Blake (the nation's future oil-supplies are at stake) are not dealt with at all. The victory is only reported in scene 21 of the following episode, where Adam tells Alexis that the newspapers have made Blake a national hero. In other words, the final element in a rounded, complete story is not given any story space worth mentioning.

Another example is the storyline about the legally invalid divorce between Mark and Krystle. A major problem here is that Krystle does not dare or want to tell Blake about the fact that legally she is a bigamist, so she keeps it a secret and tries to solve things herself, by going to Mexico to find out if Mark is telling the truth. This is of course a very stupid choice, and totally in vain, but that is what happens. Blake finally finds out where she is, and flies down for a surprise reunion. Krystle tells him the whole story, and Blake says what anyone with a minimum of intelligence would have suggested: that his lawyers should take care of the legal problem. We do get to see the two as harmoniously in love in most of a long scene here, but the shift of focus to a new storyline about serious *emotional* problems related to Krystle's previous marriage takes place in the same scene (scene 20, episode 44).

How can this constant avoidance of narrative resolution be accepted, and how does it affect the experience of the serial – and possibly life outside it?

Peter Brooks conceptualizes the 'passion for meaning' which drives readers through a literary text as 'narrative desire'. The reading of plot, 'the organizing line and intention of narrative', can be conceived as

> a form of desire that carries us forward, onward, through the text. Narra-
> tives both tell of desire – typically present some story of desire – and arouse
> and make use of desire as dynamic of signification. Desire is in this view like
> Freud's notion of Eros, a force including sexual desire but larger and more
> polymorphous, which (he writes in *Beyond the Pleasure Principle*) seeks 'to
> combine organic substances into ever greater unities'.
>
> (Brooks 1985: 37)

Narrative desire is thus 'the reader's efforts to construct meanings in ever-larger wholes, to totalize his experience of human existence in time, to grasp past, present, and future in a significant shape' (ibid.: 39). This notion of narrative desire, which ties our pleasure in narratives to the fundamental psychoanalytical notion of desire in general, is to me obviously useful as an attempt to understand the dynamics of reading (in an extended sense, including the 'consumption' of audio-visual texts), the force with which we all have experienced a drive to read on after bedtime, the strength of our involvement in the plot of a film.

But soap opera and *Dynasty* represent a textual form which not only repeatedly postpones (as all well-constructed narratives do) but *endlessly denies* the viewers a 'terminus' which might 'offer what we might call a lucid repose, desire both come to rest and set in perspective' (Brooks 1985: 61). If narrative desire is never really gratified, how can we account for so many viewers' 'hunger for more'?

Beverle Houston's formulation of what the ever 'hungry' viewer says of television may come to mind: 'I always want it as I never had it' (Houston 1984; cf. Chapter 3 above). Houston suggests that the promise of endless, twenty-four-hour flow in US television (unconsciously evoking the imaginary endless flow of the maternal breast) is part of the explanation for (US) television's continued attraction, in spite of its interruptive frustrations; the advertisements' promise of satisfaction of desire in consumption is another part of the explanation. But Norway did not have twenty-four-hour flow, and no commercials intervened to fill the gaps in the narrative circle. Even for American viewers, or those of other countries with commercial interruptions during programmes, I believe Houston's thought-provoking suggestions cannot adequately explain a specific serial's continued hold on its audiences. Such a serial must, whichever way the particular institutional supertext is organized, rely on its ability to kindle and keep alive a narrative desire related to its specific story. In other words, we need to return to the concept of narrative desire.

In a highly interesting article about how and when movie audiences are moved to tears, Steve Neale develops a more general argument about the pleasure of (melodramatic) narratives. He refers to (or rather relies on) Elizabeth Cowie, who once posited fantasy as 'the site and, in many senses the mode of existence, of desire' (Neale 1986: 13), and claimed that '[t]he pleasure of fantasy lies in the setting out, not in having the object' (Cowie 1984, cited in Neale 1986: 20). In Neale's formulation, the pleasure of fantasy 'resides in the process of articulation of a wish rather than in any representation of the attainment of its object', or, more directly related to *narrative* desire: 'In any story, pleasure comes primarily from the process of its telling, rather than from the nature of its ending' (1986: 20). This line of thinking is then taken a significant step further – from the point that the *nature* of the ending is relatively unimportant, to the point where any ending at all is unwanted. Cowie is quoted as saying that 'although we all want the couple to be united, and the obstacles to be overcome, we don't want the story to end', and that the pleasure is 'in the happening and continuing to happen; in how it will come about, and *not* in the moment of *having happened*, when it will fall back into loss, in the past' (Cowie 1984: 79f., cited in Neale 1986: 21). Neale goes on to say that an ' "unhappy" ending can function as a means of *postponing* rather than *destroying* the possibility of fulfilment of a wish. An "unhappy" ending may function as a means of satisfying a wish to have the wish unfulfilled – in order that it can be preserved and re-stated rather than abandoned altogether' (ibid.).

All of this may, at first glance, lead to the conclusion that soap opera's, and *Dynasty*'s, never-ending stories simply represent the best possible way to preserve narrative desire, and hence the pleasure of telling instead of reaching the dreaded ending of a story. But a basic problem with both Cowie's and Neale's stimulating argument(s), not untypical of much psychoanalytical theorizing in film and media studies, is that a vital distinction tends to be confused: that between desire in general and *narrative* desire. The confusion is, in other words, actually about the distinction between fiction and reality. Desire is of course never destroyed or 'abandoned altogether' by a happy (or unhappy) ending to a story. The end of *real* desire is death, absolute closure. The point of narrative is precisely to allow some sort of closure, outside death, a 'lucid repose', where 'desire [has] both come to rest and [is] set in perspective' (Brooks 1985: 61). This is something real life tends to deny us. It is true that we, as Cowie points out, may want (particularly exhilarating) stories never to end. But we normally choose 'the couple united' above the story's continuation, if that union is presented as really significant, i.e. as the focus of the story. We know that after the couple has been united, there will be little left to look or long for in that particular story – but, luckily, there are other stories, other novels, other films, another episode. The parallel to sexual desire and our general wish in that field for a 'lucid repose', or, as it has been put in French, *un petit mort*, is close at hand.

This is actually about what an ending to a story means. Neale argues that an 'unhappy' ending to a story might be more pleasurable than a happy one, and my point is that some sort of ending is anyhow not only desired but preferred. A distinction between ending as *resolution* (of conflict, of an enigma) and ending as *closure* (simply a 'stop' of some sort) is obviously needed, and I will return to this in the final chapter. If any ending is endlessly deferred, desire will eventually shrink, be withdrawn, and this goes for real life as well as for narratives. *Dynasty* (and soap opera narratives in general) endlessly defers both closure and resolution, and viewers will sooner or later learn to keep their emotional investments in the narrative at a level where their obligatory, continuous frustrations won't hurt. To the extent that the interaction with fiction bears on interaction with reality, viewers are, in a sense, trained in the art of withholding emotional investments. Useful training indeed, if one is to prepare for a modern reality in which deeper attachments to people and places are as a rule supposed to prove futile.

But both distanciated viewers and those who 'commute' between involvement and distanciation have to establish some sort of attentive relationship with the text, have to place themselves in relation to the fictional world they see unfold. If we allow the term to be used in a very loose and general way, we might say that some kind of 'identification' has to take place. The following section is an attempt to conceptualize more precisely which forms of identification *Dynasty* offered, and to show that this is where one of the most important reasons for the serial's success is located.

INVITATIONS TO INVOLVEMENT

Dynasty is a television serial. But contrary to daytime soaps, it was shot on film, with all the traditional procedures of single camera film production. In terms of visual style, it thus differs on many points from its daytime relatives. The pictures are brighter, with far better contrasts and colours, the framing is more careful than the three-camera video technique allows, etc. Even if the serial also clearly imitates daytime style in camera-work and editing (as in the monotonously repeated use of reaction close-ups at the end of practically every scene), the filmic quality of the show can be said to suggest a more cinematic viewing experience than much other television programming. The filmic use of music, played by a more or less full symphony orchestra, will, as argued on p. 196, also contribute significantly to such an effect.

It is both impossible and unnecessary for my purposes here to consider in any detail the by now quite massive amounts of work on the complicated theoretical issues of identification in cinema. Some of the most interesting and influential contributions here were made in the 1970s and draw on the Lacanian brand of psychoanalytic theory, his problematic, often too literally understood, theory of a 'mirror phase' in particular. (Anthologies like Rosen 1984 and Kaplan 1990 provide useful overviews and examples of arguments, but Metz 1982 is still, in my view, the best point of entry to this field.) I have previously touched on the notion of a generalized 'spectator' in this tradition, in Chapter 3 above. Stephen Heath's cautious parenthetical remark has not always been taken into account in the notions of spectatorship characteristic of much film analysis derived from so-called '*Screen* theory': 'What one has are films, discursive organizations, implications of spectating (the last formulation in order to avoid a "specta-tor" with its idea of a necessary unity, to stress the activity of looking . . . and hearing)' (Heath 1981: 100).

The main difference between televisual and filmic narratives, with respect to the viewer's psychic involvement in the text, lies in *the different socio-material contexts of viewing.* The specific viewing situation in the cinema, including the specific technological set-up (the projector, etc.), is a fundamental premise of the psychoanalytical account of the viewing experience, the viewer's willing psycho-logical immersion in the experience of the fictional narrative. The viewer's physical immobility in the theatre, the darkness which more or less covers up the presence of other viewers and any (other) distracting element in the room, the size of the cinema screen – all of this contributes to make the parallel between the film and the dream experience seem reasonable:

> In ordinary screening conditions, as everyone has had the opportunity to observe, the subject who has fallen prey to the filmic state (most of all when the grip of the fiction on his phantasy is sufficiently strong) feels he is in a kind of daze, and spectators at the exit, brutally rejected by the black belly of the cinema into the bright, unkind light of the foyer, sometimes have the bewildered expression (happy or unhappy) of people waking up. To leave the cinema is a bit like getting up: not always easy (except if the film was really indifferent).
>
> (Metz 1982: 117)

In reality, people's experience of the cinema has always been much more varied. Anyone who has been to an afternoon screening of a Hopalong Cassidy film for a youthful audience will know that the film was perceived more like a sports event than a dream; anyone who has been to the movies as part of adolescent dating rituals will know that the film may be far less exciting than the person next to you. There is the eating of pop corn (the fatty smell in many American cinemas) and other pleasantly unhealthy snacks, consumption of soft drinks and occasional small talk or shouting in the audience. Increasingly, it seems that people take their TV viewing habits to the cinema. In spite of all these modifications, it still appears reasonable to say that the experience of viewing television rarely approaches the level of 'immersion' in the narrative experience achieved by an effectively constructed 'classical' movie. But, importantly, this is not only related to the domestic setting in which watching television takes place, the more or less small size of the screen and the sound quality. It also has to do with the way in which the majority of broadcast television texts have been constructed so as to correspond structurally to a domestically distracted form of viewing. John Ellis (1982) has emphasized the segmentation principle as the flip side of broadcast television's characteristic audio-visual 'flow' (a concept coined by Raymond Williams 1975 after his first confused encounter with American commercial television). Ellis defines a segment as a self-contained (in terms of meaning) piece of audio-visual text, lasting a maximum of about five minutes (1982: 112), and claims that (practically) all TV programmes, fictional or non-fictional, are constructed as a series of such segments. While this principle may stem from any broadcaster's perception of domestic audience attention, it is markedly less pronounced in public service television than in commercial television channels, where programmes are interrupted by advertising. It is less pronounced in the sense that programming in public television will both most often lack the in-programme commercial breaks and also provide much more space for genres of programming where other temporal structures prevail (Hollywood or non-Hollywood feature films, theatre and ballet performances, TV drama constructed as feature films or stage drama, jazz and classical or contemporary concerts, etc.). This means, in other words, that an audience used to the relative generic variety of public service television will have a more 'cinematic', less distracted form of viewing as a part of a repertoire of viewing forms or competencies. The 'metapsychology' of TV viewing outlined by Beverle Houston (1984; see also Chapter 3 above), based on constant interruptions and the role of commercials, pointing to the supermarket as the place for the liquidation of desire, will in other words be less relevant, or at least less dominant. The Norwegian woman who told a newspaper reporter that 'words cannot describe' the disappointment she felt when a power failure made her lose an episode of *Dynasty* (see Chapter 3) must obviously have been closer to Metz's cinema 'dreamer' than to a cool TV channelhopper when watching, closer to a 'gaze' than a distanciated 'glance'.

As I have tried to argue in other sections and chapters, certain significant parts of the Norwegian audience may have retained this cinema-style viewing practice throughout at least most of the show's first run of fifty-nine episodes. As the generic principles of repetitive plotting became clear, the dominant mode of reception gradually became, so to speak, adjusted to international standards and the text's segmented, multiplot structures, i.e. came to consist in a pendular movement in and out of emotional involvement (cf. Chapter 3 above). Bernard

Timberg's (1982) description of his involvement in the narrative seems exemplary: a combination of being 'complicit' in emotions and relationships, while also 'booing and cheering, analyzing and second-guessing' – or as put by Ien Ang: 'A constant to and fro movement between identification with and distancing from the fictional world as constructed in the text [. . .] characterizes the involvement of the letter-writers who like *Dallas*' (1985: 50).

My May 1984 survey (see Chapter 3) indicated that most viewers could identify characters in the show who resembled people they knew. There was, in other words, a widespread feeling of a considerable degree of realism in the portrayal of many characters – in fact most members of the Carrington family – which was not really hindered by all the signs of an exotic, affluent lifestyle. A Bergen industrial leader also declared on the front page of *Bergens Tidende* that 'Blake Carrington is my ideal', thus signalling a traditional admiring identification with the leading male protagonist.

Admiring identification is a category of involvement with a protagonist in Hans Robert Jauss's (1977) classificatory scheme, in which the readers identify with a more or less invincible and/or invulnerable hero. This is a quite simple form of identification, represented particularly in older male-oriented popular fiction, and referred to in Freud's well-known parallel between ego-boosting daydreams and fiction writing (Freud 1977). Admiring identification with Blake is in line with Esther Shapiro's saying 'I *am* Blake Carrington' in interviews (see Chapter 1), and may occasionally take place with Alexis (the things she dares!).

However, what Jauss calls *sympathetic identification* is much more clearly suggested as a preferred mode by the *Dynasty* text. This is identification with a more everyday hero/ine, similar to the reader, suffering and struggling with problems the reader is familiar with and/or can relate to, on the basis of her/his own experiences and moral standards. It is the mode of identification suggested by the sentimental novel of the late eighteenth century, many nineteenth-century novels and various 'confessional' forms of texts. A third category is *cathartic identification*, which is identification with a character who is basically like the reader but undergoes extreme trials of one kind or another. Following Aristotle, Jauss asserts that such identification, whether tragic or comic, leads to a cathartic experience, through tragic 'shaking' or comic relief. Melodrama might typically invite such a form of identification, so probably do most Hollywood films, whether marketed as (melo)dramas or not. *Dynasty* may be said to invite such identification to the extent that, and as long as, the characters' suffering is taken seriously.

What happens in the 'to and fro' or 'in and out' form of identification with *Dynasty* (and, for instance, *Dallas*) is that the 'sympathetic' and 'cathartic' forms of identification are replaced by another form of involvement – for it is still involvement: even 'the deconstructive, ironic or camp modes of reading a popular text [. . .] are aimed at maintaining a pleasurable relation to the text' (Elsaesser 1992: 21). These modes might be of a kind Jauss calls *ironic identification*. This is a form of identification which is constantly broken up by the text. Readers are led to expect identification, but the text then turns ironical or totally denies identification. This constant frustration of expectancies, again and again, demands, according to Jauss, distanciated reflection on the side of the readers. The hero becomes an 'anti-hero', because the reader must experience her/himself as 'above' the character(s) in some way, while still recognizing something in her/him/them. In *Dynasty*, we may even, finally, in line with the 'dollhouse' metaphor, find elements of what Jauss calls *associative identification*; the mode of identification found in play, games, and certain popular festivities (such as rock concerts) where the difference between performers and audiences is reduced or non-existent.

It will by now be clear for some readers that Jauss's categories are basically not very original: they are obviously related to the classifications of heroes made by Aristotle and, a couple of millennia later, by Northrop Frye in *Anatomy of Criticism* (1957). But while Aristotle related his three categories of heroes to particular genres and Frye related his five categories to historical periods, Jauss regards all of his five forms of identification as synchronically available and, in principle, combinable in relation to one and the same text. Jauss's categories of identification are hermeneutic, not psychoanalytical, categories. Identification is defined by Jauss as 'patterns of interaction' with a fictional character, and I use his categories here mainly as descriptive terms. The point is that *Dynasty* can be regarded as inviting all five of Jauss's forms of identification or 'interaction', at different times, with different characters, for different types of audiences. This is the most striking complexity in the *Dynasty* text: the complexity of its *address*. This may be seen as related to its production (Chapter 1) and goes a long way to explaining how it could entertain very different audiences.

Krystle is constructed as an object for sympathetic and cathartic identification through a number of narrative and visual devices. I need only give a few scattered examples: in episode 16, scene 3, the shot of Alexis crossing the lawn, accompanied by ominous music, is taken from Krystle's point of view, from her bedroom, where the previous scene took place. Like subjective camera in feature films, this places the viewer in the protagonist's position. The shot conveys Krystle's experience, invites viewers to share her emotional point of view; this is reinforced by the music and by visual metaphors: Alexis appears dressed in black, and she moves from the outside towards/into the house/family. Such shots of Alexis as a serious threat alternate throughout the serial with shots in which she is practically addressing the viewers directly, with a wink of the eye, an ironic comment, etc. In the 'Mark' storyline in episodes 42–6, we are repeatedly given long flashbacks representing Krystle's memories of her previous relationship with Mark. Even if we also see Jeff's distorted vision of Kirby as Fallon, and Adam's memory of a talk he once had with a certain Dr Edwards, it is clearly the inside of Krystle's head that is given most attention throughout the serial. We do not get similar sensitive, privileged information about Blake or Alexis. In 58: 4, the final shot is a dramatic zoom out to an extreme bird's-eye view of Krystle, alone and crying in the nursery after Steven has picked up his baby son Danny, highly sentimental music accompanying. This classic and highly expressive (some would say excessive) device is never used with other characters. The crane shot of Steven and Adam on a desert airfield in 57: 22 may also be strikingly cinematic, but its meaning is less in its emotional connotations than in its underlining the simple fact that the two are miles away from anything and from Steven's dinner date with Blake and Krystle in particular. Furthermore, identification with Krystle is not a purely maso-chistic identification with a 'Polyanna' who is passively accepting whatever fate presents her with. Krystle is often shown biting back at Alexis, sometimes even wittily, as when she compliments Alexis for her desk with elephant tusks as legs: 'I love your desk. The tusks, they're so *you*!' (57: 12). Such scenes are necessary to keep Krystle as an object of sympathetic identification, never allowing her to slide into the despicably weak, which would force viewers to withdraw in order to maintain their self-esteem.

Alexis is definitely Krystle's opposite in most ways. Though we are constantly given privileged information about what she does and plans to do, we are never allowed directly into her mind, her thoughts, feelings, memories, etc. The consistently external portrayal of her is taken one important step further in the almost equally consistent theatricality of her appearance and performance. Her clothes are normally on the verge of being too elegant, and sometimes clearly crossing the line to the ridiculous (e.g. 57: 12). (Joan Braderman calls her a 'monstrous victim of fashion', but then she also says the whole cast consists of 'dressed-to-kill aliens'.) Krystle's 'natural' look, from her hairdo to her clothes, makes for a striking contrast. Alexis's manners also symbolize her role as a scheming bitch, so excessively that the humour and irony become obvious to almost anyone. This serves to make her less of a threat than a treat to the viewers. Even if they can see her as a serious problem for Krystle, she eventually becomes a largely humorous character who is more of a threat to Blake than to Krystle. This is one of the changes which occur as she moves from the garden studio to her position of power at Colbyco. In the scenes between the two in episodes 42–6 and 57–8, Krystle confronts her in a self-assured and sometimes appropriately aggressive manner (cf. above), treats her like an overbearing mother (45: 8), competes with her in a humorous way (43: 9) or starts a physical fight (58: 14). The latter two kinds of scenes are offered as pure shows, as spectacles intended to be funny. Their emblematic status for the show as a whole is reflected in the fact that the *Reunion* mini-series included a long and relatively elaborate version of a physical fight between the two. Alexis is, in '*Dynasty* as we know it', increasingly a sort of difficult sister for Krystle, not a dangerous villain. Since she is also largely what I have called a particularly irritating horsefly in her relations with Blake, it becomes clear that the 'phallic mother/woman', the 'castrating machine' (Joan Braderman) Alexis is, in a sense, herself castrated by the show, i.e. domesticated, rendered more entertain-ing than threatening. Admitting or openly enjoying a partial identification with

Alexis, admiring and ironic at different times or simultaneously, thus becomes much less of a problem (cf. Chapter 3).

Consequently, while Alexis is in some ways constructed as the ultimate bitch, her bitchiness is undercut, so that she ends up quite different from the bitches of daytime soaps. There the bitch is the one character 'whom we are allowed to hate unreservedly' (Modleski 1982: 94). Tania Modleski has seen the villainess of daytime soaps as 'the negative image of the [female] spectator's ideal self', who 'embodies the "split-off fury" which, in the words of Dorothy Dinnerstein, is "the underside of the 'truly feminine' woman's monstrously overdeveloped talent for unreciprocated empathy"' (ibid.). In contrast, Alexis cannot be hated 'unreservedly'. The ability she shares with daytime villainesses to 'transform traditional feminine weaknesses into the sources of her strength' (Modleski 1982: 95), i.e. her uninhibited use of her (and men's) sexuality in her struggle for power, is combined with 'her own skills at the kind of business manoeuvring which was previously deemed to be a masculine prerogative' (Geraghty 1991: 136). This is what creates the ground for admiring identification with her, turns her into a partially positive figure whose ruthlessness comes across more or less as an ironic, humorously acceptable feature of the ultimate competitive 'career woman' of the 1980s, the decade of male and female yuppies. In addition to this, her being undefinably middle-aged is also important. Her striking ability to attract and manipulate men by way of her sex appeal might be a particular pleasure for women of her age group and those on their way to it. Alexis demonstrates, in the words of Joan Braderman, that 'even if you're old and bitchy, if you have enough money, the right make-up man, and Nolan Miller to design your clothes, you can still get laid over fifty'.

It may be concluded from this that Alexis provides many of the central pleasures that *Dynasty* offers, i.e. distanciated forms of involvement which will tend to break the sympathetic identification centrally represented by Krystle. This pattern is, however, also produced in other ways. Viewers are cued to identify sympathetically with, for instance, Jeff, Steven and (for the most part) Kirby. (A sympathetic identification is also invited with villains and villainesses at times, as with Adam's fear of being exposed when he hears Dr Edwards is on his way to La Mirage and we get a flashback representing Adam's memory, in 58: 11.) But at the same time viewers are allowed more information than any of these characters, and in addition, as noted above, these characters often act in obviously unintelligent ways. Thus the position of superiority in which the text places the viewers is one in which empathy may be modulated by a distanciated, observational effect, not just a feeling of powerlessness in relation to developments – which is emphasized by Tania Modleski as an effect of the motherly 'multiple identification' characteristic of daytime soaps (1982: 91). If viewers have established an adequate understanding of genre conventions, the main issue raised by Adam's attempt at poisoning Jeff (episodes 42–6) is not whether Jeff will die or end up struggling with severe brain damage in the following seasons, but when and how he or someone else will come to realize what viewers have known all along. For those unaware of the mechanics of plotting, on the other hand, Jeff's suffering will call for extreme sympathy and a wish to help. It seems probable that most viewers actually belong to an intermediary category, which will tend to swing between these alternatives, and resort to the observational mode when sympathetic identification becomes too painful or humiliating.

This latter option is then indicative of the pattern of involvement in the show as a whole. '*Dynasty* as we know it' is constructed so as regularly to offer relief from potentially painful forms of identification. Evil is made playful and relatively harmless, sympathetic identification with Krystle is interrupted by offers of ironic identification with Alexis, superiority over characters in terms of story information enables an overall observational position or a kind of 'associative identification'. The point is not confrontation with and insight into the forces, conflicts and dilemmas underlying the diegetic universe and the various plotlines, it is to use them as more or less covert sources of fascination, as 'bait'.

THEMATIC RECURRENCE: INCEST – A FAMILY GAME

We will now turn from the syntagmatic organization of the storylines to their paradigmatic structures in order to analyse what the relationships and storylines chosen to appear in the serial are 'about', in what ways, and what they exclude. We are, in other words, approaching the *thematic* level of the text. A full analysis here should also have included dimensions of the text other than the narrative itself, such as mise-en-scène, editing, etc. For reasons of space, this is impossible. Suffice it to say that the conclusions of such an analysis would in part have reduplicated those of the analysis of the title sequence in Chapter 4, and that other elements of such an analysis are scattered in various other sections. I should also point out that I will return to the issue of *Dynasty*'s particular ideological character and 'message' in the final chapter of this book. In the following, the mid-season episodes 42–4 have been chosen for a closer examination of narrative themes.

If the whole range of characters is ordered according to age and sex, they largely boil down to a very few roles: father, mother, son, daughter are the basic four; a male rival for daddy must be added as a fifth. The system is made slightly more complex through duplication of each of the five basic roles – there is a good and a bad version of each – making in all ten basic roles. (A further mathematical possibility for 'complication' is suggested by the two-by-two table developed by sociologist Nora Scott Linzer, included in Cassata 1983: 92; this is based on a distinction between good and bad characters, who may be all good or all bad, or have bad and good sides.) These ten roles then make up a paradigm of characters which is structured like a duplicated nuclear family, plus a good or bad male rival representing an exterior threat to the family. Every storyline is constructed by having old or new characters fill at least two of these roles, one good and one bad, and then letting the conflict escalate. The character paradigm clearly indicates how the serial is related to melodrama by continuously playing out not only moral dramas but also versions of the Oedipal drama as conceived in Freudian theory. (Cf. Chapter 6, 'Meaning vs manipulation: melodrama vs melodramatic devices', pp. 242–8.) This does not mean that the serial is 'actually' only about 'sexual anarchy' or transgression of sexual taboos, it is also very much about the problematic instability of identities and relationships – and politics. More concretely, the basic themes of the show may be identified as follows.

In the storyline about the shale oil loan, Blake's financial powerbase is threatened by stupid politicians – and Alexis, the bad woman. The story is thus very closely tied to the power struggles in Blake's family, as evidenced also by Adam showing himself as a bad son by trying to take advantage of the situation and break his father's power. Jeff is the loyal, good son here (as usual). It is in other words a situation where the basis of father's power is challenged, and where Blake's equation of father's interests with those of the nation is not questioned by anyone or anything in the story at all. The theme here may be formulated as an opposition between an equation of father and nation with harmony and (continued) prosperity on the one hand, and an equation between a disrespectful and egoistical son and narrowminded, unproductive Washington politicians with disharmony and loss of prosperity on the other. Disruption of the power of father/capital/private enterprise equals social and economic disaster. On the other hand, Adam represents *irresponsible* private enterprise, i.e. the need to have capital checked, not by political intervention (the corrupt, bureaucratic 'Washington'), but by good old individual morality. When in episode 42, scene 12, Adam wants to use Blake's shale oil trouble to take over Denver-Carrington, and says 'the name of the game is winning', Jeff opposes this simple principle of capitalist competition: 'I mean, do we have to be barracudas to exist in this world?' Jeff here clarifies the show's Reaganite political message, and thus the position of Blake as the basically *good* patriarch, good authority, who still needs a 'female' adjustment to 'human values' and ordinary morality once in a while. This theme may be said to frame the following.

The storyline(s) about Mark is about the adventures of a lower-class tennis pro among the Carringtons. Mark's main function is always the same: that of sexually destabilizing Blake's family empire by getting involved with the women he controls or wishes to control, first Krystle, then Fallon and Alexis. Mark thus represents sexuality as potential anarchy, threatening the sexual dominance of the patriarch as he chases and attracts wives, mothers and daughters alike. This role is also signalled in his presentation in the title sequence (see p. 192). Moreover, the more or less incestuous nature of his entangled sexual relations with stepmother, mother and daughter is quite obvious. Mark is young in relation to Blake and could well be his (hitherto unknown) son. Or he could be Alexis's son from a hitherto unknown fling in her younger years, just like

233

Fallon (cf. episode 16, scene 21). As an external 'male rival', then, Mark serves to demonstrate that women's sexuality is a potential threat to the patriarch's control, as 'son' he represents the incestuous chaos resulting from keeping sexuality within the confines of the family (cf. p. 236).

The storyline about Adam's identity centres on two permanently tense relationships, that between Blake and Adam, and that between Fallon and Adam. The first of these obviously thematizes men's eternal problem with the lack of absolute certainty that they are really the fathers of children their women give birth to. It may thus be seen as another version of the 'controlling women's sexuality' problem in the 'Mark' storyline. But it may also be said to be about the uncertainty of identity in general. This is effectively dramatized in the relationship between Fallon and Adam, where incest – this time between brother and sister – is openly presented as a titillating possibility. There are quite obvious sexual implications whenever Fallon and Adam meet, signalled by proximity, glances and other non-verbal signs, and Adam is also repeatedly more or less explicit in his invitations (cf. 42: 18 and 43: 16). Fallon is, from the beginning, presented very much as daddy's girl. Speculations in the reception material about her eventually marrying Blake (see Chapter 3 above) are by no means without foundation in the text. As noted above, Alexis tells Steven (and viewers) in episode 16 that Fallon is not actually Blake's daughter, and this amplifies certain symbolic potentials in the opening scene of the same episode, where Fallon in a tiny baby-doll nightgown sits in a huge tree, riding on a solid branch, talking about how much she wishes both Krystle and Alexis would go away. (I asked the Pollocks if sexual meanings were intended in this scene, but they told me such meanings were entirely my creation. I still believe this directorial choice was based in a very long tradition in the depiction of scantily clad young women sitting on things like solid branches, and was not just an accidental choice of a locus which would emphasize Fallon's childishness.) The 'Adam' storyline thus not only thematizes the uncertainty of the patriarch's control over his women, but again also, emphatically, the uncertainty of identity.

The near deadly battle between Adam and Jeff is a sibling rivalry between the bad son and the good son. They initially seem to fight over the chief executive's office at Colbyco, which is owned 50 per cent by Alexis, 50 per cent by Jeff. Jeff has admirably managed to stay friends with both Blake and Alexis, while Adam has been mostly rejected by Blake and is also constantly reprimanded and openly threatened with rejection by Alexis, with whom he lives. Adam thus has at least three reasons for his rabid jealousy (the company, mum and dad) and the introduction of Kirby represents a fourth. However, in the very episode where the storyline gets going (Jeff demands his office, Adam buys paint), Alexis also extends a sexual invitation to Jeff which is as good as explicit (42: 17). This emphasizes a sexual, in effect incestuous, potential in their joint ownership of Colbyco. There is, then, clearly a fight over access to mother's bed component in Adam's hatred of Jeff. Incest is again lurking just millimetres beneath the surface, at times rising above it, in a maze of sexually infused power struggles and uncertain identities.

With Kirby's story, I had the pleasure of feeling 'smart' (cf. Eco 1988: 454) for a while when I recognized the story in Billy Wilder's *Sabrina* (1954), where Audrey Hepburn played a chauffeur's daughter who grew up loving William Holden but ended up loving Humphrey Bogart, the two sons of a mega-rich man whose house(hold) resembled Carrington's. But then Kirby made this intertextual reference explicit (46: 3) and my 'distinction' was gone – I was no longer in an exclusive category of viewers. Anyway, Kirby's story develops quite rapidly after her introduction in scene 10 of episode 42. In the following episode she is already sexually approached by Adam (a very dangerous version of the irresponsible William Holden) and kissing Jeff (the solid and somewhat boring Humphrey Bogart). We have also, as with Sabrina, been informed that she grew up more or less believing she was a Carrington. This means that she is about to take over her imaginary sister's husband, i.e. her imaginary cousin Jeff, who is practically Blake's son, hence also her imaginary brother. She is chased by, and appears not altogether opposed to, her imaginary brother Adam. She does not push him away when he grabs her by her naked arms and hissingly compliments her 'silken skin'. There are also other signs that Adam is in a sense speaking to the 'indecent' side of her, which viewers know of from glimpses of her life in France, revealed to Fallon in particular. So if Kirby's adventures are not *de facto* incestuous, they are very close to it. Her lower-class background is modified by her Sorbonne education (a degree in 'you know, the humanities', she says as she takes the job as Fallon's nanny in 43: 4). While it may serve to invite sympathetic identification, her father (like Sabrina's) is the only one who talks about the class difference as a problem (44: 17). Kirby's story thus not only reiterates themes of incest and identity, but also, emphatically, the theme of a split in female sexuality between the proper romance and improper, 'wild' desires, externalized in the opposition between Jeff and Adam, as Pearl's desire in *Duel in the Sun* (King Vidor, 1946) is represented by Joseph Cotten and Gregory Peck (cf. Mulvey 1989 and pp. 208–9 above).

In episodes 42–4, the storyline about Blake and Steven has Fallon acting as Blake's bad conscience. Blake reluctantly agrees to organize a search for Steven in scene 23 of episode 44, but says Fallon will have to talk him into coming home. In scene 24 we get a glimpse of Steven, before the oil rig he works on is shown exploding. Blake's problems with accepting Steven (also dropping him from his will in episode 16) are not only related to his being gay or at least bisexual. They are also tied to the repeated fact that Steven is mummy's boy, Alexis's favourite (not really surprising in view of a traditional psychoanalytic 'explanation' of homosexuality). Fallon's particular affection for Steven is also strong. Steven is thus very clearly also Blake's rival in relation to mummy/ex-wife Alexis and daughter Fallon. The Oedipal, incestuous implications hardly need pointing out. Steven's swinging between homo- and heterosexual relationships further emphasizes the 'uncertain identities' theme, and his homosexuality not only reiterates the 'anarchic' potential of sexuality, but also, in principle, represents a threat to the male hereditary line.

It may be concluded then, that incest, transgression of the most fundamental and universal taboo across the globe, is involved in all storylines except possibly the first, about the shale oil loan. I have not even mentioned the point made by Mark Finch about the 'para-incestuous' nature of the relationship between Blake and Krystle, extra- but contextually (in the US) underlined by the fact that Linda Evans once played John Forsythe's young niece (for whom Forsythe fulfilled a father's role) in the sit-com *Bachelor Father* (Finch 1986: 26). The ubiquitousness of incest is narratively a result of total concentration on a single family, and Blake's struggle to control it. Terry Lovell once remarked that 'incest is precisely the logic of all attempts to confine sexual desire to home and family' (quoted from Geraghty 1991: 70). The 'overkill' occurrence of incest in this show may have been dimly perceived by some viewers who, informally, told me they felt its atmosphere stiflingly claustrophobic, impossible to watch in the long run. Certain analytically minded or camp-oriented groups were obviously able to see that the show played with the possibility of incest, but from their relatively distanciated position, such a realization would only add to their ironic amazement at the show.

However, neither for such viewers nor for those less analytically disposed, would the incest theme appear as painful or uneasy in any way. Speculations on Fallon eventually marrying Blake did not, as I said in Chapter 3, destroy the 'family fun' experience of the show. The same goes for the incest theme regarded as an amplifying metaphor for the realistically deeply troubling lack of stability in identities and relationships. Obviously, the show was, in various ways, constructed so as thoroughly to blunt the impression of total socio-psychological crisis which its storylines actually build on. The glamour, pace, music and an intricate plotting all contributed to this effect. Viewers might thus, for instance, concentrate on its visual and other immediate gratifications or on trying to solve plot puzzles in the manner recorded by Kim Schröder (1988; cf. Chapter 3) instead of reflecting on the potentially very deeply disturbing thematic implications of the narrative(s). What is, however, perhaps the most important element in the show's deferral of attention from its dangerous thematic core, is the combined effect of all the elements that go into its dramaturgical construction, i.e. its invitation to a carefully constructed emotional rollercoaster experience in each episode. This is the topic of the final section in this chapter.

THE ORDER OF DISORDER

I noted on p. 213 that each episode roughly follows the twenty-four-hour rule of daytime soaps, i.e. that its action is supposed to take place in the course of one day. Many episodes start with a breakfast scene, and have nighttime scenes towards the end. But the temporal relations between each of the daytime and nighttime scenes are as a rule quite unclear: it is most often impossible to decide whether scenes are to be seen as taking place simultaneously or in sequence, and the temporal order of the whole episode tends to get blurred, except for the start at breakfast and the finish at night. This is a feature *Dynasty* shares with daytime soaps, and it seems to result from a historically developed, conscious strategy. While, for instance, daytime soaps used to dissolve from one scene to the next, they now use cuts, since, as an experienced writer of soaps reminds us, 'dissolve has come to imply the passage of time, and it slows up the action, whereas a *cut implies immediacy.* It is far better, then, to imply more or less simultaneous or continuous action within each act; it keeps the story going' (Rouverol 1984: 84). Whether the action is 'more or less' simultaneous or continuous is in other words of little importance, at least within each act. The ideal is, one might say, a kind of 'compressed' time; everything happens within one 'expanded' moment.

But if linear time does not decide the syntagmatic sequence in which scenes are ordered when an episode is put together, what is it then? The key to an answer is in the point I made e.g. 216f: that each episode has a carefully constructed itinerary of highs and lows in terms of dramatic tensions. This is also why I have talked about an optimum, not a maximum, of conflict (p. 219). A consideration of the emotional and affective quality of each scene, and its presumed impact on audiences, tends to decide their ordering, which storyline is 'visited' when. The show is primarily edited in accordance with the level of tensions reached in each individual storyline, so that a certain affective pattern is achieved; only secondarily in relation to chronology, the time of day or night at which incidents take place.

The affective-syntagmatic ordering of each episode is based in the various storylines, but it must still be thought of as rising above the immediate level of narrative, as a 'supra-narrative' structure. This is hardly unique to *Dynasty*. It may be a more general feature of recent television fiction that 'any form of narrativity tends to be subordinated to a dynamic on the formal and technical-structural plane', as put in a Danish analysis of *Dallas* (Kofoed and Rasmussen 1986: 54).

Peter Kofoed and Tove Arendt Rasmussen start their analysis by recognizing that the simple, stereotypical schemes of ideological ordering associated with the episodic series are dismantled by the never-ending prime-time serial (cf. my comments to Adorno on this point in Chapter 4 above.) But, they argue, the serial 'to a maximum degree becomes a slave of its own scheme of disorder' (Kofoed and Rasmussen 1986: 56). The serial constantly accumulates a mass of unresolved conflicts, which is why each episode's ability to satisfy viewers must to a significant degree be found in other registers of the text than the immediate narrative level. Kofoed and Rasmussen's point is, then, that the shifts between the various plotlines in each episode of *Dallas*, which substitute for a continuous line of narrative progress in simpler narrative forms, are ordered so as to create a relative congruence of 'ambience' or 'emotional atmospheres' within each act, i.e. between commercial interruptions. They claim (ibid.: 57) that Act I is, in general, characterized by a mixture of harmony and disharmony, and serves to present all current plotlines. Act II is dominated by various expressions of love ('threatened, false, tactical or cynical' (ibid.: 58)), and the act, while focusing on love, shows all personal relations as being threatened in some way. Act III is the most harmonious, but on the other hand both contains the strongest sexual titillation and generally has a 'disharmonious perspective' because particularly strong outbursts of aggression are found here (ibid.: 60). Act III, in other words, generally contains 'the strongest emotional titillations' (ibid.: 61). The final Act IV is then devoted totally to disharmony, and while all acts end with a scene of conflict, the final act always ends with a scene which has one of the basic troubled relationships in an exploding or near-exploding state (ibid.: 57). These central conflicts on the other hand tend to receive minimal attention in the middle two acts (ibid.: 60).

Kofoed and Rasmussen's main point is that the simple narrative structure of old-fashioned series episodes has been replaced by 'recurring schematic structures of ambience' which 'replaces the narrative logic with a formalized organization of the unfolding of dynamics' (ibid.: 69). While I have not found that Kofoed and Rasmussen's characterizations of the acts of each episode are applicable to my *Dynasty* corpus, their approach seems to me highly relevant, and in an Anglo-American context also highly original. Their ambition is precisely to explain why a massive accumulation of conflictual incidents with roots in never-resolved, deep-seated problems can attract and momentarily satisfy viewers who then beg for more.

What they do is basically to turn to emotional, affective dimensions of the bewildering mass of storylines and events, and in part abstract them from the concrete contents of the narrative. They thus suggest considering also the 'technical' and 'meaningless' dimensions of the text, such as the rapid (but significantly varying) pace of the editing, the visual titillations (sexual attractions, colours, movements) of individual shots, etc. While such visual titillations have been noted by many of those who have written about prime-time soaps, the idea that these dimensions of the text, as an *ensemble*, reproduce a temporal, pseudo-narrative structure equivalent to that of episodic series is definitely original.

Still, even Kofoed and Rasmussen do not include the role of music in their analysis. The points made about the general functions of music in the previous chapter can, however, support their basic perspective. Music effectively 'cues' the viewers' emotional responses, and it is thus indicative of the overarching purpose of each *Dynasty* episode, as well as that of other texts which

> obsessively aim at arousing a precise response on the part of more or less precise empirical readers (be they children, soap opera addicts, doctors, law-abiding citizens, swingers, Presbyterians, farmers, middle-class women, scuba-divers, effete snobs, or any other imaginable sociopsychological

238

category) [. . .] They apparently aim at pulling the reader along a pre-determined path, carefully displaying their effects so as to arouse pity or fear, excitement or depression at the due place and at the right moment.

(Eco 1984: 8)

This is Umberto Eco's definition of a 'closed' text. The main point of his definition is not that such texts are not open to a wide variety of interpretations. On the contrary, they are 'in fact open to any possible "aberrant" decoding' (ibid.), if a reader for some reason leaves the 'predetermined path' and branches out on her or his own – when for instance preparing a paper for a conference on 'postmodern' television studies. In the case of *Dynasty*, an 'aberrant' decoding is in fact directly invited by the explicit 'campiness' represented most prominently by the Alexis character. This feature, that *Dynasty* (and to a lesser degree *Dallas*) is always-already 'camped', marks a significant new development in US prime-time fiction in the 1980s, echoed in the explicit so-called 'self-reflexivity' of later shows, such as *Moonlighting*. The main function of such devices is obviously to attract audiences in the educated middle class by allowing them to feel 'smart' when actually they are only following their own 'predetermined path', in which the emotional ups and downs which other audiences are more directly involved in can be enjoyed at an invited, ironic distance.

My point, then, is that *Dynasty* is a 'closed' text in Eco's sense, and that each episode offers a largely predictable, musically supported emotional rollercoaster ride between moments of conflict and moments of harmony, complemented by a steady stream of fast-paced, exhilarating, momentous visual gratifications in bright colours (cf. the analysis of the title sequence in Chapter 4).

It is actually not very easy to demonstrate the validity of such an idea. It is about the rhythms of the 'total' emotional impression of the show, quite possibly varying significantly between individual viewers, and also hard to translate into a written or graphic code. Inspired by Kofoed and Rasmussen, I did an experiment with a kind of quantitative content analysis. Even in his quite devastating critique of quantitative content analysis Kracauer (1953) admitted it might serve as a supplement to qualitative, interpretive analysis, and my methodological experiment was actually, contrary to classical 'content analysis', both interpretive and oriented towards the textual 'whole'. The point was to try to analyse in order to synthesize, precisely not to chop up the text in unrelated pieces.

I tried to 'code' the emotional 'ambience' of each scene in my corpus to which the music contributed significantly, placing them on a scale which ranged from 'conflict++' via 'conflict+', 'conflict−', 'harmony−', and 'harmony +' to 'harmony++'. 'Conflict' would include suspense and other forms of tension. If significant emotional shifts were found within a scene, I tried to code them as well. The result was a series of graphs which I hesitate to reproduce because of their methodologically crude, subjective and experimental basis. I believe, however, that the experiment proved that a similar procedure, where a limited group of other people did the coding, could be useful in an effort to capture these 'super-' or 'supra-narrative' temporal-affective structures.

A pattern emerged which clearly has similarities with the pattern outlined by Kofoed and Rasmussen. Even if there were significant variations between episodes, the following features dominated.

Act I tends to have many rapid shifts in moods. Every scene not only tends to contrast with the previous and the following, it often has significant fluctuations within it. This is related to the use of Act I as a reminder of what goes on in all the 4–7 storylines unfolding at any time, and the frequent breakfast scenes early in this act are occasions for conversations which may turn from sweet familial harmony to hostility or conflict. On the other hand, Act I never reaches extreme levels of either harmony or conflict. Scenes of conflict or moderate disharmony clearly outweigh those of harmony, both in terms of time and in terms of numbers of scenes. The first acts tend to end with a scene of moderate conflict.

Act II is in its first parts less clearly different from Act I than I had suspected, even if it generally concentrates on fewer storylines. The most striking difference from Act I, is that the final scene most often reaches higher, twice even extreme, levels of conflict. Episode 43 is the only exception, with an Act II finale at a moderate conflict level, but an element of sex may here have been considered sufficiently titillating to bring viewers back after the commercial break. The reason for these higher levels of conflict in Act II must be that the commercial break between Act II and Act III is the longest, as in daytime soaps, so that a more solid dose of tension is needed to secure continued viewing. The climactic nature of Act II finales is further regularly emphasized by the relatively harmonious ambience of either the immediately preceding scene or the first part of the finale, making the climb in tension much more drastic than in Act I.

Act III mostly remains on levels of harmony or moderate tension. The climbs to this climactic moment also tend to be less steep than in Act II. One interesting exception to the rule is provided by the end of episode 44, in which there is a dramatic 'plunge' from a scene of conflict to a scene of extreme harmony. This is the only final scene in any act in my material in which this happens. Extreme harmony is otherwise used within acts as dramatic contrasts and as a 'platform' from which the climbs to high levels of conflict start.

Act IV is the only act which can match and actually beat Act II in the levels of conflict reached in its final scene. The climbs are regularly as steep as in Act II. A solid dose of conflict (or suspense, tension) is clearly supposed to bring back the viewers next week.

The results of this overview, then, are in a sense quite trivial. That is, however, precisely why, on the one hand, they are of fundamental importance to the viewing experience and, on the other, they tend to be overlooked in criticism bent on indulging in complexities. What we have seen is that every episode of *Dynasty* provides a predictable affective/emotional ride, with four climaxes occurring about every ten minutes, of which nos 2 and 4 stand out as most extreme, no. 4 marking a peak. Between climaxes, there are constant fluctuations between degrees of harmony and conflict, with sheer harmony sequences restricted to a minimum, often only to a part of a scene. The climaxes are of course related to the placing of commercial breaks in US television, while the fluctuations in every act are due to the multiple-plot structure, the constant shifts between plots at different stages of conflict.

Old-fashioned episodic series, concentrating on one story at a time, must also provide a distribution of tensions and titillations as required by the commercial breaks. But they will still tend to have more of a traditional dramatic curve, following their attempts to provide solutions to the conflicts the never-ending serial leaves hanging for ever. My point here is that the 'disorder' of multiple storylines and the never-ending form is contained by the supra-narrative affective/emotional structure, instead of a traditional dramatic curve. The affective/emotional structure serves the same purpose, though. Its predictable, largely standardized form unifies the experience of each episode, makes it appear as a 'whole', and reduces the possible dissatisfaction resulting from the constant frustration of narrative desire, the desire for 'complete' meaning. Meaning is simply less important than an 'emotional ride' which is produced by a cleverly organized, musically sustained series of what, from a narrative point of view, are mostly repetitive events or moments. The disturbing thematic implications of the storylines are thus effectively prevented from disturbing the enjoyment of the expected series of exciting, thrilling and touching scenes.

6

THE SOCIAL MEANINGS OF SOAP OPERA AND THE *DYNASTY* EVENT

Providing resources for citizenship does not have to smack of the lecture room. Some of the most effective contributions have come from iconoclastic comedy and from dramas that combined popularity with new ways of engaging contemporary experience. Advocating diversity entails using the full resources of television to develop programme forms that will offer a variety of pleasures as well as a variety of insights.

(Murdock 1988: 82)

This final chapter is an attempt to put the soap opera genre, the *Dynasty* text and the whole *Dynasty* event in perspective, by looking at them in the context of overarching processes in cultural and social history. The genre and the text will be discussed in relation to what some have seen as the waning of narrative, meaning and historical experience. The significance of the '*Dynasty* event' as a whole will then be briefly summarized with a view to the processes of media-political change I have seen it as representing.

MEANING VS MANIPULATION: MELODRAMA VS MELODRAMATIC DEVICES

My analysis of *Dynasty*'s narrative(s) above indicated that its paradigmatic structure clearly resembles a melodramatic universe made up of a limited number of psychic and moral positions and forces. Another route to the conclusion that *Dynasty* and other continuing serials are closely related to melodrama goes via the identification of a number of stylistic traits and narrative devices that these shows share with both classical stage melodrama and the melodramatic tradition in (Hollywood) film. Jane Feuer opened her seminal article 'Melodrama, Serial Form and Television Today' (1984) by pointing out a number of such striking similarities between *Dynasty* and Peter Brooks's (1984) description of classic melodrama. Later in the article Feuer points to the 'excessive' visual symbolism in the construction of certain frames, the use of music and the not just 'operatic' but 'positively Wagnerian' acting style (1984: 11). She argues that the visuals in various ways give priority to

242

emotionality in medium close-ups and close-ups and in the uses of zooms and freeze-frame at the end of scenes, acts and episodes. All of this is undeniably correct, and (some of) it also indicates the degree to which *Dynasty* is endebted to classical Hollywood cinema in its aesthetic regime. There are, however, still reasons to ask if *Dynasty* is a melodrama, or if it only employs melodramatic devices in its quest for strong emotional response. The answer to this question is quite revealing of the historical and cultural specificity of both soap opera narrative form and *Dynasty*.

Rune Waldecranz (1976: 177f.), lists twelve staple elements in the classic stage melodrama, based on his study of scripts by Pixérécourt, the (male) Parisian master of melodrama from about 1800 onwards. They might be summarized as follows.

1 Melodrama demonstrates a bourgeois, puritan morality by way of a plot which 'shows' that crime does not pay and that virtue will finally be rewarded.
2 Characterization is Manichaean, i.e. characters are constructed from oppositional pairs like bad–good, sinful–innocent, etc. In accordance with this basic feature, the texts are at all levels marked by a thoroughgoing play upon contrasts.
3 The plot normally starts from a moral conflict, and develops as an emotionally engaging tragedy with a happy end.
4 The plot invites identification with the hero or heroine, who is idealized but still has recognizably 'everyday' characteristics.
5 The play contains dramatic moments of surprise, and among these an almost obligatory scene with a revelation or recognition which gives the plot a new, surprising direction.
6 The extremely dynamic plot development leads to a violent, decisive settlement of the struggle between hero and crook – good and bad involved in a life-or-death battle – where the heroine is saved and the hero triumphs in the very last moment.
7 The escalation of dramatic tension is now and again broken by situation comedy featuring a clown-like bi-figure, always on the side of the good.
8 The action requires a visually fascinating or astonishing presentation of milieu/mise-en-scène.
9 The play must contain at least one spectacular or sensational sequence, like a fire, an erupting volcano, a snowstorm or an avalanche.
10 The play upon contrasts is accentuated by illustrating and ambience-creating music and sound effects.
11 The dramatic peaks of the play, and particularly the final battle between the hero and the crook, 'dissolve' into tableaux, songs and ballets.
12 The plot is normally based on a popular literary text, but this pre-text only provides the raw material for a thoroughly 'stage-oriented' theatrical production.

Waldecranz also shows in his study how melodrama provided basic aesthetic principles for the new popular entertainment medium, the cinema. This influence was a lasting one. With minor adjustments and exceptions, it is easy to recognize standard features of traditional Hollywood films of practically any genre here. Hence, there is nothing specifically 'feminine' about these drama-turgical principles. The key to the much later coding of melodrama as a 'feminine' genre can be found in shifts in the cultural coding of 'masculinity' and 'femininity' in general towards the end of the nineteenth century. The degradation of melodrama to a realm of 'the feminine' and 'the mass' happened as tragedy and realism were established as the textual forms most in line with a 'rational' view of the world, i.e. forms more capable of drawing boundaries between the masculine and the feminine. While public crying had been the expression of desirable moral sensitivity in the early part of the nineteenth century, such behaviour was regarded as an expression of 'unmanly' sentimen-talism towards the end of the century (Gledhill 1987: 34). Male critics and men in general have not been used to regarding their own favourite genres as marked by melodrama, and have largely continued to regard the historically feminine domestic and sentimental forms as utterly lowbrow. If male members of the audience spotted marks of this feminine melodramatic tradition in *Dynasty*, and experienced them as central to the serial, it would make them stop viewing, or only continue viewing while sometimes expressing their con-tempt to let wives and daughters know how simple-minded and irrational they are (cf. Chapter 3).

What makes Peter Brooks's contribution to a revised perspective on melo-drama so interesting is in the very title of his book: *The Melodramatic Imagination*. To him, melodrama is more than a genre, more than a textual mode: it basically represents a form of consciousness typical of modern society. Brooks regards the melodrama as 'a sense-making system' (1984: viii) in the desacralized modern society emerging from the French Revolution. God was no longer the ultimate signified, the meaning behind every phenomenon. Everything was now in principle debatable, no meaning was absolutely guaranteed. Melodrama was a textual machine designed to cope with the threatening black hole God left after him when he returned to his heaven. It was constructed to demonstrate the existence of an underlying universe of absolute forces and values, originally *moral* forces and values. This is why the melodramatic is an *expressionist* aesthetic, prone to hyperbole. It almost desperately strives to externalize what is under-neath the chaotic and uncertain surface of modern existence. It is worth noting that this relates the 'melodramatic imagination' to what Arnold Hauser (1972: 206ff.) regarded as the main intellectual heritage of the nineteenth century: the idea, shared by a number of prominent writers of all kinds, that something more real than 'reality' was to be found and exposed underneath its surface.

Desacralization also implied the dissolution of the God-given collectives on all levels. All bonds between people – from the family to the nation – were in principle debatable. The locus of the underlying moral universe had to be the individual, both as a 'container' of the whole universe, and, in texts, as representative of some element. Melodramatic 'good' and 'evil' are 'highly personalized: they are assigned to, they inhabit persons who indeed have no psychological complexity but who are strongly characterized' (Brooks 1984: 16). The melodramatic model could then easily accommodate the modern, psychological view of the individual, the melodrama of Freud's unconscious. Instead of representing evil, some character could represent the evil father, the good mother, the innocent daughter and so on.

Melodrama's traditional use of the spectacular, the sensational, its taste for violent effects, must then be understood in relation to the rationale sketched above. Such elements were to demonstrate the violent strength of the forces at play, their pervasiveness, the impossibility of getting around them. The battle between good and evil was about life and death. But the astonishing stage effects were not only to testify to the cosmic dimensions of the drama presented. They would also have the effect of shaking the audience, and thus possibly increasing the pedagogical effect of the play in question: melodrama was basically *didactic* drama, designed to teach the audience a lesson.

Peter Brooks also calls melodrama 'democratic art' because it provided its mass audiences with a substitute for the traditional religious understanding of life. But, as Thomas Elsaesser had earlier pointed out in his seminal essay on melodrama in film, it was also democratic in another way: it originally represented 'the struggle of a morally and emotionally emancipated bourgeois consciousness against the remnants of feudalism' (Elsaesser 1986: 281). Melodrama had an ideological side to it. It proclaimed a moral law that was the same for everyone, nobility and peasants alike. Its motifs could be seen as metaphorical representations of class conflicts: sexual exploitation and rape were drastic images of socio-economic exploitation. Elsaesser regards melodrama's transferral of social and political issues to a personalized, metaphorical form where emotionality is emphasized as being central to its dominance in popular texts for so long:

> The persistence of the melodrama might indicate the ways in which popular culture has not only taken note of social crises and the fact that the losers are not only those who deserve it most, but has also resolutely refused to understand social change in other than private contexts and emotional terms.

> (Elsaesser 1986: 282f.)

One may thus regard the popularity of melodrama as indicative of a popular resistance to abstract, theoretical ways of understanding society and history. Politics or history is only interesting in so far as it affects our everyday life and its conditions, our feelings – fears, anxieties, pleasures. The world is portrayed as governed by moral and emotional psychological values and forces anyone can understand. Characters as well as events tend to be portrayed as representations or examples of undisputable, mythic *laws* the audience is urged to get to know and live by. Confusion is only on the surface. Underneath, it's the same old stories.

Excess is a key word in making a connection between classic and film melodrama on the one hand, and *Dynasty* on the other. The 'hysterical' exaggerations found in visual symbolism, music and acting style all correspond to the 'excesses' at the hyper-dramatic narrative level. But in classic stage and film melodrama, these features correspond to the moral urgency of melodrama and its ambition to speak of what was actually unspeakable. Their function is somewhat different in the never-ending serial. Their lack of resolution profoundly affects their ability to live up to classic melodrama's ambitions and status.

Lynne Joyrich (1988) makes the argument that melodrama flourishes in various ways in contemporary American television because the US is in a deep socio-cultural crisis and has a need for the sense of security provided by melodrama:

> Melodrama helps place ourselves in a confusing world – its insistence on the validity of moral or experiential truths and its faith in the reality of the stakes creates a space from which to act. [. . .] Melodrama's promise of universally legible meaning seems to be particularly compelling in the postmodern era, experienced by many as desperately in need of some kind of grounding. It is the panic provoked by this sense of weightlessness that adds to the mode's present appeal.
>
> (Joyrich 1988: 147)

But this argument actually falls to the ground as soon as the never-ending narrative structure is considered. Joyrich touches this problem towards the end of her article (drawing on Elsaesser) by mentioning that it is often the status of the ending which 'determines melodrama's political meaning', whether it is 'happy' or not, and that 'never really ending at all, TV melodramas may not have the ability to draw attention to unresolved contradictions and excess, the key to film melodrama's subversive potential' (ibid.: 148). Christine Gledhill (1992 :112) has also pointed out that 'continuous serialization' can 'work against melodrama', and even says that at 'a structural level, for example, endless seriality may be *antagonistic* to melodrama' (ibid.: 113; my emphasis). Gledhill argues, and I agree, that melodrama depends upon closure 'in order to produce its symbols and moral lessons' (ibid.: 113). Never-ending serials will on the other hand always disrupt any equilibrium, any conclusion. This logically implies that no moral lessons can emerge – the never-ending serial can never make a definitive 'statement' on anything. It can thus hardly be didactic, and hardly 'democratic' in either Brooks's or Elsaesser's sense.

Melodrama is, in the endlessly continuing serial, somehow deprived of its existential and moral urgency, in a sense its degree of dignity. It can no longer 'endow the behavior of ordinary persons with dramatic and ethical consequence' (Gledhill 1992: 107) because any consequence is always-already conceived as temporary. Melodrama survives as a set of 'devices' (a term repeatedly used by Joyrich), but the never-ending serial ends up being about the relative insignificance of its subject-matter. Its 'moral imaginary' is no longer a 'sense-making machinery', it rather celebrates the relative insignificance of both sense and morality – in fiction, at least. Dennis Porter's characterization of the logic of soap opera's narratives may still capture something essential:

> Unlike all traditionally end-oriented fiction and drama, soap opera offers process without progression, not a climax and a resolution, but mini-climaxes and provisional denouements that must never be presented in such a way as to eclipse the suspense experienced for associated plot lines. Thus soap opera is the drama of perepetia without anagnorisis. It deals forever in reversals but never portrays the irreversible change which traditionally marks the passage out of ignorance into true knowledge. For actors and audience alike, no action ever stands revealed in the terrible light of its consequences.
>
> (Porter 1982: 124f.)

The lesson it eventually teaches its audiences was early on aptly summed up by the fans of daytime radio serials interviewed by Herta Herzog in the early 1940s, who said that their serials were about *getting into trouble and out again* (Herzog 1941: 66).

This can be related to the 'tragic structure of feeling' Ien Ang once defined in her pioneering study of letters from *Dallas* viewers. It appears to me that this is something other than the 'emotional realism' that Ang found (and my material supports) was experienced in a recognition of particular characters and the problems they encounter. The 'tragic structure of feeling', as defined by Ang, seems more of a reflection of the producer-controlled emotional ups and downs identified as the supra-narrative temporal structures (p. 236). '[T]he emotions called up are apparently what remain with the letter-writers most', Ang summarizes (1985: 45), and cites a letter-writer who 'describes *Dallas* as a sequence of ever-changing emotions' – 'suspense', 'romance', 'sadness', 'fear', 'happiness'. Instead of noting how such a listing of emotions in a sense fetishizes them, detaches them from the specific storylines out of which they derive, Ang instead lets it define the 'tragic structure of feeling', as she offers this piece of philosophy:

> What we can deduce from this is the notion that in life emotions are always being stirred up, i.e. that life is characterized by an endless fluctuation between happiness and unhappiness, that life is a question of falling down and getting up again. This structure of feeling can be called the *tragic* structure of feeling; tragic because of the idea that happiness can never last for ever but, on the contrary, is precarious. In the tragic structure of feeling, emotional ups and downs occupy a central place. [. . .] Life presents a problem according to the tragic structure of feeling, but that

247

does not mean life consists solely of problems. On the contrary, problems are only regarded as problems if there is a prospect of their solution, if, in other words, there is hope for better times. Here too we are dealing with a contrast between misery and happiness. So it is not so odd that some letter-writers want to place emphasis on 'happiness'.

(Ang 1985: 46)

One may wonder why Ang chooses to call the structure 'tragic' when many of her informants – like those of Herzog – actually emphasize its optimism; consequently, 'comic structure of feeling' might be a more adequate label. Either way, the empty banality of it would be striking. As such, it eloquently demonstrates the fundamental difference between melodrama proper and the never-ending serial – in which melodramatic devices are reduced to pure instruments for 'stirring up emotions'. In melodrama, a fall is not just an occasion to get up again in the same place. If you fall, you may well die or at least remain down, unless you struggle very hard, with or without the help of others, not to fall again, or at least not from the same position. The seriousness of melodrama is what redeems its form of banality.

THE SENSE OF AN ENDING

I tried to show, in my analysis of the *Dynasty* text, how it works to prevent conscious insight into or confrontation with a potentially deeply disturbing thematic core. The never-ending form is in itself one of the primary elements in this warding-off of insight.

The function of a story's end is precisely to provide a point from which the preceding parts of it take on meaning. This is, in part, related to the linear conception of time which in many ways dominates in modern societies, and which, at least since Aristotle, has tended to structure western narratives. Other cultures may have differently constructed narratives, marked by 'the lack of chronology' and 'the prominence of spatial relationships of events systematically related to one another in a topological way' (Thornton 1980: 171). But these cultures will typically also be without notions of social change over time, produced by conscious human action.

In his still commendable book *The Sense of an Ending*, Frank Kermode (1967: 54) talks about 'books' as 'fictive models of the temporal world', while also emphasizing

the distinction between what we *feel* is happening in a fiction when mere successiveness, which we *feel* to be the chief characteristic in the ordinary going-on of time, is purged by the establishment of a significant relation between the moment and a remote origin and end, a concord of past, present or future.

(ibid.: 50)

My point here is not to insist on some simplistic causal temporal relation between elements in a narrative chain. It is, rather, to stress the role of fiction in helping to 'make sense of our lives' (ibid.: 3).

According to Paul Ricoeur, '[t]o make up a plot is already to make the intelligible spring from the accidental, the universal from the singular, the necessary or the probable from the episodic' (Ricoeur 1985: I, 41). The point is that narratives (as other fictions, other arts) owe a great deal of their attraction and cultural function precisely to their ability to stand out from the confusing complexity of everyday experience, and serve as 'models'. Jurij Lotman, who speaks of art as a 'secondary modeling system', accordingly regards a 'frame' as something common to all art, that is, a 'boundary separating the artistic text from the non-text' (Lotman 1977: 209, quoted in Ricoeur 1985: II, 167 n.45). This frame, or boundary, is, then, not at all the same as narrative closure in the sense of 'resolution', it is simply an ending, a halt, whatever makes the text finite. J. Hillis Miller (1978: 4, 5) has argued that 'no narrative shows either its beginning or its ending' and that the 'aporia of ending arises from the fact that it is impossible ever to tell whether a given narrative is complete' (quoted in Ricoeur 1985: II, 21 n.29). But as Ricoeur correctly points out, the whole point is that 'the incidents recounted may be interminable and are in fact so in real life, but the narrative as muthos is terminable' (ibid.). Kermode quotes Henry James as saying (in the preface to *Roderick Hudson*) that '[r]eally, universally, relations stop nowhere, and the exquisite problem of the artist is eternally to draw, by a geometry of his own, the circle in which they shall happily *appear* to do so' (Kermode 1967: 176).

What I try to argue, then, is that an ending, some form of closure, is not identical to resolution, some more or less strained settling of the problems, conflicts or contradictions dealt with in the text. A confusion of the two often seems to underlie ideological denunciations of any 'closure' as inherently 'ideological', in the sense of 'false'. Endings are happy or unhappy, abrupt or well prepared, logically satisfactory or unsatisfactory. But as long as an ending is there, the text invites sense-making reflection.

Dynasty handles the problem of closure in three ways: (1) every episode, of course, has an ending, and as I have tried to show, music and (the other elements of) a 'supra-narrative' structure of emotional qualities suggest a completeness and a standardized pattern of experience, which provide a kind of closure, in spite of unresolved narrative(s); (2) the high degree of repetition in terms of themes, 'motifs' (specific storylines, events, situations, etc.) and formal devices (such as the zoom to close-up at the end of many scenes and all acts) comes in addition to the retained basic relations between central characters after the establishment of '*Dynasty* as we know it'; all of this provides a sense of 'overview', a recognition and comprehension of the diegesis at any given point; (3) any particular storyline is brought to a (temporary) closure within a limited stretch of episodes (e.g. Adam's poisoning of Jeff) or sometimes within a single episode (e.g. Claudia's attempted suicide in episode 16).

What this adds up to is that *'Dynasty* as we know it' to a large degree only *pretends* to be never-ending, in the sense of being without closure. It engages the 'narrative desire' of viewers again and again, but outside its episodic 'supra-narrative' structure delivers only in bits and pieces. Once this is acknowledged by viewers, the serial will lose much of its significance, simply become less meaningful, less important. It may still be watched with some enthusiasm of course, but then either as a show consisting of minimal variations on a set of well-known elements and devices, or for the sake of individual storylines and their (temporary) closures. It may be removed from the schedule without a strong feeling of loss, which obviously was not the case during the serial's first-year run in Norway.

US daytime serials and British soaps seem to have been able to retain a much more stable and emotionally stronger (in the long run) draw on their audiences, over decades. The reasons for this are obviously many. Since I have not done a systematic analysis of any of these varieties of the genre, I can only provide more or less qualified speculations based in available literature, my analysis of *Dynasty* and occasional watching.

SOAP OPERA AS JOURNALISM: 'INFORMATION', NOT STORYTELLING

My first hypothesis is that the more traditional US and British soaps survive because of their much greater degree of 'realism' in the sense that Ien Ang (with pejorative intentions) designates as 'empiricist realism' (Ang 1985: 36). Their diegetic worlds simply resemble the real worlds of viewers much more than the super-rich worlds of *Dynasty* and *Dallas*. This serves to strengthen the impact of their 'emotional realism'.

But this proximity to everyday life also points to a difference in meaning between the narrative structures of daytime/British soaps and *Dynasty*, in spite of their similarity. *Dynasty*, by way of its 'larger-than-life' style, supported by its symphony orchestra score, suggested a broad, grand epic – and then necessarily failed to deliver just that. US daytime serials and British soaps have, in different ways, with particular modifications for the US variety since about 1980, maintained a pronounced proximity to the everyday life of viewers, and thus managed to present their narrative format's combination of punctual, circular and linear time as a convincing mimicking of everyday time structures, not as a hoax. The five-days a week, all-year scheduling of US soaps is of course also very helpful in this respect.

This would emphasize the role of these serials as vicarious communities, as 'parallel worlds' which each individual episode *reports on*. It thus in fact funda-mentally questions their status as 'narratives' in the ordinary sense of the word. As Walter Benjamin once pointed out, 'Mnemosyne, the rememberer, was the Muse of the epic art among the Greeks' (1969: 97), and '[a]ny examination of a given epic form is concerned with the relationship of this form to historiography' (ibid.: 95). Narratives are by definition about the past, recent or distant, whether they are told by way of 'telling' or 'showing', even if the latter technique (as employed in theatrical narratives and in combination with 'telling' in film) implies an illusion of presence (cf. Branigan 1992: 146). From this point of view, then, the term used for soap opera summaries in the US press (and telephone services), 'soap opera update', is indicative of the way daytime soaps present themselves and work as continuous 'coverage' of ongoing events, as *information*, not narratives. They are then practically inseparable from television's obsession with 'now-' and 'live-ness'. This is, in the US, hysterically represented in local newscasts, where excited reporters daily recount events 'live, on the spot' – where nothing is happening (any more). But it is of course also otherwise characteristic of television's discursive regime.

From this point of view, it is in fact possible to regard soap opera form as a useful vehicle for a sort of journalistic running commentary on social life, social conflict, social change, as these phenomena affect people at a personal level, in a degree of accordance with the melodramatic spirit. British soaps are, with their emphasis on a wider, socially quite specific community and their engagement with a wider set of social concerns and character types, closer than most American daytime serials to something like that. The affinity between soap opera and topicality is also the basis for systematic use of the genre in educational efforts in countries such as Mexico and India, particularly with respect to health, hygiene, family planning, etc. (cf. for instance Rogers and Singhal 1988). But even in the US, the genre's capacity for topicality, for addressing current social issues, has been exploited at least since about 1970.

One of the two 'grand old ladies' of US daytime soaps, Agnes Eckhardt Nixon (the other was Irna Phillips), argued in 1972 that the early 1970s was a 'golden age' of soap opera particularly because a series of social issues were raised and discussed in various serials. They now had to 'stay contemporary and topical' (Nixon 1972: 51). She referred to a particularly interesting experiment which I do not think has been further developed. At a real drug rehabilitation centre in New York, where a fictional character was supposedly admitted, they 'simply taped, hour after hour, over three consecutive days, marathon group therapy sessions' with 'eight real-life teenage ex-addicts'. The tapes were then 'edited into briefer, self-contained segments, and presented throughout the summer in twenty different episodes' (ibid.: 52). Nixon also reports huge responses to episodes in which a number of diseases and issues ranging from ecology to soldiers missing in Vietnam had been treated.

What soap operas offer, then, is not primarily stories, which, in Benjamin's perspective, represent *Erfahrung* (the structured outcome of reflection on previous 'momentary' experiences), but, rather, 'coverage of' and thus access to and virtual participation in the 'soap opera community', a particular version or section of a more general 'television community':

> The relationship between viewer and medium cannot be described in terms
> of a system of representation which would allow viewers to make judgments

about whether or not they are adequately represented in the programs they watch. The point is rather that viewers experience themselves as being 'socialized', as belonging to a kind of electronically constituted society whenever and as long as they watch television.

(Rath 1989: 89)

Claus-Dieter Rath's formulation here seems to imply that the television community ends as the set is turned off. But as the mass of secondary texts about television in general and (particularly US) soaps in particular demonstrates, the sense of belonging to the electronic community is sustained far beyond the actual viewing time. It practically merges with the everyday life of viewers: 'It's like Gail in *Coronation Street*. I only watch *Coronation Street* so I can only talk about it – it's almost as if you know her, so I think "I wonder what she'll do about this baby" – almost like someone you work with in the office' (female viewer, quoted in Hobson 1989: 150). Soaps are the stuff of gossip, and as such complement viewers' real circle of acquaintances, thus obviously and more interestingly also compensating for modernity's erosion of of non-electronic communities (cf. Fiske 1987: 77ff. and Brown 1990 for debatable views on (soap) gossip as 'feminine resistance').

LINEAR TIME AND HISTORICITY VS PUNCTUAL TIME AND MYTH

The above view of soap operas, as generically closer to *information* than narrative (Benjamin's distinction, cf. above, pp. 250–1) does not mean that they do not contain 'stories'. They do, just like journalism and real life. The point is that it allows a different perspective on these texts. It places them as part of a more general historical shift, discussed by Benjamin, 'from experience to actuality' (Rath 1989: 86), eminently represented by television's preferred modes of 'now-ness'.

It is possible to regard this immense valuation of actuality, simultaneity, the momentary as evidence of a strengthening of a *punctual* sense of time in late-modern societies, which is represented in the soap opera's pendular or 'sinusoidal' (Eco) temporal structure (cf. above, p. 221). At a general social level, this does not simply mean a new degree of 'freedom' from the oppressive, 'mythic', linear time. Rather, it 'leads to an invasion of imperative pseudo-myths' (Rath 1989: 86). As Benjamin pessimistically concluded a long time ago:

This tremendous development in technology has brought along an entirely new form of poverty for mankind. And the reverse fact of this poverty is the oppressive wealth of ideas, which has come with the revival of astrology and yoga wisdom, Christian Science and palmistry, vegetarianism and gnosis, scholasticism and spiritualism, and has been spread among – or, rather, over – the people. For it is not a case of true revival, but one of galvanization.

(quoted in Rath 1989)

Soap opera's rise to a significant degree of cultural respectability, news media coverage of plotlines and stars, an increasing flora of glossy fan magazines, and increased, socially expanded audience attraction, may well be regarded as paralleled by the ubiquitous offerings of all kinds of mystic, 'spiritual' and 'exotic' religious ideas and services, from fancy 'New Age' bookstores in rich neighbourhoods to Dionne Warwick's and a dozen others' TV-advertised 'psychic phonelines', plus 'psychic's' advice on call-in radio shows. Europe ain't seen nothin' yet, if the situation in the US indicates where we are going. The point is that the 'punctual' time needs other kinds of explanation, for occurrences in each 'island' of time, for the social and cultural conditions, than those available within a linear sense of time.

In the latter, an explanation will in principle be sought for in the past, by each specific moment in time's links to those preceding it. Each moment is seen as new, in complex ways also produced by the previous one, but never identical to it. This limits the value of previous experience, but does not eradicate it. In punctual time, each momentary occurrence must be seen as the actualization of an underlying, eternal, precisely *timeless* principle. Such principles are by definition *mythic*: myths are precisely, as put by Lévi-Strauss (1966b), machines for the destruction of time. In other words, punctual time tends to deny historicity, i.e. that each moment in time, each synchronous social situation, constitutes 'a perpetually renewed field of *possibilities*' (Johansen 1984: 33). In punctual, mythic time, nothing is to be expected beyond the eternal return of the same, just as in the cyclical time typical of traditional societies based in agriculture.

To the degree that *Dynasty* and other soaps represent a punctual conception of time, they also implicitly claim that developments in time are to be understood as referring to eternal, timeless, unchangeable principles. The power relation between Blake and Krystle will always remain, as will the opposition between the femininities of Krystle and Alexis. The story is never ending, episodes keep piling up as in ancient mythic traditions, but it is basically closed already at the outset.

SOAP OPERA AND 'WOMEN'S TIME'

Soap opera's affinity to a denial of historicity, of linear time, is central to one of the more interesting attempts to tie the genre both to an essentialist notion of femininity and to central political concerns. Julia Kristeva's 1979 essay, 'Women's Time', came, it might seem, close to proclaiming that a specifically female sense of time is biologically determined:

As for time, feminine subjectivity would seem to provide a specific measure that essentially retains *repetition* and *eternity* from among the multiple modalities of time known through the history of civilizations. On the one hand, there are cycles, gestation, the eternal recurrence of a biological

253

rhythm which conforms to that of nature. [. . .] On the other hand, and perhaps as a consequence, there is the massive presence of a monumental temporality, without cleavage or escape, which has so little to do with linear time (which passes) that the very word 'temporality' hardly fits: all-encompassing and infinite like imaginary space.

(Kristeva 1986: 191)

Kristeva's argument is, however, more complex, as the 'would seem' in the first sentence of the above quote signals. She points out, for instance, that cyclical and 'monumental' time 'are traditionally linked to female subjectivity in so far as the latter is thought of as necessarily maternal', and that 'this repetition and this eternity' are fundamental conceptions of time 'in numerous civilizations and experiences', and hence shared also by men (ibid.: 192).

Kristeva was (of course) not the first to think about the links between notions of femininity and notions of time. Michelle Mattelart argued, in 1971, that

[t]he mythical hostility between the notion of woman and that of change must go back to the association – common to all cultures – between the image of femininity and that of the vital elements, water and earth, elements of permanence and fertility. The image of woman is linked with the idea of continuation, perpetuation, duration.

(Mattelart 1971, quoted in Mattelart 1986: 71)

What we seem to encounter here is in other words an age-old, cross-cultural, mythical association between 'woman' and non-linear forms of time. Mattelart defines, in line with Kristeva, 'the inflection given by femininity to time' as *repetition* and *eternity*, i.e. the eternal return of the same, 'the return of the cycle that links it to cosmic time, the occasion for unparalleled ecstasy in unison with the rhythm of nature, and along with that the infinite, womb-like dimension, the myth of permanence and duration' (ibid.: 72). The idea that this specifically female form of time has something to do with the particular fascination soap opera seems to hold for women in many parts of the world is obviously close at hand:

these lengthy tales unrolling over protracted periods by means of regular daily consignments might have much in common with this experience of repetition and eternity. These tales could well correspond to the psychic structures of women not caught up in the forward-looking idea of time, a time of change. These vast stories, delivered in small daily installments and daily repeated, would then serve, through their stereotyped rhythms, to satisfy the expectations of female subjective time. By cultivating the enjoyment of this non-forward looking sense of time, these stories tend to hold up women's access to the time of history, the time of planned action.

(ibid.: 72)

Two issues arise from this line of reasoning: the question of essentialism in conceptions of gender, and the question of the social implications of the 'female' and the 'male' sense of time.

While Mattelart may come very close to a biological grounding of the notion of femininity, she makes it clear that she is referring to how femininity has been understood, interpreted or culturally coded over hundreds of years in a variety of different societies. There are no direct references to the 'patterns of feminine sexuality' or the (not-so-)eternal return of menstruation, etc. In this way the 'female sense of time' becomes a form of experience which is shaped by a deeply entrenched mythical, cultural codification of femininity and the general, historical confinement of women to a set of reproductive functions and positions. The repetitious circularity also characteristic of basic bodily rhythms in men's lives has not hindered a cultural codification of masculinity which has tended to tie men to linear time, and thus to social functions and positions oriented towards 'planned action' for change.

Such a non-essentialist but historically aware perspective allows for a productive rethinking of the different implications of the two forms of time consciousness, along lines such as those suggested by Mattelart:

> The female sense of time is viewed in a more and more positive light as models of development are questioned and the limitations of a society governed by the rule of the highest possible GNP become plain. Increasingly social movements tell us that work and career is not everything. This new sensibility gives a heightened value to women's work and the gestures of their everyday life. The division of work between 'male' and 'female' qualities has reduced the emotional and intellectual capacity of women as much as that of men. And it is now plain that, however urgent it is to increase awareness of the productive value of household tasks, it is also vital to restore value to areas that are not directly productive.
>
> (ibid.: 73)

In this perspective, a revaluation of the 'female' sense of time is made necessary by the ecological crisis and the concomitant reduced faith in continuous economic growth of the kind hitherto more or less fetishized in modern and modernizing societies. It is, however, also clear that women's appropriation or heightened awareness of a linear sense of time (to the degree that they have been excluded from it) is also necessary, if 'planned action' for social change is to take place.

While it may be true that women as a social category have been particularly prone to experience – and have been constructed as representatives of – nonlinear forms of time, they are not at all alone in this position. Bourgeois worries about lack of time discipline in the lower classes, including the weakly developed enthusiasm for delayed gratifications, have been expressed strongly and repeatedly for centuries. Worries, contempt and anger have also been the response of western colonialists and entrepreneurs who despair at their encounter with the very different, largely non-linear forms of time-conscious-ness in non-western, non-modernized cultures. Particularly at a time when women are engaging in careers outside their traditional domain on a scale which is historically new, it is worth emphasizing that non-linear senses of time are tied to certain fields of practice and certain cultures (conceived as 'whole ways of life') rather than to either a 'real' or an 'ideal' conception of gender.

This might be helpful if one wants to avoid 'renaturaliz[ing]' (Brunsdon 1991: 365) gender identity in gender-oriented studies of media and culture by using 'men' and 'women' as unproblematically 'given' and (thus) explanatory categories:

> without the particularity of the original ethnographic enterprise, gender can be asked to explain both too little and too much. Femininity, instead of being a difficult and contradictory psychic, historical and cultural forma-tion, to which feminists have been historically ambivalent, becomes an explanatory factor. Women like these texts because they (both the texts and the women) have feminine concerns. The categories of gender, con-stituted as pure as if persons are 'just' gendered, also begin to function in a theoretical short-circuit as explanatory. This can then make it very difficult, in the classroom, to avoid either celebrating or pathologizing the pleasures of these gynocentric texts.
>
> (ibid.: 373)

AGAINST 'TEXTUALISM'

The above perspectives on soap opera, as a genre with a potential as a 'journalistic' dramatic genre and as a textual representative of a conception of time which is not without critical potential, have been introduced to modify the impression that I am unambivalently 'against' soaps as a cultural form. The genre's elements and 'rules' may be used for many purposes, and some are, from a socially critical point of view, more positive than others. The existence and popularity of soap opera are not in themselves socio-cultural and political problems. That would be a mechanical, formalist and hopelessly 'textualist' point of view.

A major problem with the form lies in the degree to which it dominates the cultural/textual menu of particular social groups, groups that would obviously benefit from an increased awareness of the possibility of real social change (as opposed to for instance endless 'resistance' when watching television). One indication of such a dominance is in the number of soap operas available and the size of their audiences, another is in the relative dominance of the plethora of *other* 'punctual', 'pendular' or 'sinusoidal' textual forms in a culture's media menu, working in combination with other formally repetitive cultural forms (cf. Gendron (1986) on Adorno; see Chapter 1 above). Since such forms tend to be prominent in television, the question here could be: 'To what degree is television the dominant medium for specific groups in a given society?' An overwhelming dominance of television, accompanied by a rapid growth in the 'mysticism businesses' (astrology, healing, psychic services, certain (other) forms of religion) and, for that matter, increasing illiteracy rates, may indicate something about the relative position of a punctual sense of time and the related mythic understanding of the world, which does not encourage planned action for significant social change.

This is why another question must also be posed, one which does not accept the medium as it is, as altogether and necessarily springing from its 'essence': what kind of television do we want? This was, basically, the question that the *Dynasty* debate in Norway was about.

THE *DYNASTY* EVENT AND THE FUTURE OF TELEVISION

Dynasty was scheduled in Norway after internal conflicts in the Norwegian Broadcasting Corporation. These conflicts were brought about not least through pressures from the nationally distributed popular press, which wrote quite extensively about the international success of its generic predecessor *Dallas*. But the show was also immediately seen as a sign of times to come as satellite and cable television was expanding rapidly. This gave a new twist to familiar debates about the (lack of) quality in transnational popular culture products. Various populist and liberalist voices were on the offensive, but equally striking was the participation in the public debate by 'ordinary' people, especially in forms organized by the popular tabloid press. The debate thus demonstrated that the most commercial press at times may serve to represent opinions not otherwise well represented in 'enlightened' public discourse. *Dynasty* appeared on Norwegian TV screens by way of the pressures of the international TV market and the most commercialized parts of the press. At the same time, it brought to light the previous exclusion of particularly women-oriented popular fiction from the menu of the 'culturally responsible' monopoly public television, where traditionally male-oriented genres had long been well-established items. In this way, 'the market' clearly had a culturally democratizing function, by breaking through the often unwittingly male chauvinist and, in part, parochial, prejudiced attitude to transnational popular culture in some (but not all) 'culturally responsible' circles.

A major difference between Norwegian and US readings was that a large, gradually diminishing portion of Norwegian viewers, unfamiliar with the soap opera format, expected the show to reach a narrative conclusion. This meant that a 'serious' reading of the show was more widespread in Norway than in the US. However, research done there by Ellen Seiter *et al.* and Andrea Press, referred to in Chapter 3 above, indicates that less-educated lower-class audiences rejected the show for its lack of realism, whereas more educated middle-class audiences would tend to recognize its 'emotional realism' while enjoying its tongue-in-cheek 'camp' mode. In Norway, the historical experience with

Hollywood films and TV shows made the 'emotional realism' more or less the only realism expected from American screen entertainment. More easily than their American counterparts, less educated Norwegians abstracted the 'emotional realism' from the glamorous, exotic setting. The strong focus on emotional realism and Krystle as a 'regular woman' in women- and family-oriented weeklies was also important here. As Norwegian audiences familiarized themselves with the never-ending format, however, 'camp' readings became more widespread in middle-class audiences and lower-class, less educated groups seem to have moved towards a form of reading which fluctuated between serious involvement and 'camp' distanciation.

The indicated differences between Norwegian and US lower-class audiences may, importantly, also be related to the wider spectrum of genre experiences provided by public television, which would tend to produce more flexible or expanded 'horizons of expectations'. The text was the same, but the supertexts are different in European public service and US commercial television, and the same goes for the 'megatexts', i.e. the entire history of programming. As a result of their 'megatextual' experiences, Norwegian audiences did not only have the ability to respond in a 'flexible' way to a new genre, the prime-time soap opera. They were also used to taking television seriously. US viewers, particularly the more educated, are not. A TV serial which quite openly says 'we know you know this is not to be taken in earnest because we're only in it for the money anyway' will be more easily understood and appreciated by middle-class audiences in a US context. The *Dynasty* experience was a learning process in this respect for Norwegian audiences. A more distanciated, ironic or 'camp' mode of viewing seemed to spread gradually during the show's three runs on the NRK, and watching *Falcon Crest* in between also helped. A new mode of viewing was added to the spectrum, while it is doubtful that a general attitude to television as a medium for ironic 'indifference' (cf. p. 260) was picked up.

The *Dynasty* event demonstrated that the NRK had failed its public service obligations by disregarding certain kinds of women-oriented fiction and – I would add – women-oriented programming in general. But it also demonstrated two central strengths of public service broadcasting: (1) its capacity for real programming diversity; and (2) its public accountability. The second point is to be seen in the way the NRK was pressured by public opinion to include US prime-time soaps in their schedule, and in the way in which a comprehensive public debate deprivatized the viewing experience. Functioning public service television is, in other words, tied to a working public sphere: its programming is not just offerings to consumers, but material for a public, cultural-political discussion among citizens. The way in which television is organized and the range of its programming is of primary importance to the 'vitality of democracy', as argued by Graham Murdock:

At the heart of this issue is the relation between television and citizenship. Full and effective citizenship requires access to the range of information, insights, arguments, and explanations that enable people to make sense of the changes affecting their lives, and to evaluate the range of actions open to them both as individuals and as members of a political community. Without these resources, they are excluded from effective participation. They become the victims not the subjects of change, unable to pursue their rights and press for their extension. Precisely because of its centrality the television system has become a key site on which the struggle to secure and develop resources for citizenship takes place. Once this is recognized, we are bound to ask how current and impending changes in this system are likely to affect its capacity and willingness to deliver and develop these resources.

(Murdock 1988: 78)

This is, in a sense, what the *Dynasty* debate, and the parallel debates about *Dallas* in many other countries, were about. The main point of my argument on this issue in this book has not been to settle a media-political debate which must be continuous. It has been that the scheduling of *Dynasty* by public service television, *in casu* the NRK, was basically a necessary step in view of public television's obligation to 'engage with the range and complexity of contemporary experience' (Murdock 1988: 78). The soap opera genre had been excluded for much too long, and the internationally successful prime-time soaps were major 'signs of the times' in the early and mid-1980s. I think this conclusion has important consequences for the way in which public service broadcasting must envisage its role in the future, in order to maintain its centrality as a provider of resources for citizenship. A true diversity of programming cannot be based on the exclusion of important popular and 'commercial' genres, whatever their ideological implications may be. Such implications are, on the other hand, a primary concern of a socially and culturally engaged television criticism, and I therefore end this book with a few notes on the role(s) of criticism.

THE ROLE(S) OF TELEVISION CRITICISM

My analysis of eight episodes of *Dynasty* differs from most other critical work on soap operas in that it looks quite closely at a concrete, limited, specific material which was chosen more or less at random. All other writing about soap operas, of any kind, either deals only with the genre in general, or with a whole serial, picking examples as illustrations, or is about a particular feature, formal, ideological or otherwise, where the researcher/writer also picks examples to illustrate a certain point. These two procedures in fact dominate the writing about television genres in general, not just soap criticism. This is also why TV programming tends to appear as more interesting in criticism than in any specific encounter with an episode or a stretch of episodes in either series or serials. If my relatively detailed discussion seemed a bit tedious, this also, I would argue, followed from the nature of the text itself. Much television is

259

actually a lot more boring than criticism has normally admitted. Academic TV criticism is normally the epitome of 'reading as poaching': taking what you want and like from a text while rejecting or forgetting about the rest.

The phrase 'reading as poaching' stems from Michel de Certeau (1988); he uses 'poaching' to describe a strategy of survival and pleasure for those in subordinate social positions. While there are good reasons to note the existence of such reading practices as signs of a relative self-determination among certain audiences, there are no good reasons for critics to celebrate texts which cannot sustain continued interest because they are largely insignificant, hence basically boring to these audiences. As once put by Grant Tinker, an already legendary executive in the US television industry: 'I think probably the biggest sin of the medium as it exists is that so little sticks to your ribs, that so much effort and technology goes into – what? It's like human elimination. It's just waste' (quoted in Gitlin 1985: 16).

One response to the insignificance of so much (US) television is that formulated by Lawrence Grossberg, who has argued that TV programmes should not be treated as 'texts to be interpreted', but rather as 'billboards to be driven past'; not 'a sign to be interpreted, but rather, a piece of a puzzle to be assembled' (Grossberg 1987: 31f.). This is in other words a strategy for a broader cultural analysis involving television primarily as a carrier of symptoms of the cultural situation which is to be characterized and interpreted. Such an approach, if legitimate for some purposes, can hardly be the only one for a television criticism which also wishes to contribute to a *critique of television*, since the present organization and use of the medium is then basically treated as a given, as 'a matter of fact'. Its readings of specific televisual texts will tend to be impressionistic and hence somewhat superficial. The approach does not involve a comparison between different existing television institutions and programming policies, and closes off speculations about alternative, possible or thinkable forms of television. It will often tend to end up as more or less informed, more or less entertaining and enlightening essayistic laments about, or celebrations of, the cultural situation in general.

What is needed is an improved theoretical understanding of television, one which accommodates the real historical and global multifariousness of the medium, related to in-depth empirical analyses of specific institutional, textual and reception instances. Importantly, a critique of television cannot wait for the always elusive moment when our understanding of the medium is finally 'correct'. Critique will simply have to be a necessary part of research and the social obligations of researchers, drawing on a set of 'values', ideas about what the medium ought to be, ought to be doing.

Just as television is different from one context to another across the globe, so the conditions for the effectiveness of television criticism vary. In general, it is probably the case that smaller nation-states offer better opportunities for critical intervention than larger ones, by way of public debate and by way of direct contact with broadcasting institutions. But the attitudes of scholars, the interest in influencing what actually goes on in media institutions, is also of great importance, anywhere. These attitudes are, however, not just a personal responsibility. They are culturally determined, produced by the traditions and social positions of academic institutions over long stretches of time. They may encourage *engagement* with political world issues outside academia proper, or dismiss for instance contributions to public discourse as irrelevant, as 'bullshit on the side', to quote one (anonymous) American professor of literary studies (Miller 1988: 5). Institutional norms may, however, be changed, and where needed, work in the direction of such change should start straight away.

The effectiveness of traditional television criticism has been questioned on many grounds, however. One of the more interesting arguments here was once made by sociologist Oskar Negt and film maker Alexander Kluge in their *Öffentlichkeit und Erfahrung* [Public Sphere and Experience] (1974: 110). According to Negt and Kluge, external critique will tend to remain either too abstract or too piecemeal (focusing on individual programmes), hence ineffective in relation to television as a historically established apparatus with a particular relation to the social conditions of production in general. It is primarily those who work in television who understand the medium as a specific organization of production, and they can normally show that it is unhelpful to make complaints which do not take into consideration the practical possibilities for alternative methods of production.

I think Negt and Kluge's dismissal of traditional television criticism is too pessimistic, particularly since providing audiences with critical resources is also a major, worthwhile aim. But their point needs to be seriously considered as an impetus to renewed attention to the relation between academic criticism and the education of media personnel in academic institutions. The wall between departments or sections of film/TV production on the one hand, and criticism on the other, is often much more than a practical, organizational one in many universities. It needs to be dismantled, and replaced by a productive dialogue.

Increased critical engagement with television as it is requires discussion of what television should be, i.e. of values, the question of 'quality'. This issue has been almost taboo for many years, for many reasons, among media scholars. Both certain political tendencies and dominating scholarly traditions have opposed the idea that notions of quality should play any role in media research and academic criticism (Gripsrud 1991b: 227f.). There is no space here for a full rehearsal of my (tentative) arguments on this issue, published elsewhere (1989a, 1991b). Suffice it to say that a general guideline could be the following: 'All texts are trivial until the opposite is proven in each individual case' (Johannesen 1979: 469). This implies that it is possible (and necessary) to distinguish between more and less significant and valuable texts, but that the distinction should not be made on the basis of simplistic prejudices concerning certain cultural or institutional forms, media or genres. On the other hand, any given genre, at any given time, privileges particular perspectives on the human condition or elements in/of it. There are limits to what a text within a certain genre can do. This book could not have been turned into a comic or a collection of sonnets without consequences for what it says. This is why, from certain points of view, with regard to certain values, some genres may be regarded as being more valuable or important than others. Still, since every genre, every mode of discourse, is different from the others, only history can render them obsolete. Finally, the criteria for all judgements in television criticism should be explicated, so as to open even them to critical debate.

Researchers, teachers, students, media professionals and ordinary folk make judgements of significance and value along similar lines every day. It is a central obligation of media scholars to contribute to making these judgements as well informed as possible.

APPENDIX

Descriptions of episodes 16, 42–6, 57–8

ABBREVIATIONS USED

Alexis-b	Alexis's (apartment) building
C	Carrington
C-m	Carrington mansion
Coco	Colbyco
CU	Close-up
DC	Denver-Carrington
DC-b	Denver-Carrington building
D-theme	*Dynasty*-theme
ECU	Extreme close-up
ES	Establishing shot
MCU	Medium close-up
MS	Medium shot

EPISODE 16

Directed by Richard Kinon
Music by Richard Warren
Preceded by (Saturday) late night news

NRK announcer: 'And now, we're going to Denver, Colorado again, that is, to a new episode of *Dynasty*.'
'Last week, on *Dynasty*' (voice over): time 1′ 05″
Title sequence: time 1′ 26″

ACT I - Total time 11′ 53″

Scene 1
Time 3′ 20″
ES C-m. Morning: Fallon in baby-doll nightgown climbs her childhood's favourite tree. Jeff wakes up, goes out. Fallon talks about her love for her father, dislike of Krystle and contempt for her mother. Jeff comforts, kisses her – and is unfairly reprimanded for wanting sex at an inappropriate time. Jeff angrily tells Fallon to grow up. Final CU on Fallon.

Scene 2
Time 0′ 33″
Blake on his way to the office, in tender morning exchange with Krystle.

263

Scene 3
Time 2' 33"
High longshot of Alexis, dressed in dark blouse and riding trousers, crossing the lawn towards C-m. Dramatic, ominous music. Talks to Mrs Gunnarson in the kitchen about luxury 'necessities' she wants ordered. Joseph in, ironic/negative. Krystle in, dressed in white, asks Alexis to come with her. They leave the kitchen.

Scene 4
Time 3' 04"
Confrontation between Alexis and Krystle. Alexis condescending, ironical. Krystle angry, shows contempt. [Highly excessive/stylized melodramatic acting by Collins/Alexis.]

Scene 5
Time 2' 23"
ES DC-b. Lawyer Andrew talks to Blake about his probation, buying Alexis out of her deed to the studio and about Claudia. Finally, Blake says he wants Steven removed from his will. Zoom in to CU of Andrew, burst of music, fade to black.

ACT II – Total time 10' 21"

Scene 6
Time 1' 29"
ES pompous public building. Blake waiting in queue with common criminals. Comic misunderstanding. Blake wants to be treated differently by police, does not succeed. Near total shot of frustrated Blake at end.

Scene 7
Time 1' 42"
ES Memorial Hospital. Andrew (lawyer) follows Claudia out. Tells her Matthew and her daughter are in South America. Claudia walks into CU and out.

Scene 8
Time 1' 55"
Object ('clay pigeon') shot to pieces in the air. Fallon is practising with a shotgun. Complains to Alexis about Krystle, signals hostility to mother. Alexis almost mildly, humorously reprimands her. Fallon misses 'clay pigeon'. Alexis grabs shotgun and makes a perfect hit.

Scene 9
Time 1' 30"
Limousine drives to ordinary house. Andrew follows Claudia to door. Sad music. *Dissolve.*

Scene 10
Time 1' 03"

ES DC-b, tilted, 'still' of top. Andrew and Blake. Blake orders Andrew to offer Alexis $500,000 to give up the studio. Zoom to CU of Andrew.

Scene 11
Time 1' 41"
ES Claudia's house. Claudia in child's room, with dolls, teddy bears, etc. Cries, hugs teddy, empties a glass of pink pills. Continuous sad music with touch of 'children's' music. CU of Claudia. *Dissolve.*

Scene 12
Time 1' 01"
ES DC-b. Blake has called Claudia, secretary says she doesn't understand what Claudia

says. Crosscutting sleepy Claudia/Blake. CU of Claudia's phone on floor, with empty pill glass. Blake rushes out. Burst of music, fade to black.

ACT III – Total time 13′ 51″

Scene 13
Time 3′ 29″
Blake's limo towards camera, ending in low, wide-angled ECU of front. Nick Toscanni, M.D., arrives in sports car. Nick tries hard to wake Claudia up, continuously talking about his childhood while walking her up and down the floor, takes her to bathroom to throw up. Blake watches all. Camera follows (pans) Nick's and Claudia's movements in MCU and total, in unusual degree of mobility. [Nick's monologue and his acting fine little piece of almost poetic realism.]

Scene 14
Time 2′ 41″
ES unusual aerial shot of C-m's gardens. Alexis painting in garden, Andrew arrives to present Blake's offer of $500,000. They exchange cool compliments. Alexis says she doesn't want money, prefers a simple life and painting. Andrew: 'Marie Antoinette in her little Trianon, eh?' Alexis: 'And who has no intention of having her head dumped in a basket again.' Andrew finally mentions Blake removing Steven from his will. CU of shocked Alexis. *Dissolve.*

Scene 15
Time 3′ 14″
More traditional ES of C-m, zoom on bedroom window. Nick talks to Claudia about what has happened. [Again fine writing and acting.] Claudia is in bed. No music during talk until end. Cut when Nick leaves.

Scene 16
Time 3′ 08″
Nick walks down the impressive staircase, into library. Blake wants him to visit Claudia regularly, overseeing her recovery. Nick declines, aggressive. MCU of Blake.

Scene 17
Time 0′ 32″
Flute plays as Krystle in peach dress enters house from outside. Collides with Nick on his way out. Zoom to CU of Nick, looks as if he's had a nasty idea.

Scene 18
Time 0′ 47″
Blake and Krystle in harmonious baby-talk. Nick comes in, says he's changed his mind. MCU of Nick, looks smilingly ominous. Music burst, fade to black.

ACT IV – Total time 7′ 55″

Scene 19
Time 1′ 13″
Aerial ES C-m. Fallon talks on the telephone about a chauffeur Blake has fired. [Background: Fallon had an affair with him.] Krystle, still in peach dress, says she's pregnant. Zoom to CU of Fallon, shocked.

Scene 20
Time 2′ 19″
ES motel neon sign at night ('adult movies' etc.). Fallon waits by her red sports car, Jeff arrives in less conspicuous car. Fallon has brought food and wine, suggests they spend night at hotel – wants to have a baby. Humour in dialogue.

Scene 21
Time 3′ 35″
House on street with some traffic, night. Alexis in Steven's apartment, has prepared dinner (by ordering it to be delivered). Steven enters, has left job with DC. Alexis wants him to 'patch up with Blake'. Tells Steven (who gets angry) that Blake is not Fallon's father. Dramatic music.

Scene 22
Time 0′ 48″
House in darkness. Telephone rings. Nick in, answers. Tells his sister he came to Denver to get at Blake, says he's now found a way.

Total episode time (excluding summary, title sequence and end credits) 44′ 00″

END CREDITS
Followed by jazz concert, 'Miles Davis Live in Europe'.

EPISODE 42

Directed by Irving J. Moore
Music by Peter Myers
Preceded by magazine-format programme on ecology/nature.

NRK announcer/host: 'And now we'll do a long leap. We're going from Norwegian nature to Denver, Colorado, and the Carrington dynasty.'
Title sequence (the version where Alexis is presented with pool and palms, sporting a cigarette; cannons with skyscrapers and black limousine with skyscrapers between Alexis and final bird's-eye shot of the Carrington mansion): time 1′ 27″

'LAST TIME, ON *DYNASTY*:
1. Blake to Adam at La Mirage: 'Why are you so hostile?'
2. Fallon to Adam: 'You're a fraud.'
3. Blake to Krystle: 'Is he my son?'
4. Mark to Alexis: 'For my last money I bought a legal divorce.' Alexis: 'Except it was a phoney document, you're still married to Krystle.'
5. Mark to Fallon: 'I'm the right man for the job.'
6. Alexis talks to Fallon about preparing 'a nice surprise' for Krystle.
7. Scene involving Jeff, Adam and Alexis: Jeff is joining Colbyco.
8. Alexis to Adam: '*I* will decide if Jeff is a real threat, not you.'
Fade to black
Time 1′ 01″
Music: Continuous, with dramatic burst at the end.

ACT I – Total time 12′ 39″

Scene 1
Time 3′ 20″
Story/visuals: More credits during chopper ES of C-m. Breakfast table. Blake angrily talking about oil politics and the government's failure to understand the situation. A suggestion from Fallon is pushed aside. Jeff instructed to look into a government loan [for the development of the shale oil process] and Congressman McVane. Jeff will do so even if he's about to move to Colbyco. After he's left, Blake: 'I'll miss him.' Fallon: 'That makes one of us.' Blake: 'Don't be cute with me, young lady.' Reprimandingly instructs Fallon to accept that Jeff remains in the mansion, and that Adam is her brother, because Denver-Carrington is in trouble. Fallon answers by reminding Blake of Steven's unknown

whereabouts. Blake asks if anything has happened between Fallon and Adam that he doesn't know about. Fallon looks distant. CU on Blake and Fallon, final shot CU of Fallon.

Music: D-theme starts just before and lasts during ES and credits, ends at start of dialogue. Deep string instrument (cello?) solo sets in after Blake's question about Adam, signalling tristesse, afterthought, etc.; turning into bridge across cut to next scene.

Scene 2
Time 0′ 12″

Story/visuals: Krystle meets Blake in corridor. She has been out riding. Short display of mutual affection. Krystle walks towards camera, cut at MCU of her.

Music: Bridge shifts to bright, harmonious mode as flute takes lead when Krystle appears, music continues across cut to next scene.

Scene 3
Time 0′ 13″

Story/visuals: Blake in library, telephones Adam at Alexis's apartment.

Music: Shift to dark suspense, ends when number dialled and Adam answers, thus bridging the two locations/scenes.

Scene 4
Time 1′ 52″

Story/visuals: Adam agrees to meet Blake at Blake's office (cross-cutting Blake/Adam). Breakfast with Alexis/Adam, luxurious food, waiter in warmly yellow jacket. Adam thinks Blake still investigates his background. [Adam once went to Yale and lived in New York afterwards.] Does Alexis trust him, or does she mistrust him as Blake does? Alexis: 'Darling, you know how much you mean to me.' Article in newspaper about DC spells 'big trouble'. Alexis looks pleased, eager to act.

Music: No music during most of conversation. Dramatic, disharmonious, high strings after 'big trouble'; bridge across cut to next scene.

Scene 5
Time 0′ 25″

Story/visuals: ES: Tilt up DC-b, Jeff enters Blake's office with the contract on DC's shale oil loan, pulled from a secret file. Blake says he'll put it back after lunch with Congressman McVane who is in town, leaves document on his desk. MS of Blake behind desk.

Music: Strings note from sc.4 taken over by trumpet playing a variation of the D-theme as camera tilts in ES. No music after Jeff's entry.

Scene 6
Time 0′ 21″

Story/visuals: Front office, with secretary. Adam in as Jeff exits Blake's office. Jeff tells secretary he's going home. Adam: 'Good morning, Jeff.' Jeff: 'Is it?' Adam asks secretary for permission to enter Blake's office.

Music: No music.

Scene 7
Time 2′ 41″

Story/visuals: Adam and Blake in office. Camera first shows Blake's office desk from side, the two on opposite sides. In the course of dialogue, in rapid traditional shot-reverse-shot technique, variously showing speakers and listener's reactions, camera moves from MCU to CU, ending with 'interlocking gazes'. Blake says he's sorry for remarks about Alexis the day before. 'We used to have a strong bond between us. After we lost you, a terrible barrier built up. Even after Fallon was born, and then Steven, we couldn't tear that barrier down. We finally divorced.' Blake hopes his relations with Alexis won't destroy his relation to Adam. 'I want to be a father to you. You are my son. I want that very much.' Blake called out to front office before Adam answers. Adam in MCU, sees confidential shale oil contract, picks it up and has a brief look, hastily puts it back as Blake re-enters. Adam shakes hands with Blake, displaying excessively false smile and laughter, leaves. CU of pensive but smiling Blake in profile.

Music: No music at the beginning of dialogue, not even when Blake gets sentimental towards Adam. [Makes emotions less believable.] Starts as Blake is called out, in somewhat undecidable mood between sentimental harmony (cf. Blake's speech) and slight suspense suggested by three notes continuously repeated on piano before Adam sees contract marked 'Confidential'. Suspense becomes dominant but still restrained as Adam looks at document, 'mickey-mousing' occurs as he hastily puts document back, suspense and disharmony ('threat') contradict handshake and smile. Bridge to next scene.

Scene 8
Time 3′ 35″

Story/visuals: La Mirage exterior (with name of hotel on sign) – standard ES. Location shots from tennis court, young, shapely players. Pan to Alexis at outdoor café table. Mark instructs Barbie-doll blonde, embracing her from behind as part of instruction; seen from Alexis's point of view. Mark over to Alexis's table. Alexis asks why Mark is in Denver after turning down her offer in New York. Mark doesn't reply. Alexis wants him to meet Krystle 'to get her back'. Mark says he may not want her back; tells Alexis to stay away, won't answer questions about Krystle. Alexis leaves, Mark back to court. Alexis gets into her Rolls Royce, from back seat telephones 'Catherine' who has telephoned Krystle without saying her name, getting Krystle to come to see Mark. CU on Alexis. Fade to black.

Music: Bridge formed by musical 'wipe' on xylophone or similar instrument, leads into festive-sounding La Mirage motif (sounds a bit like a theme heard in Westerns when nature or 'home' is celebrated). Same mood continued playfully through Alexis's first appearance and Mark's instruction, touch of disharmony and 'atonality' added as Mark approaches Alexis. Music stops at start of dialogue, resumes after Mark's final line in 'atonal' slight suspense mood, MCU of Alexis. Deep, rising addition of something ominous comes as Alexis goes through lounge to her car. Dramatic burst at CU of Alexis and fade to black.

ACT II – Total time 12′ 06″

Scene 9
Time 4′ 39″

Story/visuals: ES La Mirage. Krystle arrives in her blue convertible Rolls Royce. Krystle enters café/restaurant, stops as she sees Mark on tennis court. Zoom in on Mark, zoom in on Krystle. CU on Krystle gets 'wavy', i.e. Krystle remembers. In a scene-within-the-scene, where voices have echo-effect and the colours are warmly yellow, brown and red, Mark comes home drunk to Krystle, who has different hairdo from in the 'present'. Krystle's initial resentment gives way to long kiss: 'Why do I love you so much?' Back in the present, Mark walks over to Krystle in what seems to be a tracking or crane shot [extremely rare in the serial]. Krystle explains she thought Blake would be there, Mark asks how she is, claims to read something in her eyes, Krystle says he could never read her. Last line: 'Leave me alone, Mark!' Cut to next scene.

Music: Starts before image lights up, continuous throughout entire scene. Opening shot accompanied by La Mirage theme 'over' a particularly passionate string version of D-theme at Krystle's arrival. Strong dissonance as Krystle sees Mark. Memory sequence and its 'wavy' visual introduction is underscored and aurally continued by repetitive three-note mini-motif on xylo- or vibraphone with strings, volume dramatically increases as they kiss. Single note continues out of memory sequence into 'reality', bass/drum beat added, signalling suspense/expectation/destiny, as Mark approaches. Touches of something sentimental, melancholy, 'wound' appears during conversation. Krystle's final line is punctuated, but not very strongly. Music continues across cut to next scene.

Scene 10
Time 3' 39"
Story/visuals: ES C-m, garden. Kirby arrives in taxi, wearing dark blue jacket and hat, white blouse and skirt, looking somewhat like British school uniform. Wanders in garden, camera showing luscious park, pool, etc. Talks to turtle named 'Geoffrey' when Jeff comes out of mansion and they see each other. Jeff does not recognize her, says 'That happens to be my name.' Kirby explains she called turtle Geoffrey when she was a child. Jeff: 'You're little Kirby?! I'll be damned!' Kirby asks for a hug, and gets it. 'Welcome home, Kirby.' She's been a student in Paris. Kirby says Jeff has become 'a very distinguished man in these five years', 'distinguished and handsome, oh! there I said it![. . .] I had this gigantic crush on you.' Jeff was only interested in Fallon then, but now he explains to Kirby that they don't live together even if they're in the same house. Kirby: 'I'm sorry, I really am!' Long CU of Kirby smiling to herself. Joseph into garden as Jeff leaves: 'Kirby!' Kirby: 'Papa!' [Pronounced with un-American emphasis on second syllable.] Kirby runs upstairs to embrace Joseph. Low angle total of the two embracing. *Dissolve* to next scene.
Music: Bridge becomes horn variations of the pompous D-theme with ES, shifts to extremely sweet, romantic melody played by solo flute as Kirby arrives. Continuous, strongly romantic music as Kirby wanders in garden. Full orchestra at full volume as Kirby turns round to see Jeff and we get cross-cut interlocking gazes. Music ends as conversation gets going. Kirby's super-sweet leitmotif plays again as she smiles when Jeff leaves. Music continues until Joseph enters the garden. Strings picked in rapid, joyous climb as 'mickey-mousing' of Kirby's climbing of a few stairs to embrace her 'papa'.

Scene 11
Time 1' 36"
Story/visuals: Overwhelming greenery and brightly coloured flowers in garden, Joseph and Kirby appear, walking and talking. Kirby is now in very red, tight-fitting, short dress, black hair hanging long and loose. She tells Joseph how friendlily she's been received by everyone, especially Krystle. 'I know you find this hard to believe, papa, but Kirby Anders is not a child any more.' Kirby has been engaged to a Jean-Paul in Paris, Joseph laments their break-up, Kirby only talks about Jeff and Fallon. No more French! Promises Joseph not to interfere with Jeff and Fallon, but smiles sweetly with a touch of the shrewd again as she walks into (and out of) profile CU before cut to next scene.
Music: The mickey-mousing at end of sc. 9 turns into a bridge across cut; romantic music during introductory shots from garden stops as dialogue gets going. Resumes with final CU on Kirby, barely introducing her sweet motif before music shifts radically to something dramatically suspenseful, ominous, about one second before cut.

Scene 12
Time 2' 22"
Story/visuals: ES (zoom in on entrance to) Coco building. Adam in office, Jeff enters. Adam suggests Coco lends DC money needed to go on with shale oil process, in return for access to the secret process. Jeff strongly rejects idea, saying process is worth much more than loan, and that he, contrary to Adam, doesn't want to break or take over DC. Adam says 'the name of the game is winning', and talks about 'noble words from my always noble brother-in-law'. Adam asks how Jeff can work in Coco and keep ties to DC. Jeff says there is room for both empires 'if they are healthy. I mean, do we have to be barracudas to exist in this world?' Jeff also reminds Adam that Blake is his father. Jeff ends up by saying he wants to take over his uncle Cecil's old executive office from Adam

when he moves to Coco – 'the *owner's* office'. Zoom in to CU of Adam, who is very angry. Fade to black.

Music: The dramatic music from sc. 10 accompanies ES of Coco building, reduced volume under shot of Adam in office, ends as Jeff enters. Resumed as ominous, dramatic, played by brass (horn of some sort) after Jeff has declared his refusal of Adam's plan. Continues through rest of scene, building to dramatic climax at final zoom in on angry, dangerous Adam.

ACT III – Total time 9' 31"

Scene 13
Time 2' 21"
Story/visuals: ES CU of flowers, zoom out to view of bushes, pan to C-mansion, cut to young servant in uniform serving Blake and McVane having lunch on terrace. Blake talks of his responsibility for more than a thousand employees, McVane says government/ congress won't listen. Blake says shale oil process will increase daily production by 15–30 per cent etc. McVane says that's impressive but still . . . Blake reminds him: 'You've always had a good and very helpful friend in me. And you want it to remain that way, no question. [. . .] You twist their arm [. . .] for *my* company and *your* future. Not to mention the future of this country!' Cut to next scene.

Music: Strong, loud music starts just before image lights up, D-theme variations played in a harmonious, sweeping fashion. Ends as conversation starts. Begins again after 'a friend in me', harmonious and proud/pompous though also ominous [= righteous threats], turns into dramatic D-theme fanfares after Blake says 'this country', slides into La Mirage theme at cut.

Scene 14
Time 1' 55"
Story/visuals: ES La Mirage. Fallon aggressive at someone on telephone. Cut to Blake outside, looking at Mark instructing a whole group of Barbie-doll blondes again. Lesson's over, Mark passes Blake who says 'You're good' and wants to play him one day. Fallon comes in background, waits until Mark leaves, says to Blake it's a surprise to see him after 'the discussion yesterday'. Blake: 'Who remembers yesterday? I just stopped by to see your pretty face and to say I'm sorry . . . and take a look at my investment. You seem to have done a good job here. That fellow Mark is gonna be a winner!'

Music: Bridge ends after ES. A solo horn starts after 'a good job here' and becomes bridge across cut to next scene.

Scene 15
Time 1' 33"
Story/visuals: ES (tilt up) Alexis-b. Fallon wants to call off 'Mark meets Krystle' project. Alexis doesn't. Fallon: 'What I want to make sure is that my father won't get hurt.' Alexis calls Krystle 'Blake's pseudo-wife, who is not worthy of him', and tells Fallon to relax and let things develop. CU of uncertain Fallon, then of confident Alexis.

Music: Dramatic at ES, ends at dialogue. Resumes after Alexis's last line as 'atonal', threat/suspense, continuous across cut.

Scene 16
Time 0' 56"
Story/visuals: ES C-mansion. Kirby in kitchen with other servants, Jeanette in particular. Fixes baby bottle, says: 'This makes me want to be a mother.' Kirby asks about Fallon and Jeff. 'They just don't seem to agree on anything.' Jeanette confirms her impressions and says she hopes they can find a nanny to take care of their baby soon. CU on smiling Kirby.

Music: Kirby theme starts directly at shot of mansion, miraculously developed out of the ominous motif immediately preceding it without break. Ends at start of talk, resumes towards end after the Kirby line quoted above, again based in Kirby theme. Bridge across cut to next scene.

Scene 17
Time 2′ 40″
Story/visuals: ES shot of Alexis-b. Alexis meets with Jeff to discuss shale oil. Alexis and Jeff own Coco 50/50. Alexis: 'That Blake and I are divorced doesn't mean that we're mortal enemies. So if he needs money to get out of a tight spot and some of it happens to be mine, so what?' Jeff says there's no need for help, since McVane has now arranged a government loan. Alexis, openly flirting, invites Jeff to move in with her – 'there's always a spare bed here!' Jeff recognizes the sexual invitation by smiling in a mildly humorous, slightly bashful way, exchanging cross-cut glances with Alexis. Jeff leaves, and Alexis picks up phone, calling Washington, asking for McVane – 'he'll remember me'. CU on Alexis, fade to black.
Music: Kirby motif from last scene gets 'distorted' into something ominously dramatic at ES. No music during first part of talk. But sweet music appears as Alexis first mentions McVane – even if it serves mainly to underscore her flirting invitation to Jeff. Continues into suspense mood as Jeff leaves, builds to dramatic climax at final shot and fade to black.

ACT IV – Total time 9′ 14″

Scene 18
Time 2′ 06″
Story/visuals: ES La Mirage – this time zoom out. Fallon has received flowers with high praise of her on accompanying card. Adam in without knocking. He wants them to be friends. 'Because I admire you . . . and then there's your son. All of Colbyco is going to be his one day!' Fallon says Jeff is not stupid in matters of business, and rejects Adam's invitation to reconciliation. She starts to leave office. Adam grabs both of her arms, moves up very close and says: 'I'm your brother, we can't be on opposite sides.' Fallon: 'You're not my brother.' Adam: 'If not, why don't we pick it up where we left it, remember?' [Referring to their first encounter, in which mutual sexual attraction was played out.] Adam leaves, CU on Fallon before cut to next scene.
Music: The vivacious, energetic La Mirage theme accompanies ES, continues at low volume until Adam enters, then ends. Starts again as Adam says 'I'm your brother' at low volume, as if at a distance, first dreamy/a little melancholy, then becomes ominous and finally more normally dramatic under final CU on Fallon. Bridge across cut to next scene.

Scene 19
Time 2′ 07″
Story/visuals: ES Alexis-b. Alexis is painting – on her balcony? Instructs Adam that she'll handle Jeff from now on, using her 'honey' instead of Adam's 'vinegar'. 'Honey attracts small flies better than vinegar.' Talks about how Blake has treated her violently, and how Adam has inherited this trait from Blake. Still makes defensive remarks about Blake's role in the death of Steven's lover. Adam vehemently declares that he 'strongly dislikes' Jeff. Alexis promises to order dinner for them at 8.30, 'prime rib the way I know you like it – blood rare'. Adam rushes out, Alexis continues to paint. Last shot shows Adam rushing out of door.
Music: Single last tone from the previous scene becomes starting point for dramatic music at ES. No music during first part of talk, picks up again towards the end, at first low and vaguely romantic but ominous, then very dramatic, full volume, with 'singing' drumbeats and a low, strong, ominous string note (bass). Becomes bridge across cut to next scene.

Scene 20
Time 2' 01"
Story/visuals: Cut directly to MCU on Krystle. It later turns out she's in the C-m garden, with flowers. 'Wavy' picture signals memory, about Mark. Dominant curtain behind Mark is roughly the same as Krystle's clothing in 'reality' part of scene. Mark wants to drink again, depressed because of career problems. Krystle supportive, but he has packed a suitcase and is on his way to Mexico to get a divorce he'll send her in the mail. Cut back to reality with CU on Krystle as she is stung by thorn on rose. Krystle turns round, walks with determination up towards C-m. *Dissolve* to next scene.
Music: The bridge drops in volume, shifts to the xylo-/vibraphone or glockenspiel motif signalling memory sequence as 'wavy' picture appears. Continuous 'dreamy' music during this sequence, shift to romantic, melodious mood (after mimicked 'sting') at the return to 'the present'. Dramatically 'climbing' phrases as Krystle ascends stairs in garden, increasing tempo as well [signalling: Action!]. Continues through *dissolve* into next scene.

Scene 21
Time 1' 21"
Story/visuals: Krystle arrives at La Mirage and angrily tells Fallon she knows Fallon brought Mark to make trouble. [Krystle's energy here is striking.] Krystle: 'It's going to backfire on you. [. . .] Do you hear that?! Do you understand that?!' Final MCU on Fallon, sort of blank expression, shocked.
Music: Climbing bridge (from previous scene) reaches dramatic top and then drops at Krystle's entry into Fallon's office. Starts again to accentuate dramatically Krystle's challenging questions to Fallon, reaches top with MCU of Fallon, continues as bridge across cut to next scene.

Scene 22
Time 0' 49"
Story/visuals: ES Coco building. Adam in Jeff's new office, tells secretary he wants to redecorate it as a welcoming present. Secretary says Cecil Colby had it redecorated with expensive panels just before he died. Adam says it still looks dingy; wants to order paint himself. MCU on bewildered secretary, Adam stops to think in front office, CU of him final shot.
Music: Bridge transformed to march-beat dramatic mode at ES. Shifts to low-volume 'atonal' background at cut to office, continuous during dialogue. A couple of ominously emphasized beats as Adam exits office, a very low string note played up at final CU of Adam, becomes bridge across cut to next scene.

Scene 23
Time 0' 50"
Story/visuals: Opening shot of builder's store/hardware store/warehouse. Adam has asked for a kind of paint which is to be used under boats for protection. Salesperson insistently, slowly, repeatedly explains to Adam that the paint is extremely dangerous, fumes may cause brain damage and death. Adam says he knows this very well, and smiles, displaying a large number of teeth. Image freezes, credits appear as extra dramatic effect, in bright yellow, large letters, filling the screen (executive producers Aaron Spelling, Douglas Cramer/Richard and Esther Shapiro). Fade to black.
Music: Continuous from bridge, low-volume, high-pitch woodwind and low strings seemingly playing in minor key take turns in dominating, signalling suspense, undecided-ness, not reaching a high volume climax until credits dramatically fill the screen, over Adam's frozen smile.

END CREDITS over bird's-eye shot of C-mansion.
Time 0' 28"
Music: Final part of D-theme, ends as in title sequence.

EPISODE 43

Directed by Irving J. Moore
Music by Marvin Laird
Preceded by magazine on current movies.

NRK announcer/host: 'The Movie Magazine was hosted by Pål Bang Hansen and Randi Weum. And then we're ready for a new episode of *Dynasty*.'
Title sequence

'LAST TIME, ON *DYNASTY*' (voice over):
Time 1' 52"
1) Blake to Fallon at breakfast: Accept Adam!
2) Krystle to Mark: You never could read me/ That's ancient history.
3) Krystle yells at Fallon.
4) Kirby with Fallon, they talk about Jeff and Fallon.
5) Blake with McVane about oil loan.
6) Jeff talks with Adam on DC/Coco.
7) Alexis and Adam talk about Jeff.
8) Adam gets the dangers of boat-paint spelled out.
Fade to black
Music: Continuous. Suspense at 1), the rest low-volume, romantic, burst at end.

ACT I – Total time 9' 46"

Scene 1
Time 1' 09"
Story/visuals: ES lights up – Denver by night, C-m at night. Blake and Krystle returning home after formal business dinner. She has been looking weary and uncommunicative all evening. Krystle turns down Blake's invitation to a brandy and talk in the library, says she's tired and goes to bed. Blake walks downstairs, turns towards library.
Music: Grandiose opening music: tremolos become D-theme at mansion ES. Volume reduced very much to become continuous string background for dialogue; volume increased again to form bridge across cut to next scene.

Scene 2
Time 0' 59"
Story/visuals: Jeff already in library. Fireplace in use. Blake and Jeff talk about shale oil and why McVane can't be found, and Blake explains that McVane is so important that other channels of influence are not tried. MCU of Blake. *Dissolve* to next scene.
Music: Music (bridge) ends as dialogue starts, returns at end of scene to form bridge across dissolve to next scene. A 'wipe' (xylophone?) is heard at dissolve.

Scene 3
Time 3' 10"
Story/visuals: Krystle and Blake in bed, can't sleep. Krystle brings up the tennis coach, Mark. Her nightgown is low cut and elegant. Krystle thought Blake and Fallon hired Mark to put her to a test. Blake says he was not involved, Krystle embraces Blake. Krystle tells Blake that Fallon set up a fake meeting with Blake to have her meet Mark at La Mirage. Blake offers to fire Mark. Krystle says this is not necessary, she only had to know Blake was not in on the hiring. Blake: 'I'm glad we talked.' Interlocking tender gazes, kiss,

embrace, sex suggested. Slow zoom to CU of kissing couple, Krystle lying in bed, Blake sitting. Cut to following scene.

Music: Bridge turns into continuous romantic background music, associated with Mark and Krystle memories. Increased volume as Krystle says 'I was married to him once', then music stops for a while until Blake says he's glad they talked. Heavily romantic strings becomes bridge across cut.

Scene 4
Time 3' 12"
Story/visuals: C-m courtyard/driveway, morning. Mercedes sports model arrives. Inside, Jeff downstairs. Kirby out of door, looks at Jeff, as Fallon comes in from outside. Fallon mentions to sulky Jeff that she spent the night at the hotel to prepare for party. She meets Kirby for the first time – happiness/joy. Fallon says, looking down over Kirby's body: 'Three years ago in Paris you were this scrawny kid – and now, competition!' Adds: 'Steven should have seen you.' Kirby: 'Where is he?' Fallon says he's travelling around the globe, doesn't know where. Fallon says she has to give her baby a bath. They both go to nursery, look at baby, who makes sweet baby babble throughout conversation. Fallon says the situation with Jeff is 'just the end of a mistake, we're both on different wavelengths'. Kirby says she took care of four-month-old baby on yacht in Greece 'last August'. Fallon knows about Kirby's 'engagement' with Jean-Paul. Kirby suggests herself as nanny. Fallon says she's 'overqualified' – 'Oh, I know you graduated from the Sorbonne. What kind of degree, anyway?' Kirby: 'Oh, you know, the humanities.' That settles it: she's hired as nanny, they hug, talk of salary is unimportant, says Kirby. CU on baby, Fallon and then on Kirby, looking at Fallon, not baby.
Music: Continuous, melodious music until Fallon and Kirby meet. No music until almost end of scene, but cute baby babble continues in background. At final shots a short, sweet bridge across cut to next scene starts.

Scene 5
Time 1' 16"
Story/visuals: Fallon and Blake at breakfast, servant assisting. Blake brings up Mark. Fallon says she was not the one who told Krystle to meet Blake at La Mirage, and that Mark got the job when he asked for it after Fallon one day saw him play tennis at the hotel. Joseph in with express letter to Fallon, Steven's handwriting on envelope. He's in Hong Kong. CU on Blake, who leans forward, serious, tense. Fade to black.
Music: Bridge ends when dialogue starts. Low music starts just before Joseph's entry, as Blake says 'so you weren't the one who left that message for Krystle', erupts into dramatic climax at 'Hong Kong!' and CU of Blake.

ACT II – Total time 12' 43"

Scene 6
Time 1' 36"
Story/visuals: ES: rarely used aerial shot of Denver. ES La Mirage. Mark outside with Alexis, who has paid for tennis lesson but prefers 'a game where the ball just falls into my lap'. Alexis pushes Mark to meet Krystle, no immediate success: Mark won't talk to Alexis about it. Alexis says Mark should fight, Blake is in 'a very vulnerable position right now'. CU of Alexis.
Music: Harp opening into first shot, variations of La Mirage theme under opening ESs. No music during dialogue. Romantic music starts after Alexis's line about Blake, with reaction CU of Mark, accompanies final shot of Alexis, becomes bridge across cut to next scene.

Scene 7
Time 1' 50"
Story/visuals: ES DC-b. Blake on the phone, commands someone to find Steven in Hong

Kong. Krystle is in office. Quotes from Steven's letter about friend Bent Reynolds. Bent is lucky according to Steven because he's a loner with no family or expectations to live up to. Steven has obviously not forgiven Blake. Loving confidence between Krystle and Blake. Krystle: 'Give him some time, Blake.' They hold hands. Blake can't have lunch with her, has to find McVane. Talk about Fallon's party at La Mirage same evening. Krystle will spend afternoon buying dress for party. Blake follows her to door, arm around her and vice versa. Krystle stops just outside door, zoom to CU of her.

Music: Bridge does not become D-theme fanfares. No music during dialogue. Blandly romantic as they walk to door, shift, with a brief fragment of dizzy 'memory' motif, to strong 'Mark' love theme with zoom to CU on Krystle. Becomes bridge.

Scene 8
Time 1' 15"

Story/visuals: ES Coco building. The painter in Jeff's new office wonders why a beautiful panel is covered in paint and complains about smell and dizziness. Adam answers arrogantly. Alexis enters, asks about paint. Adam claims it is to wish Jeff welcome and make friends. And Alexis accepts this explanation immediately, saying 'we've got enough enemies as it is, darling, without inventing new ones'. Turns and leaves. Zoom to CU of Adam.

Music: Peaceful background continues from bridge, a little 1920s jazzy burst as Alexis takes a dance step on her way out. Bridge across cut to next scene.

Scene 9
Time 2' 20"

Story/visuals: ES costumers store (sign on building). Krystle and Alexis in same dress shop, putting on dresses in booths side by side. Witty exchange of hostilities, Krystle shows strength. They leave their booths simultaneously – wearing identical costumes, clearly performing for the camera. They flip a coin to find out who is going to wear it at Fallon's party – Krystle wins. CU on smiling Krystle.

Music: Basically light bridge ends at dialogue. Light comedy music, 1920s pastiche, starts as Alexis says 'Boring? Me?' Drumbeat marking jazzy show performance along with increased volume as they come out of booths. Music continues through cut to outside store (next scene).

Scene 10
Time 0' 59"

Story/visuals: Krystle leaves store. Mercedes sports car prominently parked behind her Rolls. Mark comes running towards Krystle outside store, says he's got important things to say. Krystle says he's lost the right to talk to her, gets into her Rolls. Mark: 'Let's go some place for coffee.' Krystle: 'Try Brazil!' Drives off, Mark staring in her direction. Camera catches Alexis observing the scene from inside the store, smiling.

Music: Sweeping Gershwinesque blues heard as Mark appears, mood then becomes indecisive, dies at start of dialogue. Weak city traffic noise in background. Dramatic music picks up again when Krystle starts car and drives off, under CU of Mark, even more pronounced with cut to final zoom shot of Alexis. Bridge across cut to next scene.

Scene 11
Time 1' 07"

Story/visuals: ES C-m, night, zoom in on bedroom window [very rare shot]. Krystle doing her make-up etc. Maid helps. Blake in: 'My God, you look beautiful!' Krystle turns round and shows herself. Compliments Blake's looks, adds: 'Darling, that loan, that whole mess, forget Neil McVane, just for tonight.' Blake says he doesn't understand why McVane can't be reached, but agrees to forget for the night: 'if you're game, I'm game'. Laughs, embrace.

Music: Touch of D-fanfare at ES. Continuous music, moving between 1920s party music and romantic, Gershwinesque, bluesy 'tenderness'. No real bridge to next scene, but there is still continuity in soundtrack (cf. next scene).

Scene 12
Time 1' 45"
Story/visuals: ES La Mirage exterior at night, veteran cars, Rolls and bundles of balloons outside. Inside: large, crowded costume party, 'Welcome to the roaring 20's' on large placard on wall. Fallon hostess, wearing shiny red dress and even redder and shinier wig/ hat shaped like 1920s hairdo. Fallon calls for attention and makes short welcome speech, particularly thanking her father.
Music: Outside location sounds of old cars mixed with seemingly diegetic 1920s music playing inside. Music increased in volume inside, band not visible. Music stops during Fallon's speech, then picks up again, forming bridge to next scene.

Scene 13
Time 1' 51"
Story/visuals: ES Alexis-b, night. Inside, Alexis descends stairs wearing glitzy, short white dress with fringes and 1920s accessories. Wants to open champagne bottle, kicks around as if doing the Charleston. Elevator door in her living room opens, McVane enters, compliments Alexis on her looks. They talk about previous encounters in Spain, he particularly remembers 'those siestas'. Alexis: 'The night is young, Congressman!' Later, Alexis: 'I'm a Gemini, many different women.' Asks about his trip to Washington, he says he managed but he now owes more favours than he likes to. Alexis helps him with his tie. CU on happy Alexis. Fade to black.
Music: 'Happy' 1920s music, the Charleston tune, until McVane arrives. Music then briefly turns a little sensual before it disappears. Picks up again with bluesy, sensual clarinet, interspersed with humorous effects, towards end of conversation as Alexis moves in, getting more definitely playful, increasing to a final burst just before fade to black.

ACT III – Total time 10' 57"

Scene 14
Time 1' 29"
Story/visuals: Party at La Mirage, outside, lots and lots of people moving around, dancing. Fallon introduces French Count Pierre to Blake and Krystle: 'Pierre's family owns a couple of Alps and I met him when I was skiing there, in Chamonix.' Now he'll try Aspen. Blake leaves with count. Fallon alone with Krystle, says the count couldn't take his eyes off her, but knows she's married, so not to worry. Zoom to MCU of Krystle.
Music: Diegetic 1920s party/dance music, continues through all following scenes. Here: 'Yes, sir, that's my baby'.

Scene 15
Time 1' 12"
Story/visuals: Dancing, inside. Lavish scene, colours, lights, music, party noise. Alexis arrives with Congressman McVane. Fallon goes to meet them, is introduced to him. Fallon stares in amazement after her mother as she vanishes in crowd, discreetly shaking her head.
Music: Party music.

Scene 16
Time: 1' 09"
Story/visuals: Fallon administrates staff. Adam approaches, reminding her not only of their last talk but also of 'the first time we met'. Jeff arrives, compliments Fallon on the

hotel and the party, asks Adam why he had his office painted. Adam says it was a 'gesture of welcome' and leaves. Fallon: 'Be careful with him, Jeff, never turn your back on him.' Long CU of Jeff.
Music: Party music, cf. above.

Scene 17
Time 1′ 03″
Story/visuals: Dancing, in garden. Mark in white suit with white cap (stylish version of a sixpence). Blake spots him while dancing with Krystle, suggests they go in, but Krystle chooses confrontation: introduces Blake to Mark. Blake says he still wants to play tennis, Mark says 'Any time'. Blake and Krystle return to dance floor. CU of Mark looking in their direction.
Music: Party music.

Scene 18
Time: 00′ 39″
Story/visuals: Alexis talks with McVane, suggests they go and find 'privacy', gives him a key to a room in the hotel where she implies they should meet. Very heavy exchange of glances. CU on excessively flirtatious Alexis.
Music: Party music.

Scene 19
Time 1′ 18″
Story/visuals: Fallon and Count Pierre in the crowd as Kirby arrives, wearing a simple but nice white dress, no costume. The count says he knows her. Kirby denies that they have met previously at a party in Monte Carlo. The count insists, and says to Fallon after Kirby has moved on: 'Whoever she is, she gets around.' CU of wide-eyed Fallon, looking in Kirby's direction.
Music: Party music.

Scene 20
Time 1′ 04″
Story/visuals: Kirby walks around, meets Adam for the first time. He comes on to her very strongly. Jeff comes and takes her away by asking her to dance. Adam looks in their direction, very clearly not pleased. Long CU of Adam before he turns and walks away.
Music: Party music.

Scene 21
Time 00′ 17″
Story/visuals: Alexis asks McVane if he has the key, they leave together.
Music: Party music.

Scene 22
Time 0′ 25″
Story/visuals: Blake and Krystle dancing outside, Blake suggests having a look at a new bar inside hotel.
Music: Party music.

Scene 23
Time 0′ 41″
Story/visuals: Fallon in crowd. Mark approaches, puts arm around her shoulder and suggests a drink. Fallon says she's had her quota, but agrees to have one more. They go to outside bar together.
Music: Party music.

Scene 24

Time 00′ 40″

Story/visuals: Blake spots Alexis and McVane moving through inside crowd at a distance, follows them, stops as they go into room. Krystle goes up to Blake from behind, says: 'What's wrong? You look as though you've just seen a *ghost!*' Blake says he hasn't seen a ghost but something a lot more dangerous. Zoom to CU on Blake, fade to black.

Music: Party music fades as Blake sees Alexis and McVane. Only party chatter heard a little while; as Blake follows the couple D-theme variation develops, played with deep strings, sounding sentimental, almost melancholy [thus contradicting Blake's expressed sentiment]. Increase in volume/force until dramatic burst at zoom and fade to black.

ACT IV – Total time 10′ 48″

Scene 25

Time 2′ 25″

Story/visuals: ES La Mirage exterior, night. In garden, Fallon dancing Charleston on the diving board. Mark laughing and looking in the crowd, the two communicate with looks. Band is shown. Fallon invites Mark to join her, he does, they dance on the board until Fallon falls into pool, Mark jumps in after her with drink in hand, they laugh and kiss. Jeff watching with Kirby, who defends Fallon.

Music: Starts before image lights up. Continuous, loud 1920s party music: Charleston.

Scene 26

Time 00′ 30″

Story/visuals: Blake dancing with Krystle in crowd, they exchange humorous remarks: Krystle needs to powder her nose, Blake says he'll behave as long as the band doesn't play a tango.

Music: Party music.

Scene 27

Time 1′ 37″

Story/visuals: Blurred CU of reflector globe/ball hanging from roof. More dancing crowd, Blake and Krystle still dancing. Blake sees Alexis and McVane coming out of their room. Alexis wipes McVane's face, their dialogue makes it even more evident they have had sex. Alexis has also promised to support him 'generously' in the upcoming election. Cecil Colby always made sure he had sufficient financial means to survive if things went wrong, contrary to 'my ex-husband' [as if C. Colby wasn't her most recent ex]. Cut to MCU on Blake, who looks angrily at McVane, walks over and takes him with him more or less against his will. CU on triumphantly smiling Alexis who joins party.

Music: Loud party music. Reduced volume when Blake spots the couple. Music ends, no music during Alexis/McVane talk. Dramatic music starts at MCU of Blake, 'atonal'/disharmonious dramatic music last until final CU on smiling Alexis, when a playful little motif is introduced which becomes bridge.

Scene 28

Time 1′ 24″

Story/visuals: Blake in hotel room with McVane. He has double-checked about the Washington shale oil loan, and McVane has not told the truth. Blake says he has heard certain rumours about McVane's moral conduct which he might make public. McVane: 'And blackmail me?' Blake: 'Blackmail? I don't operate that way. Let's say survival, for me, my company, my country.' And: 'We're going to talk, right now.' CU of Blake over McVane's shoulder, then on very obviously uneasy McVane over Blake's.

Music: Bridge dies out as conversation starts. No music rest of scene. [NB: Almost unique]

Scene 29
Time 1' 04"
Story/visuals: Dancing. Jeff and Kirby dancing. Count Pierre toasts Kirby at a distance. Kirby wants to leave. Drops something from her bag on the way out. Adam immediately there on bended knees to help her, grabs her arm: 'It's so lovely, it's just like silk.' Kirby seems passive, looking at Adam with no particular expression. Jeff approaches from behind Adam, pushes him over so he falls on the floor, smiles triumphantly as he follows Kirby to the door. Adam smiles to the crowd, but sends evil look after Jeff and Kirby.
Music: Party music.

Scene 30
Time 00' 35"
Story/visuals: Jeff and Kirby on the way out: 'Drive carefully, after all you're my favourite little girl.' Kirby: 'I'm *not* a little girl any more, *truly*, I'm not!' Kirby kisses Jeff on the mouth at the door and looks him in the eyes: 'for helping me out'. MCU on Jeff, contented smile.
Music: Quiet, slower dance music, muted trumpet makes it sound romantically erotic.

Scene 31
Time 1' 35"
Story/visuals: Blake with McVane, says: 'And believe me, America will be grateful!' Alexis enters, asks if they have talked about her, 'comparing notes?' When confirmed, she says: 'And did I come out on top, as it were?' McVane: 'Alexis, I won't be able to accept your offer after all, Blake and I already have an agreement.' Alexis, laughing: 'Neil, you scum. You double-crossing scum' – and: 'Enjoy your title while you can.' McVane leaves. Blake's facial expression deadly determined but also signals a degree of respect for her techniques and what he calls her 'boudoir charms', but he strongly warns her against further interference. Alexis does not look scared but defiant. Still replicates respect by way of her expression. Rapid cross-cutting of CUs of the two, final one of Blake.
Music: No music at start. Begins as Blake answers Alexis first time – largely suspense, but a dash of playfulness at 'you scum'. Phrases by unusual instrument (harpsichord? electronic?) as McVane leaves. Continued drama/suspense until cut. Bridge.

Scene 32
Time 1' 25"
Story/visuals: At party. Mark says to Krystle she's not Blake's wife, she's still married to him. The divorce was never filed in Mexico. Krystle protests, but eventually steps outside. Looks desperate in CU as she hears Mark's voice again, with echo effect, saying that she's still married to him. Says as she's overcome by her need to cry, still in CU: 'My God! It can't be true!' Sobs, sobs. Fade to black.
Music: Bridge ends as soon as Mark meets Krystle. Romantic theme ('Krystle/Mark theme'?) starts as Mark says 'we were never divorced', with piano chords à la Richard Claydermann, powerful dramatic burst in the end, where names of executive producers are superimposed as usual.

EPISODE 44

Directed by Philip Leacock
Music by Peter Myers
Preceded by documentary and discussion on the role of (communist) resistance in northern Norway during World War II.

NRK announcer: 'And at that all is clear for another episode of *Dynasty*.'
Title sequence (Alexis still with pool and palms)

Fade to black
'Last time, on *Dynasty*' (voice over)
Time 1' 20"
1. Fallon and Blake with letter from Steven
2. Fallon hires Kirby as nanny
3. Jeff asks Adam at party why he had office painted – Fallon's warning
4. Adam with Kirby at party, compliments her silken skin
5. Kirby kisses Jeff
6. Two sequences from final scene with McVane, Alexis and Blake
7. Mark's talk to Krystle at party – Krystle sobbing outside
Fade to black
Music: Disharmonious/suspense, getting harmonious at 2) (Kirby), then variations between D-theme and suspense. Music is in other words continuous but highly variable in terms of mood; emphasis on suspense/conflict.

ACT I – Total time 14' 11"

Scene 1
Time 3' 17"
Story/visuals: ES C-m front yard/driveway, a Rolls and a black limo parked outside, more credits superimposed in yellow capital letters. Inside, Blake is packing, is going to Washington. Krystle dressed in blue outfit, helps Blake absentmindedly. 'Replays' Mark's message the previous night, but this time the scene is in daylight, seen from the side so that the lobby's fireplace appears prominently between the two. Return to 'present': Krystle and Blake chit-chat in harmony. Joseph enters, shows half-humorous resentment at not having been given the privilege of packing for Blake (he would have chosen everything in grey, Blake explained previously). Krystle uses the phrase 'I do', and Blake says they've been married for two years. As Blake is about to leave, Krystle says 'Blake' as if she's about to tell him what Mark said. But instead, she says 'I sometimes wonder if you know how much I love you.' Blake: 'Well now, that's the kind of send-off that a husband really needs.' Embrace. Final CU of Krystle.
Music: D-theme at ES, played with strings, continues as background variations through Krystle's memory, slightly dramatic burst at end of memory. No music until Joseph arrives: low, humorous variations, becoming romantic after he leaves, D-theme dominant in increased volume during final romantic sequence – becomes bridge.

Scene 2
Time 0' 47"
Story/visuals: ES Alexis-b. Inside Alexis on phone to Washington. Orders a Mr Spencer to stop Blake's loan. CU of Alexis. *Dissolve* into next scene.
Music: Bridge turns dramatic at ES. No music during first part of talk, suspense music towards end, as Alexis threatens Spencer, becomes bridge.

Scene 3
Time 1' 19"
Story/visuals: ES private jet in air. McVane and Blake inside. McVane has another Bloody Mary. Blake: 'Neil, you know that money is mother's milk to a politician, particularly when he's running for re-election.' McVane says Blake wants a voice for himself and his company in Washington, Blake: 'for the country, dammit!' Recommends McVane takes coffee instead.
Music: Bridge becomes dramatic tremolo (?) at ES. Vague plane noise throughout talk. Slow 'serious drama' cello takes over towards end, music increasing in volume and dramatic effect (touch of D-theme, horns added), becomes bridge of monotone high violins.

Scene 4

Time 0′ 20″

Story/visuals: Unusual ES of C-m (MCU of front entrance with pillars). Krystle at home, still in blue, tries in vain to reach Mark by phone. Asks if he can be paged.

Music: Continuous variations from bridge to bridge.

Scene 5

Time 2′ 39″

Story/visuals: ES Coco building. Jeff in his new office. Kirby enters with flowers from garden. Kiss on cheek. Modern art prominent in picture, particularly large modern sculpture ('pseudo-primitive', stylized sitting human). Kirby [with degree in, you know, the humanities] comments only on the new furniture. Talk about Fallon's behaviour and party in general. Kirby compliments and thanks Jeff for his gallant aid in her awkward situation with Adam, apologizes for having kissed him. Jeff gets phone call from Hong Kong, Kirby leaves. MCU of Jeff at desk.

Music: Bridge becomes vigorous at ES, stops as talk begins. Sweet Kirby theme begins as she thanks Jeff. More 'serious' music begins with phone call, Kirby's theme follows her out as bridge.

Scene 6

Time 00′ 45″

Story/visuals: Kirby out to lift, where Adam exits. He apologizes for previous night, she accepts. Adam says she should get children of her own instead of being nanny for his nephew. Kirby: 'You have your babies, I'm busy.' MCU on laughing Adam.

Music: Kirby theme without strings becomes bridge. Music changes a little during talk with Adam, but Kirby's theme continues until shift to medium-low drama after her final line.

Scene 7

Time 1′ 59″

Story/visuals: ES: zoom in on upper window at C-m. Fallon and Kirby in nursery. Kirby tells Fallon what *she* says Count Pierre has already told her about sinful life in France. Kirby says it would be cruel to break Joseph's illusions about her, Fallon says that's Kirby's problem. CUs of Fallon and Kirby.

Music: Energetic Kirby-theme variation (strings) at ES. Baby babble and rattle noise during talk, no music during most of talk, Kirby-theme variation with a little drama accompanies final part, becomes bridge with a 'wipe' (on vibra-/xylophone?) at cut.

Scene 8

Time 3′ 05″

Story/visuals: Mark and Krystle arrive at countryside meeting place, Krystle in her Rolls convertible, Mark in Porsche. Speed and power emphasized by clouds of dust behind cars, etc. *Dissolve* to talk. Krystle dressed in striking red outfit. Talk gives details from their marriage, Mark stole $1,000 from Krystle's savings when leaving for Mexico, etc. Mark says he doesn't want money from Krystle, only that she believe him when he says the divorce was fake, bought for $100 from lawyer in bar in Guadalajara. Alexis has told him this won't hold legally. Krystle is surprised [!] to hear Alexis is involved, says Mark has sunk to new levels, record unholy alliance. MCU on Mark. Fade to black.

Music: Bridge has become flute variations on 'baroque' part of D-theme, ends when talk starts. Resumes at certain line from Mark ('you're still, at least technically, my wife!'). Continues as low background, deep, ominous bass strokes added as Alexis is mentioned, builds to dramatic burst at final shot and fade to black.

ACT II – Total time 5′ 08″

Scene 9
Time 0′ 35″
Story/visuals: ES La Mirage. Fallon in lobby, Mark arrives, sulky/angry. Fallon criticizes him for leaving his work without permission. Mark bites back, aggressive. Zoom to MCU of Fallon. *Dissolve* to next scene.
Music: La Mirage theme at ES. Continuous music during talk. Bridge to next scene.

Scene 10
Time 1′ 53″
Story/visuals: Mark half naked after shower (white towel around hips), gold chain around neck on hairy chest. Knock on door: 'Room service'. Fallon enters with champagne, says she's sorry. Mark still sulky/angry, short conversation, pushes Fallon out. She says she understands he didn't get his way with Krystle, 'maybe you've lost your touch'. Mark grabs her in door opening, says 'who says?', kisses her for several seconds. Fallon: 'I was wrong.' Mark wants to continue, Fallon says: 'I just came by to protect my investment' while looking down over Mark's body. Leaves. Zoom to MCU of Mark, who turns to face the camera, towel not showing.
Music: Bridge ends at knock on door. Music starts again at 'lost your touch', now jazzy, with dominant saxophone. Instrumentation changes as music becomes bridge.

Scene 11
Time 00′ 41″
Story/visuals: CU of flowers and photo of baby in window, Jeff moves into picture to look. Jeff is in Fallon's office. He's obviously not feeling well, dizzy, massaging his head and neck. Exchanges slightly unfriendly lines with Fallon as she arrives. Tells Fallon Steven is on an oil rig in Java Sea, Indonesia.
Music: Bridge becomes 'dizzy' as Jeff massages himself, then ends. Starts again as Steven is mentioned, dramatic, becomes bridge.

Scene 12
Time 1′ 15″
Story/visuals: ES: very dark shot of oil rig at sea, JAVA SEA, INDONESIA superimposed in bright yellow capital letters. Worker's cabin with bunk beds. Steven lying with back to camera, a friend facing camera says Steven is stupid to run away from family. Steven says he envies friend with no family. Friend repeats Steven is stupid.
Music: Bridge gets high-volume 'oriental theme' added at ES. No music during most of talk, vaguely dramatic background during final part of talk contains D-theme fragments played on soft/muted/melancholy horn, becomes bridge.

Scene 13
Time 0′ 44″
Story/visuals: ES C-m, luxury car (limousine) outside. Krystle ready to leave for Mexico. Refuses (with authoritative tone) to tell Joseph more precisely where she is going and why. MCU on Joseph. Fade to black.
Music: Touch of vigorous D-theme (strings) at ES. Continuous music, still vaguely dramatic, more dramatic burst at fade.

ACT III – Total time 13′ 44″

Scene 14
Time 1′ 27″
Story/visuals: ES: overview of city, ACAPULCO superimposed in yellow capital letters across screen. Inside room lawyer confirms Mark's story to Krystle, who insists the person who

signed divorce document must be found before she'll return to Denver. Lawyer leaves. Total of Krystle, 'frozen' after closing door.

Music: D-theme variation, strings, during ES (not 'Mexican'). No music during talk until lawyer says 'Adios'. Low, romantic music builds towards bridge.

Scene 15
Time 4′ 03″

Story/visuals: ES DC-b. Blake in his office, searching for Krystle by phone. Adam enters, knows about Krystle leaving for Mexico. Blake asks him if he knew what Alexis tried to do with the loan, Adam gives no clear answer. Blake tells him the loan is now OK. Blake also says he and Alexis really *are* enemies. Says Alexis 'operates on her passions', while Adam is 'cool and logical' and therefore should 'ride herd on' his mother. Adam says his mother is very strong and asks what Blake would do if he had to fight both Alexis and him. Blake: 'I'd fight, fight hard, both my ex-wife and my son.' Adam shows a few teeth, looks ironical, slightly amused, mildly dangerous. Blake gets telephone call about where Krystle was yesterday, says in irritated tone that that isn't good enough. CU of Blake, angry and worried.

Music: Dramatic horns and rhythmic punctuation at ES. No music during most of talk, low background towards end, where Adam shows teeth, also minor dramatic effects (such as 'warning' trombones) punctuating final parts of talk, becomes bridge.

Scene 16
Time 3′ 24″

Story/visuals: ES C-m, zoom in on conservatory. Jeff inside. Wipes sweat off forehead, acts dizzy. Kirby enters, a light-hearted conversation includes Kirby telling Jeff he snores, which is news to him. Kirby says he works too hard, gives him massage of neck and shoulders. Pleasant intimacy. As Jeff leaves for office, camera first moves with Kirby to frame her with flowers on grand piano, she stops. Cut to Joseph, who has been watching through window. Looks serious. CU of Kirby.

Music: Bridge becomes 'dizzy' at Jeff. Shift to sweet Kirby theme played by flute as she enters. No music for a while. Variations on Kirby's theme start again as Jeff leaves, turning to drama/suspense when Joseph is seen, becomes bridge.

Scene 17
Time 1′ 54″

Story/visuals: Joseph rushes servants out of kitchen for serious talk with Kirby. Joseph warns against involvement with Carrington family: 'These people *use* people', then says Jeff 'is a married man'. Orders Kirby to repair her relationship with Jean-Paul in Paris and marry him: 'Kirby! You're my daughter! I want you to do as I ask!' Kirby, crying: 'I can't. He *is* married!' CU of Kirby hugging daddy's chest, CU of Joseph, confused and worried.

Music: Bridge ends with servants out. No music during first part of talk. Starts again as Kirby starts to cry, mildly dramatic, probably built on Kirby theme. Becomes bridge.

Scene 18
Time 1′ 43″

Story/visuals: ES Coco building. Jeff in office, very visibly feeling sick and irritable. Calls in Adam, asks about missing report. Adam demonstrates Jeff is forgetting things. CU of Jeff, pressing fingers to his temples.

Music: String variations of Kirby theme at ES, continuous music becomes suspenseful, then dizzy – bridge.

Scene 19
Time 1′ 13″

Story/visuals: ES: tilt up hotel in darkness. Lawyer talks to Krystle. A signature from the clerk who supposedly signed the divorce document shows signature on the document was forged. Lawyer leaves, Krystle alone a few seconds. Knock on door: Blake at door. Tears of overwhelming joy, ECU of Krystle in energetic embrace. Fade to black.

Music: Bridge continues at somewhat higher volume at ES. No music during talk with lawyer. A touch of 'Spanish'/Latin melancholy melodic fragment as Krystle is alone, then dramatic shift to sweeping romantic mood at Blake's appearance and their embrace – D-theme variations . . . final burst.

ACT IV – Total time 9' 58"

Scene 20
Time 2' 40"
Story/visuals: ES top of hotel in darkness. Krystle has told Blake everything. Blake says he would have dropped his trip to Washington to settle this. Krystle says she wanted to protect him since he has other serious worries. Blake: 'Since when did anything come before you?' Says his lawyers will find a way out of the problem. They kiss and say 'I love you', etc. for a while. Blake orders a splendid dinner to their room. Picture gets 'wavy' and Krystle remembers romantic scene with Mark, drops a wine glass and says 'Blake, I love you, I do!'
Music: Light D-theme variations start just before ES lights up. No music until rising romantic strings variation of D-theme start as they kiss. Continues to become bridge.

Scene 21
Time 2' 43"
Story/visuals: ES Alexis-b. Alexis and Adam at breakfast. Newspapers have made Blake a hero because of shale oil process/loan. Adam criticizes his mother. Alexis: 'Just who do you think you are?' Points to Steven as ideal son in terms of love and respect for mother. Adam rushes out, CU/MCU of Alexis.
Music: Bridge becomes 'sick', sort of falling strings, signalling discord. No music during most of talk. Starts again towards end as mild background, getting ominous towards bridge.

Scene 22
Time 2' 42"
Story/visuals: ES C-m garden. Krystle in garden. Morning. Blake comes out, tells her lawyers will fix everything shortly. They may remarry in ninety days, during which time they'll have to 'live in sin' (humorous). Blake suggests immediate second honeymoon to Hawaii. Krystle not happy. It isn't over, she says. She wants to talk to Mark before Blake's lawyers do, in order to 'explain what I was going through'. Blake angry because Mark seems to be so important to her, says 'forget Hawaii', leaves, slamming door. Krystle: 'Blake!' CU on Krystle. *Dissolve.*
Music: Bridge gets D-theme bursts at ES, ends as talk starts. Picks up again after Blake has suggested trip to Hawaii. A soft string melodic line signals shifts between sentimental memories and disharmony/threat. Gradually more ominous towards Blake's exit. Tristesse at Krystle alone, becomes bridge.

Scene 23
Time 1' 14"
Story/visuals: ES DC-b. Blake in office, Fallon enters, claims Blake doesn't care about Steven, says it's a question of priorities. Blake is willing to start search for Steven but says Fallon will have to talk him into coming home.
Music: DC-theme played by horns at ES. No music until Fallon has begged Blake to find Steven, then soft, 'sensitive' music played into bridge.

Scene 24
Time 00' 39"
Story/visuals: ES oil rig at sea in darkness, JAVA SEA, INDONESIA superimposed. Steven and

other workers get up as alarm sounds. Distant total of rig exploding. Picture frozen, first credits almost fill screen with bright, dramatically yellow letters (repeating colour of flames from explosion).

Music: Strongly suspenseful music (accompanied by alarm) until explosion, dramatic burst at credits.

END CREDITS

Next programme on NRK: Reportage about geography and culture of North Atlantic Faroe islands, it rains a lot there.

EPISODE 45

Directed by Jerome Courtland
Music by Ben Lanzarone
Preceded by magazine on serious music, focusing on modern composer's opera version of Strindberg's *Miss Julie.*

NRK announcer talks about the opera's success in Germany, very brief introduction of *Dynasty.*
Title sequence
'Last time, on *Dynasty*' – time: 1′ 17″
1. McVane and Blake on plane to Washington. 2. Krystle argues with Mark. 3. Adam with Jeff. 4. Mark and Fallon kiss. 5. Alexis talks to Adam. 6. Fallon talks with Jeff. 7. Exploding oil rig.

ACT I – Total time 13′ 27″

Scene 1
Time 5′ 02″
ES C-m, night. Krystle by mirror in bedroom, looks sad. Blake wants to know about Mark, why she can't leave the divorce to lawyers. Blake is called to telephone from Hong Kong. CU on Krystle, bright memory of her with Mark. Blake back with news about explosion – Steven not found.

Scene 2
Time 1′ 51″
ES C-m, morning. Limousine outside. Breakfast with Blake, Jeff, Fallon. Blake says he feels closer now to Steven than ever before, says he's got to go alone to find him. A number of short segments with bits of conversations between the three mentioned plus Krystle and Joseph.

Scene 3
Time 1′ 18″
Krystle in bedroom, packing. Blake in, says he's got to go alone, says aggressively: 'I don't need anybody to help me fight my battles!' CU of Krystle.

Scene 4
Time 1′ 21″
ES Alexis-b. Jeff arrives, met by Adam. Jeff wants to talk to Alexis, but Adam says he can talk to him. Jeff gives the news about Steven, Adam reacts as if he's seriously shocked. MCU on serious Adam.

Scene 5
Time 2′ 18″
ES C-m, bedroom window. Fallon grieves in Steven's room. Krystle enters, Fallon is

hostile when Krystle tries to be friendly. Krystle says she's going to meet Mark – final CU of Fallon.

Scene 6
Time 1′ 37″
ES Alexis-b. Alexis in deep grief. Adam holds her in his arms, from behind. Alexis wants to go to Indonesia with Blake. Zoom to CU of evil-looking Adam.

ACT II – Total time 10′ 02″

Scene 7
Time 2′ 09″
ES C-m. Alexis arrives in the hall with Adam, Fallon says Adam is not welcome. Alexis and Fallon talk about Steven in the library. Alexis gets angry when told Blake has already left. She sees Krystle in the garden and goes out. Total of confused Fallon.

Scene 8
Time 1′ 48″
In the garden, Alexis attacks Krystle for having brought Sammy Jo to the house and consequently (!) being responsible for Steven's death. Krystle reminds Alexis that she was the one who paid Sammy Jo to leave Steven. Otherwise she says she does not want to fight a mother in grief. Alexis's anger is stylized/overdone.

Scene 9
Time 2′ 17″
ES La Mirage. Mark instructs a blonde named Barbie. Krystle appears, dressed in blue. Krystle wants to go somewhere private. Mark says 'My place'.

Scene 10
Time 1′ 45″
Garden outside a wing of La Mirage. Mark asks why Krystle has come over herself to take care of divorce formalities. Krystle: 'We shared some wonderful years.' Romantic music. CU of Mark.

Scene 11
Time 2′ 06″
ES aeroplane in the air, skies red/yellow. Blake sits in sofa on first class, Alexis enters from tourist class (she was too late for a first class ticket). She angrily blames Blake for not letting her come with him. Blake: 'This is between me and my son, it has nothing to do with you.' The quarrel rapidly develops into a physical fight where it seems as if Blake is about to strangle Alexis. But he stops, CU of Blake in sombre profile.

ACT III – Total time 10′ 24″

Scene 12
Time 2′ 05″
ES CU of flowers in garden, C-m. Fallon by the pool, 'sees' Steven lying in it, face down. Adam arrives, they have mild talk about Steven, Adam's brotherly love and sympathy accepted. CU of Adam.

Scene 13
Time 2′ 01″
Kirby practises classical ballet while taking Fallon's baby for a walk in the park. Adam stops his car next to her, apologizes for last encounter. He almost gets physical in intense come-on, invites Kirby to dinner, she declines.

Scene 14
Time 2' 12"
ES Coco building. Jeff in his office. Joseph arrives to ask Jeff not to encourage Kirby. Jeff becomes extremely aggressive, loses control, then snaps back to normal and apologizes, confused, looks sick.

Scene 15
Time 2' 31"
ES C-m, night. Krystle reads in library. The disgusting father of Sammy Jo, Frank, arrives, wearing a terribly tasteless tie. He says he has come to see if there was anything he could do after Steven has died, Krystle is tough on him and says he's just after a part of his daughter's possible inheritance. Frank leaves, threatening Krystle in an unspecific way.

Scene 16
Time 1' 35"
BALI in bright yellow letters superimposed on tropical-looking white building(s) in a more or less tropical setting. In a hotel, Blake angrily reprimands Cassidy, an American seemingly responsible for searching for lost oil workers, i.e. Steven. Alexis is there, too. Blake wants to fly to the area in spite of a typhoon. Fade to black.

ACT IV – Total time 9' 15"

Scene 17
Time 1' 10"
Rare ES C-m, starting at the little 'chapel' tower representing Kirby in the title sequence, pan to main building. Fallon and Krystle at breakfast. Phone call from Mark, he's dressed in red and wants Krystle to come over. Fallon suspicious.

Scene 18
Time 1' 49"
Gate to C-m, Krystle exits in her Rolls Royce. Her brother-in-law Frank follows her in old, beaten-up car. Outside La Mirage, Frank acts very aggressive with Krystle. Mark saves her by knocking Frank around a little. Krystle and Mark embrace. Music: romantic version of D-theme.

Scene 19
Time 1' 43"
ES La Mirage garden wing. Mark and Krystle at outside table, he gives her a locket. He had once stolen and pawned it, later paid to get it back and kept it since. He returns it to Krystle as part of their final divorce settlement. CU of Krystle.

Scene 20
Time 1' 32"
Tropical beach at night. Hotel in darkness. Blake angry with Cassidy, but apologizes. Cassidy is himself going to fly Blake out to the area where Steven is lost. Alexis enters as Cassidy leaves, so there is no cut to next scene.

Scene 21
Time 3' 01"
Alexis complains about the hotel, says she doesn't want an argument with Blake. Blake calls home, learns from Fallon that Krystle has gone to see Mark. Alexis acts in a friendly, almost inviting way, Blake is suspicious. Alexis gets angry and warns him that he thought he had, he may never have had . . .

END CREDITS – 0' 28"

APPENDIX

EPISODE 46

Directed by Alf Kjellin
Music by Peter Myers
Preceded by: documentary on fascist repression of trade unions in Turkey.
NRK announcer provides additional information about the situation in Turkey, then says:
'But now to something entirely different – a new episode of *Dynasty.*'
Title sequence
'Last time, on *Dynasty*':
Time: 1' 18"
1) Jeff aggressive with Joseph, 2) Fallon angry with Krystle, 3) Adam gets message about Steven from Jeff, 4) Blake tells Krystle he doesn't need help from anybody, 5) Blake and Alexis fight on plane.

ACT I – Total time 12' 23"

Scene 1
Time 1' 58"
ES BALI, hotel. Blake's room, very early morning, Alexis enters, wants to join Blake on plane. Cassidy enters, ready to go.

Scene 2
Time 2' 06"
ES C-m, nursery. Kirby consoles Fallon, who gives Kirby the rest of the day off, lifts the baby out of his bed.

Scene 3
Time 2' 19"
ES Coco building. Jeff has a drink in his office, Kirby enters (music: Kirby theme) in pink, tight dress generously cut in front. She talks about her childhood and says 'My father thinks I'm Sabrina, you know, the movie.' Jeff does not want to go with her to a movie. 'Dizzy' music. Kirby stops to think a little outside the door.

Scene 4
Time 0' 36"
ES C-m, night. Krystle in library. Joseph brings her letter from Frank, who thanks her for help via Mark. *Dissolve*, voice over. The transition from this scene to the next one is unique. Krystle's voice reads the letter across dissolve and ES in next scene.

Scene 5
Time 1' 46"
ES La Mirage. Krystle finishes reading Frank's letter for Mark. They are in the lobby, in front of the fire, which is prominent in the frame. Mark has given Frank $1,000 to get rid of him for good and to repay an old debt to Krystle. There is literally a fire burning between them.

Scene 6
Time 3' 38"
ES BORNEO. Alexis and Blake visit badly burned survivor from the explosion in hospital, who can tell them nothing about Steven. [Possible to call it change of scene after this.] Outside, in the corridor, Cassidy brings additional bad news. Blake is angry, won't give up. Alexis leans her head against his shoulder. Fade to black.

ACT II – Total time 14′ 05″

Scene 7
Time 2′ 58″
ES Coco building, at night. Jeff in his office, sweating heavily, talks to photograph of
Fallon. Kirby enters. Jeff sees her become Fallon. He kisses Kirby, who talks about the
movie she has been to see. Jeff sees her as Fallon again, says 'Fallon!' and kisses her again.
Kirby runs out, disharmonious music. Low CU on miserable-looking Jeff.

Scene 8
Time 0′ 45″
Kirby exits from the lift on the ground floor. Meets Adam, who talks her into accepting
an invitation to dinner.

Scene 9
Time 1′ 53″
ES BALI hotel. Blake and Alexis are in the room. Cassidy enters, presents Steven's jacket,
found at sea. It has bloodstains. Cassidy says they can't continue the search any longer.
Blake is angry, Cassidy sad but determined.

Scene 10
Time 3′ 15″
Blake sits down, Alexis cries. Blake tries to remember the name of a male psychic. Alexis
talks sentimentally about the past. Blake suddenly remembers the name. Alexis is angry
with him for not accepting the facts. Zoom in on tense Blake.

Scene 11
Time 1′ 12″
ES C-m, night. Jeff with Krystle in conservatory (?). Jeff is sick. Krystle is worried, calls a
doctor. Jeff faints.

Scene 12
Time 4′ 02″
ES Alexis-b, night. Home-alone dinner, Adam and Kirby. Kirby is convincingly drunk.
The fireplace is active in the background. They dance in front of the fireplace. Kirby says
the baby she is taking care of is rich. Adam gets her down on the floor and starts taking
off her dress by force. She refuses and struggles, but then becomes passive.

ACT III – Total time 6′ 50″

Scene 13
Time 1′ 20″
ES Alexis-b, night. Kirby has been to the bathroom, now sober. Adam apologizes, Kirby
blames herself, calls for a taxi. *Dissolve.*

Scene 14
Time 0′ 52″
ES C-m, night. Jeff in his bed, awake. Fallon enters, she is 'really concerned'. The doctor
has said he is overworked. CU of Jeff, as he looks away when Fallon leaves.

Scene 15
Time 1′ 03″
Kirby arrives at C-m outer door, cries, meets Joseph in the hall, doesn't want to talk.
Upstairs, she meets Fallon, and says she has been to see a 'comedy of errors, just like life'.
CU of pensive Fallon.

Scene 16
Time 2' 00"
ES C-m, morning. Limo outside for Krystle, who is going to L.A. to meet Blake. Kirby in nursery with baby, Jeff enters and tries to explain about the night before, Kirby says she 'understands'. They attend to baby.

Scene 17
Time 1' 35"
ES plane in the air. Alexis and Blake on board, first class. Blake is going to Los Angeles to meet psychic. Alexis says she will organize a memorial service for Steven in Denver. Blake says, 'No!' Alexis says: 'You killed him!' Rapidly cross-cut CUs of both of them, fade to black.

ACT IV – Total time 9' 55"

Scene 18
Time 2' 00"
ES beach-front house, yellow capital letters: MALIBU, CALIFORNIA. Inside the psychic Dehner's stylish house – Blake and Krystle. Dehner touches letters from Steven, says the contact is weak. *Dissolve.*

Scene 19
Time 2' 25"
ES airplane in the air. The psychic again tries to concentrate. Krystle and Blake talk lovingly, Blake is really into his belief in the psychic. Krystle is wearing the locket she got back from Mark, and that creates a little tension between the two. *Dissolve.*

Scene 20
Time 1' 05"
ES C-m, limo outside. Blake, Krystle and Dehner arrive. Fallon cries and embraces daddy. Joseph tells Krystle that Jeff is still strange, different. CU of Krystle.

Scene 21
Time 1' 42"
ES Coco building. Jeff in his office, seems about to fall apart. Adam plays cool, offers to have the room redecorated in case Jeff has a problem with the colour. CU of Jeff, very dramatic music.

Scene 22
Time 1' 18"
ES C-m. Blake with Krystle, who does not quite share Blake's trust in Dehner. Blake looks at her locket, says: 'Please keep your negative thinking out of this hallway, I don't want this man's concentration hurt!'

Scene 23
Time 0' 41"
Blake enters Steven's room, where Dehner is. Dehner says: 'If your son is alive, Mr Carrington, he will come to me here.' Blake says, 'Yes!'

Scene 24
Time 0' 44"
ES builder's store. Adam buys more poisonous compound for paint. Very dramatic music.

END CREDITS
Followed by: Pop/rock magazine.

EPISODE 57

Directed by Philip Leacock
Music by (not included, end titles shortened)
Preceded by sports magazine

Title sequence – now with Rolls Royce representing Alexis
'Last time – on *Dynasty*' – 1' 12"
1) Alexis talks to the board of Denver-Carrington, 2) Blake talks to board of D-C, 3) Steven talks to lawyer, wants a divorce, 4) Steven, Alexis,?? 5) Blake threatens Alexis, 6) Mark kisses Fallon, Alexis watches/spies in the background, 7) Alexis calls a newspaper.

ACT I – Total time 9' 29"

Scene 1
Time 2' 14"
ES C-m, morning. Blake, Krystle and Steven with Steven's baby son Danny in the nursery. Steven now works for Alexis at Colbyco. He wants to have Danny with him in his own apartment, Blake will not permit it. Steven leaves, no cut before next scene [which could consequently have been counted as part of this one].

Scene 2
Time 0' 52"
Blake tells Krystle to stay out of the conflict between him and Steven. CU of Krystle with baby, she says 'Not OK'.

Scene 3
Time 1' 52"
Blake down the stairs, Joseph tells him Congressman McVane is in the library. McVane says his private life is still being investigated, even if he has done what Blake told him to do. Blake says he is not behind it.

Scene 4
Time 2' 16"
ES Alexis-b. Steven enters, finds a female journalist waiting. She tries to trick him into giving an interview, asks questions about Claudia (now recovering at a psychiatric institution). Steven leaves.

Scene 5
Time 0' 33"
Alexis with journalist, asks why the story about McVane and the teenage daughter of a Governor has not been printed.

Scene 6
Time 1' 42"
ES DC-b. Krystle in Blake's office, suggests a reconciliation dinner with Steven. Blake is reluctant and angry. Krystle reminds him of what he said when Steven was missing in Sout East Asia.

ACT II – Total time 9' 23"

Scene 7
Time 1' 49"
ES Coco building. Steven and Alexis talk in her office about Steven's conflict with Blake. They compliment each other warmly, and Alexis talks about bonds between them which Blake's 'cruelty' has not been able to break.

Scene 8
Time 1′ 26″
ES DC-b. Blake in his office with Jeff. Blake calls up Alexis, says she must come over. Alexis says he should come to her, Blake says no, since he has something she wants to know. Alexis agrees to come over, Blake and Jeff smile at each other.

Scene 9
Time 1′ 26″
ES Coco building. Kirby enters (now just married to Jeff?), asks for Jeff but walks into the wrong office, Adam's. He reminds her of their sexual encounter. Jeff comes in, acts suspicious.

Scene 10
Time 2′ 07″
ES La Mirage. Kirby and Jeff have lunch. They have been married one month. Jeff complains about Kirby and Adam, Kirby complains about Jeff and Fallon. She wants to move out of the Carrington mansion, into a house of their own. Jeff won't say when. Kirby cries, nearly faints when she gets up. Jeff says she must see a doctor.

Scene 11
Time 2′ 40″
ES Coco building. Steven is in Alexis's office. Krystle enters, invites him to to dinner with Blake. Krystle and Steven talk sentimentally, warm and friendly. Steven finally accepts the invitation. Alexis enters. No cut before next scene.

Scene 12
Time 1′ 55″
Alexis wears a hat one is tempted to call hysterical, and she is dressed in purple. Krystle is a perfect contrast with her 'natural'-looking blonde hair and light-grey outfit. Alexis angrily says Krystle has no right to interfere in the Blake/Steven conflict. Krystle keeps cool, and gets the final line, about Alexis's glass-top desk with legs made of full-size elephant tusks: 'I love your desk. The tusks, they're so *you*!' CU of angry Alexis.

ACT III – Total time 12′ 03″

Scene 13
Time 2′ 42″
ES DC-b. Alexis, smoking, in Blake's office. Blake says Alexis has underestimated the value of Denver-Carrington and its shale oil process. But the big news is that he, personally, has purchased the rights to the shale oil process, and he is not going to let just anybody use it. Alexis is *very* angry, and accuses Blake of playing dirty. Blake says 'Not dirty, just tough', and adds that 'The oil business is *my* turf.' Alexis is furious, but beaten. CU of a complacent Blake.

Scene 14
Time 4′ 22″
ES Meadowland Sanatorium. Claudia is out jogging when Steven arrives. Claudia says Krystle has visited her several times, Steven hasn't been there before. The dialogue also provides background: Claudia has been at the sanatorium since she was found on the roof with a doll she thought was her daughter Lindsay and viewers thought was Fallon's baby.

Scene 15
Time 2′ 16″
ES Alexis-b. Alexis and Mark talk about their relationship so far. Mark is now in a relationship with Fallon, after she divorced Jeff in Haiti ('background'). Alexis offers

Mark money if he is willing to leave, but Mark says he loves Fallon. After he is gone, Alexis writes a note 'from Mark' to Fallon, asking her to meet him at five in his room.

Scene 16
Time 3' 25"
ES La Mirage, garden wing. Alexis knocks on Mark's door. He is dressed only in a towel (again), comes right out of the shower. He tells Alexis to get out, opens the door to emphasize the message, but then returns to the bathroom without checking that she actually leaves. Alexis takes off her fur coat, adorns the room with stockings etc. and jumps under the covers in Mark's bed, seemingly undressed because of her strapless dress. Seconds later, Fallon arrives according to the fake note from Mark. She is shocked at seeing her mother in Mark's bed; him coming from the bathroom after a shower does not improve her impression. She runs out, not willing to listen to Mark's not very competent attempt to explain.

Scene 17
Time 0' 22"
Mark out after Fallon, sees her get into her car, she won't stop when he calls her, Mark sees her drive off.

ACT IV – Total time 9' 22"

Scene 18
Time 1' 48"
ES Alexis-b. Alexis and Adam at breakfast. Alexis wants Adam and Steven to go on a mission for Colbyco together. Adam is angrily reproaching Alexis for favouring Steven, Alexis threatens Adam.

Scene 19
Time 0' 55"
Tennis court, La Mirage. Mark is instructing a man [for once], ends the lesson in order to talk to Fallon, who passes. She refuses to talk to him, and Mark [in a remarkably insensitive/unintelligent move] criticizes her personality.

Scene 20
Time 1' 26"
ES plane in the air. Adam and Steven on their way to visit a remote oil field. Adam tries to tell Steven something, but Steven is aggressively talking about how little Adam knows about the oil business since he has never had oil on his hands, never really worked, just read his law books.

Scene 21
Time 0' 46"
Very rare ES C-m – the mansion 'comes down' from heaven (where the plane was). Krystle is in the kitchen with Mrs Gunnarson, the cook, talks about Steven's real homecoming dinner, which is already being prepared.

Scene 22
Time 1' 28"
A landrover/jeep with Adam and Steven in it drives through a dusty desert landscape, late afternoon light. An airfield (single strip of concrete) is empty, no plane is there to pick up Steven and Adam. Adam has done what Alexis instructed him to do – deliberately delayed the return journey so Steven won't be able to come to the reconciliation dinner. Adam says he tried to tell Steven on the way out there. Final shot is a rare, very high crane shot of Steven on the desert airstrip.

Scene 23
Time 2' 59"
ES C-m, night. Krystle in formal evening dress. Blake enters, will not accept Steven's explanation for not coming. Krystle gets angry with him, and says 'You're like a man on a mountain. [. . .] From now on, take care of your own problems on your own!'

END CREDITS
NRK announcer: 'The Carrington family and all their problems will show up again next Wednesday. And now we're ready for Late Night News.'
Time 2' 16"

EPISODE 58

Directed by Bob Sweeney
Music by Peter Myers
Preceded by a sunny, folkloristic documentary from Åland, a semi-independent group of islands in the Baltic sea, between Sweden and Finland, the score one of Mozart's piano concertos.

NRK announcer: 'And so we're going, for the second-last time, to Denver, Colorado. We're ready for the 58th episode of the American serial *Dynasty*.'

Title sequence
'Last time, on *Dynasty*' – time 1' 26"
1) McVane talks to Blake about being investigated, 2) Alexis quarrels with Adam, 3) Steven and Adam quarrel on plane, 4) Blake triumphs over Alexis in his office, 5) Jeff and Kirby quarrel, 6) The Mark/Alexis/Fallon farcical situation, 7) Krystle's final angry line to Blake.

ACT I – Total time 12' 04"

Scene 1
Time 3' 07"
ES C-m, morning. Krystle alone at breakfast, wearing pink outfit, low shot. Blake enters, blames Krystle for avoiding him. They quarrel about Steven. Joseph brings the newspaper, McVane scandal on the front page, Blake takes the paper with him to the office without asking Krystle if she's interested.

Scene 2
Time 2' 13"
CU of sleeping Kirby. Jeff kisses her from behind. Tender lines exchanged, both apologize for the quarrel they had the day before. They kiss, again. Kirby seems to be sleeping naked – she shows her naked shoulders, arms and a thigh or two to the camera. The room is very dark, in a warm colour tone.

Scene 3
Time 0' 50"
Jeff down the stairs as Fallon comes in the main entrance with Blake Jr. A display of harmony between mother, father and baby follows, watched by Kirby from the top of the stairs. Music signals shift to tension/suspense.

Scene 4
Time 2' 07"
Toys and dolls in the light-blue nursery. Krystle holds Danny. Steven and a nanny are there. Harmony and tristesse. Steven and nanny leave. Extraordinary shot follows: zoom out to a very high bird's-eye shot of crying Krystle, very alone.

Scene 5
Time 1′ 50″
ES DC-b. Blake in his office, McVane enters. Blake gets the opportunity to state a principle: 'My family comes first, then business!' He says that Alexis is behind the scandal because McVane has helped Blake to postpone the merger between Colbyco and DC. McVane is very surprised to hear this!

Scene 6
Time 1′ 57″
ES Alexis-b. McVane calls to talk to Alexis, Adam answers and Alexis refuses to come to the phone. She reminds him of when he tried to poison Jeff with paint. Adam warns Alexis.

ACT II – Total time 7′ 03″

Scene 7
Time 2′ 01″
Rare ES La Mirage. Steven has lunch with his lawyer, Chris. They talk about Danny and custody rights. Chris highly understanding of Steven's gay experiences.

Scene 8
Time 0′ 41″
Mark enters Fallon's office, wants to explain. Fallon refuses to listen, asks if Mark has ever gone to bed with Alexis, Mark shuts up.

Scene 9
Time 1′ 40″
ES Coco building. Jeff in his office, Kirby arrives to say she is pregnant. She almost faints again. Jeff compares her condition to that of Fallon when she was pregnant, Kirby dislikes the comparison.

Scene 10
Time 1′ 48″
ES La Mirage, this time CU of sign outside. Adam talks to Fallon in her office. Wants them to be friends, reminds her of their first (sexually tense) encounter. Now he wants to be accepted as a brother, particularly to Steven. An employee enters, talks to Fallon about a congress for MDs, and the name of Dr Edwards from Billings, Montana, is mentioned. Adam does not say that he recognizes the name, but he clearly does. Adam leaves.

Scene 11
Time 0′ 53″
Adam stops outside the door, remembers (visualized) a conversation with Dr Edwards about his (Adam's) drug experiments and a nervous breakdown. Zoom in to CU of Adam, fade to black.

ACT III – Total time 10′ 50″

Scene 12
Time 3′ 26″
ES Steven's apartment. Chris knocks on door, he brings sherry. Fire already burning. Chris says the story of his life is much like Steven's – 'I'm gay.' They toast – 'to friendship'.

Scene 13
Time 2′ 02″
ES C-m. Fallon arrives in her Mercedes sport model. Alexis is in the library. She explains

to Fallon that Mark had to be exposed. Fallon says Alexis is bad, while Krystle is good. Alexis sees Krystle outside, in the garden.

Scene 14
Time 3′ 39″
Krystle sits on a bench by the lily pond, dressed in blue. Alexis out, more or less yelling abuse. Calls Krystle 'Mrs Jennings'. Krystle jumps at her, and they fall into the pond in slow motion. Funny fighting in the pond. Blake arrives in his black limo, sees his two ladies fight. He gets out and paternally reprimands Krystle while helping Alexis climb out. She walks towards the house, in one high-heeled shoe.

Scene 15
Time 1′ 43″
In Blake and Krystle's bedroom. Blake tries to stop Krystle from moving to La Mirage with a suitcase or two. Krystle is determined: 'You humiliated me in front of the woman who cost us our child!' Blake follows her, stops at top of stairs, camera emphasizes the distance between them. *Dissolve.*

ACT IV – Total time 13′ 04″

Scene 16
Time 5′ 20″
ES La Mirage. Krystle and Mark sit in lobby bar [the following day?]. Blake enters, Krystle goes to talk to him in the lobby, where she talked to Mark in an earlier episode. This time there is no fire in the fireplace. Blake wants to make up, asks her to come home in a heartbreakingly well-prepared speech. Krystle refuses: 'Alexis never really left you, Blake.' She says she needs time on her own.

Scene 17
Time 2′ 02″
ES C-m, zoom on kitchen window. Kirby is drinking water. Joseph enters, Kirby asks if her mother had morning sickness that early in her pregnancy, Joseph can't remember. Kirby leaves, Alexis enters. She threatens to reveal something to Kirby about her mother. Joseph seems to take the threat seriously.

Scene 18
Time 5′ 42″
City in darkness. CU of newspaper, Alexis, dressed in black, is reading it: McVane is rejected as candidate for his party this time. Alexis calls Blake about McVane and a meeting. McVane enters without knocking while she is on the phone. He angrily pulls out the phone from the jack. He picks up a long, sharp paper knife, pours himself a drink. He is obviously out of control. Alexis is frightened, tries to escape. McVane grabs her by the throat and is about to strangle her when Blake arrives, just in time to save her neck. He sends McVane home, and tells Alexis she won't survive if she keeps on ruining people's lives. Zoom to close-up of frightened Alexis.

END CREDITS
Followed by: Late Night News and sports magazine.

BIBLIOGRAPHY

Other sources are mentioned concurrently in the text.

Adorno, Theodor W. (1941) 'On Popular Music' (with the assistance of George Simpson), *Zeitschrift für Sozialforschung/Studies in Philosophy and Social Science*, vol. 9: 17–48.

Adorno, Theodor W. (1969) 'Scientific Experiences of a European Scholar in America', in D. Fleming and B. Bailyn (eds), *The Intellectual Migration: Europe and America, 1930–1960*, Cambridge, Mass.: The Belknap Press of Harvard University Press.

Adorno, Theodor W. [1957] (1972) 'Sociologi og empirisk forskning' ('Sociology and empirical research'), in his *Kritiske modeller* ('Critical models'), Copenhagen: Rhodos.

Adorno, Theodor W. [1962] (1976) *Inledning till musiksociologin* ('Introduction to the sociology of music'), Kristianstad (Sweden): Bo Cavefors Bokförlag.

Adorno, Theodor W. [1963] (1991) 'Culture Industry Reconsidered', in his *The Culture Industry. Selected Essays on Mass Culture* (edited and with an introduction by J.M. Bernstein), London: Routledge.

Adorno, Theodor W. [1938] (1991) 'On the Fetish Character in Music and the Regression of Listening', in his *The Culture Industry. Selected Essays on Mass Culture* (edited and with an introduction by J.M. Bernstein), London: Routledge: 26–52.

Adorno, Theodor W. [1954] (1991) 'How to Look at Television', in his *The Culture Industry. Selected Essays On Mass Culture* (edited and with an introduction by J.M. Bernstein), London: Routledge.

Adorno, Theodor W. [1977] (1991) 'Free time', in his *The Culture Industry. Selected Essays on Mass Culture* (edited and with an introduction by J.M. Bernstein), London: Routledge.

Adorno, Theodor W. and Horkheimer, Max [1947] (1981) *Upplysningens dialektik* ('The dialectic of enlightenment'), Gothenburg: Röda Bokförlaget.

Adorno, Theodor W. *et al.* (1950) *The Authoritarian Personality*, New York: Harper.

Alasuutari, Pertti (1992) ' "I'm Ashamed to Admit it but I Have Watched *Dallas*": the Moral Hierarchy of Television Programmes', *Media, Culture and Society*, vol. 14: 561–82.

Allen, Robert C. (1983) 'On Reading Soaps: A Semiotic Primer', in E.A. Kaplan (ed.), *Regarding Television*, The American Film Institute *Monograph* Series, vol. 2, Frederick, Md: University Publications of America Inc.

Allen, Robert C. (1985) *Speaking of Soap Operas*, Chapel Hill and London: The University of North Carolina Press.

Althusser, Louis (1971) 'Ideology and Ideological State Apparatuses (Notes Towards an Investigation)', in his *Lenin and Philosophy and Other Essays*, New York: Monthly Review Press.

Altman, Rick (1986) 'A Semantic/Syntactic Approach to Film Genre', in B. Grant (ed.), *Film Genre Reader*, Austin: University of Texas Press.

BIBLIOGRAPHY

Ang, Ien (1985) *Watching 'Dallas'. Soap Opera and the Melodramatic Imagination*, London: Methuen.

Ang, Ien (1989) 'Wanted: Audiences. On the Politics of Empirical Audience Studies', in E. Seiter, H. Borchers, G. Kreutzner and E.-M. Warth, *Remote Control: Television, Audiences and Cultural Power*, London and New York: Routledge: 96–115.

Bakke, Marit (1986) 'Culture at Stake', in D. McQuail and K. Siune (eds), *New Media Politics. Comparative Perspectives in Western Europe*, London, Beverly Hills, New Delhi: Sage Publications.

Barnouw, Eric (1975) *Tube of Plenty. The Evolution of American Television*, Oxford, New York, Toronto, Melbourne: Oxford University Press.

Barthes, Roland [1964] (1977) 'The Rhetoric of the Image', in his *Image – Music – Text* (essays selected and translated by Stephen Heath), London: Fontana.

Barthes, Roland [1968] (1982) 'The Death of the Author', in his *Image – Music – Text* (essays selected and translated by Stephen Heath), London: Fontana.

Barthes, Roland [1971] (1982) 'From Work to Text', in his *Image – Music – Text* (essays selected and translated by Stephen Heath), London: Fontana: 155–64.

Bazin, André [1957] (1968) 'La politique des auteurs', in P. Graham (ed.), *The New Wave*, London: Secker & Warburg.

Benjamin, Walter [1936] (1969) 'The Storyteller: Reflections on the Works of Nikolai Leskov', in his *Illuminations*, New York: Schocken Books: 83–109.

Bennett, Tony (1983) 'Texts, Readers, Reading Formations', *Bulletin of the Midwest Modern Language Association*, no. 16, spring.

Biltereyst, Daniel (1991) 'Resisting American Hegemony: A Comparative Analysis of the Reception of Domestic and US Fiction', *European Journal of Communication*, vol. 6: 469–97.

Bjørkvold, Jon-Roar (1988) *Fra Akropolis til Hollywood*, Oslo: Freidig Forlag.

Bobo, Jacqueline (1988) '*The Color Purple*: Black Women as Cultural Readers', in E.D. Pribram (ed.), *Female Spectators. Looking At Film and Television*, London and New York: Verso: 90–109.

Bogart, Leo [1982] (1985) 'Media and a Changing America', in R.E. Hiebert and C. Reuss (eds), *Impact of Mass Media: Current Issues*, New York and London: Longman.

Bordwell, David (1985) *Narration in the Fiction Film*, London: Methuen.

Bordwell, David (1989) *Making Meaning: Inference and Rhetoric in the Interpretation of Cinema*, Cambridge, Mass., and London: Havard University Press.

Bordwell, David, Staiger, Janet and Thompson, Kristin [1985] (1988) *The Classical Hollywood Cinema. Film Style and Mode of Production to 1960*, London: Routledge.

Bourdieu, Pierre (1979) *Outline of a Theory of Practice*, Cambridge, London, New York and Melbourne: Cambridge University Press.

Bourdieu, Pierre (1984) *Distinction. A Social Critique of the Judgement of Taste*, Cambridge, Mass.: Harvard University Press.

Branigan, Edward (1992) *Narrative Comprehension and Film*, London and New York: Routledge.

Brincker, Jens, 1985: 'Musik til billeder' ['Music with images'], in R. Pittelkow (ed.), *Analyser af TV*, Copenhagen: Medusa.

Brooks, Peter [1976] (1984) *The Melodramatic Imagination*, New York: Columbia University Press.

Brooks, Peter (1985) *Reading for the Plot: Design and Intention in Narrative*, New York: Vintage Books/Random House.

Brown, Mary Ellen (1990) 'Motley Moments: Soap Opera, Carnival, Gossip and the Power of the Utterance', in her (ed.) *Television and Women's Culture: The Politics of the Popular*, London, Newbury Park and New Delhi: Sage Publications: 183–98.

298

Browne, Nick (1984) 'The Political Economy of the Television (Super) Text', *Quarterly Review of Film Studies*, vol. 9, no. 3, summer: 174–82.

Brunsdon, Charlotte (1983) '*Crossroads*: Notes on Soap Opera', in E.A. Kaplan (ed.), *Regarding Television*, The American Film Institute *Monograph* Series, vol. 2, Frederick, Md: University Publications of America Inc.: 76–83.

Brunsdon, Charlotte (1991) 'Pedagogies of the Feminine: Feminist Teaching and Women's Genres', *Screen*, vol. 32, no. 4, winter: 364–81.

Buckingham, David (1987) *Public Secrets: 'EastEnders' and Its Audience*, London: British Film Institute.

Burns, Tom (1977) *The BBC: Public Institution and Private World*, London and Basingstoke: Macmillan.

Buscombe, Ed (1980) 'Creativity in Television', *Screen Education*, no. 35, Summer: 5–17.

Cantor, Muriel (1971) *The Hollywood TV Producer: His Work and His Audience*, New York: Basic Books.

Cantor, Muriel (1981) (2nd edn 1992) *Prime Time Television. Content and Control*, Beverly Hills and London: Sage Publications.

Cantor, M. and Pingree, S. (1983) *The Soap Opera*, Beverly Hills, London and New Delhi: Sage Publications.

Cassata, Mary (1983) 'The More Things Change, The More They Are The Same: An Analysis of Soap Opera From Radio to Television', in M. Cassata and T. Skill, *Life on Daytime Television: Tuning-In American Serial Drama*, Norwood, NJ: Ablex Publishing Corporation.

Caughie, John (1991) 'Adorno's Reproach: Repetition, Difference and Television Genre', *Screen*, vol. 32, no. 2, summer: 127–53.

de Certeau, Michel (1988) *The Practice of Everyday Life*, Berkeley, Los Angeles and London: University of California Press.

Connell, Ian (1983) 'Commercial Broadcasting and the British Left', *Screen*, vol. 24, no. 6: 70–80.

Corner, John (1991) 'Meaning, Genre and Context: The Problematics of "Public Knowledge" in the New Audience Studies', paper presented to the Fourth International Television Studies Conference, London 1991.

Coward, Rosalind (1986) 'Come back Miss Ellie: on character and narrative in soap operas', *Critical Quarterly*, vol. 28, nos 1, 2, spring, summer: 171–8.

Cowie, Elizabeth (1984) 'Fantasia', *m/f*, no. 9: 71–105.

Crotta, Carol (1985) Interview with Esther Shapiro, *Los Angeles Herald Examiner*, 4 February.

Culler, Jonathan [1981] (1983) *The Pursuit of Signs: Semiotics, Literature, Deconstruction*, Ithaca, NY: Cornell University Press.

Dahl, Hans F. (1981) *Fra Gutenberg til Gjerde*, Oslo: Aschehoug.

Dahl, Hans F. (1983) Commentary, *Dagbladet*, 2 November.

Denzin, N.K. (1970) *The Research Act: a Theoretical Introduction to Sociological Methods*, Chicago: Aldine.

Doane, Mary A. (1990) 'Remembering Women: Psychical and Historical Constructions in Film Theory', in E.A. Kaplan (ed.), *Psychoanalysis and Cinema*, New York and London: Routledge.

Dreier, Peter [1983] (1985) 'The Corporate Complaint against the Media', in R.E. Hiebert and C. Reuss (eds), *Impact of Mass Media: Current Issues*, New York and London: Longman.

Dyer, Richard (1981) 'Entertainment and Utopia', in Rick Altman (ed.), *Genre: The Musical. A Reader*, London: Routledge & Kegan Paul.

Eco, Umberto [1964, 1978] (1984) *Apokalyptiker und Integrierte. Zur kritischen Kritik der Massenkultur*, Frankfurt. a.M.: S. Fischer Verlag.

Eco, Umberto [1979] (1984) *The Role of the Reader. Explorations in the Semiotics of Texts*, Bloomington: Indiana University Press.

Eco, Umberto (1985) 'Innovation and Repetition: Between Modern and Post-Modern Aesthetics', *Daedalus*, vol. 114, no. 4: 161–85.

Eco, Umberto [1979] (1988) '*Casablanca*: Cult Movies and Intertextual Collage', in D. Lodge (ed.), *Modern Criticism and Theory*, London and New York.

Elliott, Philip (1972) *The Making of a Television Series*, London: Constable.

Elliott, Philip (1986) 'Intellectuals, the "Information Society" and the Disappearance of the Public Sphere', in R. Collins *et al.* (eds), *Media, Culture and Society. A Critical Reader*, London, Beverly Hills, Newbury Park and New Delhi: Sage Publications: 105–15.

Ellis, John (1982) *Visible Fictions. Cinema, Television, Video*, London: Routledge & Kegan Paul.

Elsaesser, Thomas [1972] (1986) 'Tales of Sound and Fury: Observations on the Family Melodrama', in B.K. Grant (ed.), *Film Genre Reader*, Austin, TX: University of Texas Press: 278–308.

Elsaesser, Thomas (1992) 'TV through the Looking Glass', *Quarterly Review of Film and Video*, vol. 14, nos 1–2: 5–27.

Enzensberger, Hans Magnus (1987) 'Norsk utakt' ('Norwegian off-beat'), in his *Akk, Europa! Inntrykk fra syv land med en epilog fra år 2006* ('Oh, Europe! Impressions from seven countries and an epilogue from the year 2006'), Oslo: Universitetsforlaget.

Espinosa, Paul (1982) 'The Audience in the Text: Ethnographic Observations of a Hollywood Story Conference', *Media, Culture and Society*, vol. 4, no. 1.

Evensmo, Sigurd (1967) *Det store tivoli* ('The great amusement park'), Oslo: Gyldendal.

Faludi, Susan [1991] (1992) *Backlash. The Undeclared War Against Women*, London: Vintage.

Feuer, Jane (1984) 'Melodrama, Serial Form and Television Today', *Screen* vol. 25, no. 1, January–February: 4–16.

Feuer, Jane (1989) 'Reading *Dynasty*: Television and Reception Theory', *South Atlantic Quarterly*, vol. 88, no. 2, spring: 443–60.

Feuer, Jane, Kerr, Paul and Vahimagi, Tise (eds) (1984) *MTM: 'Quality Television'*, London: British Film Institute.

Finch, Mark (1986) 'Sex and Address in *Dynasty*', *Screen*, vol. 27, no. 6, November–December: 24–42.

Fish, Stanley (1980) *Is There a Text in this Class? The Authority of Interpretive Communities*, Cambridge, Mass., and London: Harvard University Press.

Fiske, John (1987) *Television Culture*, London and New York: Methuen.

Fiske, John (1989a) *Understanding Popular Culture*, Boston, London, Sydney and Wellington: Unwin Hyman.

Fiske, John (1989b) 'Moments of Television: Neither the Text nor the Audience', in Ellen Seiter *et al.* (eds), *Remote Control: Television, Audiences and Cultural Power*, London and New York: Routledge.

Flitterman-Lewis, Sandy (1988) 'All's Well that Doesn't End – Soap Opera and the Marriage Motif', *Camera Obscura*, no. 16, January: 119–27.

Foucault, Michel [1969] (1979) 'What Is an Author?', in J.V. Harari (ed.), *Textual Strategies. Perspectives in Post-Structuralist Criticism*, Ithaca and New York: Cornell University Press.

Freud, Sigmund [1908] (1977) 'Der Dichter und das Phantasieren' ['The creative writer and daydreaming'], Danish edition in J. Dines Johansen (ed.): *Psykoanalyse, Litteratur, Tekstteori*, Copenhagen: Borgen.

Frye, Northrop (1957) *Anatomy of Criticism*, Princeton: Princeton University Press.

Gadamer, Hans Georg (1960) *Wahrheit und Methode*, Tübingen: Mohr; 2nd English edition, 1979, *Truth and Method*, London: Sheed and Ward.

Galtung, Johan and Gleditsch, Nils P. (1975) 'Norge i verdenssamfunnet' ('Norway in the world community'), in N. Rogoff Ramsøy (ed.), *Det norske samfunn* ('The Norwegian society'), vol. 2, Oslo: Gyldendal Norsk Forlag: 742–806.

Gans, Herbert J. (1957) 'The Creator-Audience Relationship in the Mass Media: An Analysis of Movie Making', in B. Rosenberg and D. White (eds), *Mass Culture: The Popular Arts in America*, New York: Free Press: 315–24.

Garnham, Nicholas (1984) 'Introduction', in A. Mattelart, X. Delcourt and M. Mattelart, *International Image Markets. In Search of an Alternative Perspective*, London: Comedia.

Garnham, Nicholas (1990) *Capitalism and Communication. Global Culture and the Economics of Information*, London, Newbury Park and New Delhi: Sage Publications

Gendron, Bernard (1986) 'Adorno meets the Cadillacs', in Tania Modleski (ed.), *Studies in Entertainment. Critical Approaches to Mass Culture*, Bloomington and Indianapolis: Indiana University Press: 18–38.

Geraghty, Christine (1981) 'The Continuous Serial – a Definition', in R. Dyer *et al.*, *Coronation Street*, London: BFI Publishing: 9–26.

Geraghty, Christine (1991) *Women and Soap Opera. A Study of Prime Time Soaps*, Cambridge: Polity Press.

Gitlin, Todd (1978) 'Media Sociology: The Dominant Paradigm', *Theory and Society*, 6: 205–53.

Gitlin, Todd [1983] (1985) *Inside Prime Time*, New York: Pantheon Books.

Glaser, B.G. and Strauss, A.L. (1967) *The Discovery of Grounded Theory: Theoretical Sensitivity*, Mill Valley, Calif.: Sociology Press.

Gledhill, Christine (1987) 'The Melodramatic Field: An Investigation', in her (ed.) *Home Is Where the Heart Is*, London: British Film Institute.

Gledhill, Christine (1992) 'Speculations on the Relationship between Soap Opera and Melodrama', *Quarterly Review of Film and Video*, vol. 14, nos 1–2: 103–24.

Goodwin, Andrew, (1993) 'Fatal Distractions: MTV Meets Postmodern Theory', in S. Frith, A. Goodwin and L. Grossberg (eds), *Sound and Vision: The Music Video Reader*, London and New York: Routledge.

Gorbman, Claudia (1987) *Unheard Melodies: Narrative Film Music*, London: BFI Publishing, and Bloomington and Indianapolis: Indiana University Press.

Gripsrud, Jostein (1981) *La denne vår scene bli flammen . . . Perspektiv og praksis i og omkring sosialdemokratiets arbeiderteater ca 1890–1940* ('Let our stage be the flame . . . Perspectives and practice in and around the worker's theatre of the social democrats 1890–1940'), Oslo: Universitetsforlaget.

Gripsrud, Jostein (1989) 'The *Dynasty* Event in Norway: The Role of Print Media', *Edda. Scandinavian Journal of Literary Research*, vol. 27, nos 3–4: 26–33.

Gripsrud, Jostein (1989a) 'High Culture Revisited', *Cultural Studies*, vol. 3, no. 2, May: 194–207.

Gripsrud, Jostein (1990) *Folkeopplysningas dialektikk. Perspektiv på norskdomsrørsla og amatørteateret 1890–1940* ('The dialectic of popular enlightenment. A perspective on the New Norse movement and its amateur theatre 1890–1940'), Oslo: Det Norske Samlaget.

Gripsrud, Jostein (1991) 'The Aesthetics and Politics of Melodrama', in P. Dahlgren and C. Sparks (eds), *Journalism and Popular Culture*, London, Newbury Park and New Delhi: Sage Publications.

Gripsrud, Jostein (1991b) 'Modernizing Hierarchical Modernism: On the Problems of Evaluating Texts', in H. Rønning and K. Lundby (eds), *Media and Communication: Readings in Methodology, History and Culture*, Oslo: Norwegian University Press: 227–38.

Gripsrud, Jostein (1994) 'Intellectuals as Constructors of Cultural Identity', in *Cultural Studies*, May.

Grossberg, Lawrence (1987) 'The In-Difference of Television', *Screen*, vol. 28, no. 2, spring: 28–45.

Habermas, Jürgen (1971) *Borgerlig offentlighet* ('Bourgeois public sphere', original title: 'Strukturwandel der Öffentlichkeit'), Oslo: Gyldendal Norsk Forlag.

Hall, Stuart (1981) 'Note on Deconstructing "the Popular" ', in R. Samuel (ed.), *People's History and Socialist Theory*, London: Routledge & Kegan Paul: 227–40.

Hauser, Arnold (1972) *The Social History of Art*, vol. IV: *The Film Age*, London: Routledge & Kegan Paul.

Heath, Stephen [1977/8] (1981) *Questions of Cinema*, Bloomington: Indiana University Press.

Herzog, Herta (1941) 'On Borrowed Experience. An Analysis of Listening to Daytime Sketches', *Zeitschrift für Sozialforschung / Studies in Philosophy and Social Science*, vol. IX, no. 1: 65–95.

Hjorth, Anne (1984) *Når kvinder ser TV – om medieforskning og reception* ['When women watch TV – on media research and reception'], M.A. dissertation, Department of Literary Studies, University of Copenhagen (*AIL* 140). [English language version published 1986 by The Media Research Department at the Danish Broadcasting Corporation.]

Hobson, Dorothy (1989) 'Soap Operas at Work', in E. Seiter, Hans Borchers, Gabrielle Kreutzner and Eva-Maria Warth, *Remote Control: Television, Audiences, and Cultural Power*, London and New York: Routledge.

Höijer, Birgitta (1992) 'Reception of Television Narration as a Socio-cognitive Process: a Schema-theoretical Outline', *Poetics*, 21: 283–304.

Hollander, Norman N. (1992) 'Film Response from Eye to I: The Kuleshov Experiment', in J. Gaines (ed.), *Classical Hollywood Narrative: The Paradigm Wars*, Durham and London: Duke University Press.

Hoskins, Colin and Mirus, Rolf (1988) 'Reasons for the US Dominance of the International Trade in Television Programmes', *Media, Culture and Society*, vol. 10: 499–515.

Høst, Sigurd (1983) *Bruk av massemedier i Norge* ('Uses of mass media in Norway'), Oslo: Institutt for presseforskning.

Houston, Beverle (1984) 'Viewing Television: The Metapsychology of Endless Consumption', *Quarterly Review of Film Studies*, vol. 9, no. 3, summer: 183–95.

Huyssen, Andreas (1986) 'Mass Culture as Woman: Modernism's Other', in T. Modleski (ed.), *Studies in Entertainment. Critical Approaches to Mass Culture*, Bloomington, Indianapolis: Indiana University Press.

Ingarden, Roman [1930] (1973) *The Literary Work of Art*, Evanston, Illinois: Northwestern University Press.

Intintoli, Michael James (1984) *Taking Soaps Seriously: The World of 'Guiding Light'*, New York, Philadelphia, Eastbourne (UK), Toronto, Hong Kong, Tokyo and Sydney: Praeger.

Iser, Wolfgang (1974) *The Implied Reader: Patterns of Communication in Prose Fiction from Bunyan to Beckett*, Baltimore, Md.: Johns Hopkins University Press.

Iser, Wolfgang (1978) *The Act of Reading: A Theory of Aesthetic Response*, Baltimore, Md.: Johns Hopkins University Press.

Jakobson, Roman (1956) 'Two Aspects of Language and Two Types of Aphasic Disturbances', in *Fundamentals of Language*, Gravenhage: Mouton, 45–96 (2nd revised edition 1971, The Hague: Mouton.)

Jakobson, Roman [1960] (1988) 'Linguistics and Poetics', in D. Lodge (ed.), *Modern Criticism and Theory: A Reader*, London and New York: Longman.

Jameson, Fredric (1971) *Marxism and Form*, Princeton, NJ: Princeton University Press.

Jankowski, N.W. and Wester, F. (1991) 'The Qualitative Tradition in Social Science Inquiry: Contributions to Mass Communication Research', in K.B. Jensen and N.W. Jankowski (eds), *A Handbook of Qualitative Methodologies for Mass Communication Research*, London and New York: Routledge.

Jauss, Hans Robert [1970] (1974) *Literaturgeschichte als Provokation*, Frankfurt: Suhrkamp.

Jauss, Hans Robert (1975) 'Racines und Goethes Iphigenie. Mit einem Nachwort über die Partialität der rezeptionsästhetischen Methode', in R. Warning (ed.), *Rezeptionsästhetik: Theorie und Praxis*, Munich: W.S. Fink Verlag: 352–400.

Jauss, Hans Robert (1977) *Ästhetische Erfahrung und Literarische Hermeneutik I*, Munich: W.S. Fink Verlag.

Jick, T. (1979) 'Mixing Qualitative and Quantitive Methods: Triangulation in Action', *Administrative Science Quarterly*, no. 24, December: 602–11.

Johannesen, Georg (1979) 'Trivialbegrepet og den norske lyrikken' ['The "trivial" and Norwegian poetry'], in A. Tvinnereim (ed.), *Underholdningslitteratur, Masselitteratur, Trivialitteratur*, Bergen, Oslo and Tromsø: Universitetsforlaget.

Johansen, Anders (1984) *Tid är makt, tid är pengar* ['Time is power, time is money'], Gothenburg: Röda Bokförlaget.

Joyrich, Lynne (1988) 'All that Television Allows: TV Melodrama, Postmodernism and Consumer Culture', *Camera Obscura*, no. 16, January: 129–53.

Kaplan, E. Ann (ed.) (1990) *Psychoanalysis and Cinema*, New York and London: Routledge.

Katz, Elihu and Liebes, Tamar (1986) 'Mutual Aid in the Decoding of *Dallas*: Preliminary Notes from a Cross-cultural Study', in P. Drummond and R. Paterson (eds), *Television in Transition*, London: British Film Institute: 187–98.

Katz, Elihu, Blumler, Jay G. and Gurevitch, Michael (1974) 'Utilization of Mass Communication by the Individual', in J.G. Blumler and E. Katz (eds), *The Uses of Mass Communications. Current Perspectives on Gratifications Research*, Beverly Hills and London: Sage Publications.

Kermode, Frank (1967) *The Sense of an Ending: Studies in the Theory of Fiction*, London, Oxford and New York: Oxford University Press.

Klein, Joe (1985) 'The Real Star of *Dynasty*. Esther Shapiro and her Empire', *New York Magazine*, 2 September: pp. 34ff.

Klinger, Barbara (1991) 'Digressions at the Cinema: Commodification and Reception in Mass Culture', in James Naremore and Patrick Brantlinger (eds), *Modernity and Mass Culture*, Bloomington and Indianapolis: Indiana University Press.

Kofoed, Peter and Rasmussen, Tove Arendt (1986) *DALLAS. Skabelon og struktur i den moderne TV-Serie* ['DALLAS. Stereotype and structure in the modern TV serial'], Aalborg, Denmark: Aalborg Universitetsforlag.

Kolbjørnsen, Tone Kr. (1993) 'Betatt av "Tatt av vinden"': Scarlett, Rhett Butler og det kvinnelige publikum' ['Taken by "Gone With the Wind"': Scarlett, Rhett Butler and the female audience'], in J. Gripsrud (ed.), *Mediegleder* ['Media pleasures'], Oslo: Ad Notam/Gyldendal.

Kracauer, Sigfried (1953) 'The Challenge of Qualitative Content Analysis', *Public Opinion Quarterly*, vol. 16, no. 2: 631–42.

Kreutzner, Gabrielle and Seiter, Ellen (1991) 'Not all "Soaps" are Created Equal: Towards a Cross-cultural Criticism of Television Serials', *Screen*, vol. 32, no. 2, summer: 154–72.

Kristeva, Julia [1979] (1986) 'Women's Time', in T. Moi (ed.), *The Kristeva Reader*, Oxford: Basil Blackwell: 188–213.

Larsen, Peter (1988) 'Betydningsstrømme: Musikk og moderne billedfiktioner' ['Currents of signification: music and modern visual fictions'], *Studia Musicologica Norvegica* 14, Oslo: Universitetsforlaget: 19–52.

Larsen, Peter (ed.) (1990) *Import/Export: International Flow of Television Fiction (Reports and Papers on Mass Communication*, no. 104), Paris: UNESCO.

Lazarsfeld, Paul F. (1941) 'Remarks on Administrative and Critical Communications Research', in *Zeitschrift für Sozialforschung/Studies in Philosophy and Social Science*, vol. 9: 2–16.

Lévi-Strauss, Claude [1965] (1966) 'The Culinary Triangle' (originally 'Le Triangle culinaire', *L'Arc*, no. 26: 19–29), in *New Society*, 22 December.

Lévi-Strauss, Claude (1966b) *The Savage Mind*, London.

Liebes, Tamar and Katz, Elihu (1990) *The Export of Meaning. Cross-Cultural Readings of 'Dallas'*, New York and Oxford: Oxford University Press.

Lotman, Jurij (1977) *The Structure of the Artistic Text*, Ann Arbor: University of Michigan Press.

Lull, James (1990) *Inside Family Viewing: Ethnographic Research on Television's Audiences*, London and New York: Routledge.

Lundberg, D. and Hultén, O. (1968) *Individen och massmedia*, Stockholm: EFI.

Mahamdi, Yahia (1988) 'Algerian Television and the *Dallas* Phenomenon: Cultural Imperialism or Appropriation?', paper presented to the 16th Congress of the International Association for Mass Communication Research, Barcelona. (Re)printed in the IAMCR collection *Mass Communication and Cultural Identity*, vol. 1.

Marx, Karl (1973) *Grundrisse*, Harmondsworth: Penguin Books.

Matelski, Marilyn J. (1988) *The Soap Opera Evolution: America's Enduring Romance with Daytime Drama*, Jefferson, NC and London: McFarland & Company.

Mattelart, Michelle (1986) 'Women and the Cultural Industries', in R. Collins *et al.* (eds), *Media, Culture and Society: A Critical Reader*, London, Beverly Hills, Newbury Park and New Delhi: Sage Publications.

Medhurst, Andy (1991) 'That Special Thrill: *Brief Encounter*, Homosexuality and Authorship', *Screen*, vol. 32, no. 2: 197–208.

Metz, Christian [1977] (1982) *The Imaginary Signifier. Psychoanalysis and the Cinema*, Bloomington: Indiana University Press.

Miller, J. Hillis (1978) 'The Problematic of Ending in Narrative', *Nineteenth Century Fiction*, 33: 3–7.

Miller, Mark Crispin (1988) *Boxed In: The Culture of TV*, Evanston, IL: Northwestern University Press.

Mills, C. Wright (1967) 'IBM Plus Reality Plus Humanism = Sociology', in I.L. Horowitz (ed.), *Power, Politics and People. The Collected Essays of C. Wright Mills*, New York: Oxford University Press: 568–76.

Modleski, Tania (1982) 'The Search for Tomorrow in Today's Soap Operas', in her *Loving With a Vengeance*, Hamden, Conn.: The Shoe String Press.

Monaco, James (1981) *How to Read a Film*, 3rd edition, New York and Oxford: Oxford University Press.

Morley, David (1980) *The 'Nationwide' Audience*, London: British Film Institute.

Morley, David (1992) *Television, Audiences and Cultural Studies*, London and New York: Routledge.

Morley, David (1992) 'Where the Global Meets the Local: Notes from the Sitting Room', in his *Television, Audiences and Cultural Studies*, London and New York: Routledge.

Morse, Margaret (1986) 'Talk, talk, talk', *Screen*, vol. 26, no. 2: 2–17.

Mukarovsky, Jan [1931] (1970) *Aesthetic Function, Norm and Value as Social Facts*, Ann Arbor.

Mulvey, Laura [1981] (1989) 'Afterthoughts on "Visual Pleasure and Narrative Cinema" Inspired by *Duel in the Sun*', in her *Visual and Other Pleasures*, London: Macmillan.

Murdock, Graham (1977) 'Fabricating Fictions: Approaches to the Study of Television Drama Production', *Proceedings of the Meeting on Organization and Structure of Fiction Production in Television*, Vol. 1: *Introductory Reports*, Turin: Edizione RAI (Radiotelevisione Italiana).

Murdock, Graham (1988) 'Television and Citizenship: In Defence of Public Broadcasting', in A. Tomlinson (ed.), *Consumption, Identity, and Style: Marketing, Meanings and the Packaging of Pleasure*, London and New York: Routledge.

Murdock, Graham [1980] (1993) 'Authorship and Organisation', *Screen Education* no. 35, summer; reprinted in M. Alvarado, E. Buscombe and R. Collins (eds), *The Screen Education Reader: Cinema, Television, Culture*, London: Macmillan: 123–43.

Neale, Steven (1980) *Genre*, London: British Film Institute.

Neale, Steven (1986) 'Melodrama and Tears', *Screen*, vol. 27, no. 6, November–December: 6–22.

Negt, Oskar and Kluge, Alexander [1972] (1974) *Offentlighet og erfaring* (original title *Öffentlichkeit und Erfahrung*, 'Public sphere and experience'), Nordisk Sommer-universitets skriftserie, no. 3.

Newcomb, Horace (1974) *Television: the Most Popular Art*, Garden City, NY: Anchor Press/Doubleday.

Newcomb, Horace (1983) Introduction, in M. Cassata and T. Skill (eds), *Life on Daytime Television: Tuning-In American Serial Drama*, Norwood, NJ: Ablex Publishing Corporation.

Newcomb, Horace (1983) 'A Humanistic View of Daytime Serial Dramas' in M. Cassata and T. Skill (eds), *Life on Daytime Television: Tuning-in American Serial Drama*, Norwood, NJ: Ablex Publishing Corporation: xxiv–xxxv.

Newcomb, Horace and Alley, Robert S. (1983) *The Producer's Medium*, New York and Oxford: Oxford University Press.

Nixon, Agnes Eckhardt (1972) 'In Daytime TV, the Golden Age Is Now', *Television Quarterly*, vol. X, no. 1, fall: 49–54.

Nochimson, Martha (1992) *No End to Her: Soap Opera and the Female Subject*, Berkeley/Los Angeles/Oxford: University of California Press.

NRK (1987) *NRK mot år 2000* ('NRK toward the year 2000'), Oslo.

Paterson, Richard [1980] (1993) 'Planning the Family: The Art of the Television Schedule', *Screen Education*, no. 35, summer; reprinted in M. Alvarado, E. Buscombe and R. Collins (eds), *The Screen Education Reader: Cinema, Television, Culture*, London: Macmillan: 144–53.

Porter, Dennis (1982) 'Soap Time: Thoughts on a Commodity Art Form', in H. Newcomb (ed.), *Television: The Critical View*, 3rd edn, New York and Oxford: Oxford University Press: 122–31.

Prendergast, Roy M. (1992) *Film Music – A Neglected Art. A Critical Study of Music in Films*, 2nd edn, New York and London: W.W. Norton & Company.

Press, Andrea (1991) *Women Watching Television. Gender, Class, and Generation in the American Television Experience*, Philadelphia: University of Pennsylvania Press.

Radway, Janice (1984) *Reading the Romance. Feminism and the Representation of Women in Popular Culture*, Chapel Hill: The University of North Carolina Press.

Rasmussen, Tove A. (1988) 'Fiktion og reception i det interpersonelle rum' ('Fiction and reception in the interpersonal space'), Hans Jørn Nielsen (ed.), *Kultur, identitet og kommunikation*, Aalborg (Denmark): Aalborg Universitetsforlag.

Rath, Claus-Dieter (1989) 'Live Television and its Audiences: Challenges of Media Reality', in E. Seiter, Hans Borchers, Gabrielle Kreutzner and Eva-Maria Warth (eds), *Remote Control: Television, Audiences, and Cultural Power*, London and New York: Routledge: 79–95.

Reitan, Lorentz (1987) 'Analyse av musikkbruken i to episoder av *Dynasty*' ['An analysis of the use of music in two episodes of *Dynasty*'], unpublished paper, Department of Mass Communication, University of Bergen.

Ricoeur, Paul (1985) *Time and Narrative*, 2 vols, Chicago and London: The University of Chicago Press.

Robbe-Grillet, Alain [1963] (1966) 'Ny roman og virkelighet' ('The new novel and reality'), *Vinduet* (first presented as a lecture at the Institut de Sociologie de l'Université Libre de Bruxelles, and printed in a special issue of *Revue de l'Institut de Sociologie*, Brussels).

Rogers, E.M. and Singhal, A. (1988) 'Television Soap Operas for Development in India', paper presented at the International Communication Association Conference, Montreal.

Rokkan, Stein (1966) 'Norway: Numerical Democracy and Corporate Pluralism', in Robert A. Dahl (ed.), *Political Oppositions in Western Democracies*, New Haven: Yale University Press.

Rokkan, Stein (1967) 'Geography, Religion and Social Class: Crosscutting Cleavages in Norwegian Politics', in S.M. Lipset and S. Rokkan (eds), *Party Systems and Voter Alignments*, New York: Free Press.

Rorty, Richard (1980) *Philosophy and the Mirror of Nature*, Princeton: Princeton University Press.

Rosen, Philip (ed.) (1984) *Narrative, Apparatus, Ideology: A Film Theory Reader*, New York: Columbia University Press.

Rouverol, Jean (1984) *Writing for the Soaps*, Cincinnati, OH: Writer's Digest Books.

Sarraute, Nathalie [1963] (1966) 'Ny roman og virkelighet' ('The new novel and reality'), *Vinduet* (first presented as a lecture at the Institut de Sociologie de l'Université Libre de Bruxelles, and printed in a special issue of *Revue de l'Institut de Sociologie*, Brussels: 107–13.

Schatz, Thomas (1981) *Hollywood Genres: Formulas, Filmmaking and the Studio System*, New York: Random House.

Schröder, Kim Chr. (1988) 'The Pleasure of *Dynasty*: The Weekly Reconstruction of Self-Confidence', in Phillip Drummond and Richard Paterson (eds), *Television and its Audience. International Research Perspectives*, London: British Film Institute.

Seiter, Ellen (1981) 'The Role of the Woman Reader: Eco's Narrative Theory and Soap Operas', *Tabloid*, no. 6.

Seiter, Ellen (1990) 'Making Distinctions in TV Audience Research: a Case Study of a Troubling Interview', *Cultural Studies*, vol. 4, no. 1, January: 61–84.

Seiter, Ellen, Borchers, Hans, Kreutzner, Gabrielle and Warth, Eva-Maria (1989) ' "Don't Treat us Like We're so Stupid and Naïve": Toward an Ethnography of Soap Opera Viewers', in their (eds) *Remote Control. Television, Audiences and Cultural Power*, London and New York: Routledge.

Sennett, Richard [1977] (1986) *The Fall of Public Man*, London and Boston: Faber & Faber.

Shapiro, Esther (1984) 'Introduction', *Dynasty. The Authorized Biography of the Carringtons*.

Shklovsky, Victor ([1917] (1988) 'Art as Technique', in D. Lodge (ed.), *Modern Criticism and Theory: A Reader*, London and New York: Longman.

Silj, Alessandro *et al.* (1988) *East of Dallas: The European Challenge to American Television*, London: BFI Publishing.

Silverman, Deborah L., Cassata, Mary, Skill, Thomas (1983) 'Setting the Mood: An Analysis of the Music of *General Hospital* and *As the World Turns*', in M. Cassata and T. Skill, *Life on Daytime Television: Tuning-In American Serial Drama*, Norwood, NJ: Ablex Publishing Corporation.

Skiles, Marlin (1976) *Music Scoring for TV and Motion Pictures*, Blue Ridge Summit, Pa.: Tab Books.

Sklar, Robert (1976) *Movie-Made America: A Cultural History of American Movies*, New York: Vintage Books.

Sontag, Susan (1966) *Against Interpretation*, New York.

Staiger, Janet (1992) *Interpreting Films: Studies in the Historical Reception of American Cinema*, Princeton, NJ: Princeton University Press.

Swanson, Gillian (1981) '*Dallas*', parts 1 and 2, *Framework*, 14–17.

Syvertsen, Trine (1992) *Public Television in Transition*, Ph.D. dissertation, University of Leicester, published as *Levende Bilder* no. 5/92, Oslo: KULT/NAVF.

Taylor, Helen (1989) *Scarlett's Women. 'Gone With the Wind' and Its Female Fans*, New Brunswick, NJ: Rutgers University Press.

Thompson, Kristin (1985) *Exporting Entertainment: America in the World Film Market 1907–1934*, London: BFI Publishing.

Thornton, Robert J. (1980) *Space and Culture among the Iraqw of Tanzania*, New York.

Timberg, Bernard (1982) 'The Rhetoric of the Camera in Television Soap Opera', in H. Newcomb (ed.), *Television: The Critical View*, 3rd edn, New York and Oxford: Oxford University Press.

Todorov, Tzvetan [1978] (1990) *Genres in Discourse*, Cambridge, New York, Port Chester, Melbourne and Sydney: Cambridge University Press.

Towers, Wayne M. (1977) 'Lazarsfeld and Adorno in the United States: A Case Study in Theoretical Orientations', in *Communication Yearbook I*, New Brunswick.

Tulloch, John and Alvarado, Manuel (1983) *'Doctor Who': The Unfolding Text*, New York: St Martin's Press.

Tynjanov, Jurij [1927] (1971) 'On Literary Evolution' in L. Matejka and K. Pomorska (eds), *Readings in Russian Poetics: Formalist and Structuralist Views*, Cambridge, Mass. and London: The M.I.T. Press.

Vianello, Robert (1984) 'The Rise of the Telefilm and the Networks' Hegemony Over the Motion Picture and Television Industries', *Quarterly Review of Film Studies*, vol. 9, no. 3, summer: 204–18.

Vodicka, Felix (1976) *Die Struktur der literarischen Entwicklung*, Munich.

Waldecranz, Rune (1976) *Så föddes filmen* ['How film was born'], Stockholm: Prisma.

Weber, Max (1968) *Economy and Society: An Outline of Interpretive Sociology*, vol.1 (ed. G. Roth and C. Wittich), Berkeley, Los Angeles and London: University of California Press.

Weber, Max (1969) *The Methodology of the Social Sciences* (5th edn), New York: The Free Press.

Wheen, Francis (1985) *Television*, London: Century Publishing.

White, Hayden [1973] (1990) *Metahistory: The Historical Imagination in Nineteenth-Century Europe*, Baltimore and London: The Johns Hopkins University Press.

Williams, Raymond (1975) *Television. Technology and Cultural Form*, New York: Schocken Books.

Winston, Brian [1981] (1985) 'Showdown at Culture Gulch', in R.E. Hiebert and C. Reuss (eds), *Impact of Mass Media: Current Issues*, New York and London: Longman: 473–81.

Wober, M. (1981) 'Psychology in the Future of Broadcasting Research', *Bulletin of the British Psychological Society* 34.

Wren-Lewis, Justin (1983) 'The Encoding/Decoding Model: Criticisms and Redevelopments for Research on Decoding', *Media, Culture and Society*, vol. 5, no. 2, April: 179–97.

Østbye, Helge (1982) 'Norsk Rikskringkasting: Ett monopol – to medier', in *NOU 30 Maktutredningen: Rapporten om massmedier*, Oslo: Universitetsforlaget 1.

INDEX

Note Characters from *Dynasty* are entered in single quotes to distinguish them from real people

308